Introduction ............................................ ... 7

Identity and Nationalism in the ']        tif
for the New Age in Japan
   Ian Reader.................................................................................. 13

War Memorials in modern Japanese context: The transformation of
nationalistic representation
   Awazu Kenta ............................................................................. 37

The Quest for Religious and National Identity of Japanese Protestants
before 1945 – Anti-, or Philo-Semitism as the Framework of Reference –
   Kubota Hiroshi ........................................................................ 51

Buddhism and *kokutai* (National Polity) in Modern Japan: The Case of
the Nichirenist Movement of Tanaka Chigaku
   Ōtani Eiichi.............................................................................. 75

Nishi Hongan-ji and National Identity in Bakumatsu and early Meiji
Japan
   Peter Kleinen .......................................................................... 87

Nationalism and Japanese Buddhism in the late Tokugawa period and
early Meiji
   Fujii Takeshi ......................................................................... 107

The *chinkon kishin*: Divine help in times of national crisis
   Birgit Staemmler ................................................................... 119

Constructing the 'Other Modernity': Religion and 'Indigenous Identity'
in Contemporary Japanese Cultural Discourse
   Lisette Gebhardt ................................................................... 133

Prophets of salvation coming out of the forests of Japan – Introducing
some of the so called "spiritual intellectuals"
   Inken Prohl .......................................................................... 149

Hachiman – Protecting *kami* of the Japanese Nation
   Martin Repp........................................................................... 169

Land of the *Kami* and Way of the *Kami* in Yoshida Shintō
   Bernhard Scheid ................................................................... 193

Matching *kami* with Modernity: an early Meiji intellectual's thought on
electric light
   Michael Wachutka.................................................................. 217

6

**The Emperor, Shintō Ultranationalism and Mass Mobilization**
Walter A. Skya ................................................................................ 235

**The Cosmology of Shintō and National Identity in Modern Japan**
Endō Jun ....................................................................................... 249

**Shintō and *kokutai*: Religious Ideology in the Japanese Context**
Klaus Antoni .................................................................................. 263

**'*Nihon no kuni wa tennō o chūshin to suru kami no kuni*' – The Divine Country Debate 2000**
Johann Nawrocki ........................................................................... 289

The Contributors ........................................................................... 301

Klaus Antoni, Hiroshi Kubota, Johann Nawrocki,
Michael Wachutka (eds.)

# Religion and National Identity in the Japanese Context

# BUNKA

Tübinger interkulturelle und linguistische Japanstudien
Tuebingen intercultural and linguistic studies on Japan

herausgegeben von/edited by

## Klaus Antoni und/and Viktoria Eschbach-Szabo

(Universität Tübingen)

Band/volume 5

LIT

Klaus Antoni, Hiroshi Kubota, Johann Nawrocki,
Michael Wachutka (eds.)

# Religion and National Identity in the Japanese Context

LIT

Gedruckt mit Unterstützung des Fördervereins japanisch-deutscher
Kulturbeziehungen e. V., Köln (JaDe)


**Die Deutsche Bibliothek – CIP-Einheitsaufnahme**

Religion and National Identity in the Japanese Context / Klaus Antoni ; Hiroshi
Kubota ; Johann Nawrocki ; Michael Wachutka (eds.). – Münster : LIT, 2002
    (BUNKA – Tübinger interkulturelle und linguistische Japanstudien/
    Tuebingen intercultural and linguistic studies on Japan ; 5)
    ISBN 3-8258-6043-4


© LIT VERLAG Münster – Hamburg – London
    Grevener Str. 179    48159 Münster    Tel. 0251-23 50 91    Fax 0251-23 19 72
    e-Mail: lit@lit-verlag.de    http://www.lit-verlag.de

Distributed in North America by:

**Transaction Publishers**
New Brunswick (U.S.A.) and London (U.K.)

Transaction Publishers
Rutgers University
35 Berrue Circle
Piscataway, NJ 08854

Tel.: (732) 445 - 2280
Fax: (732) 445 - 3138
for orders (U. S. only):
toll free (888) 999 - 6778

# Introduction

On February 1-3, 2001, an international symposium on "Religion and National Identity in the Japanese Context" was held at the University of Tuebingen, organized by Klaus Antoni, Hiroshi Kubota, Johann Nawrocki and Michael Wachutka. The organizers were glad and obliged that it became possible after nearly two years of preparatory work, to meet at Castle Hohentübingen for this occasion and to welcome speakers and participants from Japan, the United States, Great Britain, Austria and various parts of Germany.

The symposium was the third one in a series of such events under the formal umbrella of the AJR ("Arbeitskreis Japanische Religionen", an informal study group on Japanese religions). At the starting point of this group stood the insight that an increasing interest in questions concerning the reality of Japanese religions can be found in the scientific as well as in the popular world, being far away from those widespread 'exotistic' constructions of for instance, 'Zen as the heart of the Japanese culture'. On this basis an informal circle of Japanologists who scholarly and critically work on some aspects of Japanese religious history formed a working group in the year 1994 at the University of Trier. This first meeting was not yet dedicated to any central main topic, but sought to at first plumb relevant themes within the scope of Japanese religions.

As a result it was decided, to organize a small symposium on questions of ritualization and standardization of Japanese religions in March 1995, again in Trier. Due to the still experimental nature of the meeting there was only one lecture presented by the late Nelly Naumann (Freiburg University) on "Standardization and Ritualization in Japanese religions"[1].

Encouraged by the two first meetings the working group decided to organize a symposium on questions of the ritualization among Japanese religions in the year 1996, this time however within a larger organizational framework and with international participation. The meeting was once again organized in Trier and comprised of several presentations within the main thematic frame of "Rituale und ihre Urheber – 'Invented Traditions' in der japanischen Religionsge-

---

[1] Tragically we now have to bemoan deeply that Professor Naumann has passed away in September 2000. She was an unequalled teacher and paragon for all of us.

schichte" ("Rituals and their causers – 'Invented Traditions' in the Japanese religious history"). The contributions to this workshop were published as a book in 1997, edited by Birgit Staemmler.

It was not until March 1999 that a consecutive symposium could take place, this time in Berlin at the Japanese-German Center, in cooperation with the Free University. The organization was managed by two colleagues, Hartmut Zinser and Inken Prohl, from the Department of the Science of Religions at Free University. The topic of this exceptionally stimulating conference was the appearance of "Japanese Religions in Europe". The conference proceedings will be currently published, under the supervision of Inken Prohl.

The topic of the present symposium is called "Religion and National Identity in the Japanese Context". As indicated by this title, the workshop, or symposium, focused upon the relationship between religion and socio-cultural or socio-political aspects in the history of religions in Japan. We believe that political, cultural and religious elements are closely interrelated in Japanese history as well as in most modern societies. Such interconnectedness may be noticed in every region of the world before the onset of secularization, but also in modern nation-states today. In some of these nation-states the formation of the political and national identity, and the coincidence of political, national, and cultural issues are religiously and ideologically justified. A comparative approach therefore is appropriate. In this context the connection between religious, political and cultural ideas in modern as well as premodern Japan need to be addressed, as for instance the emergence and formation of nativism (*kokugaku* 国学) and State Shintō.

Various approaches were conceivable, e.g. concerning the self-consciousness of a nation, the questions of traditionalism and nativism as well as the religiously motivated concept of state that uses religious 'traditions', or more correctly, ideas that are supposed to have been traditionally transmitted.

Other questions were the relationship between religion and politics or the historiography as well as religious movements within the Japanese context.

Within the wide framework of the symposium's topic we had the opportunity to listen to and discuss various presentations, starting with a lecture given by Professor Ian READER from Lancaster University, who spoke about: "Identity and Nationalism in the 'New' New Religions: Buddhism as a Motif for the New Age in Japan", followed by AWAZU Kenta, from the National Museum of Japanese History in Tōkyō, with a presentation on: "The Transformation of

Nationalistic Representation: A Historical Study of War Memorials in Modern Japanese Context". The final speech of the first day was given by KUBOTA Hiroshi, concerning the topic: "The Quest for Religious and National Identity of Japanese Protestants before 1945: Anti- or Philo-Semitism as the Reference Frame-work".

On the following day the series of lectures was opened by ŌTANI Eiichi (International Institute for The Study of Religions, Tōkyō) on: "Buddhism and *kokutai* (National Polity) in Modern Japan: The Case of the Nichirenist Movement of Tanaka Chigaku". Peter KLEINEN from Bonn University also focused on Buddhism with a presentation on: "Nishi Hongan-ji and National Identity in Bakumatsu and Early Meiji Japan", followed by the lecture of Martin REPP (NCC Center for the Study of Japanese Religions, Kyōto) concerning: "Hachiman – The *kami* for the Protection of the Japanese Nation". Buddhism continued as the main topic with the presentation given by FUJII Takeshi (Tōkyō Gakugei University) on: "Nationalism and Japanese Buddhism in Early Meiji period".

Three lectures on questions concerning the New Religions, historically ranging from late Tokugawa times up to the present, concluded the second day's presentations: Birgit STAEMMLER (Tübingen University) on: "The *Chinkon Kishin*: Divine Help in Times of National Crisis", Lisette GEBHARDT (Trier University) on: "Constructing the 'Other Modernity': Religion and 'Indigenous Identity' in Contemporary Japanese Cultural Discourses" and Inken PROHL (Free University, Berlin) on a very recent trend in Japanese society: "Introducing some of the so called 'Spiritual Intellectuals'".

On the final day Bernhard SCHEID (Austrian Academy of Sciences, Vienna) opened the session on Shintō with his lecture on: "Land of the *kami* and Way of the *kami* in Yoshida Shintō". Reinhard ZÖLLNER (Erfurt University) followed with: "*Eejanaika* – Religion, Nation and Politics". The question of Shintō and nationalism was discussed by Walter SKYA (Loyola Marymount University, Los Angeles) who lectured about the main results of his soon appearing study on: "The Emperor, Shintō Ultranationalism and Mass Mobilization". ENDO Jun (International Institute for the Study of Religions, Tōkyō) afterwards delivered a paper on: "The Cosmology of Shintō and National Identity in Modern Japan". The concluding afternoon session saw presentations by Klaus ANTONI on: "Shintō and *kokutai*: Religious Ideology in the Japanese Context" and finally Johann NAWROCKI (Tübingen University), who dealt with an up-to-date topic of political debate in present day Japan: "'*Nihon no kuni wa tennō o chūshin to suru kami no kuni desu*' – The Divine Country Debate 2000". This was the final lecture of our symposium, which was supported by the German Research Foundation (DFG) and the German East Asian Science Forum. Within the present work, an additional paper by Michael WACHUTKA – who also did the editing of this volume – on the topic: "Matching *kami* with Modernity: an early Meiji intellectual's thought on electric light" was included.

Regarding the topic of the symposium, some short remarks may be added here. In the present world, data based on the various cultures has grown so immense that we theoretically became able to take under consideration nearly every relevant region when talking about universal categories like 'nation' and religion. Furthermore, it is not because of our own coincidental preoccupation with Japan that one should be convinced of the fact that Japan provides one of the most striking insights into this general and global pattern of problems.

From the beginning of documented history throughout the centuries, we find, among scholars and priests of Shintō, Buddhism and Confucianism alike, a definite religious debate in Japan about the question of what it means to be 'Japanese' as distinguished from the outside world. Modern *Nihonjinron* 日本人論, the thinking and self reflection about Japan by native thinkers and ideologists themselves, indeed has a very long intellectual history. It is the fault of many Western historians to be convinced of the idea that thinking in such terms – and hence early forms of nationalism – in Japan only started after the contact with the West in the second part of the nineteenth century.

Of course the European idea of the nation-state deeply influenced modern Japanese nationalism since the Meiji period. But this Eurocentric view on Japanese history is unable to recognize the most fascinating fact that Japanese ideological thinkers themselves, during Tokugawa times and even previous historical epochs, developed their own kind of 'national idea'. It centered on the concept of a Japanese 'imagined community' – to use the well known term coined by Benedict Anderson – which later manifested as the idea of a distinct Japanese *kokutai* 国体 ('national polity') under the Emperor's rule.

In Japan it became especially the construct of a postulated common ethnicity that was fundamental to this concept. It founded the myth of common origin of all Japanese in the Age of Gods. Such religious thinking had always, even since the early days of *ritsuryō* 律令, a clearly political connotation, i.e. the mere utopian idea, or ideology, of constant imperial rule. The theoretical constructions were handed down, regardless of their historical reality, through centuries. This marks the main difference between orthodox, emic Shintō worldview, which declares the unbroken line of imperial rule as a historical fact, and etic critical research that can state only the persistence of such idealistic utopian constructs regarding 'unbroken' Imperial rule.

Of course we could not elaborate these ideas exhaustively, but it became comprehensible that, when speaking about the development of the global idea of the nation in relation to religious ideas, one may not omit the Japanese case without simultaneously sacrificing one of the most valuable examples for understanding the whole universal pattern. Japan is an island in geographical terms, of course, but not in regard to her development in religion, culture, society, political ideas and history. The alleged isolation of Japanese culture itself marks an ideological construction, and in this sense pointing out the fact of Japan being a part of the world is an important task for Japanese studies inside and outside Japan. The Japanese context will contribute deeply to the understanding of the global pattern, i.e. those questions of religion and identity that have become so important in our present world. The fact that discussions on such basic questions can unite researchers from all over the world was best documented by this symposium.

Klaus Antoni, on behalf of the organizers
July 2001

# Identity and Nationalism in the 'New' New Religions: Buddhism as a motif for the New Age in Japan

Ian READER

## *Introduction*

Just before I left Japan in early 1989 to move to the UK, one of my best and brightest Japanese students – a young woman taking my courses on Buddhism and Japanese Religions at my then-university – informed me that she had become extremely interested in the 'new' new religion Kōfuku no Kagaku 幸福 の科学. One of the things that had attracted her to it, she informed me, was its emphasis on Buddhist ideas, and the ways in which its leader, Ōkawa Ryūhō 大 川隆法, managed to present and explain those ideas in a way that, in her view, could be readily understood by, and appear highly relevant to, young Japanese people such as herself in the present day.

This young lady told me that she used to be disinterested in Buddhism: like many of her generation, she conceived of Buddhism in Japan as little more than a funereal religion of arcane rituals related to death rather than life. However, she had then gone on to spend a year in the USA as an exchange student, during which time she had been exposed to a very different culture and felt her sense of identity being challenged. This caused her to reflect on her cultural roots and to recognise the importance of Buddhism as part of her Japanese cultural heritage. This in turn spurred her to study Buddhism. However, she continued to feel uncomfortable with the traditional Buddhism of Japan, because, with its close associations with death and funerals, it appeared to be out of step with her orientations as a young, internationally minded person living in the modern world.

By contrast, Kōfuku no Kagaku, as a new religious movement emphasising its roots as a Buddhist movement in modern Japan, had a great appeal for her. Shortly after graduating and moving to Tōkyō to work, and after having begun to acquire and read various books by its leader, she became a member of the movement. Subsequently she spoke at length to me about why she had joined, emphasising that Ōkawa's teachings provided her with a spiritual focus she had previously lacked, and of how they spoke both to her sense of national identity as a Japanese and as a citizen of the world beyond Japan. Kōfuku's teaching, she emphasised, contained universal meanings bound up with its Buddhist orientations – yet ones with a special resonance for Japanese people since they emphasised Japanese centrality in this universal world (a point that will be illustrated later in this article). These ideas were closely bound up with Kōfuku's self-identity as a Buddhist-oriented movement, in its belief that Ōkawa was a Buddhist teacher with a special mission to revive Buddhism and who, in spreading its message to the world at large, would engender a world spiritual renewal – a point emphasised by Ōkawa himself in 1991, when he proclaimed himself to be the eternal Buddha.[1]

In asserting that it taught a new form of Buddhism – one that would bring about universal transformation or salvation – Kōfuku no Kagaku was not unique in late twentieth century Japan. Such affirmations have been a predominant feature in the rhetoric of several of the 'new' new religions in Japan (i.e., movements that have flourished in the last decades of the twentieth century) of Buddhist orientation, including Agonshū 阿含宗 and Aum Shinrikyō オウム真理教. These affirmations have also been closely linked to a series of millennial beliefs that all these movements in some way or other have shared, and in which images of cataclysm and disaster have been juxtaposed with concepts of transformation, salvation and world renewal. The rhetoric that such movements have used in their promises of a new Buddhist revival contains some strikingly nationalist images that place Japan at the centre of, and affirm its special destiny in, any such world spiritual transformation. In such terms, several of the 'new' new religions either explicitly or implicitly create or affirm close links between their self-identity as Buddhist revival movements, the millennial perspectives they espouse, and assertions of Japanese destiny in the world. The primary focus of this paper is on how three such movements (Agonshū, Aum Shinrikyō and Kōfuku no Kagaku) do this, and on how they articulate nationalist themes through their emphasis on Buddhist revival, millennialism and national destiny. It particularly focuses on the teachings of these movements in the latter part of

---

[1] On these developments in Kōfuku no Kagaku see Astley (1995).

the 1980s and in the early 1990s, before the 1995 Aum attack on the Tōkyō subway dramatically affected the situation and affected the ways in which new movements presented themselves.[2] I will also focus on why it is that Buddhism has been the religious tradition that these movements have turned to in their construction of a nationalist and millennialist discourse.

### New new religions, the 'crisis of expectancy' and the 'revival of Buddhism'

Aum, Agonshū and Kōfuku no Kagaku have all variously been described as 'new' new religions (Japanese: _shin shin shūkyō_ 新新宗教) – a term used by several scholars to refer to the types of new religion that attracted prominence and attention from the 1980s onwards. Space does not permit more than a brief introductory overview of these movements here, save to note that (as indeed the case of the young lady cited above indicates) they have widely been regarded as appealing especially to urban-based younger, well educated Japanese as a result of having tapped into a general dissatisfaction with, and distrust of, the modern scientific rationalism that forms the basis of the Japanese education and work systems. Their development can also be seen in part as a reaction to the pervasive influence of modernisation which, as has been widely pointed out, is often equated with the incursion of Western cultural influences in Japan and which is seen as having provided material wealth but afforded its members little in the way of spiritual satisfaction or meaning. This general unease and belief that the present system is failing has led to aspirations for change on temporal and spiritual levels, and to a search for new meanings and paradigms, often framed in 'catastrophic' millennial terms (i.e., in the belief that world renewal requires some form of dramatic and cataclysmic scenario to happen).[3]

---

[2] It is evident that in the 'post-Aum era' [see Reader (2001)] several of the religious movements that previously espoused dramatic millennialist stances have modified their tone somewhat. This is an issue about which I intend to write at a later stage.

[3] On the 'new' new religions in general see Reader (1988), (1991), pp. 208-233 and (1994) (all of which focus particularly on Agonshū), Shimazono (1992), Numata (1995) and Shimada (1995). In Reader (2000a), pp. 47-52, I discuss the millennial impulses behind these movements. For further discussion of the term 'catastrophic millennialism' see Wessinger (1997), pp. 47-59. While millennial themes were also prominent in the early development of older new religions such as Tenrikyō 天理教 and Ōmoto 大本 they have become less so as these movements grew in age [see Reader (2000b), pp. 199f.], and it has

Such millennialist views were rooted both in a sense of crisis, fear and despair relating to the future (in which environmental worries and the ever-present awareness of nuclear weapons have led many Japanese to believe that some form of world crisis or catastrophe is inevitable) and in a sense of expectation that some form of radical upheaval will necessarily occur in order to transform the world and overturn the materialism of the present order. In late-twentieth century Japan the popularity of such millennial views has owed much to Western influences, both in terms of the Western calendar which provided a ready date for any such projected event to occur, and through the prophecies of Nostradamus, which first appeared in Japanese translation in 1973 and which have gained great popularity in Japan since then. These prophecies (and especially the notion, featured prominently in Japanese renditions, that a saviour from the East would appear at the end of the century to save the world) have figured prominently in the interpretations and prophetic perspectives of the founders of all three of the movements discussed here and all of whom have managed to identify themselves with this prophesied saviour.[4]

At the same time, the millennialism of the 'new' new religions has been impelled by a latent hostility to Western cultural incursions into Japan. It has also drawn inspiration from the Buddhist tradition, and from the concept of karma, which plays a significant part in the thinking of the three religious movements under discussion here. Certainly it is through the concept of karma – both in individual and collective terms – that these movements understand why the world is faced with cataclysm in the modern day. According to Kiriyama Seiyū 桐山靖雄, the founder and leader of Agonshū, the imminent disasters and potential millennial catastrophe that he predicted (from the 1970s onwards) would occur at the end of the century were caused by the collective karma of humanity, in which he included the spirits of the dead for whom the correct memorial services have not been performed and which therefore, in his

---

been among the 'new' new religions that such themes have been most prominently articulated in Japan in the last part of the twentieth century.

[4] On Nostradamus's prophecies and their impact on Japanese popular culture see Shimada (1995), pp.106f and Kisala (1997). In Aum and Kōfuku respectively, Nostradamus' prophecies are discussed in several publications such as Asahara (1991) and Ōkawa (1990a) and (1991).

understanding, remained unsettled and capable of causing unrest. The eradica-
tion of this accumulated bad karma could only come about through spiritual
practices and rituals, which would, in Kiriyama's terms, 'cut' the negative
karma that had accrued on individual and collective levels.[5] Asahara Shōkō 麻原
彰晃, who founded Aum Shinrikyō after spending some time in Agonshū, and
who drew many influences from Kiriyama's teachings, also saw a direct causal
relation between the end-of-century catastrophes he prophesied, and the
accumulation of negative karma in the world. His solution to these problems
also revolved around karmic cleansing on an individual level (through ascetic
practice) and, eventually, on a wider level through more drastic means.[6]

In developing a link between karma and the potential for world destruction,
movements such as Agonshū and Aum also implicitly critiqued established
Buddhism in Japan as being incapable of providing spiritual solutions for
modern problems, and claimed that it was their destiny and mission to develop a
new form of Buddhism suitable for the modern world. This was a Buddhism
that, while speaking to the needs of the modern age, also 'restored' or reaffirmed
the spiritual purity of Buddhism's origins. Indeed, these movements portrayed
themselves as having a mission to revive 'original Buddhism' (_genshi bukkyō_ 原
始仏教) – a term used particularly by Aum and Agonshū – and to spread it to the
world at large, thereby eradicating the collective negative karma of the world
and bringing about a global spiritual transformation.

### Buddhism for a new age: Agonshū's sense of mission in the modern day

These themes are perhaps best seen in Agonshū, the oldest of the three
movements discussed here.[7] While Agonshū, from its earliest foundations in
1954, has combined an eclectic mixture of concepts, beliefs and practices from

---

[5] See Reader (1988) for a discussion of these teachings: Kiriyama's views are set out in
   various of his publications such as Kiriyama (1981).
[6] Asahara's teachings on these matters are found in a variety of his publications, notably
   Asahara (n.d. [c. 1994]), passim. Both Shimazono (1997) and Reader (2000a) present
   extended discussions and analyses of Asahara's teachings.
[7] This discussion of Agonshū is based largely on my earlier work on the movement [e.g.,
   Reader (1988, 1994)] coupled with subsequent reading of Agonshū materials following the
   Aum affair.

Buddhism, Shugendō 修験道 and traditional Japanese folk religion, its primary frame of self-identity has always been as a Buddhist movement.[8] Its ritual practices are drawn largely from esoteric Buddhism making particular use, for example, of the *goma* 護摩 fire rite, which is performed regularly at Agonshū centres (and which Kiriyama has also performed in tandem with leaders from the Tibetan Buddhist tradition, including the Dalai Lama) as well as in a huge performance at its annual *Hoshi matsuri* 星まつり (Star Festival) each year outside Kyōto. Tibetan Buddhist symbols (which have proved a constant source of interest and fascination for young Japanese people, and which figured also in Aum Shinrikyō) are prevalent also in Agonshū, while the movement also emphasises basic meditation practices which have their roots in what Kiriyama terms 'original Buddhism' (*genshi bukkyō* 原始仏教), and makes use of early Buddhist sutras such as the Āgama (Japanese: Agon) sutras in its teachings.

As was mentioned earlier, Kiriyama has also incorporated millennial themes into his teachings with his warnings that some form of world crisis or disaster would occur before the end of the twentieth century unless spiritual action were taken to ward it off. It is in this context that Agonshū's self-proclaimed notion of 'original Buddhism' comes to the fore, for central to Kiriyama's teaching is his conviction that he and Agonshū have a mission to bring about a Buddhist revival through the restoration of 'original Buddhism' to the world. It is through the transmission of the teachings of this Buddhism (which, according to Agonshū interpretation, is a re-presentation of early Buddhist ideas expressed through esoteric forms and guided by Kiriyama) that the karmic unease of the world can be resolved, the unhappy spirits of the dead pacified, and the threat of world disaster negated.

Agonshū's self-proclaimed mission of world salvation owes much to an experience Kiriyama had in 1981 when he visited the ancient Buddhist site of Sahet Mahet (also known as Sravasti, the location of the first Buddhist monastery) in northern India. While there he claimed to have 'felt' a vibration emanating from Shakyamuni the Buddha that was directed to him. In his mind

---

[8] In various discussions with Agonshū officials and believers, they have always emphasised that, in their view, Agonshū is a Buddhist movement. Aum followers and officials have made similar points to me. I should note that in this paper I focus on the self-perceptions of the movements discussed here.

this was a direct awakening and a direct message to him from the Buddha, anointing of ratifying him as a successor in the modern day.[9] The experience convinced Kiriyama that his mission was to spread 'original Buddhism' to the world in order to save it – and that, in so doing, he was to build what Agonshū has since described as the 'new Sahet Mahet' (a temple symbolising and representing the first ever Buddhist monastery) in Japan. This was to be the spiritual centre from which Buddhist-inspired peace would spread across the globe. In this process, the power of Buddhism was passed, via Kiriyama's transmission, from India to Japan, effectively transforming Japan into the new Buddha land. Thus Agonshū began work in the 1980s on a new main temple, its 'new Sahet Mahet', on a hillside at Yamashina outside Kyōto (this work was completed in the early 1990s), and it is at this location, too, that Agonshū's major annual public ritual (and mass spectacle) the *Hoshi matsuri* takes place.

In 1986, too, Agonshū acquired a Buddhist relic from Sri Lanka and while this relic is but one of many thousand Buddhist relics to be found throughout Asia, it has been firmly proclaimed in Agonshū that this is, indeed, one of the few genuine relics of the Buddha. To Agonshū it is not just a piece of bone but a living, powerful entity that manifests and radiates the spiritual power of the Buddha. The bequest of this has also been presented in Agonshū literature as recognition, by one Buddhist country, Sri Lanka, of Agonshū's mission to the world, and the relic now serves of Agonshū's chief focus of veneration and worship.[10]

Agonshū has thus equipped itself with two potent symbols – the Buddha relic from Sri Lanka and the spiritual transmission from the Buddha at Sahet Mahet – which legitimate its holy centre at Yamashina, which stand at the centre of its proclaimed mission to the world, and which symbolise its restoration of 'original Buddhism' to the world. It is, of course, evident that in this claiming, or appropriation of symbols of legitimacy, that Agonshū has sought to move the centre of Buddhism away from India and to Japan. While Buddhism first spread

---

[9] In 1988, I was shown a video at Agonshū's main office in Tōkyō in which Kiriyama spoke about his experience of receiving this direct transmission at Sahet Mahet.
[10] On this relic and its meaning, and on the background to its donation see Reader (1991), pp. 216f.

from northern India across Asia, now it was to spread again from Japan in a second wave of renewal, but this time across the whole world.

Despite these seemingly universalising dimensions to Agonshū's mission, it is not difficult to discern a rather nationalist and Japan-centred undertone to its world mission. This can be seen not just in the appropriation to Japan of Buddhist images, or in the claim that Japan was to be the new centre of Buddhism, but also in the visual symbols on display at the *Hoshi matsuri* itself. The festival itself is held, ostensibly to maximise public attendance, on a public holiday, February 11th, which is now known as Constitution Day. This public holiday date is significant, however, in that it used to be National Foundation Day – the day according to Shintō/ nationalist myths when Jinmu, the legendary first Emperor and descendant of the Sun Goddess Amaterasu came down to earth to establish the nation of Japan. Such nationalist undertones resulted in the proscription of this name after the war and the renaming of this public holiday with the new, secularised and sanitised name Constitution Day.

The nationalist undertones are hardly lost on those who attend, not just because of the date or, indeed, the ubiquitous Japanese flags erected throughout the ritual site. The invocations made before the fires of the *goma* 護摩 are lit, have, on the occasions I have attended, been full of nationalist imagery, calling on the spirits of past Emperors, making reference to the 'great country of Japan' (*Dainipponkoku* 大日本国), and invoking the native Japanese spirit (*yamato-damashii* 大和魂).[11] Despite such an apparent emphasis on national symbols and images, the proclaimed overarching theme of the festival is universal, and centres on praying for world peace. However, despite such an overarching and universal ambition, the more immediate focus of prayers and rituals centred on the two *goma* pyres centres on distinctly Japanese religious themes – praying for worldly benefits and seeking solace for one's ancestors – through which world peace may be attained. The universal meanings of the festival are thus expressed primarily through localised Japanese concerns, and thus world salvation is effectively tied in with and becomes part of the expression of Japanese needs and concerns.

---

[11] See Reader (1991), p. 221-225 for a fuller description of this event.

The messages of world peace and harmony are emphasised, however, by the presence of invited religious leaders from around the world, whose presence is designed to provide an international and ecumenical flavour to the occasion. In 1988, for example, a group of Egyptian Muslim leaders were among the invited guests. Their presence and participation in a ritual for world peace and religious harmony appeared to be at odds with the invocations to the Japanese spirit and the nationalist symbols linking state and religion, and it was evident, to this observer at least, that the international/ ecumenical dimension of the festival – and of Agonshū's mission – was in fact subjugated within, and subservient to, expressions of Agonshū's nationalism. Yamashina, the new Buddha land on earth, from whence the spirit of peace was to be spread across the globe, was equally the setting for a festival suffused with nationalistic symbols and expressive declarations of Japanese power and glory. As I have indicated elsewhere, the festival reflects a central theme in Agonshū's dynamic, in which the movement affirms a particularist focus of Japanese identity framed around major nationalist symbols, and strengthens that message in the eyes of its followers by placing it in the context of a universal message. Agonshū followers can, by participating in its festivals and rituals, 'touch base' with the roots of their culture and affirm the unity of their faith and national sense of belonging, yet also feel they are doing 'something' for world peace and harmony: they are taking part in a mission to save the world and spread Agonshū's newly revived Buddhism across the globe, while emphasising the centrality of Japan and of their identity as Japanese in the process.[12]

### Aum Shinrikyō, Buddhism and Nationalism

As I have discussed at length elsewhere, Aum Shinrikyō eventually developed a highly negative view of the world, and a deeply aggressive perspective in which it came to view mass destruction as an inevitable part of the salvation process.[13] However, in its early days in the mid-1980s, it expressed views similar to those of Agonshū, with pessimistic visions of world destruction being offset by an optimistic sense that the crisis could be avoided, negative karma

---

[12] See Reader (1991), pp. 227-232 for a fuller and more extensive discussion of the linked themes of particularity and universal motifs in Agonshū.
[13] See Reader (2000a) for a full discussion of the Aum affair and Aum's turn to violence.

eradicated, and a new age of salvation achieved non-violently through religious means. Like Agonshū it saw world salvation coming about through the restoration of 'original Buddhism', and it drew extensively on Buddhist teachings, particularly those relating to the relationship between materialism, desire, suffering and enlightenment, in this context. Like Kiriyama, Asahara saw India as a sacred land and source of spiritual sustenance, legitimation and empowerment, and he too had visited and found inspiration at Buddhist sites there, including Sahet Mahet.

Aum also emphasised its mission to save the world from imminent destruction. However, unlike Agonshū, Asahara's mission was built around images of a sacred war between good and evil in which materialism (evil) and spirituality (good) would struggle for supremacy, with the latter triumphing to bring about the advent of a new world. Underlying Asahara's mission of world salvation was a virulent antipathy to the materialism of modern society, which had to be combated by the forces of spiritual transcendence. Asahara found scriptural legitimations for this polarised view of the world, and for his belief in the necessity for the forces of good to confront and defeat the realms of evil, in the Tibetan Buddhist Kālacakra Tantra, which tells of how a sacred king from the mythical Kingdom of Shambhala arises to lead the forces of good in a final victorious battle against the forces of evil.[14] Although primarily intended as an allegorical account of the eventual triumph of Buddhism, the Kālacakra Tantra clearly contains a vision of military triumph, one which proved highly attractive to Asahara, who visualised such a contest enacted on the earthly plain in which he would lead an army of followers in a final battle against evil. Aum also developed what it called its 'Shambhala plan' intended to transform this world into an earthly spiritual paradise through the construction of communes (called, in Aum, 'Lotus Villages').

Asahara's vision of conflict, while legitimated by Buddhist sources, had its roots also in his concerns to save Japan from foreign dominance. In studies of Aum this side of Asahara's teaching has often been subsumed because of the antipathy Asahara expressed towards Japanese materialism, because of his murderous attitude, as evidenced by the Tōkyō subway attack, to the Japanese

---

[14] On this text and its apparent symbolism see Newman (1995).

population at large, and because, in the period immediately prior to the subway attack, he appeared to damn Japan. Yet, even amidst his condemnations, there always were hints of a rather different, and less hostile, view of Japan and its people: at root Asahara conceived of his mission as one in which he was to save Japan from materialism and foreign dominance, and in which Japan was to be turned into the spiritual centre through which the world at large could be transformed.

Such messages began to be expressed by Asahara soon after he established his movement in 1984. He was influenced by the predictions of the pre-war nationalist Sakai Katsuisa 酒井勝軍 that a final war would erupt and that only a lineage of compassionate sages led by a saviour from Japan (a reference Asahara clearly saw as referring to himself), would survive, Asahara travelled in 1985 to Mount Goyō 五葉山 in Iwate prefecture, which is associated with Sakai, and had a visionary encounter there that further affirmed his mission.[15] In his travels in India in 1986, too, Asahara claimed that many of the holy people he met either entrusted to him or prophesied for him the mission of saving his own country by people he met in India: in journeying to the birthplace of Buddhism, in other words, he received an empowering message to save his own country.[16]

If Asahara's mission was shrouded in images of conflict and struggle from the outset, it was also one that, as the above comments show, focused especially on the salvation of Japan and the triumph of Buddhism. At times the struggle he envisaged involved a conflict between religions in which Buddhism (the force of good) would confront and finally defeat Christianity (evil).[17] It also, it is important to note, was framed around dark vision of an 'other' that symbolised and epitomised the presence of evil in the world and that explicitly threatened Japan in such terms. In practical terms it is clear that for Asahara this 'other' was the United States, which he saw not just as the world's prime symbolic representative of the forces of materialism, but as a threat to Japan in cultural and other terms.

---

[15] Cf. Shimazono (1995). p. 395.
[16] Cf. Reader (2000a), pp. 78f and pp. 89f.
[17] Cf., for example, Asahara (1995a), p. 306.

The image of America as a dangerous force capable of destroying Japan (as it had done before in 1945) ran through many of Asahara's thoughts. Even in 1993 – a time when his messages had all but failed in Japan – he continued to argue in sermons that Japan could become a strong power capable of defeating the USA. He publicly lamented Japan's military weakness in comparison to the USA, blaming Japan's defeat in 1945 on its technological deficiencies and criticising the Japanese of that era for being 'an ignorant people who had tried to fight against atomic weapons with bamboo spears'.[18] To counter the continuing imbalance in military terms, he advocated that Japan should pursue a programme of manufacturing chemical weapons (including sarin).[19] It was, in fact, in his demands that Japan should make sarin in order to resist external aggression that he first spoke publicly about this chemical weapon that became the ultimate symbol of Aum's violence.

Aum's increasingly violent theology of confrontation not only emphasised the need to physically destroy the forces of materialism but also became increasingly obsessed with complex conspiracy theories alleging that Japan was being subverted by evil forces intent on crushing Aum and achieving world domination. Central to such conspiracy theories was the belief that an influential group of people in Japan was conspiring with outside forces (primarily American) to undermine the country and brainwash its people, so as to destroy Aum and to facilitate the world domination that the conspirators planned.[20] The 'conspirators' were basically people in the privileged elite who had been embraced, seduced and corrupted by the forces of materialism, and who were in thrall to Western culture and to the USA. It was such people (who included the Imperial family, along with Crown Princess Masako, doubly elitist because she was married into the most elite family in Japan and because she came from a privileged diplomatic background and had studied in the USA) who were condemned as conspirators planning to subjugate Japan for their own ends and for those of a foreign power.

While Asahara expressed deep resentment against, and dissatisfaction with, Japan, it is evident here that his ire was especially focused on what he saw as a

---

[18] Asahara (n.d. [c. 1994]), p. 235.
[19] Cf. ibid. p. 231.
[20] On Aum's conspiracy theories and their meanings see Reader (2000a), pp. 188-191.

Japan dominated and perverted by privilege cliques, and that he never wholly gave up the hope that Japan could escape the grip of such people. Indeed, even as he condemned humanity in general for having sold out to materialism, he continued to hope that Japan might 'wake up' to the truth and fight its external enemies. In his last book, _Bōkoku Nihon no kanashimi_ 亡国日本の悲しみ ('The sadness of the ruined country Japan'), produced just before and published just after the subway attack, Asahara dwelt on the likely occurrence of war between the USA and Japan, in which the Japanese people would finally have to make up their minds whether (as he hoped) they would stand up and fight, or whether they would supinely submit to subjugation.[21] In other words, even at the point at which he and his cohorts were readying themselves to inflict mass murder on the Japanese population, Asahara and Aum never abandoned the hope of inspiring the Japanese nation to join their Buddhist-inspired crusade against, and envisioned defeat of, the forces of evil.

### _Kōfuku no Kagaku, Buddhism and the triumph of Japan_

Of the movements discussed here, the one that appeared, at least in the earlier part of the 1990s, to exhibit the most aggressive nationalist orientations, and to most directly link millennial catastrophe to Japanese triumph and the rise of a new Japan-led Buddhism has been Kōfuku no Kagaku 幸福の科学, founded by Ōkawa Ryūhō 大川隆法 in 1986. Interestingly, in its early days Kōfuku no Kagaku had been a rather eclectic movement, centred on the person of Ōkawa who claimed to receive and transmit messages from the spiritual realms, from a variety of holy figures from across the religious pantheon. These included not only figures from the Buddhist pantheon, but from Christianity, Islam and other traditions as well. However, gradually, Buddhist themes and images began to dominate and prevail in the movement, especially as it underwent rapid growth and expansion in Japan at the turn of the 1990s.

In this period of rapid expansion, too, Ōkawa's teachings took an increasingly militant millennial form in which the world was depicted as heading towards disaster and as being in need of a spiritual transformation that would destroy the

---

[21] Cf. Asahara (1995b), pp. 270ff.

threatening forces of evil. These ideas came to be closely linked to strident nationalist images that depicted Japan as the emergent spiritual centre of the world, and Kōfuku and Ōkawa as the guiding forces in this process.

In the early 1990s Kōfuku began a campaign of mass proselytisation that was instrumental to its rapid growth, centred on a series of books (including two that were translated into English as *The Laws of the Sun* and *The Laws of Gold*). These books combined an emphasis on Ōkawa's teachings relating to karma, transmigration and other themes drawn from Buddhism, with a powerful evocation of millennial themes. In particular they expressed dramatic images of destruction, with Ōkawa envisaging cataclysms ranging from earthquakes and wars to pestilence that would sweep away the foundations of the current era, causing mass destruction and the collapse of Western civilisation. Amidst this destruction, however, Japan would survive to stand out as a beacon, as the light through which the new civilisation would materialise:

> "*When the world sinks into darkness, Japan will shine as the sun...
> those who are born in this age are the chosen people, to whom many
> missions have been assigned.*"[22]

This image of Japan shining like the sun expressed in *The Laws of the Sun* was further developed in *The Laws of Gold*, which spoke of Japan as providing a 'Light of Hope' for the world and becoming its new spiritual centre: Japan, would, Ōkawa pronounced, lead the world into a new golden age of spiritual truth and to the creation of Utopia on earth.[23] At the turn of the 1990s, too, Ōkawa claimed to have received a series of prophecies from the spirit of Nostradamus, in which it was foretold that the United States would suffer cataclysmic destruction and defeat, that Russia and China (two countries traditionally seen in Japan as threatening neighbours) would be laid waste by disaster, and that Japan would emerge as the new centre of the world.[24]

As Kōfuku no Kagaku's millennialism became more strident and nationalis-tic, its focus on Buddhism became more pronounced. In 1991, for example,

---

[22] Ōkawa (1990b), p. 179.
[23] Cf. Ōkawa (1990c), p. 31 and pp. 191f.

Ōkawa declared himself to the eternal Buddha and proclaimed that his wife was as an incarnation of Monju 文珠 (Manjushri).[25] As the eternal Buddha, Ōkawa was no longer a prophet of the world to come: henceforth he was its saviour, the Buddha who had returned to this world to bring about the spiritual transformation of humanity and to oversee the triumph of Japan.

Not only was Kōfuku no Kagaku a Buddhist movement, but also Buddhism was proclaimed as superior to other faiths. Although Ōkawa had, in Kōfuku's earlier eclectic days, drawn on Christian imagery in his teachings, by 1992 he had begun to emphasise the differences he saw between Christianity and Buddhism, and to state that the latter was a higher and more exalted religion than Christianity, while Buddha was superior in spiritual terms to Jesus.[26] In later pronouncements he was to state that Christianity was out of touch in the new age, and that it was no longer a valid or adequate religion for the needs of modern people.[27] By contrast his religion was well suited to do this, and his followers (who he had come to describe as Bodhisattvas and Buddhas radiating truth to the world[28]) would lead the Japanese people (*kokumin* 国民) to true religious belief, and make Japan the source of light and a centre of world salvation.[29] The next century would see the dawn of the 'Japanese era' (*nihon no jidai* 日本の時代), heralding a new age in which the light of Buddha would come into the world and bring about Utopia on earth.[30]

In the first half of the 1990s, then, as it grew rapidly, Kōfuku no Kagaku came to espouse a fervent nationalistic and triumphalist millennialism in which Japan would 'shine like the sun' and bring about a Japanese-dominated age of Buddhist world ascendancy led by Ōkawa and his young Japanese followers. By contrast, one might add, places that were obvious rivals and cultural threats to Japan such as the USA, faced destruction through various disasters and calamities as a result of accumulated karmic faults. Ōkawa and Kōfuku, in other words, had woven together a religious agenda that offered potential Japanese followers

---

[24] Cf. Ōkawa (1990a), pp. 23-45.
[25] Cf. Numata (1995), p. 204.
[26] Cf. Ōkawa (1992), p. 210.
[27] Cf. Ōkawa (1995a), pp. 155-160.
[28] Cf. ibid., p. 19.
[29] Cf. ibid, pp. 95-98.

the chance to stand in the vanguard of that new order, as Japanese leaders of the new age that would dawn across (and dominate) the rest of the world, while Japan's rivals were destroyed or swept aside. Like the movements discussed earlier in this paper, then, Kōfuku no Kagaku had linked together a sense of national identity to a message of universal triumph in ways that spoke to the concerns and aspirations of its Japanese followers seeking, like the lady mentioned at the beginning of this paper, a sense of identity and meaning both in localised cultural terms and in the context of the wider world, coupled with a message of triumph over those forces that appeared to offer the greatest cultural threat to Japan.

### Concluding comments

The ways in which Japanese new religions may link together particularist and universal themes so as to affirm a sense of national identity have been commented on in previous academic studies. Michael Pye, for example, has demonstrated how Byakkō Shinkōkai 白光真宏会 transmits universal messages about world peace, expressed through its peace prayer and rituals in ways that enable its Japanese members to connect to, and express feelings about, the world at large. At the same time its members are able to reaffirm their localised sense of identity through Byakkō's religious practices (such as spiritual healing) that are oriented very much towards a Japanese audience. These two processes thus operate together in a dynamic in which universality is thus predicated upon the affirmation of Japanese identity.[31]

Catherine Cornille, too, has commented on such issues in discussing the apparently universal rhetoric of Japanese new religions in the context of establishing world peace and saving humanity.[32] Yet, Cornille argues, while such missions for peace may be a religious articulation of these movements' awareness of internationalisation and globalisation, they are also strongly underpinned by a potent nationalist agenda in ways that enable such movements to

---

[30] Cf. Ōkawa (1995b), p. 123.
[31] Cf. Pye (1986), pp. 234-241.
[32] Cf. Cornille (1999), p. 228.

'remain fundamentally and essentially Japanese'.[33] Cornille also emphasises that the new religions often make use of millennial ideas in such contexts, articulating universal themes of salvation in which the disunities of the past will be replaced by a new spiritual order centred on Japan. Often, as Cornille notes, this may assume rather triumphalist forms – a point she particularly notes in connection with Kōfuku no Kagaku.[34]

While my analysis largely fits with those of Pye and Cornille, it also draws attention to factors not particularly discussed in their studies. These are notably the importance, in the rhetoric of the three movements discussed here, of Buddhism as a force in the process of world salvation and renewal, and the link that is made in all three groups between millennialist discourse and nationalist triumph. In Agonshū, Aum and Kōfuku no Kagaku, millennial themes, images of Buddhist revival, and nationalistic visions relating to Japanese identity and destiny are woven together. All three, in different terms, visualise Japan at the centre of a world renewal, which necessitates the subjugation of opposing and alien forces that threaten Japanese identity and cultural integrity. Hence the 'new world order' or new spiritual dawn envisaged by these movements has a distinctly Japanese hue to it, as well as one cloaked in the images of a newly revived Buddhism, in which Japan becomes the centre of a mission to spread a new (yet 'original') Buddhism to the world. In all three, millennial visions have thus been used to answer questions of cultural uncertainty and worries about the apparent cultural domination of Japan by external forces and forms, and to promise and envisage a future in which Japan will triumph.

The use of Buddhism in this process is especially fascinating, for it is this that has provided each of these religious groups with a core theme of identity and a focus through which they can define and locate themselves on the religious spectrum. It has also served as a critical mechanism through which they could express their future visions and express themselves as Japanese religious movements within a wider, universal context. Affirming their orientation as a Buddhist movement enables them to place their rationale and dynamic of world salvation within a universalising context, in the sense that Buddhism is a world

---

[33] Cf. ibid., p. 238.
[34] Cf. ibid., p. 235.

religion that transcends borders. Yet simultaneously their use of Buddhist imagery reinforces their 'Japanese' core, for it associates them with a tradition that is an essential element within Japan's cultural heritage. It thus binds them into a powerful nationalist sentiment that is important in terms of identity formation and in terms of the construction of cultural defences *against* universal and global themes in the present day.

The emphasis the movements mentioned here have placed on Buddhism, and the ways in which Buddhism frames their and their followers' sense of identity, indicates that Buddhism remains highly relevant for late 20th century Japan – a point clearly understood by the young lady mentioned at the start of this paper, when she found herself in another land and thinking about her own sense of identity. In so doing, she found herself thinking not, in religious terms, about Shintō, but about Buddhism. Likewise, Buddhism remains so important to such issues of religious identity in Japan that numerous militant new religions have found it vital to appropriate and articulate it as an image of revival and to use it as a means of affirming their relevance both in Japanese cultural terms and in the context of demonstrating their potential universality.

Indeed, I would argue that Buddhism alone of the various elements of the Japanese religious tradition has the cultural resonance to be viable in future global contexts. By contrast, the tradition most commonly associated with nationalism in modern Japan, Shintō, is incapable of accommodating the sort of internationalist-global perspectives and dimensions that are needed in the modern world to deal with the concerns of people such as the young woman introduced earlier, who are conscious of other lands and languages, and yet who need reassurance about their intrinsic cultural identity in relation to the wider world. Shintō, which has been singularly poor at sustaining a presence beyond Japan even among Japanese communities,[35] is too tied to the limited and parochial nationalism of those who know little about the wider world – and too closely associated, I suspect, with older generations – to appear relevant to the global age of the coming century.

---

[35] Here one could draw attention to Hawaii, where Shintō has been unable to maintain its shrines at any serious level of functionality despite the presence of a sizeable Japanese-American population that continues to support Buddhist temples and Japanese new religions.

By contrast, the type of imagery projected by the 'new' new religions of Buddhist persuasion operates within a more global, macrocosmic frame of identity. Buddhism as a world religion – yet one with a distinct connection to Japanese heritage and identity – provides an 'international' side to the world missions of the 'new' new religions, and serves as the medium through which they can express their millennial and universal goals while simultaneously asserting their sense of Japanese power and pride. Those who identify and feel at home with such ideas are people who are well aware of global issues and of other cultures, and understand that Japan cannot exist within an insular framework. Such people – young, urban, educated Japanese like the young woman mentioned earlier (and, indeed, like Ōkawa himself, who was studying and working in New York when he had his first religious visions) – are at home with the signs and symbols of other cultures in terms of food, music, mass communications, experiences and so on. Often, too, they are people who appear to have more in common with those who live in similar environments: one could argue, for example, that in many respects the young, educated Tōkyōite has much more in common with his/ her counterparts in New York, London and Paris than with, say, elderly Japanese farmers, fishermen and housewives in Shimane, Akita or the islands of the Inland Sea. Yet they may, as a result of their very internationalism (or at least their familiarity with the trappings and challenges of other cultures) be more in need of new modes of identity that emphasise their cultural difference (and, as a result, help assuage any sense of cultural insecurity) than would be, for example, someone in a rural Japanese village.

It is in such contexts that one can discern one of the primary appeals of the 'new' new religions, with their focus on Japanese identity and their assertions of Japanese cultural and spiritual predominance. The Buddhist images they utilise enable them to function them within a Japanese cultural context while allowing them to interpret their missions in a universal context of global salvation. When, as has happened with Agonshū, Aum and Kōfuku no Kagaku, this is also tied to millennialist visions that articulate underlying concerns about the future, that emphasise the need for world renewal and promise eventual Japanese ascendancy, we can see how particularised issues of cultural and religious identity are woven into, and placed at the very apex of, global religious development.

## References

Asahara (1991)

Asahara, Shōkō 麻原彰晃: *Nosutoradamusu himitsu no daiyogen: 1999-nen no nazo* ノストラダムス秘密の大予言: １９９９年の謎. Tōkyō: Oumu Shuppan, 1991.

— (1995a)

Asahara, Shōkō: *Disaster Strikes the Land of the Rising Sun*. Tōkyō: Aum Publishing, 1995.

— (1995b)

Asahara, Shōkō 麻原彰晃: *Bōkoku Nihon no kanashimi* 亡国日本の悲しみ. Tōkyō: Oumu Shuppan, 1995.

— (n.d. [c. 1994])

Asahara, Shōkō 麻原彰晃: *Vajrayana kōsu: Kyōgaku shisutemu kyōhon* ヴァジラヤーナコース: 教学システム教本. [Internal unpublished Aum training document consisting of a collection of Asahara's main sermons between 1988-1994].

Astley (1995)

Astley, Trevor: "The transformation of a recent Japanese new religion: Ōkawa Ryūhō and Kōfuku no Kagaku", in: *Japanese Journal of Religious Studies*. Vol. 22/3-4 (1995), pp. 343-380.

Cornille (1999)

Cornille, Catherine: "Nationalism and Japanese New Religions", in: *Nova Religio*. Vol. 2/2 (1999), pp. 228-244.

Kiriyama (1981)

Kiriyama, Seiyū 桐山靖雄: *1999 nen karuma to reishō kara no dasshutsu* １９９９年カルマと霊障からの脱出. Tōkyō: Hirakawa Shuppansha, 1981.

Kisala (1997)

Kisala, Robert: "1999 and beyond: The Use of Nostradamus' Prophecies by Japanese Religions", in: *Japanese Religions*. Vol. 23/1 (1997), pp. 143-157.

Newman (1995)

Newman, John: "Eschatology in the Wheel of Time Tantra", in: Lopez, Donald S. (ed): *Buddhism in Practice*. Princeton, NJ: Princeton University Press, 1995, pp. 284-289.

Numata (1995)

Numata, Kenya 沼田健哉: *Shūkyō to kagaku no neoparadaimu: shin shin shūkyō o chūshin to shite* 宗教と科学のネオパラダイム：新新宗教を中心として. Ōsaka: Sōgensha, 1995.

Ōkawa (1990a)

Ōkawa, Ryūhō 大川隆法: *Nosutoradamusu no shinyogen* ノストラダムスの新予言. Tōkyō: Kadokawa Bunko, 1990.

—      (1990b)

Ōkawa, Ryūhō: *The Laws of the Sun*. Tōkyō: Institute for Research into Human Happiness, 1990.

—      (1990c)

Ōkawa, Ryūhō: *The Laws of Gold*. Tōkyō: Institute for Research into Human Happiness, 1990.

—      (1991)

Ōkawa, Ryūhō 大川隆法: *Nosutoradamusu senritsu no keiji* ノストラダムス戦慄の啓示. Tōkyō: Kōfuku no Kagaku Shuppan, 1991.

—      (1992)

Ōkawa, Ryūhō 大川隆法: *Shūkyō no chōsen* 宗教の挑戦. Tōkyō: Kōfuku no Kagaku Shuppan, 1992.

—      (1995a)

Ōkawa, Ryūhō 大川隆法: *Kiseki no jidai o ikiru* 奇跡の時代を生きる. Tōkyō: Kōfuku no Kagaku Shuppan, 1995.

—      (1995b)

Ōkawa, Ryūhō 大川隆法: *Jinsei seikō no hisaku* 人生成功の秘策. Tōkyō: Kōfuku no Kagaku Shuppan, 1995.

Pye (1986)

Pye, Michael: "National and International Identity in a Japanese Religion (Byakkō Shinkōkai)", in: Hayes, V. (ed.): *Identity Issues and World Religions: Selected Proceedings of the XVth Congress of the International Association for the History of Religions*. South Australia: Australian Association for the Study of Religion, 1986, pp. 234-241.

Reader (1988)

    Reader, Ian: "The 'New' New Religions of Japan: an Analysis of the Rise of Agonshū", in: *Japanese Journal of Religious Studies*. Vol. 15/4 (1988), pp. 235-261.

—    (1991)

    Reader, Ian: *Religion in Contemporary Japan*. Basingstoke, UK: Macmillans, 1991.

—    (1994)

    Reader, Ian: "Appropriated Images: Esoteric Themes in a Japanese New Religion", in: Astley, Ian (ed.): *Esoteric Buddhism in Japan*. Copenhagen and Aarhus: Seminar for Buddhist Studies, 1994, pp. 36-63.

—    (2000a)

    Reader, Ian: *Religious Violence in Contemporary Japan: The Case of Aum Shinrikyō*. Richmond, UK: Curzon Press, 2000.

—    (2000b)

    Reader, Ian: "Japan", in: Landes, Richard (ed.): *Encyclopedia of Millennialism and Millennial Movements*. New York: Routledge, 2000, pp. 198-202.

—    (2001)

    Reader, Ian: "Consensus Shattered: Japanese Paradigm Shifts and Moral Panics in the Post-Aum Era", in: *Nova Religio*. Vol. 4/2 (2001).

Shimada (1995)

    Shimada, Hiromi 島田裕巳: *Shinji yasui kokoro: wakamono ga shinshin shūkyō ni hashiru riyū* 信じやすい心：若者が新々宗教に走る理由. Tōkyō: PHP Kenkyūjo, 1995.

Shimazono (1992)

    Shimazono, Susumu 島薗進: *Shinshin shūkyō to shūkyō būmū* 新新宗教と宗教ブーム. Tōkyō: Iwanami Bukkuretto, 1992.

—    (1995)

    Shimazono, Susumu: "In the Wake of Aum: The formation and transformation of a universe of belief", in: *Japanese Journal of Religious Studies*. Vol. 22/ 3-4 (1995), pp. 381-415.

—    (1997)

    Shimazono, Susumu 島薗進: *Shūkyō no kannōsei: Oumu Shirnikyō to bōryoku* 宗教の可能性：オウム真理教と暴力. Tōkyō: Iwanami Shoten, 1997.

Wessinger (1997)

    Wessinger, Catherine: "Millennialism With and Without the Mayhem", in: Robbins, Thomas J./ Palmer, Susan J. (eds.): Millennium, Messiahs, and Mayhem. New York: Routledge, 1997, pp. 47-59.

# War Memorials in modern Japanese context:
# The transformation of nationalistic representation

AWAZU Kenta

## 1. Introduction

In recent studies of nationalism, it is important to note that Benedict Anderson agrees that nationalism performs an ideological function but he has also examined the deep attachment to it as well: "*[....] it is doubtful whether either social change or transformed consciousness, in themselves, do much to explain the attachment that people feel for the inventions of their imaginations – [....] why people are ready to die for these inventions*" [Anderson (1991), p. 141].

Although a large number of researches have been conducted into this imagination, little is known about its representations of fatality. In his recent article, Balakrishnan, a Marxist theorist, has pointed out that "*Marxism lacked a concrete conception of a people, a political anthropology.*" [Balakrishnan (1995), p. 69]. In other words, the questions that Anthony Smith has examined are still worthwhile examining: 'why are men and women willing to die for their countries? Why do they identify so strongly with their nations?' [cf. Smith (1986), p. 8].

Anderson has tried to examine this fatality and has gone further in this direction.

> "*[....] in everything 'natural' there is always something unchosen. In this way, nation-ness is assimilated to skin-colour, gender, parentage and birth-era – all of those things one can not help. And in these 'natural ties' one senses what one might call 'the beauty of gemein-schaft'. To put it another way, precisely because such ties are not chosen, they have about them a halo of disinterestedness. [....] Dying for one's country, which usually one does not choose, assumes a moral grandeur which dying for the Labour Party, the American Medical Association, or perhaps even Amnesty International can not rival, for these are all bodies one can join or leave at easy will.*"
> [Anderson (1991), p. 143f.]

It is reasonable to suppose that war memorials and monuments to the war dead can be seen as one of the representations of fatality, because they, at least, indicate the fact that many people have already died for their nation in the past.

The primary consideration for a study of memorials and monuments should be their forms and contents. The monuments have been simply treated as a display of hegemonies or as manipulative devices. Anderson expressed his disappointment as follows: 'Few observers have recognized that monuments are a type of speech or tried to discern concretely what is being said, why form and content are specifically what they are' [cf. Anderson (1990), p. 174]. John Bodnar, a social historian in the U.S., seeks historical approach towards these forms of speech and describes their multivocal nature [see Bodnar (1992)]. It seems appropriate to apply this type of study to the monuments in Modern Japanese context.

## 2. The Monument to the War Dead in Modern Japan

Picture 1: *Chūkonhi* 忠魂碑                Picture 2: *Shōkonhi* 招魂碑

*Chūkonhi* 忠魂碑 and *shōkonhi* 招魂碑 as well, are typical names of war memorials in Japan. The monuments have been constructed increasingly at local public places (e.g., the precincts of a shrine, temple or school) from the Russo-Japanese War period to the end of World War II.

The National Museum of Japanese History has been engaged in a project of 'the national inventory of war memorials in Japan' since 2000. This ongoing project identified 28 prefectures that already have their own researches on memorials, while 19 prefectures have not. The total number of identified war memorials are 12 241 and the Museum estimated that more than 30 000 war memorials exist throughout the Japanese Islands.

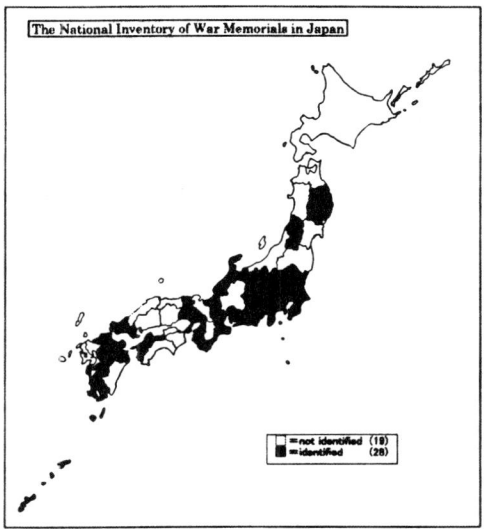

Figure 1: *NIWMJ statements*

This paper mainly investigates historical documents relating to the monuments in Saitama Prefecture.

The documents contain opinions and perceptions of both the people and the Government. All related documents include an application form, a written consent by the landowner, the permissions of local police, local governor and prefectural governor, and the response from the Home Ministry. In these official documents, which are housed in the Saitama Prefectural Archives, there were 23 rejected applications in 230 official documents. These rejected applications are concentrated in the Meiji era, and only two of them were rejected after Meiji 34

(1901), namely in Meiji 40 and Meiji 42. Out of a total of 85 applications for monuments to the war dead, 81 were for those of the Russo-Japanese War, and therefore concentrated in within several years after Meiji 37 (1904).

In addition to the Meiji Documents, there are 21 applications in the Taishō era and 22 applications in the Shōwa era.

| Years | R-J War | others | rejected | total |
|---|---|---|---|---|
| Meiji era (1868-1912) | 81 | 4 | 23 | 85 |
| Taishō era (1912-1926) | 21 | – | – | 21 |
| Shōwa era (1926-1945)<br>[only until the end of WWII] | 22 | – | – | 22 |

Figure 2: *Documents of war related monuments housed in the Saitama Prefectural Archives*

The nation-building period in Modern Japan may be understood as a period of warfare. Almost every ten years, Modern Japan was involved in civil or international wars in which modern military forces were mobilized: The Boshin Civil War (1868-1869), the Satsuma Rebellion (1877), the Chichibu Incident (1884), the Sino-Japanese War (1894-1895) and the Russo-Japanese War (1904-1905). Amongst other things, the Russo-Japanese War may be understood as the first experience of huge warfare in terms of total war. The Japanese people had to be engaged in the war on the Home Front as well as on the battlefields. The Russo-Japanese War required a huge number of sacrifices, which the Japanese people never before had experienced. In the Sino-Japanese War, 5 000 soldiers had died, but 118 000 soldiers died in the Russo-Japanese War [cf. Irokawa (1985)].

Under these conditions, in 1886 the Home Ministry, which regulates the control of a newly built shrine or temple and the construction of monuments on state-owned land, issued instructions on administrative divisions of Japan. These instructions have been referred to as indicating the general principles for monuments. Article 5 on the *"Prohibition of construction of monuments on state-owned land"* reads:

*"Exceptions: A monument to a person who has rendered distinguished services to the state, considered worthy of being publicised, and which is subject to permission obtained from the Home Ministry.*
*A monument should be of a certain material that celebrates a person who has rendered distinguished service, evokes the sentiments of*

*people in general, and encourages action which contributes to the public well-being."* [The Home Ministry, Instruction no. 397]

In the Ōoka Village 大岡村 case of 1895 (Meiji 28), the people of the village planed to dedicate a memorial service in a folk religious ceremony for dead (*segaki* 施餓鬼) in front of the monument. This case was rejected. In Agano Village 吾野村 in 1898 (Meiji 31), the people of the village intended 'to mourn for the death of the soldiers of their village'. Even the word 'mourn' itself was a trouble for the Ministry and this case was also rejected.

As Kagotani has pointed out [see Kagotani 1984], it is apparent that the Home Ministry rejected applications which implied the intention: ① to perform any rituals in front of the monument; ② to dedicate religious worship to the monument; ③ to pay a charge to an officiating Shintō priest (*shinshoku* 神職); ④ to dedicate sacred sake (*omiki* 御神酒) or to make any offering to the monument.

In 1897, people living in Hoshikawa Village 星川村 attempted to build a monument to their local soldiers who survived after war periods, but this attempt was rejected for one simple reason. The reason why the Home Ministry rejected their application was that this monument was intended to be for survivors. It appears that the Ministry considered that monuments should exclude religious elements, but at the same time, contradictorily, they should be only for the dead.

However natural it was that people who faced mass death needed to interpret it in folk religious ways with which they were already familiar, the Home Ministry did not give permission to dedicate or worship monuments. People were deprived of the opportunity of expressing in their own words their condolences concerning the death of their neighbours. In this sense, *chūkonhi*, or War Memorials in Japan, were standardized monuments that were reduced varieties of folk knowledge amongst pre-modern or rural communities.

### 3. Formalized rationality

On June 15, 1906 (Meiji 39), the Home Ministry issued an official notice about monuments. In this notice, the Ministry again stressed that the construction of monuments virtually indistinguishable from gravestones was not permitted.

*"It is not permitted to construct monuments to the war dead, such as* chūkonhi 忠魂碑 *[lit. monument to the loyal soul],* chōkonhi 弔魂碑 *[lit. monument to grieve for the soul] and* chūshihi 忠死碑 *[lit. monument to the loyal death], in the style of gravestones.*
*Postscript: If there is an application seeking to build more than two monuments in a municipality, only one selected monument will be allowed."*

In the Archive, there are in total 7 instructions given repeatedly to local governors during the Meiji-era. As mentioned previously, rejected applications are concentrated in the middle of the Meiji era, with only two rejected applications after Meiji 34 (1901). These instructions to local governors moulded the people's attitudes and, subsequently, stereotypical applications emerged.

In the Yoshimi Village 吉見村 case of 1900 (Meiji 33), the application interpreted modern war in Japan as a manifestation of 'the authority of the Emperor spread throughout the world'. And the purpose of constructing the monument as 'to memorialise this great achievement of the Emperor and of us his subjects permanently'. In the Jion-ji Village 慈恩寺村 case of 1913 (Taishō 2), to build a monument to 'the honour of the loyal death' is understood as 'to raise the morale of the people'.

Words such as 'mourn' and 'condolences' or others with religious connotation had been completely swept out of these applications and, alternatively, they consist of words with standardized meaning, glorifying the nation and its greatness.

By the notice of 1906, the Home Ministry delegated its authority for the construction of monuments to the local self-governing bodies and made clear their location policy for war memorials: principally, a monument should not be a religious monument, and there should be only one monument in each city, town and village. Even today, despite the replacement of monuments on state-owned lands and the reformation of local self-governing bodies after the end of WWII, this formalized rationality of configurations of the monuments in cities, towns and villages can be seen.

Such formalized rationality on the configurations of location is also represented by the reorganization of Shintō Shrines in modern Japan. Although its intention was not fully completed, the Home Ministry reduced 190 000 shrines into 120 000 by the end of the Russo-Japanese War. In accordance with the

Principal Regulations of Local Shrines, communities could have only one monument, just like they could have only one shrine (1871; Meiji 4). The monument should represent the specific local governmental body as a sign of a pledge to the nation, not as its vernacular religious symbol.

## 4. From Sign to Symbol

After the outbreak of the Manchurian Incident, monuments became objects of worship as if they were religious symbols of the nation. This period can be described as a process in which Japan had been losing civilians in its decision-making processes.

Picture 3: *Shōkonshi* 招魂祠

On February 27, 1939, the Ministry of Army issued an official notice which declared that 'the monuments to the war dead should not be just memorials, they should be objects of worship'. And, on July 7, the Great Japan Foundation for Celebrating the Loyal Souls (*Dainippon chūrei-kenshō-kai* 大日本忠霊顕彰会) was established.

New types of monuments – *shōkonshi* 招魂祠 and *chūreitō* 忠霊塔, small shrines and huge towers to the war dead within which soldier's ashes were placed – appeared, and other monuments to the war dead were interpreted with this new meaning as well.

The form of a *chūreitō* (lit. tower to the loyal soul) is derived from the Buddhist traditional stupa. A 'stupa' is a Buddhist commemorative monument usually housing sacred relics associated with the Buddha or other saintly persons; it is an architectural symbol of Buddha's *parinirvana*, or death. The hemispherical form of the stupa appears to have derived from pre-Buddhist burial mounds in India.

The Meiji government officially adopted the Imperial era year (*kōki* 皇紀) from *Nihongi* 日本紀 in Meiji 5 (1872) and enacted it simultaneously with the adoption of the solar calendar. The year 1872 of the Christian calendar was then interpreted as year 2532 of the Imperial calendar, starting with the reign of Emperor Jinmu. And therefore, the Christian year 1940 was equivalent to the Imperial year 2600.

At both, the national level and local level, there were many commemoration projects planed for this aimed at year 2600, especially during the 1930's. Initially the Japanese Government tried to held the world fair and the Olympics, though both events were declined after all. The 'Great Japan Foundation for Celebrating the Loyal Souls' was indeed active in these commemoration trends, raised money to construct monuments, not only interior but also in other Asian countries, and invited the public to submit suggestions of design for this kind of modern stupa.

Picture 3 is a photocopy of an article that first appeared in a newspaper [TNNS (1939)] and later was published by the Foundation as an official understanding of the monuments. At the beginning of the article, the Unknown Soldier of the Westminster in London, the triumphal arch (Arc de Triomphe) in Paris, and, especially, the war memorial in Munich (München), are mentioned.

Picture 4: article mentioning "*Sie werden auferstehen*"

At the local level, Mikashima Village 三ヶ島村 in Saitama Prefecture is a good example. In this application of 1942, the applicants – a local governor and a chief of the 'Association of ex-soldiers' (*Zaigō-gunjin-kai* 在郷軍人会) with people's approval – understood soldiers who died for the Emperor as being Gods and, therefore, the monument was understood as a Grave Stone of Gods.

People were encouraged to dedicate worship to them. In front of the monuments they performed and were also encouraged to perform religious or religion-like rituals, which celebrated the nation.

### Conclusion

Japanese leaders, for better or worse, decided that the country should become a colonizer rather than being colonized. It is important to note that the nation building process in Japan itself had occurred in the context of a certain colonial crisis, and, therefore, forced modernization caused distorted growth. This might be taken into account when we try to understand Modern Japanese history and society. Kamishima Jirō 神島二郎 has pointed out that Japanese society had been covered with a certain nihilistic atmosphere, which affirmed sacrifices in this rapid change [cf. Kamishima (1972)]. People were deprived of their language and were forced to express their grief and emotions by using nationalistic words.

In the emergence of both, stereotypical applications and formalised rationality related to the location of monuments and Shintō Shrines, 'governmentality' in Foucault's sense appeared. By the term 'governmentality' or 'governmental rationality' it is implied that this kind of rationality in the religious domain can be understood as 'conduct of conduct' in which 'governed individuals are willing to exist as subjects' [cf. Gordon (1991), p. 48].

As Marshall pointed out, 'this is a form of activity which attempts or aims at the conduct of persons; it is the attempt to shape, to guide, or to affect not only the conduct of people but, also, the attempt to constitute people in such ways that they can be governed' [cf. Marshall (1995)]. This formalised rationality cultivated people as subjects of the Emperor and united them emotionally as a nation.

To sum up the documents on War Memorials in Japan: whereas people tried to construct their member's monuments privately and religiously, the Home Ministry initially intended that monuments to the war dead should not be religious, but later, in the 1930's, shifted them to be religious. It is clear that the dichotomy of sign (metonymy) and symbol (metaphor) is not a stable distinction. Alternatively, it could be argued that the same monument could be transformed from sign to symbol in a certain socio-historical context.

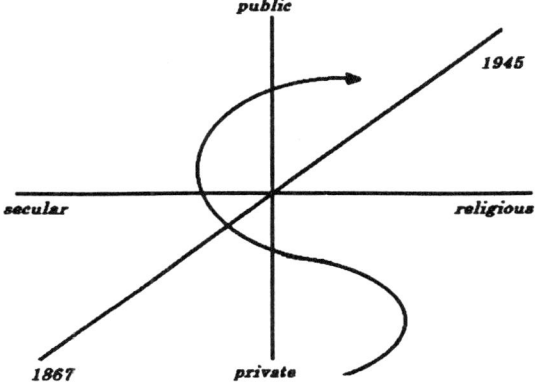

Figure 3: *Transformation of representations*

Although there are some definitions of symbols and signs in the social sciences [cf. Leach (1976); Sperber (1974)], it is important to examine transformations of representations and their socio-historical context more closely. Since nationalism itself is a very modern idea and thought – as Hans Kohn pointed out almost half of century ago [cf. Kohn (1965)] –, it seems that Japanese nationalistic representations of war dead have a very hybridised nature. In terms of their forms, these monuments could be understood as the amalgams of not only Buddhist or other religious traditions and different kinds of folk knowledge, but also of the western idea of monuments.

However, we still have little knowledge of how memorials might be understood theoretically, therefore, more intensive and interdisciplinary study on this subject matter is needed.

*References*

Anderson (1990)
    Anderson, Benedict: *Language and power: exploring political cultures in Indonesia*. Ithaca: Cornell University Press, 1990.

— (1991)
Anderson, Benedict: *Imagined Communities: Reflections on the Origin and Spread of Nationalism.* [revised ed.] London, New York: Verso, 1991.

Balakrishnan (1995)
Balakrishnan, Gopal: "The National Imagination", in: *New Left Review*, series I, no. 211 (May-June 1995), pp. 56-69.

Bodnar (1992)
Bodnar, John: *Remaking America: public memory, commemoration, and patriotism in the twenties century.* Princeton, N.J.: Princeton University Press, 1992.

Irokawa (1985)
Irokawa, Daikichi: *The culture of the Meiji period.* [transl. ed. by Marius B. Jansen] Princeton, N.J.: Princeton University Press, 1985.

Kagotani (1984)
Kagotani, Jirō 籠谷次郎: "Senbotsusha-hi to 'chūkonhi': aru chūkonhi soshō ni yosete 戦没者碑と「忠魂碑」：ある忠魂碑訴訟によせて", in: *Rekishi hyōron 歴史評論*, no. 406 (1984), pp. 27-55.

Kamishima (1972)
Kamishima, Jirō 神島二郎: *Kokka mokuhyō no hakken 国家目標の発見.* Tōkyō: Chūō-kōron sha, 1972.

Kohn (1982)
Kohn, H.: *Nationalism: Its Meaning and History.* [reprint of 1st rev. ed., Princeton: Van Nostrand, 1965] Malabar, Fla.: Krieger, 1982.

Leach (1978)
Leach, Edmund: *Culture and Communication: the logic by which symbols are connected.* Cambridge: Cambridge University Press, 1978.

Marshall (1995)
Marshall, James D.: "Foucault and Neo-Liberalism: Biopower and Busno-Power" [1995], Online Hyper-text of The University of Auckland: <http://www.ed.uiuc.edu/COE/EPS/PES-Yearbook/95_docs/marshall.html>, (15.08.2001).

Smith (1986)
Smith, Anthony D.: *The Ethnic Origins of Nations.* Oxford: Blackwell, 1986.

Sperber (1974)
> Sperber, Dan: *Rethinking Symbolism.* Cambridge: Cambridge University Press, 1974.

"Stupa", in: *The Encyclopaedia Britannica.* [Web-Edition]:
> <http://www.britannica.com/eb/article?eu=71861&tocid=0>, (15.08.2001).

TNNS (1939)
> *Tōkyō nichi-nichi shinbun* 東京日日新聞, 3 Aug. 1939.

SPAD
> *Saitama-ken kōbunsho* 埼玉県公文書 (Saitama Prefectural Archive Document):
> No. m-2353-3.
> No. m-2353-6.
> No. m-2354-5.
> No. m-2377-10.
> No. m-2379-2-11.
> No. m-2399-22.
> No. s-4247-34.
> No. t-178-8.

# The Quest for Religious and National Identity
# of Japanese Protestants before 1945
# — Anti-, or Philo-Semitism as the Framework of Reference —

KUBOTA Hiroshi

In this paper, a historical investigation shall be made into certain forms of the quest for religious identity by those Japanese Protestants whose political stance was strongly influenced by the widespread ideology of *kokutai* 国体 (national polity). The period to be dealt with shall concentrate on the 1930's and 40's, because it was in this period that the suppression of the Christian churches by the civil and military authorities increased. Parallel to this, the negative perception of Christianity was strengthened in society,[1] so that the study of the conditions in Christian churches in this period can provide an insight into their struggle for religious and national identity. Firstly, the historical situation of the church shall be outlined. This offers the religious and religio-political background for the activities and ideologies of three nationalistically orientated Protestant leaders to be treated later: Nakada Jūji 中田重治, Imaizumi Genkichi 今泉源吉, and Sakai Katsuisa 酒井勝軍.

## 1. Protestant Churches and their Involvement in the Totalitarian and Militaristic Process in the 1930's and 40's

Since the beginning of Protestantism in Japan in the 1870's, a strong nationalist inclination lay firmly embedded in the political stance of early Japanese converts. In the first phase of the missionary activities of the Western Protestant churches and the foundation of the first Protestant church in Japan in the 1870's,

---

[1] It is worth mentioning that the authorities, especially the Special Political Police (*tokkō* 特高), paid little attention to Christian churches until 1936. But, from 1939 on, it began to register increasingly and intensively various cases of "anti-Christian movements" in society as an independent chapter in its internal reports. See Dōshisha Daigaku (1972-73), vol. 1, p. 10 and p. 25. For my subsequent line of argument, it may be useful to suggest here that anti-Christian movements denounced Christianity partially because of its "Jewish" character; cf. ibid., vol. 1, p. 293 and vol. 2, pp. 43f. On the characteristics of these internal reports, see ibid., vol. 2, pp. 6ff.

the majority of the Japanese converts who accepted the Christian faith belonged sociologically to a certain intellectual class that originated from the former warrior class, which had more or less lost their social and political significance in the newly forming Meiji-state.[2] Accordingly, the ideological tendency of these early converts was mainly characterized through their strong longing for the establishment of a Christian morality, as a continuum of their feudalistic moral consciousness.[3] Through this moral endeavor, they, whether consciously or not, consolidated and justified the emerging modern nation state. Their framework of reference, therefore, remained undeniably the "national polity" advocated by the Meiji government, especially after a lèse-majesté affair of Uchimura Kanzō 内村鑑三 (1861-1930) in 1890 and the following controversy about the potential inconsistency of Christianity with national polity.[4] These incidents made most Christians, especially Protestants, quite conscious of their religious, and moreover, political standpoint in society, as they were almost convinced that no contradiction existed between being a Christian and being a faithful subject in the political system led by the State Shintō policies.[5] Therefore, they began to harmonize their Christian existence with the given political ideology in form and content. Of course, there were also avowed opponents to these compromising parties within the Protestant churches, too. Yet, this harmonizing tendency characterized strongly the church history of the 1930's and the early 1940's, when the Religious Organization Law (*Shūkyō dantai hō* 宗教団体法) came into force in 1940.[6] One year later, the United Church of Japan (*Nihon Kirisuto Kyōdan* 日本基督教団), a united Protestant church comprising most of the various Protestant denominations, was founded according to this new law.[7] In spite of the apparently restrictive nature of this law, church leaders obeyed the regime's religio-political instructions without any hesitation. They justified the forced church union and even the Japanese

---

[2] Cf. Kaneda (1985), p. 6.

[3] Cf. Dohi (1975), p. 51.

[4] Cf. Dohi (1975), p. 145; Kaneda (1985), pp. 8ff.; Takeda (1967), pp. 22ff.

[5] This stance can definitely be observed among the initiators of the so-called "Japanese Christianity" to be mentioned later. Cf. Kaneda (1985), pp. 11f.; Takeda (1967), pp. 335ff.

[6] On the relevance of this law in Christianity, see Takamichi (1965), pp. 45-56.

[7] Concerning the religio-political relationship between the Religious Organization Law and the foundation of the United Church of Japan, see Dohi (1975), pp. 214ff.; Hara (1999a); Kaneda (1985), pp. 182-187; Kasahara (1978), pp. 151ff.

invasion in Asian countries on the grounds of the enlargement of their mission-ary activities.[8]

This co-operative and compromising manner can be seen not only in collaboration on the surface, but also in the theological rationale for building up a so-called 'Japanese Christianity' (_nihon teki kirisutokyō_ 日本的基督教).[9] Especially in the 1930's and 40's, a number of prominent Protestant theologians advocated this theological standpoint that refuted the popularly maintained opinion of the latent, or, apparent contradiction between Christianity on the one hand, and national polity and moral consciousness in Japan on the other, and endeavored to conciliate the Christian message with traditional religious elements, especially with the pseudo-religious demands of State Shintō. These theologians were of the opinion that only this reinterpreted Christianity could contribute to the prosperity of the quintessence of Japanese spiritual and politi-cal virtue. Some even went so far as to say that it embodied the moral and religious ideals of national polity itself.[10] This so-called 'Japanese Christianity' in itself was surely neither the official standpoint, nor the most influential current in the whole Christian church in Japan, but, practically, church leaders promoted this trend in public, not only forced by the authorities that demanded the 'Japanization' of Christian doctrines, but also and more strongly on their own initiative.[11]

---

[8] Cf. Dohi (1975), pp. 173-182 and p. 294; Han (1988), pp. 84ff. The Special Political Police also observed this trend. Cf. Dōshisha Daigaku (1972-73), vol. 1, p. 82 and p. 171.

[9] Concerning "Japanese Christianity", see Hara (1999b); Kasahara (1974); Morioka/ Kasahara (1974), pp. 48ff. and pp. 91f.

[10] Cf. Hara (1999b), p. 96.

[11] Cf. Hara (1999b), pp. 91f.; Dōshisha Daigaku (1972-73), vol. 2, pp. 177f. and p. 185. Concerning the demand of the "Japanization" of Christianity through the authorities, see, for example, ibid, vol. 1, p. 189. But, the authorities regard the endeavors of the Protestant church to "Japanize" the Christian doctrines often as the expression of opportunism, or camouflage, and simultaneously point out that they are not sufficient enough to reform anti-Japanese teachings fundamentally. See, for example, ibid., vol. 1, p. 39, p. 81, p. 148 and p. 189.

## 2. The Case of the Holiness Churches[12] and Anti-, or Philo-Semitism as the Framework of Reference

While the mainstream of the Protestant churches, especially after 1941, was totally under the control of the militaristic and totalitarian regime, a number of larger and smaller Protestant groups were oppressed under the restrictive legislation of the Peace Preservation Law (*Chian iji hō* 治安維持法), which was revised in 1941.[13] The Holiness Churches belonged to these oppressed Christian groups. Two Holiness groups affiliated with the United Church of Japan and an independent one were suspected of denying national polity and defiling the dignity of Shintō shrines because of their doctrine concerning the Second Coming of Christ and their belief in millennialism.[14] A certain nationalistic tendency of the Holiness Churches made the authorities suspicious of them, because it deviated definitely from the nationalism officially approved by the regime, although this was not the directly stated official reason for their oppression.[15] One of the main teachings of the founder of this denomination, Nakada Jūji 中田重治 (1870-1939)[16], consisted of the Japanese nation being

---

[12] Concerning the history of the Holiness Churches in Japan and of their oppression during the war, see Yoneda (1964), and Hōrinesu-Bando (1983). Concerning the involvement of the Special Political Police in the oppression affair, see, for example, Dōshisha Daigaku (1972-73), vol. 2, pp. 234-248.

[13] On the influence of the law and its revision on the Christian churches, see Hara (1999a), pp. 7f. and pp. 15ff.; Sasaki (1966), pp. 39-77.

[14] Cf. Dōshisha Daigaku (1972-73), vol. 2, pp. 241-243. After the oppression affair of the "Watch-Tower, Bible and Tract Society (*tōdaisha* 灯台社)" in 1939, the Special Political Police became suspicious of the doctrine on the Second Coming of Christ and the millennialism. See Dōshisha Daigaku (1972-73), vol. 1, pp. 199-204; Sasaki (1966), p. 76.

[15] The official reason for the oppression was the charge with the denial of national polity and the defilement of Shintō shrines. Cf. Dōshisha Daigaku (1972-73), vol. 2, pp. 241f. Yet, the authorities remark that the ultimate aim of the Holiness Churches consists in "*building a world-wide consolidated state under the control and rule of the Jewish people*", ibid., vol. 2, p. 234. The authorities knew, on the other hand, the patriotic orientation of the Holiness Churches as well. Cf. for example, ibid., vol. 1, p. 106.

[16] In 1917 the *Tōyō Senkyōkai Nihon Hōrinesu Kyōkai* 東洋宣教会日本ホーリネス教会 ('The Oriental Missionary Society, Japan Holiness Church'), whose leader was Nakada Jūji, was founded. Nadaka's first contact with Christianity was the Methodist Church and the Methodist-affiliated Tōō Gijuku 東奥義塾, then he studied at the Tōkyō Eiwa Gakkō 東京英和学校 (later: Aoyama Gakuin Daigaku 青山学院大学). After being a pastor in Hokkaidō and Akita, he went to the USA in 1897, where he studied at the Moody Bible Institute. After his return to Japan, he founded the Holiness Church above mentioned, and organized a series of lectures concerning the Second Coming of Christ in 1918 with Uchimura Kanzō. Cf. NKRD, p. 990.

charged of a special mission in world history, which had been prophesied in the Old and New Testament. According to Nakada, Japanese Christians have the duty to pray for the Jewish people and their national recovery, in order that the Japanese people, entrusted also with a special mission for the Jewish people, will be redeemed simultaneously.[17] Moreover, the so-called Great East Asia War (_dai tōa sensō_ 大東亜戦争) is the first step toward the fulfillment of the Biblical prophecies. It is said to be the so-called 'Armageddon', the final war between Good and Evil[18], in which the Japanese army plays an important role in the liberation of the Jewish people and in the restoration of a Jewish state.[19] In this way, the militaristic and expansionist policy of the regime was religiously justified and the notion of the 'Whole World Under One Roof' (_hakkō ichiu_ 八 紘一宇) was interpreted as an explanation for the Japanese mission prophesied in the Bible.[20]

This way of interpreting the Bible was not restricted to the Holiness Churches. The Special Political Police (abbr. _tokkō_ 特高) registered this kind of interpretation of the war frequently in various Protestant groups, and considered it a misunderstanding of the significance of the 'Holy War' (_seisen_ 聖戦).[21] However, for the analysis of the self-understanding of the Holiness Churches, the fact should be taken into consideration that a unique superiority of Japan was supposed to be the quintessence of Biblical prophecies. Consequently, a religious, historical, and political position of Japan and the Japanese people was seen in their relationship to the so-called 'chosen people'.

This can be regarded as one type of Christian-motivated quest for religious and political identity at that time. It might naturally be categorized as one form of 'Japanese Christianity' which aimed at the 'Japanization' i.e., indigenization of Western-style Christianity[22], but differs from it notably in the adventurous

---

[17] Concerning the special mission of Japan in the world history, see Nakada: _Nihon seito no shimei_ 日本聖徒の使命, in: NJZ (1973-75), vol. 6, p. 374. The criticism against Nakada also illustrates his Judeo-centric interpretation of the Bible. Cf. Yoneda (1996), pp. 461ff.

[18] Cf. Dōshisha Daigaku (1972-73), vol. 2, p. 234 and pp. 238f.

[19] Cf. Nakada, Jūji: "Seisho yori mitaru nihon 聖書より見たる日本", in: NJZ (1973-75), vol. 2, pp. 122f. and p. 131.

[20] For example, see Dōshisha Daigaku (1972-73), vol. 2, p. 36.

[21] Cf. Dōshisha Daigaku (1972-73), vol. 1, p. 147 and pp. 282f; ibid., vol. 2, p. 69, pp. 71f., pp. 230f. and p. 243.

[22] Mullins points out as fostering factors for the formation of indigenous versions of Christianity in Japan "_the anti-Western social climate, growing nationalism, and dissatisfaction with Western missionaries_", Mullins (1998), p. 43.

reinterpretation of the traditional Christian message on the basis of characteristic dispensationalism and the great emphasis on the relationship between the Jewish and Japanese people. Therefore, the preoccupation with the so-called *yudayajin mondai* 猶太人問題 ('Jewish problem') provided certain Japanese Christians with a framework of reference that enabled them to seek their religious identity. They 'discovered', or were at least confronted with, the spiritual or religious origin of Christianity, and felt that they were obliged to deal with it in order to find their true religious roots, while the majority of the Protestants accepted the vulgarized anti-Semitism influentially propagated by a part of the military and being widespread in society, and denounced the Western-style Christianity they supposed to be deformed under the influence of the Jewish world conspiracy.[23] But, no matter how such "discoverers" of Judaism might react to this pre-Christian religious tradition, their commitment to the Jewish problem was inevitably based on an affirmation of the given socio-political status quo. This means that their final aim consisted in the establishment of a kind of Christianity suitable to the Japanese mentality, which was strongly conditioned by the given political order. This kind of Judaism-orientated understanding of Christianity, whether with anti-, or philo-Semitic orientation, was consequently combined with a religious and political consciousness of Japanese superiority. This feature can also be clearly seen in Imaizumi's and Sakai's works.

## 3. Imaizumi Genkichi and the Mikuni Movement[24]

In contrast to Nakada and the initiators of 'Japanese Christianity', these two attempted – especially through their adventurous reinterpretation of the traditional Christian faith – to realize religious-political reconciliation independent

---

[23] Cf. Dōshisha Daqigaku (1972-73), vol. 3, pp. 58-64.

[24] Until now, Imaizumi and his movement have not been sufficiently investigated, but the following two monographs are available: Fujimaki (1983) and Komuro (1993). The evaluation of Imaizumi and his movement in the church history is, consequently, still controversial, and more comprehensive analysis, especially about their relation to the main stream of the Protestant church, their reception and acceptance both in the institutionalized church and outside it, for example, among anti-Christian groups, and also the sociological influence of the movement, is necessary in order to judge the significance of Imaizumi's movement correctly in the context of the history of religions before and during the war.

of institutionalized churches, which finally resulted in the transformation, and even complete denial, of the form and content of traditional Christianity.

The religious struggle of Imaizumi Genkichi 今泉源吉 (1891-1969), a former senior pastor in the Presbyterian Church of Japan (_Nihon Kirisuto Kyōkai_ 日本基督教会)[25], was caused by the conflict between his Christian faith and his affirmation of the political status quo. It led him finally in 1935 to the decision to publish the monthly magazine _Mikuni_ みくに[26], gather like-minded people, and establish an organized movement with the name "Mikuni Association (_Mikuni Kai_ みくに会)".[27]

His religious thinking was based on an understanding of religion according to natural theology, which enabled him to acknowledge divine attributes in political entities, and also to sharply criticize Western-style mission churches, which he thought propagated only Western political teachings, not Christianity itself. Accordingly, he recommended to read the Bible and practice its teachings with Japanese spirit (_yamato damashii_ 大和魂)[28]. Imaizumi referred in this connec-

---

[25] The following description is based on Dohi (1975), p. 153, pp. 186f.; Fujimaki (1983), pp. 1-5; Fujimaki (1988a); Fujimaki (1988b); Komuro (1993), pp. 9-13.
Imaizumi Genkichi, a graduate of the Imperial University of Tōkyō (Faculty of Law), was ordained as a minister of the Presbyterian Nakashibuya Church, after a position as a judge at the Tōkyō District Court. In the 1920's, he made a name for himself by taking a leading part in opposition movements against the enactment of the "Law on Religion (_Shūkyō Hōan_ 宗教法案)" in 1927 and 1929, as one of the most talented lawyers of the Protestant church. After resigning from his pastoral post in 1929, he again began to study the religious policy of the Meiji-government at the graduate school of the Imperial University of Tōkyō. Nevertheless, he continued to be actively involved in church issues as a leading member of the _Fukuin Dōshikai_ 福音同志会 (Association of Evangelical Fellows) founded by Takakura Tokutarō 高倉徳太郎 (1885-1934), and as an active contributor to church magazines also after he founded the _Mikuni Kai_ みくに会 (Mikuni Association). After 1945, he returned to the Protestant church.

[26] The periodical was monthly published from January 1935 to December 1943, whereby the December number of the year 1939 did not appear. As publisher, firstly "_Mikuni Sha_" was named, but since the second year it was "_Mikuni Kai_".

[27] Main activities of the _Mikuni Kai_ were, according to Fujimaki (1983), pp. 1-5: ① The publication of the periodical _Mikuni_ (number of circulation: 800) from 1935 to 1943, and of various books and pamphlets; ② Regular Sunday services in the parishes: Tōkyō, Yokohama (I), Yokohama (II), Kamakura, Yamanashi, Nara, Ōsaka, and Kyūshū; ③ Mikuni Conventions (_Mikuni Taikai_ みくに大会): no. 1 in August 1935 in Kamakura (about 40 participants), no. 2 in August 1936 in Kōfu (89 participants), and no. 3 in August 1937 in Tōkyō (73 participants); ④ Public lectures; ⑤ Study groups; ⑥ Theatrical activities (_Mikuni Gekidan_ みくに劇団).

[28] Cf. Imaizumi, Genkichi: "Kirisutokyō sonnō aikoku no teishō 基督教尊王愛国の提唱", in: _Mikuni_, vol. 1, no.1 (Jan. 1935), pp. 13f.

tion to a famous expression by Uchimura Kanzō – "the Two Js (Jesus and Japan)" – in order to justify his intention, and simultaneously to emphasize his Christian conviction.[29]

In spite of this moderately nationalist tenor, the future of Imaizumi's struggle was already decided when the Mikuni Movement began. In the preface of the magazine's founding issue in 1935, he explains its title "Mikuni". According to him, *mikuni* means not only the 'Kingdom of God', but also the 'Imperial Land' (*kōkoku* 皇国).[30] He states further: "*I believe that the rise and fall of the Imperial Land is a divine issue which is crucial to the glory of the Kingdom of God*"[31]. Thus, his natural theological thinking is based on the self-image of the given political entity, and the acknowledgement of its holy feature. Thereby, he adds a Christian pose to his political stance, regarding it as the aim of his movement to "*clarify national polity through Christ*"[32]. This affirmation of national polity can be irrefutably recognized in the self-definition of the movement as "*Christianity that follows the spirit of the Imperial Way*"[33] (*kōdōka sareta kirisutokyō* 皇道化 された基督教). This adjustment to the given polity became undeniable, particularly after the Marco Polo Bridge Incident in July 1937 and the promulgation of the National Mobilization Law (*Kokka sōdōin hō* 国家総動員法) in April 1938. In these political changes, the Mikuni Movement began to show its full willingness to co-operate religiously with the expansionist policy and to integrate religious powers according to the intention of the law mentioned above.

Although Imaizumi repeatedly and emphatically maintained that the Christianity he and his movement propagated was the true Christian form[34], it cannot be denied that he regarded Christianity as an instrumental doctrinal system according to which one could grasp the quintessence of national polity. Thereby, the traditional theological scheme was applied to the political status quo and to current events. For example, one of the members of the movement compares Christ with Japan, saying "*Christ is the Spirit of God whom God sent to this world in the form of a person, and the Divine Land, Japan, is also the Spirit of*

---

[29] Cf. ibid., p. 14.
[30] Cf. Imaizumi, Genkichi: "Hakkan no ji 発刊の辞", in: *Mikuni*, vol. 1, no. 1 (Jan. 1935), p. 1.
[31] Ibid., pp. 1f.
[32] Ibid., p. 2.
[33] Fujimaki (1983), p. 1.
[34] Cf. Imaizumi, Genkichi: "Kenkokuseishin to kirisutokyō 建国精神と基督教", in: *Mikuni*, vol. 1, no. 12 (Dec. 1935), p. 2.

_God in the form of a state_"[35]. Imaizumi further claims, referring to Ōkuni Takamasa 大国隆正 (1792-1871), that God's most valuable Creation and Revelation is the Unbroken Imperial Line (_kōtō renmen_ 皇統連綿).[36] He states further: "_The Kingdom of God, Christ taught of, is Japan, where His Majesty the Emperor stands_"[37]. In this way the ideology of national polity was interspersed with theological terms, at least on the surface. However, it is quite apparent that even this theological thinking was strongly modified through a certain political perception. A quite obvious example for this shift of theological argumentation is the following statement: "_Ah! Really His Majesty was alone crucified instead of us!_"[38]

The religious statements by this movement show vividly how theological terms functioned, when Japanese Christians attempted to justify the political status quo without losing their Christian identity. This theological reinterpretation can be surely understood as a reform movement that emerged from the inside of the Westernized and institutionalized church, aiming at the establishment of an indigenous form of Christianity. Yet, Imaizumi's movement finally left the ground of Christianity, totally abandoned any Christian decorations, and became an anti-Christian movement. The main reason for this change lay in its understanding of the so-called Jewish problem.

After the Marco Polo Bridge Incident in 1937, the theory of the Jewish conspiracy suddenly appeared in the periodical _Mikuni_. Imaizumi's characterization of the Jewish people allows the assumption that he had internalized the widespread stereotypes of anti-Semitism. He understands the Jews as those who plan to corrupt national consciousness and produce international-orientated people by making full use of the press under their control and propagating liberalism, individualism, democracy, anarchism, Marxism, and so on. [39] Following this conspiracy theory, he begins to criticize that traditional Christianity has been deceived by the Jewish conspiracy, and has become its

---

[35] Matsuno, Shigemasa 松野重正: "Shinkoku nihon o hiteisuru mono 神国日本を否定する者", in: _Mikuni_, vol. 3, no. 11 (Nov. 1937), p. 20.

[36] Cf. Fujimaki (1983), p. 9.

[37] Imaizumi, Genkichi: "Aa, Ikeda Chitose kokushu あゝ池田千寿国手", in: _Mikuni_, vol. 6, no. 8 (Aug. 1940), p. 27.

[38] Iwakoshi, Gen'ichirō 岩越元一郎: "Kōdō no taigi 皇道の大義", in: _Mikuni_, vol. 1, no. 5 (May 1935), p. 13.

[39] Cf. Fujimaki (1983), p. 19f.

instrument. It is making people worship Jehovah, who is only a tribal god of the Jews, and propagating democratic ideas.[40] He therefore identifies the Western church with "Jewish Christianity" and attributed to it a program aiming at the destruction of Japanese national polity and mentality.[41]

His identification of the traditional Christian church with the Jewish conspiracy, however, led Imaizumi to criticize Christianity as a whole, whose purification he had energetically pursued since the beginning of the 1930's. He claims: "Amaterasu Ōmikami 天照大御神 *is the genuine Deity, although the Christians think that Jehovah is the genuine God*"[42]. Consequently, the Jewish self-perception of being the chosen people led him to the conviction that the war now going on was a religious war between *Amaterasu Ōmikami* and Jehovah[43], i.e., between the descendants of the true goddess and the people chosen by the Jewish tribal god. Finally, he self-confidently asserts: "*All people, whether they are Christians or not, are saved through national polity*"[44].

It is, therefore, quite understandable that the Mikuni Movement, which became converted to anti-Christian nationalism, was on good terms with the authorities, especially the Special Political Police.[45] This shows quite clearly how religious and national identity among nationalist-orientated Christians could be formed, and even transformed. And this forming or transforming of identity was strongly dependent on the acceptance of vulgarized and stereotyped anti-Semitism.

---

[40] Cf. Imaizumi, Genkichi: "Kami-no-kuni undō no shōtai 神の国運動の正体", in: *Mikuni*, vol. 8, no. 10 (Oct. 1942), p. 21.

[41] Cf. Fujimaki (1983), p. 27. Not only Imaizumi, but also the main stream of the Protestant church has this criticism against Christianity as "Jewish Christianity" in common. See Dōshisha Daigaku (1972-73), vol. 3, pp. 57-61.

[42] Imaizumi, Genkichi: "Shinkoku mondō 神国問答", in: *Mikuni*, vol. 4, no. 11 (Nov. 1938), p. 16.

[43] Cf. Fujimaki (1983), p. 20.

[44] Imaizumi, Genkichi: "Shisōteki seisen ni tatsu 思想的聖戦に立つ", in: *Mikuni*, vol. 4, no. 1 (Jan. 1938), p. 9.

[45] Cf. Fujimaki (1983), p. 29f.

## 4. *Sakai Katsuisa and his philo-Semitism*[46]

In contrast to Imaizumi, Sakai Katsuisa 酒井勝軍 (1874-1940) and his movement[47] stressed Christian character more profoundly. This emphasis on Christianity, however, differs greatly from that of so-called 'Japanese

---

[46] Until the present time, Sakai and his movement have been dealt with mostly in the context of "popular science" – for example, in the context of the so-called *chō kodai* 超古代 ('hyper-ancient times') or *nichi-yu dōso ron* 日猶同祖論, a theory according to which the Japanese and the Jews have the same ancestry – and most of the publications concerning Sakai have been written by those who themselves are involved with such "popular science". One example for this trend is: Shinpi [kaisetsuhen] (1982). Consequently, there is, to my knowledge, only one series of articles that deals with Sakai more or less in academic terms, Aizawa (1983 - 1989) Goodman/ Miyazawa (1995) certainly also treat this topic, but only under the aspect of the reception and prevalence of anti-Semitism in Japan. Accordingly, they do not deal with the modality of Sakai's quest for religious and national identity as a Protestant. Although Aizawa (1988) delivers a short sketch of Sakai's life and activities in an encyclopedia of church history in Japan, neither his relevance and significance in the history of Christianity in Japan nor that of "Japanese Christianity" have been sufficiently elucidated.

[47] The following description is mainly based on Aizawa (1983, 1988); "Shinsei fukko sekai dōmei undō kaishi 神政復古世界同盟運動開始", in: Shinpi, no. 19 (April 1938), n.p.; Shinpi [kaisetsuhen] (1982), pp. 3-46.
Sakai Katsuisa became a member of the *Kirisuto Itchi Kyōkai* 基督一致教会 ('Presbyterian Union Church') at the age of fifteen. After studying at and graduating from the *Sendai Shingakkō* 仙台神学校 ('Sendai Theological Seminary', later: *Tōhoku Gakuin Daigaku* 東北学院大学), which was affiliated with the German Reformed Church, and the ordination as presbyter, he went to the USA and pastored young Japanese Christians in San Francisco. After that, he studied at the Moody Bible Institute and at a music academy in Chicago. After returning to Japan, he became the initial founder of the *Tōkyō Shōka Gakkō* 東京唱歌学校 ('Tōkyō School of Singing'), and devoted his energies to the propagation of the significance of church hymns for religious life. He published a periodical called *Sanbi no tomo* 讃美の友 ('Friend of the Praise of God') which was later renamed *Shion* シオン ('Zion'), and simultaneously founded the *Nihon Sanbi Shōrei Kai* 日本讃美奨励会 ('Association for the Promotion of the Praise of God in Japan'). After that, this association became the main body of Sakai's religious activities, it was later renamed *Nihon Sanbi Dan* 日本讃美団 ('Association for the Praise of God in Japan'), and then once more *Kokkyō Senmei Dan* 国教宣明団 ('Association for the Proclamation and Clarification of National Religion'). Finally, in 1932, he founded the *Nichi-yu Kyōkai* 日猶協会 ('Association for Japanese-Israelism'), and, after 1936, reorganized these associations into one body: *Shinsei Fukko Sekai Dōmei* 神政復古世界同盟 ('World Federation for the Restoration of Theocracy'). He began publishing the magazine *Shinpi no Nihon* 神秘之日本 ('Japan, the Divine Secret') [see Shinpi], which continued until his death. Sympathizers of Sakai's ideas and his movement were found chiefly in the army and navy, for example, Koiso Kuniaki 小磯国昭, Shirakawa Yoshinori 白川義則, Yamamoto Eisuke 山本英輔, or Hata Shinji 秦真次, and also among certain members of the *Ōmoto* 大本.

Christianity', because of Sakai's Christian fundamentalist thinking patterns and his curious philo-Semitism.

Yet, the comparison of Sakai with Imaizumi is quite interesting, because the theological terminology used by the former was more one-sidedly limited on certain doctrinal issues than that of the latter. Imaizumi strove for the reinterpretation of almost all the doctrinal issues according to his thinking pattern of 'Imperial Way', but such a comprehensive treatment cannot be seen in Sakai's thoughts. His theological and religious key idea consists exclusively in millennialist dispensationalism, i.e., the millennialist understanding of world history under the aspects of Divine Providence, with which Sakai probably became acquainted during his studies at the Moody Bible Institute in Chicago. Here, it is worth mentioning that Nakada also studied at Moody Bible Institute, which had a strong fundamentalist orientation, and later preached his theory concerning a Japanese special mission in the world history. Another aspect that Sakai and Nakada have in common was – contrary to Imaizumi – a positive concentration on the so-called 'Jewish problem', which resulted in a high assessment of the religious and political significance of the Jewish and the Japanese people.

Certainly, even in his early years, while Sakai appreciated the superiority of Japanese feudalistic morality, he still remained a strong admirer of the American spirit and American-style democracy.[48] But, after working for the army as an interpreter during the Russo-Japanese War in 1904, he converted to a warmon-ger. In 1914, confronted with an extraordinary phenomenon in the moon, he experienced a spiritual awakening which led him to the conviction that a worldwide war – Armageddon – was imminent, and that secretly Japan was a divine land chosen by God.[49] Parallel to this nationalist and spiritual change, he began to deal with the so-called Jewish problem and from this moment on to regularly publish various books and pamphlets concerning it. Finally, his interest in this issue culminated in his theory on so-called 'Japanese-Israelism'. According to this theory, the Japanese people and the Jewish people have the

---

[48] Cf. Aizawa (1983), p. 17 and p. 23; Aizawa (1986), p. 90; Shinpi [kaisetsuhen] (1983), p. 4. In 1902 moreover, the influential anarchist Kōtoku Shūsui 幸徳秋水 endeavored to come into contact with Sakai, because Sakai advocated destroying the given political system under the State Shintō policy. Cf. Aizawa (1983), p. 24.

[49] Cf. Aizawa (1983), p. 24.

same ancestry.[50] His preoccupation with the Jewish problem resulted in the foundation of various organizations to promote the propagation of his philo-Semitic theory, which seems, however, at first glance, rather anti-Semitic.[51]

Certainly, Sakai partially accepted the vulgarized stereotype of the Jewish conspiracy in the world, but reinterpreted it according to his dispensationalist understanding of history and his peculiar opinion on Judaism. He claims that World War I was undoubtedly the result of the Jewish worldwide conspiracy.[52] However, this conspiracy is nothing but Divine Providence, according to which God gave them a special mission to accomplish the union of the world and to restore theocracy.[53] Furthermore, Sakai defines Judaism as something similar to Shintō. He says Judaism is not a system of teachings and doctrines, but _shintō_,

---

[50] Still in 1924, Sakai confesses that he does not know if the Japanese and the Jews have the same ancestry, but is convinced that there exists "_a mysterious relationship_" between both [Sakai (1924b), p. 211]. Yet, at the same time, he mentions that the Japanese Empire is the successor of the Kingdom of Israel and that the Unbroken Imperial Line of the Japanese Imperial Household suggests the close relationship between the both people [ibid.]. But, in 1928, he arrived at the conviction that the Kingdom of Israel and the Japanese Empire have the same national polity and the same Imperial Line, and that Japan is one of the twelve lost tribes of Israel; cf. Aizawa (1987), p. 116; Sakai (1928), pp. 303ff. Further, he affirms that the heavenly descendants – i.e., the Japanese – are, in reality, the chosen people – i.e., the Jewish people – and that Zion, which the Jewish people have desired to be realized, is nothing but the Japanese Empire; cf. Sakai (1928), p. 543. Yet, from the beginning of the 1930's Sakai began shifting the framework of his theory by maintaining that all civilized people originate in the Japanese Imperial Household. This is practically the reverse argumentation of his former theory. On the basis of this theoretical shift, he concludes that the Japanese Emperor will reign the world as the Emperor of the world, i.e. as the Messiah; cf. Aizawa (1989), p. 42, pp. 45f., p. 48. In spite of this shift, his "Japanese-Israelism" remains further unchanged, only the stress is now no longer placed on the Jewish origin of the Japanese people, but on the Japanese origin of all the civilizations in the world, among which the Jewish people have incomparable significance besides Japan. This standpoint is apparently seen in the magazine _Shinpi no Nihon_ [see Shinpi], published from 1936 to 1940. See, for example, Shinpi, no. 17 (Feb. 1938), p. 40.

[51] Goodman and Miyazawa throw Sakai's thoughts totally into the category of the anti-Semitic discourse of his time; cf. Goodman/ Miyazawa (1995), p. 82; Miyazawa (1982), p. 71. Although Sakai's language usage can easily lead us to the assumption that his main motive may be derived from anti-Semitic prejudice, and one cannot deny that his "philo-Semitic" ideas bespeak partially a type of the popular anti-Semitism as also seen in Nakada, the whole picture of his thoughts cannot be put into the category of anti-Semitism. As Aizawa repeatedly emphasizes, Sakai's philo-Semitic motivation also can be clearly discerned in his works; cf. for example Aizawa (1983), p. 47; Aizawa (1989), p. 69; Shinpi [kaisetsuhen] (1982), p. 27.

[52] Cf. Sakai (1924a), _Jijo_ 自序, p. 3.

[53] Cf. Sakai (1924a), p. 181.

i.e., the 'Way of God'.[54] It is realized only through the Jewish people who are practicing it, and can therefore be translated with 'Jewish Way' (*yudaya dō* ユダヤ道) or 'Jewish spirit' (*yudaya seishin* ユダヤ精神), and it is identical with 'Japanese spirit' (*yamato damashii* 大和魂). He goes so far as to say that Judaism is nothing but genuine Shintō, *kannagara no michi* 惟神道.[55]

Similar to Nakada, for Sakai the religious and political significance of Japan is based on certain Biblical prophecies. Yet, what distinguishes him from Nakada is that he identifies the Imperial Household with one of the lost Israelite tribes[56] – using a vulgar etymological method which is in reality nothing but making puns[57] – and concludes that the Zion the Bible is prophetically referring to, is not an ideal land which will be realized in the future in Palestine, but Japan which exists now and is appearing on the stage of the world.[58] But, this can be realized only at the moment of the Second Coming of Christ from heaven. It will enable the Jewish people and the Japanese state to be united, and lead to the realization of a theocratic land which has Christ, the Son of God, as the King, the Jewish people as the subjects, and Japan as the state form.[59]

In order to understand this confusing theory, one should investigate his specific understanding of Christianity, Japan, and their mutual relation. He vehemently criticizes an Americanized form of Christianity, whereby he mainly attacks missionary activities. Sakai claims that American missionaries preached not Christianity, but only an 'American Religion' (*amerika shū* アメリカ宗) which coincided with the Americanization of Japanese culture[60], distorted the holy teachings of Jehovah and the spirit of Christ, and schemed even for the subversion of Japan.[61] In other words, they taught not the teachings of Christ, i.e., theocracy, but democracy[62], and concentrated only on an individualistic doctrine concerning atonement.[63] Therefore, the American missionaries led the

---

[54] Cf. Sakai (1924a), pp. 180f.
[55] Cf. Sakai (1924a), pp. 180f.; Sakai (1924b), pp. 22f.
[56] Cf. Aizawa (1985), pp. 88f.
[57] Examples of this "popular etymology" can be found in: Shinpi, no. 4 (1936), pp. 62f.
[58] Cf. Sakai (1924a), p. 351 and pp. 465f.
[59] Cf. ibid., pp. 469f.
[60] Cf. Sakai (1924b), pp. 193f.
[61] Cf. Sakai (1924b), p. 329.
[62] Cf. Sakai (1924b), pp. 193f.
[63] Cf. Sakai (1928), p. 51.

Japanese people with their democratic ideas to the false understanding that
"_Christianity and our national polity are incompatible with one another_" and, as
a result, Japanese Christians denied Japanese national polity, while those
Japanese who defended national polity came to refuse Christianity.[64] This criticism shows that Sakai understands Christianity only as a religio-political system
to be realized according to certain Biblical prophesies, which reminds us of
Nakada's theory. But, although Nakada saw the quintessence of Christianity still
in the salvation or redemption of individual souls, even this theological aspect
was totally denounced by Sakai as an American misinterpretation of the teachings of Jesus Christ. For him, genuine Christianity has a clearly political feature,
theocracy, as Jesus once preached in his Sermon on the Mount: "_But seek ye first
the kingdom of God and his righteousness_" [Matt. 6:33].[65] Sakai calls this theocracy also the Shintō of Christ (_kirisuto no shintō_ 基督の神道).[66] Therefore, his
quest for Christian identity cannot be detached from his quest for national, and
political identity. His political conviction that Japan, because of her incomparable superiority, has to become a realization of theocracy like Old Israel, brought
him to his unique reception of Christianity.

This political conviction can be demonstrated in his opinion that the Japanese
Empire was build as a Divine Empire which God had secretly concealed for a
long time[67], and that only in the form of an Empire chosen by God Japan has her
raison d'être.[68] Sakai openly declares that this opinion is based on the official
dogma concerning the Unbroken Imperial Line.[69] Yet, he repeatedly based his
political stance on religious arguments in the Christian fashion. For example,
this feature can be clearly recognized in his reinterpretation of the doctrine of
incarnation. He argues that _kannagara no michi_ became an individual person in
Jesus, a nation among the Jewish people, and a state in Japan, and all of these are
manifestations of the 'Word of God'.[70]

In the 1930's, Sakai came into conflict with the authorities, i.e., the Special
Political Police and the Military Police. His publications were suppressed, and

---

[64] Cf. Sakai (1924b), p. 317.
[65] Cf. Ibid., p. 315; Sakai, Katsuisa: "Yo no owari chikazukeri kui aratameyo 世の終り近づけ
り悔い改めよ", in: Shinpi, no. 5 (Feb. 1937), p. 43.
[66] Cf. Sakai (1924b), p. 294.
[67] Cf. Aizawa (1987), p. 117.
[68] Cf. Sakai (1924b), p. 199.
[69] Cf. ibid., p. 211 and pp. 241f.
[70] Cf. Sakai (1924c), pp. 219f.

he was charged with lèse-majesté and disrespect toward the Imperial Household.[71] This was mainly because his interpretation of Japanese history with regard to the religio-political significance of Japan – in short, his 'Biblical and mythological nationalism' – deviated in essential points remarkably from the officially approved version. He was accused of involvement in the *Amatsukyō* 天津教, a Shintōistic religious organization, which delivered a supra-nationalistic interpretation of Japanese history. Sakai and Takeuchi Kyomaro 竹内巨麿 (1874-1965), the founder of the *Amatsukyō*, were of the opinion that the *Kojiki* 古事記 and the *Nihongi* 日本紀, two 'holy scriptures' for the State Shintō system, were not sufficient enough for the solid foundation of national polity. They based their arguments on some historical pseudographs (for example, *Uetsufumi* 上記), on the basis of which they could maintain that there had already been a number of Emperors and a firm Empire before the allegedly first Emperor Jinmu. As mentioned above, Sakai also elaborated a dispensationalist historiography, according to which the outbreak of the war between China and Japan in 1937 was the first step of the worldwide Great War, Armageddon.

Despite this tension between him and the authorities, it is also undeniable that his religious conviction, i.e., his dispensationalist theory, is founded on a firm affirmation of the religious and political superiority of Japan, and a future conquest of the whole world under the Japanese leadership through the union of Christ, the Jewish people, and Japan.[72] Accordingly, the fundamentalist scheme of his religious thinking has a certain similarity to that of Nakada, who eagerly pursued his Christian and Japanese identity without any doubt about the given polity. Sakai's and Nakada's ideologies stood in contrast to the Mikuni Move-

---

[71] Concerning the suppression of his publications, see Aizawa (1989), pp. 42ff., pp. 47ff., pp. 51f.; Shinpi, no. 8 (April 1937), p. 11. On his involvement in the *Amatsukyō*, see ibid., pp. 52ff. On *Amatsukyō* and Takeuchi Kyomaro, see Inoue (1990), pp. 497f., pp. 701f. and p. 890.

[72] Cf. Sakai (1926), pp. 59f. Here one reads the following passages: "*Japan is the only Divine Land of the Son of God. And this land is now growing. [...] Certainly, its root does not move, but we can not deny at all that its branches are destined to grow to the East and to the West, to become dense in the North and the South, and finally, to cover the whole world. However, this does not mean an invasion. This is the growth God permitted gracefully. Then, the Japanese state will neither annex nor merge the world, but become the Divine Land of the Son of God. Accordingly, the Kingdom of Zion for which the Jewish people have longed for 2600 years, and the appearance of which they have continuously and earnestly desired, is in fact this Divine Land of the Son of God, i.e., our Japan*".

ment, because they would not sacrifice their Christian identity for the official political mythology. Certainly, it is peculiar to Sakai that, for him, the religious and political superiority of Japan was derived chiefly from his philo-Semitic premise that the Jews as 'God's chosen people' (_shinsen minzoku_ 神選民族) and the ancestors of the Japanese as 'the heavenly descendants' (_tenson minzoku_ 天孫民族) have the same ancestry.[73] It follows that both were assigned to the same divine mission for the recovery of Zion, the realization of Christ's teachings, i.e., theocracy, by means of the present Japanese political order.

## 5. Summary and conclusion

The majority of the Protestant churches, willingly or not, were put under the control of the regime and its religious politics. However, they sought an indigenous version of Christian theology and church formation, and struggled for its firm position and raison d'être in society. On the one hand, as seen above, the 'Japanization' of Christianity by the Mikuni Movement inevitably meant the denial of its Christian origin and character, inspired by the popular anti-Semitic discourse. On the other hand, their unique understanding of Judaism and the Jews allowed Nakada and Sakai to keep their Christian identity, or precisely speaking, to develop a perplexing religio-political concept. Here, one can see that the so-called 'Jewish people', who do not necessarily correspond with historical reality, but are a mental and imaginary construct, play an important role in making these three Protestants discover, or recognize, the religious and political position of Japan in the world.

In order to understand why the preoccupation with the Jewish problem could become so significant at all, it should be taken into consideration that the anti-Semitism, taken on in a quite vulgarized form, was even dominant in the general atmosphere of the military and of certain political groups, and was partially used to control political and religious thoughts. The affair of the oppression of the Holiness Churches can also be interpreted in this context as an expression of this anti-Semitic attitude of the authorities.[74] Generally, the authorities naïvely assumed that Christianity was closely related to Judaism,

---

[73] With regard to the terms _shinsen minzoku_ and _tenson minzoku_, see Sakai (1938).
[74] Cf. Miyazawa (1982), pp. 122f.

and, accordingly, was utilized for the worldwide Jewish conspiracy. The mainstream of the Protestant churches however, for instance the United Church of
Japan, took on this anti-Semitic discourse and endeavored to differentiate
'Jewish' Christianity – i.e., Christianity preached by Western missionaries –
from 'Japanized' Christianity. From this position, Imaizumi only went a little
further when he identified every form of Christianity with the Jewish conspiracy.

In the 1930's, when Sakai actively began propagating his philo-Semitic teachings, the political control over the religious treatment of the Jewish problem was
not as strong as in the years after 1941, but, as mentioned above, certain tensions
already existed between him and the authorities. Although Sakai's
philo-Semitism was inherently in danger of being understood as anti-Japanese,
he insisted on his theory, paradoxically, in order to consolidate national polity
propagated by the regime. Therefore, his religious thoughts can be considered a
deformation of vulgarized *kokugaku* 国学 in a Christian shape.[75] Since the
beginning of the 20th century, a number of like-minded Protestants had a similar
personal history as Nakada and Sakai.[76] All of them were graduates of Protestant
schools, studied abroad, were actively involved in church service, and all of
them were ultimately convinced that the ancestors of the Japanese people were
the Israelites. Their life, in which a Protestant education, study abroad, especially in the USA, and church activities seem to have played a significant role,
was apparently unusual in comparison with that of average Japanese intellectuals, and even among ordinary Christians at that time. It confronted them with a
crisis in their understanding of national and religious identity, and led them to a
unique acceptance of the Judeo-Christian tradition in the Japanese context.
Consequently, Sakai's theory can also be considered part of this quest for an
indigenous, i.e., 'Japanized' form of Christianity, which does not contradict the
vulgarized *kokugaku* concepts in principle. However, it remains only the product

---

[75] Cf. Miyazawa (1982), p. 66.

[76] Inter alios, the member of the Anglican (Episcopal) Church and scholar of Chinese
Nestorianism Saeki Yoshirō 佐伯好郎 (1871-1965); the former pastor at a Congregational
church Oyabe Zen'ichiro 小谷部全一郎 (1867-1941); the pastor at some Japanese
Presbyterian churches in the USA and Doctor of Theology Kawamorita Eiji 川守田英二
(1891-1960) etc. [cf. Goodman/ Miyazawa (1995), pp. 64ff]. With regard to Kawamorita,
see also Aizawa (1983), pp. 2ff.; Aizawa (1989), pp. 64ff.; NKRD, p. 341. With regard to
Saeki, see also Miyazawa (1982), pp. 63ff.; NKRD, p. 560. Concerning Oyabe, see also

of certain 'marginal, alienated' outsiders[77] in Protestantism, which in itself was also a minority in society. In other words, it was an expression of the self-assertion, or self-justification of a religious minority that was more or less supposed to be anti-Japanese in the ideologically unified society.

To conclude, it should be mentioned that vulgarized anti-Semitism, as Imaizumi espoused, has continued unbroken as a latent underground current. It has been met with positive acceptance, and most of its supporters belonged to Protestant groups. Similarly, the Judeo-Japanese theory by Sakai has also been highly appreciated and further cultivated chiefly by fundamentalist Protestants. In both cases, a strong nationalist inclination can be observed.[78] It must be further studied which socio-political and social psychological factors determine the repeated occurrence of these trends in the history of Japanese Protestantism after 1945, although the so-called "Jews" in Japan remain what they have always been: an imaginary product that has been nursed in political and religious discourse in Japan.

### Bibliography

Dōshisha Daigaku (1972-73)
 Dōshisha Daigaku Jinbunkagaku Kenkyūsho 同志社大学人文科学研究所 / Kirisutokyō Shakaimondai Kenkyūkai キリスト教社会問題研究会 (ed.): _Senjika no kirisutokyō undō_ 戦時下のキリスト教運動. 3 vol., Tōkyō: Shinkyō shuppansha, 1972-73.

Mikuni
 _Mikuni_ みくに, vol. 1, no. 1 (Jan. 1935) – vol. 9, no. 12 (Dec. 1943), Tōkyō: Mikuni sha [from vol. 2 on: Mikuni kai].

NJZ (1973-75)
 Nakada Jūji Zenshū Kankōkai 中田重治全集刊行会 (ed.): _Nakada Jūji zenshū 中田重治全集._ 7 vols., Tōkyō: Inochi-no-Kotoba sha, 1973-75.

---

Miyazawa (1982), pp. 65ff.; NKRD, p. 268. Concerning Sakai's "Japanese-Israelism" Miyazawa points out an inferiority complex towards the USA; cf. Miyazawa (1982), p. 75.
[77] Cf. Miyazawa/ Goodman (1995), p. 73.
[78] Cf. Miyazawa/ Goodman (1995), pp. 159f., pp. 225ff.; Mullins (1998), pp. 105-127.

Sakai (1924a)
   Sakai, Katsuisa 酒井勝軍: *Yudayajin no sekai seiryaku undō* 猶太人の世
   界政略運動. Tōkyō: Naigai shobō, 1924.

—   (1924b)
   Sakai, Katsuisa 酒井勝軍: *Yudaya minzoku no dai inbō* 猶太民族の大陰謀.
   Tōkyō: Naigai shobō, 1924.

—   (1924c)
   Sakai, Katsuisa 酒井勝軍: *Sekai no shōtai to yudayajin* 世界の正体と猶太
   人. Tōkyō: Naigai shobō, 1924.

—   (1926)
   Sakai, Katsuisa 酒井勝軍: *Tenshi seiji o kōshō seyo* 天子政治を高唱せよ.
   Tōkyō: Kokkyō senmeidan, 1926.

—   (1928)
   Sakai, Katsuisa 酒井勝軍: *Shinshū tenshikoku* 神州天子国. Tōkyō:
   Banrikaku shobō, 1928.

—   (1938)
   Sakai, Katsuisa 酒井勝軍: *Tenson minzoku to shinsen minzoku* 天孫民族
   と神選民族. Tōkyō: Shinpi no Nihon sha, 1938.

Shinpi
   *Shinpi no Nihon* 神秘之日本, vol. 1 (1936) – vol. 45 (1940), Tōkyō:
   Shinpi no Nihon sha [Reprint: Tōkyō: Hachiman shoten, 1982].


*Secondary Literature*

Aizawa (1983)
   Aizawa, Genshichi 相沢源七: "Sakai Katsuisa no 'Shinshū tenshikoku'
   ron ni tsuite (jō) 酒井勝軍の「神州天子国」論について（上）", in: *Tōhoku
   Gakuin Daigaku Tōhoku Bunka Kenkyūsho kiyō* 東北学院大学東北文化
   研究所紀要, vol. 15 (1983), p. 1-52.

—   (1985)
   Aizawa, Genshichi 相沢源七: "Sakai Katsuisa no 'Shinshū tenshikoku'
   ron ni tsuite (chū) 酒井勝軍の「神州天子国」論について（中）", in: *Tōhoku
   Gakuin Daigaku Tōhoku Bunka Kenkyūsho kiyō* 東北学院大学東北文化
   研究所紀要, vol. 17 (1985), p. 43-107.

— (1986)
Aizawa, Genshichi 相沢源七: "Sakai Katsuisa no 'Shinshū tenshikoku' ron ni tsuite (ge no ichi) 酒井勝軍の「神州天子国」論について（下の一）", in: *Tōhoku Gakuin Daigaku Tōhoku Bunka Kenkyūsho kiyō* 東北学院大学東北文化研究所紀要, vol. 18 (1986), p. 81-114.

— (1987)
Aizawa, Genshichi 相沢源七: "Sakai Katsuisa no 'Shinshū tenshikoku' ron ni tsuite (ge no ni) 酒井勝軍の「神州天子国」論について（下の二）", in: *Tōhoku Gakuin Daigaku Tōhoku Bunka Kenkyūsho kiyō* 東北学院大学東北文化研究所紀要, vol. 19 (1987), p. 103-150.

— (1988)
Aizawa, Genshichi 相沢源七: "Sakai Katsuisa 酒井勝軍", in: *Nihon kirisutokyō rekishi daijiten* 日本キリスト教歴史大事典. Tōkyō: Kyōbunkan, 1988, p. 561.

— (1989)
Aizawa, Genshichi 相沢源七: "Sakai Katsuisa no 'Shinshū tenshikoku' ron ni tsuite (ge no san) 酒井勝軍の「神州天子国」論について（下の三）", in: *Tōhoku Gakuin Daigaku Tōhoku Bunka Kenkyūsho kiyō* 東北学院大学東北文化研究所紀要, vol. 21 (1989), p. 35-83.

Dohi (1975)
Dohi, Akio 土肥昭夫: *Nihon purotesutanto kyōkai no seiritsu to tenkai* 日本プロテスタント教会の成立と展開. Tōkyō: Nihon Kirisutokyōdan shuppankyoku, 1975.

— (1980)
Dohi, Akio 土肥昭夫: *Nihon purotesutanto-kirisutokyōshi* 日本プロテスタント・キリスト教史. Tōkyō: Shinkyō shuppansha, 1980.

Fujimaki (1983)
Fujimaki, Takayuki 藤巻孝之: *Mikuni undō no kiseki: hitotsu no shōgen* みくに運動の軌跡：一つの証言. Numazu: Kirisutokyō shidankai, 1983.

— (1988a)
Fujimaki, Takayuki 藤巻孝之: "Imaizumi Genkichi 今泉源吉", in: *Nihon kirisutokyō rekishi daijiten* 日本キリスト教歴史大事典. Tōkyō: Kyōbunkan, 1988, p. 132.

— (1988b)
Fujimaki, Takayuki 藤巻孝之: "Mikuni undō みくに運動", in: *Nihon kirisutokyō rekishi daijiten 日本キリスト教歴史大事典*. Tōkyō: Kyōbunkan, 1988, p. 1351.

Goodman/ Miyazawa (1995)
Goodman, David G./ Miyazawa, Masanori: *Jews in the Japanese mind: The history and uses of a cultural stereotype*. New York : The Free Press, 1995.

Hara (1999a)
Hara, Makoto 原誠: "Nihon kirisuto kyōdan to fashizumu jidai 日本基督教団とファシズム時代", in: *Kirisutokyō kenkyū 基督教研究*, vol. 61, no. 1 (June 1999), p. 1-27.

— (1999b)
Hara, Makoto 原誠: "Senjiki no kirisutokyō shisō: nihonteki kirisutokyō o chūshin ni 戦時期のキリスト教思想：日本的基督教を中心に", in: *Kirisutokyō kenkyū キリスト教研究*, vol. 61, no. 2 (Dec. 1999), p. 15-41.

Han (1988)
Han, Sokki 韓晢曦 [Han Sŏk-ki 한석기]: *Nihon no chōsen shihai to shūkyō seisaku 日本の朝鮮支配と宗教政策*. Tōkyō: Miraisha, 1988.

Hōrinesu-Bando (1983)
Hōrinesu-Bando Shōwa Kirisutokyō Dan'atsushi Kankōkai ホーリネス・バンド昭和キリスト教弾圧史刊行会 (ed.): *Hōrinesu-bando no kiseki: ribaibaru to kirisutokyō dan'atsu ホーリネス・バンドの軌跡：リバイバルとキリスト教弾圧*. Tōkyō: Shinkyō shuppansha, 1983.

Inoue (1990)
Inoue, Nobutaka 井上順孝 et al. (ed.): *Shinshūkyō jiten 新宗教事典*. Tōkyō: Kōbundō, 1990.

Kaneda (1985)
Kaneda, Ryūichi 金田隆一: *Senjika kirisutokyō no teikō to zasetsu 戦時下キリスト教の抵抗と挫折*. Tōkyō: Shinkyō shuppansha, 1985.

Kasahara (1974)
Kasahara, Yoshimitsu 笠原芳光: "'Nihonteki kirisutokyō' hihan 「日本的キリスト教」批判", in: *Kirisutokyō shakaimondai kenkyū キリスト教社会問題研究*, vol. 22 (March 1974), p. 114-139.

—    (1978)
Kasahara, Yoshimitsu 笠原芳光: "Nihon kirisutokyōdan seiritsu no mondai 日本基督教団成立の問題", in: Dōshisha Daigaku Jinbunkagaku Kenkyūsho 同志社大学人文科学研究所 (ed.): _Senjika teikō no kenkyū: kirisutosha, jiyūshugisha no baai_ 戦時下抵抗の研究：キリスト者、自由主義者の場合. vol. 1, Tōkyō: Misuzu shobō, 1978 [2nd ed.], pp. 140-187.

Komuro (1993)
Komuro, Naoko 小室尚子: _'Mikuni undō' ni okeru kirisutokyō dochakuka no mondai_ 「みくに運動」におけるキリスト教土着化の問題. [MA-thesis] Tōkyō Union Theological Seminary, Graduate School, 1993.

Miyazawa (1982)
Miyazawa, Masanori 宮沢正典: _Zōho yudayajin ronkō_ 増補ユダヤ人論考. Tōkyō: Shinsensha, 1982.

Morioka/ Kasahara (1974)
Morioka, Iwao 森岡巌/ Kasahara, Yoshimitsu 笠原芳光: _Kirisutokyō no sensō sekinin: nihon no senzen, senchū, sengo_ キリスト教の戦争責任：日本の戦前、戦中、戦後. Tōkyō: Kyōbunkan, 1974.

Mullins (1998)
Mullins, Mark: _Christianity made in Japan: a study of indigenous movements_. Honolulu: University of Hawai'i Press, 1998.

NKRD
Nihon Kirisutokyō Rekishi Daijiten Henshū Iinkai 日本キリスト教歴史大事典編集委員会 (ed.): _Nihon kirisutokyō rekishi daijiten_ 日本キリスト教歴史大事典. Tōkyō: Kyōbunkan, 1988.

Sasaki (1966)
Sasaki, Toshiji 佐々木敏二: "Chian iji hō kaiaku to kirisutokyōkai 治安維持法改悪とキリスト教会", in: _Kirisutokyō shakaimondai kenkyū_ キリスト教社会問題研究, vol. 10 (April 1966), p. 39-77.

Shinpi [kaisetsuhen] (1982)
_Shinpi no Nihon: kaisetsuhen_ 神秘之日本：解説篇. [published as appendix to the reprint of the magazine "Shinpi no Nihon"] Tōkyō: Hachiman shoten, 1982.

Takamichi (1965)
Takamichi, Motoi 高道基: "Fashizumu taiseika no shūkyō ファシズム体制下の宗教", in: _Kirisutokyō shakaimondai kenkyū_ キリスト教社会問題研究, vol. 9 (April 1965), p. 45-56.

**Takeda (1967)**
Takeda, Kiyoko 武田清子: *Ningenkan no sōkoku* 人間観の相剋. Tōkyō: Kōbundō, 1967 [revised ed.].

**Yoneda (1996)**
Yoneda, Isamu 米田勇: *Nakada Jūji den* 中田重治伝. Tōkyō: Ōzora sha, 1996.

**Yoneda/ Takayama (1964)**
Yoneda, Yutaka 米田豊/ Takayama, Keiki 高山慶喜: *Shōwa no shūkyō dan'atsu: senji hōrinesu junanki* 昭和の宗教弾圧：戦時ホーリネス受難記. Tōkyō: Inochi-no-Kotoba sha, 1964.

# Buddhism and *kokutai* (National Polity) in Modern Japan: The Case of the Nichirenist Movement of Tanaka Chigaku

ŌTANI Eiichi

## Introduction

The purpose of this paper is to analyze the relationship between religion and politics in modern Japan.

I will focus specifically on the case of Nichirenism (*Nichiren-shugi* 日蓮主義) advocated by Tanaka Chigaku 田中智学 (1861-1939). He was the founder of the *Kokuchū-kai* 国柱会, a lay Buddhist association, and asserted a nationalistic version of Nichiren Buddhism before the Second World War. His thought and activities had an important effect on intellectuals, the military, educators and capitalists. Some people inspired by his teachings include Ishihara Kanji 石原莞爾, a military officer who took part in the invasion of Manchuria (*Manshū jihen* 満州事変), Inoue Nisshō 井上日召, a terrorist responsible for the Ketsumeidan incident (*Ketsumeidan jiken* 血盟団事件) and the esteemed author Miyazawa Kenji 宮沢賢治.[1]

Over the past few decades, many scholars have criticized Tanaka's Nichirenism, decrying it as a philosophy of militarism and imperialism that contributed to the rise of militarism in modern Japan [cf. Tokoro (1967, 1972); Nakano (1977)]. But little is known about the entirety of his thought and activities.[2] When we examine his essential philosophy of Nichirenism, we must especially look more carefully into his thought about the relationship between religion and politics.

Tanaka reconstructed Nichiren's traditional teachings regarding this relationship between religion and politics (*hōkoku sōkan ron* 法国相関論), adapting it to fit the modern nation-state. His intention was to organize a nationalistic religious movement that proposed to transform the world into a utopia through the unity of religion and politics (*hōkoku-myōgō* 法国冥合, *ōbutsu-myōgō* 王仏冥合,

---

[1] For effects of Nichirenism in modern Japan, see Tamura/ Miyazaki (1972).

[2] For a discussion of the entirety of Tanaka's thought and activities, see Ōtani (2001).

*risshō-ankoku* 立正安国). The question I wish to address is how Tanaka interpreted the relationship between Nichiren Buddhism and the nation-state, in other words, the connection between Nichirenism and nationalism.

In this paper, I would like to focus on his *kokutai* 国体 ('national polity') ideology. Tanaka shaped the original theory of *Nihon kokutai* (*Nihon kokutai gaku* 日本国体学), which connected Nichirenism with *kokutai* ideology. '*Kokutai*' can be defined as an ideology that legitimates modern Japan as nation-state, and as Tanaka negotiated the connection between *kokutai* ideology and Nichiren Buddhism, he designed a specifically Japanese national identity from a Nichiren Buddhist point of view.

From the beginning of the 1900's he claimed that Nichiren Buddhism was to become the established religion of Japan, and systematized his theory of *Nihon kokutai* through the 1910's and 1920's. Though the details of his entire life are important in order to analyze his thought about the relationship between religion and politics, I will limit the discussion to his thought formation from the 1900's to 1920's, the latter part of his life.

I will reconsider the relationship between religion and politics in modern Japan by analyzing the process of adaptation between Buddhism and *kokutai* ideology.

### Studies on Religion and kokutai Ideology in Modern Japan

#### The Definition of kokutai Ideology

I will use the term '*kokutai* ideology', otherwise known as '*tennō-sei ideorogī*' 天皇制イデオロギー, to refer to the knowledge system used to justify the authority of the Emperor (*tennō* 天皇) and the Emperor system (*tennō-sei* 天皇制) and to legitimate the nation-state of modern Japan. The Emperor system was an 'invented tradition' that constructed nationals (*kokumin* 国民) and state (*kokka* 国家) in the name of a sacred older tradition.[3]

*Kokutai* ideology became implicit among the Japanese people by spreading through its formulation in state ceremony, education, army, mass media and

---

[3] For further details of the relationship between nation-state building and the Emperor system in modern Japan, see Yasumaru (1978, 1992).

other forms. The turning point in the establishment of a national consciousness was the Sino-Japanese War (*Nisshin-sensō* 日清戦争) of 1894-1895 and the Russo-Japanese War (*Nichiro-sensō* 日露戦争) of 1904-1905. Not least due to these victories, Japan established its nationalism between the 1890's and 1910's. As a result, *kokutai* ideology was diffused through the consciousness of the Japanese people.

### *Studies on Religion and* kokutai *Ideology*

Over the past few years, several studies have been published regarding the relationship between religion and *kokutai* ideology in modern Japan.

Tsushima Michihito 対馬路人 studied 'end-prophecy religion' (*shūmatsu-yogen shūkyō* 終末預言宗教) from the Taishō 大正 (1910's) to the early postwar era [see Tsushima (1985, 1988)]. This included Japanese new religious movements that emphasized eschatology, such as Ōmoto 大本, Tenri Honmichi 天理本道, Jiu 爾宇, and Shinsei ryūjinkai 神政龍神会. Tsushima reasoned diffusion of *kokutai* ideology, thus he states:

> "*It has been recognized that the diffusion and fixation of the myth of the modern Emperor system prevented the development and representation of religious imagination within the new religions. On the other hand, that diffusion and fixation contributed to the activation of end-prophecy religions.*" [Tsushima (1985), p. 102]

Tsushima points out three reasons for this: ① since the *amatsu-hitsugi* 天津日嗣 belief (belief in a living God) permeated into the consciousness of the Japanese people, the idea of a Messiah came to be accepted; ② since the myths contained in *Kojiki* 古事記 and *Nihon shoki* 日本書紀 (*kiki shinwa* 記紀神話) were emphasized as actual, literal history, it aroused within religion the legitimacy of grasping the history of the Japanese nation and state from the viewpoint of mythology; and ③ the ideas espoused by the new religions did not necessarily value the *Kojiki* and *Nihon shoki* myths as the official myth systems of the Japanese people [cf. Tsushima (1985), p. 103].

Tsushima states that the myths espoused by Ōmoto and Tenri Honmichi were artificially reconstructed to include the *Kojiki* and the *Nihon shoki* myths, which demonstrates that end-prophecy religion was formed by borrowing from the official system ideology. However, it is important to point out that end-prophecy religion did not accept the actual living Emperor and Emperor system, but rather designed an idealized version thereof that aimed to transcend the existing structure. In other words, these religious movements incorporated *kokutai* ideology into the system of their doctrine and ritual by borrowing from the established framework of the official system of ideology.

Also Nishiyama Shigeru 西山茂 points out:

> *"When the ritual of Emperor worship spread to the Japanese people after the late Meiji era or the beginning of the Taishō era, new types of religious movements that incorporated Emperor worship into their doctrine and ritual were developed. These were religious movements such as the Nichirenism of Tanaka Chigaku and Kōdō Ōmoto 皇道大本 of Deguchi Onisaburō 出口王仁三郎."* [Nishiyama (1998), p. 8]

According to Nishiyama, Tanaka Chigaku reconstructed Nichiren's traditional teachings and constructed the theory of *kokutai* from the standpoint of Nichirenism, while simultaneously borrowing from the *Nihon shoki*. I shall discuss this in detail by analyzing Tanaka's thought formation.

### The relationship between Nichiren Buddhism and kokutai between the 1880's and 1920's

#### Outline of the Nichirenist Movement

When Tanaka Chigaku in the early Meiji-period lost his parents at an early age, he took the tonsure and entered the Nichiren Buddhist sect as a priest. However, soon after he contracted a serious illness, and simultaneously began to have doubts about the sect's state of feudal system and conservative doctrine at that time.[4]

Due to these conflicts, he left the sect and organized a lay Buddhist association. In 1884, at the age of 23, he formed the *Risshō ankoku-kai* 立正安国会 in Tōkyō. Though he reformed the society into the *Kokuchū-kai* 国柱会 in 1914,

---

[4] For further details of Tanaka's life , see Tanaka (1977) and Tanaka (1974).

he remained the head of this lay Buddhist movement throughout the rest of his life.

The history of this movement can be divided into two stages. In the first stage, between the 1880's and 1900's, this reform movement of the Nichiren sect emphasized the notion: 'reform the sect (*shūmon-kakumei* 宗門革命) and return to Nichiren (*sodō-fukko* 祖道復古)'. With the publication of his *Nihon kokutai gaku* 日本国体学 ('Theory of *Nihon kokutai*') in 1903, his movement entered a second stage. In the 1910's and 1920's the group developed into a nationalistic *kokutai* movement, a so-called enlightenment movement that preached the credo: 'be conscious of the concept of *kokutai*' (*kokutai-kannen o jikaku seyo* 国体観念を自覚せよ). Throughout both of these stages, this was a nationalistic religious movement that aimed to transform the world into a utopia through the unity of religion and politics based on the *Hokke-kyō* 法華経 ('Lotus Sūtra').

*Nichiren Buddhism and the Nation-State in the 1900's*

In 1901 Tanaka published an essay entitled *Shūmon no ishin* 宗門之維新 ('The Restoration of the Nichiren Sect'). In this essay, he wrote:

> "*The heart of my plan is the complete restoration of the original doctrine, while simultaneously establishing a progressive institutional structure. Moreover, we must maintain an aggressive attitude at all times.*" [Tanaka (1901), p. 15]

By 'aggressive attitude' Tanaka meant the unification of humankind through the Lotus Sūtra. He predicted the unity of the whole world in this essay. The pre-condition was the unity of religion and politics in Japan. After the Nichiren sect was restored, he said, Nichiren Buddhism (*Honge myōshū* 本化妙宗) was to become the religion of the establishment in Japan within fifty years. This in turn would lead to the establishment of the so-called 'national ordination platform' (*kokuritsu kaidan* 国立戒壇). Thus Tanaka strongly asserted that religion should be directly connected with the nation-state.

In 1902, Tanaka wrote a work entitled *Honge myōshū shikimoku* 本化妙宗式目 ('Nichiren's Religious System'). This work was a systematic formulation of Nichiren's teaching and the doctrinal system of the *Risshō ankoku-kai*. Tanaka opened a full-year lecture series in Ōsaka in April 1903, to explain the *Myōshū shikimoku*. Transcripts of these lectures were published the following year [cf. Tanaka (1904-13)]. In these works, he formulated a process of the unity of religion and politics (*hōkoku-myōgō* 法国冥合) by means of establishing the 'national ordination platform' *kokuritsu kaidan*.

Tanaka based his interpretation of how to establish this platform on a paragraph contained within Nichiren's *Sandai hihō hinjō ji* 三大秘法稟承事 (or *Sandai hihō shō* 三大秘法抄).[5] He described the process in three steps: ① the unity of religion and politics (*nihō-myōgō* 二法冥合); ② establishing the 'national ordination platform' (*jidan-jōju* 事壇成就); and ③ the unity of the whole world (*enbu-tōitsu* 閻浮統一). The first step was divided into developing a public consciousness of the idea of *kokutai* (*ōbō-myōbutsu* 王法冥仏) and the diffusion of Nichiren Buddhism throughout the whole state (*buppō-keiō* 仏法契王). The second step was divided into the proclamation by the Emperor declaring Nichiren Buddhism as the national faith (*taishō-kanpatsu* 大詔渙発), and a resolution to revise Nichiren Buddhism and to establish the 'national ordination platform' at the National Diet (*ikkoku-dōki* 一国同帰), to be proposed directly by the Emperor himself. The third step was the unity of all of thought, religion, morals, society and politics through the power of *Myōhō-renge-kyō* 妙法蓮華経, i.e., through the essence of the Lotus Sūtra.

Tanaka warned that when Japan declared the establishment of the 'national ordination platform' to the whole world, many states would rise up in opposition. This would inevitably result in a World War, a conviction buttressed by a reference to a paragraph of Nichiren's *Kanjin honzon shō* 観心本尊抄. At that time, the *kennō* 賢王 (Messiah), in the form of the Bodhisattva Jōgyō (*Jōgyō bosatsu* 上行菩薩) would enter and assume supreme leadership. In the lecture transcripts, the *kennō* was to be the *tennō*, or Emperor. Thus to Tanaka, the *tennō* was to play the triple role of proposer of the ordination platform, Bodhisattva and Messiah.

In November 1903, Tanaka went on a pilgrimage to the mausoleum (*kofun* 古墳) of Emperor Jinmu 神武 at Nara. He subsequently lectured on the Japanese nation and its relation to Nichiren's thought, in a presentation entitled *Kōsō no*

---

[5] On the authenticity of Nichiren's authorship of *Sandai hihō shō*, see Sueki (1999).

*kenkoku to honge no daikyō* 皇宗の建国と本化の大教. It was in this lecture that he advocated the theory of *Nihon kokutai* for the first time. This lecture was published as a booklet under the title *Sekai-tōitsu no tengyō* 世界統一の天業 ('The Heavenly Task of the Unity of the Whole World') the following year.

This lecture stressed that the notion of *kokutai* was derived directly from the *Nihon shoki*. In the context of the strained international situation at that time, he declared the importance of the moral unity of Japan in the face of the avaricious unity of Russia. He explained that the morality of the Japanese people was also based on the *Nihon shoki*. According to Tanaka, the Japanese nation had inherited the philosophy of *kokutai* from the *Nihon shoki*, and was charged with the mission of the unity of the whole world, a duty that has existed since Emperor Jinmu founded the Japanese nation [cf. Tanaka (1904)]. In this lecture, Nichirenism was characterized as essentially linked to *kokutai* ideology, and was justified as a religiously vindicated nationalism.

### *Nichiren Buddhism and* kokutai *in the 1910's and 1920's*

After the First World War, democracy and socialism rather than nationalism prevailed among the Japanese people. However, during that time *kokutai* ideology continued to spread. In April 1919, accepting a request from the Nichiren sect, Tanaka lectured in Tōkyō on *Nihon kokutai* from a Nichiren Buddhist point of view.

In this lecture and his later *Nihon kokutai no kenkyū* 日本国体の研究 ('Studies in Japanese *kokutai*') published in 1922, he definitively formulated the theory of *kokutai*.

The theme of the lecture was the idea of a nation (*kokka* 国家, *kuni* 国) based on Nichirenism and the relationship between Nichiren Buddhism and *kokutai*. His theory is based on the concept of the originally existing land (*hon kokudo* 本国土) founded in Nichiren Buddhist teachings. *Hon kokudo* means the transcendental ideal land. In Buddhism there is an idea of a realm of land in which sentient beings exist, known in Japanese as *kokudo seken* 国土世間. In Nichiren's use of the term 'nation' (*kokka, kuni*), what he was referring to was primarily not a socio-political structure, but rather a realm of land.[6] But then nation means a socio-political structure in Nichiren's teachings, too. Tanaka also makes reference to this, distinguishing between a realm of land and a socio-political structure.

Strictly speaking, Tanaka's usage of the term 'nation' can be classified into three categories: land, nation-state, and *kokutai*. The nation-state exists on land, and the Japanese nation is founded in the ideology of *kokutai*. He discusses that these are based on the originally existing land from the standpoint of Nichiren Buddhist teaching, explaining it as follows:

> "*When I explain Japanese* kokutai *from the standpoint of the originally existing land, scholars complain that an ideal land is not within the capacity of actual states, but only of the spiritual world. However, Nichiren said that Japan is the originally existing land explained by the Lotus Sūtra for more than 600 years.*" [Tanaka (1932), p. 115]

Tanaka thus suggested that the transcendental ideal land was identical to the Nichiren concept of *kokutai*, the essential Japanese nation-state.[7]

In his *Nihon kokutai no kenkyū* ('Studies in Japanese *kokutai*'), Tanaka explains the origins, contents, and mission of *Nihon kokutai* through references to the *Nihon shoki*. According to him, the Japanese nation was built by the 'three guides of nation-building' (*kenkoku no santaikō* 建国の三大綱) derived from the *Nihon shoki*. Those are the concepts of *yōsei* 養正, *chōki* 重暉, and *sekikei* 積慶. *Yōsei* means carrying out justice, *chōki* means enlightening the world through wisdom, and *sekikei* means being merciful to sentient living beings. In tandem with this, Nichiren Buddhism has the 'three great secret Dharmas' or *sandai hihō* 三大秘法. They are *honzon* 本尊, *daimoku* 題目, and *kaidan* 戒壇, revealed in the original teachings or *honmon* 本門 of the Lotus Sūtra. The *honzon* is the principal object of worship, the *daimoku* is the Lotus Sūtra essentialized in the seven sacred syllables '*Namu-myōhō-renge-kyō*' 南無妙法蓮華経, and the *kaidan* is the 'ordination platform', a solid foundation of this faith. Tanaka explains that as the three guides correspond to the three great secret Dharma, Nichiren Buddhism coincides with *Nihon kokutai*.

---

[6] See Satō (1999) for Nichiren's view of nation, where this point is argued.
[7] For further details of Tanaka's view of nation, scf. Ōtani (2001), pp. 246-252.

That is to say, in his interpretation the foundations of the Japanese nation and its subsequent incarnation in the form of a modern nation-state are inherently resonant with the tenets of Nichiren Buddhism.

## Conclusion

I have examined the manner in which Tanaka interpreted the relationship between Nichiren Buddhism and the Japanese nation-state. His Nichirenism was a reformulation of Nichiren's traditional teachings that connected with *kokutai* ideology derived from the *Nihon shoki*.

In the beginning of the 1900's, he declared that Nichiren Buddhism was to become the established religion of Japan. He reinterpreted the contents of the *Sandai hihō shō* and described the unity of religion and politics by means of the establishment of a 'national ordination platform'. He emphasized Nichiren Buddhism's relevance to the political and social structure of the Japanese nation-state, and advocated the theory of *kokutai* and incorporation of *kokutai* ideology into Nichiren Buddhism under the influence of the rise of nationalism.

Through the 1910's and 1920's, Tanaka formulated the theory of *Nihon kokutai* and interpreted *kokutai* from a Nichirenist point of view. In order to establish the unity of religion and politics, he proposed a public consciousness of the idea of *kokutai*.

In conclusion, Tanaka claimed to justify the notion of the modern nation-state from the venerable standpoint of Nichiren Buddhism. He ultimately asserted that Nichirenism would link up with the nation-state through the medium of *kokutai* ideology.

## References

Nakano (1977)
    Nakano, Kyōtoku 中濃教篤: "Tanaka Chigaku 田中智学", in: Nakano, Kyōtoku (ed.): *Kindai Nichiren kyōdan no shisōka* 近代日蓮教団の思想家. Tōkyō: Kokusho kankō-kai, 1977.

Nishiyama (1998)
Nishiyama, Shigeru 西山茂: "Kindai bukkyō kenkyū no shūkyō shakai-gaku-teki kenkyū 近代仏教研究の宗教社会学的研究", in: *Kindai bukkyō 近代仏教*, vol. 5 (1998), pp. 5-14.

Ōtani (2001)
Ōtani, Eiichi 大谷栄一: *Kindai Nihon no Nichiren-shugi undō 近代日本の日蓮主義運動*. Kyōto: Hozō-kan, 2001.

Satō (1999)
Satō, Hiroo 佐藤弘夫: "Nichiren's view of Nation and Religion", in: *Japanese Journal of Religious Studies*, vol. 26/3-4 (1999), pp. 307-324.

Sueki (1999)
Sueki, Fumihiko 末木文美士: "Nichiren's problematic works", in: *Japanese Journal of Religious Studies*, vol. 26/3-4 (1999), pp. 216-280.

Tamura/ Miyazaki (1972)
Tamura, Yoshirō 田村芳朗/ Miyazaki, Eishū 宮崎英修 (eds.): *Nihon kindai to Nichiren-shugi 日本近代と日蓮主義*. Tōkyō: Shunjū-sha, 1972.

Tanaka (1901)
Tanaka, Chigaku 田中智学: *Shūmon no ishin 宗門之維新*. Tōkyō: Shishiō-bunko, 1901.

— (1904)
Tanaka, Chigaku 田中智学: *Sekai-tōitsu no tengyō 世界統一の天業*. Tōkyō: Shishiō-bunko, 1904.

— (1904-13)
Tanaka, Chigaku 田中智学: *Honge myōshū shikimoku kōgiroku 本化妙宗式目講義録*. 5 vols., Tōkyō: Shishiō-bunko, 1904-13.

— (1922)
Tanaka, Chigaku 田中智学: *Nihon kokutai no kenkyū 日本国体の研究*. Tōkyō: Tengyō-minpō-sha, 1922.

— (1932)
Tanaka, Chigaku 田中智学: "Honge shūgaku yori mitaru Nihon kokutai 本化宗学より見たる日本国体", in: *Shishiō-zenshū 師子王全集*. [36 vols. in 3 parts] part 1, vol. 2, Tōkyō: Shishiō-bunko, 1932, pp. 1-402.

— (1977)
Tanaka, Chigaku 田中智学: *Tanaka Chigaku jiden: Waga heshi ato 田中智学自伝：我が經しあと*. 12 vols., Tōkyō: Shishiō-bunko, 1977.

Tanaka (1974)

Tanaka, Hōkoku 田中芳谷: *Tanaka Chigaku sensei ryakuden* 田中智学先生略傳. Tōkyō: Shishiō-bunko, 1974.

Tokoro (1967)

Tokoro, Shigemoto 戸頃重基: *Nichiren kyōgaku no shisōshi-teki kenkyū* 日蓮教学の思想史的研究. Tōkyō: Toyama-shobō, 1967.

— (1972)

Tokoro, Shigemoto 戸頃重基: *Kindai shakai to Nichiren-shugi* 近代社会と日蓮主義. Tōkyō: Hyōron-sha, 1972.

Tsushima (1985)

Tsushima, Michihito 対馬路人: "Shūmatsu yogen shūkyō no keifu 終末預言宗教の系譜", in: *Shinri to sōzo* 真理と創造, vol. 24 (1985), pp. 94-106.

— (1988)

Tsushima, Michihito 対馬路人: "Shin-shūkyō ni okeru tennō-kan to yonaoshi-kan 新宗教における天皇観と世直し観", in: Kōmoto, Mitsugi 孝本貢 (ed.): *Ronshū nihon bukkyōshi* 論集日本仏教史. [9 vols.] vol. 9, Tōkyō: Yūzankaku-shuppan, 1988, pp. 189-214.

Yasumaru (1978)

Yasumaru, Yoshio 安丸良夫: *Kamigami no Meiji-ishin* 神々の明治維新. Tōkyō: Iwanami-shoten, 1978.

— (1992)

Yasumaru, Yoshio 安丸良夫: *Kindai tennō-zō no keisei* 近代天皇像の形成. Tōkyō: Iwanami-shoten, 1992.

# Nishi Hongan-ji and National Identity
# in Bakumatsu and early Meiji Japan

Peter KLEINEN

A critical examination into the scientific relevance of the very topic under discussion, namely the question of Nishi Hongan-ji's 西本願寺 part in the construction and maintenance of a specifically Buddhist national identity, may immediately identify a whole range of related questions. With respect to the composition of the title of this paper, some among those may be as follows: Firstly, why, in comparison with other Buddhist traditions in the Japanese context, should Nishi Hongan-ji be of any particular importance to the shaping of a 'national identity'? Secondly, exactly how should we conceive of a concept superficially as self-explanatory and natural, but, upon closer consideration, as complex and prone to evade definition as 'national identity'? In other words, what, as for one thing, is identity, and in what sense do *national* identities differ from other types of identity? (It goes without saying that propositions in the realm of this second question-complex are not without repercussions on the first question) Thirdly, and finally, one may ask why it should have been the Bakumatsu 幕末 and early Meiji 明治 periods, the years between, say, 1853 and 1889 or 1894/95, which were of any particularly great significance to Nishi Hongan-ji and the genesis of its national consciousness? After all, certain notions of Japaneseness among Buddhist clerics may well have existed centuries before Japan's second large-scale encounter with Western powers in the 1850s. And, on the other hand, it is well known that a central thesis of Carol Gluck's highly influential and widely accepted study on *Japan's Modern Myths* claims that "*what is now called 'emperor system' ideology*", for most of us undisputedly one of the major constituent parts of modern Japan's national identity, "*did not begin to emerge in earnest until around 1890*" [Gluck (1985), p. 17]. Again, it should be evident that the treatment of such a time question is closely interlinked with our understanding of the socio-psychological phenomenon we choose to address as 'national identity'. For this reason, before dealing with the Bakumatsu and early Meiji history of Nishi Hongan-ji – or, to be precise about that, clerics such as (Shaku 釈) Gesshō 月性 (1817–1858) and Shimaji Mokurai 島地黙雷 (1838–1911), two outstanding royalist priests or *kinnōsō* 勤王僧 belonging to a circle of spiritually and politically akin comrades in arms, which I shall call the Hongan-ji's Chōshū-faction and which in Japanese is commonly referred to as 'those from Suō and Nagato' (*bōchō shussin-sha* 防長出身者) – it seems appropriate to engage in a brief theoretical discussion of the most crucial concepts at stake, that is 'nation', 'nationalism', and 'national identity'.

There is another, more specific, reason for meddling with theory for a while: As anyone familiar with the literature will acknowledge, this paper, just as the contributions of Ōtani Eiichi 大谷栄一 and Fujii Takeshi 藤井健志 to this volume, is situated within a young and still somewhat under-represented genre in the province of Japanology. Issues related to Japanese Buddhist nationalism, institutional Buddhism's collaboration with the so-called 'emperor-system' state, and, consequently, its 'war responsibility' have long marked a rather neglected field of research. The examination of what in the early post-war academic world almost always used to be identified as the ideological cradle of modern Japan's national-chauvinism, imperialistic aggression and so forth – namely of what is commonly referred to as 'State-Shinto' – was probably given too much attention to discern in Japanese Buddhism much more than a most unfortunate victim of blunt religious suppression ever since the anti-Buddhist iconoclasm (*haibutsu kishaku* 廃仏毀釈) of early Meiji had thrown its institutions into their most severe crisis of the entire modern era. Since the 1980s, however, Western historiography on Japan has gradually begun to reconsider the case of modern Buddhism, that is, in principle, to treat it as a serious political actor and subject of Japan's national history. Consciousness is constantly growing that *"Buddhism"*, to put it in Kevin Doak's words, *"was not merely the 'victim' of a state-centered nationalism that privileged State Shinto and oppressed all other religions. The position of the emperor in religious ideology, the privileged position of State Shinto, and the 'emperor-system' nature of the prewar Japanese state cannot be ignored. However, an overemphasis on these factors, coupled with too simplistic an understanding of the nature of national-ism in prewar Japan, have all to often led to the conclusion that Buddhism maintained an Asian, if not universal, value-structure in the face of state oppression. This was true, of course, in some cases. Yet, nationalist and reli-gious sentiments were deeply rooted and often subtly intertwined to the degree that no religious group was totally immune from nationalist inclinations and no nationalist formulation could completely ignore the powerful appeals of Buddhism in all its sectarian forms"* [Doak (1995), pp. 174f.]. Well, even though I could not agree more with Kevin Doak's overall characterization of large parts of the older relevant literature, it is exactly the 'understanding of the nature of nationalism' as exposed by those few colleagues who have made long overdue endeavors at a reassessment of the socio-political stance and history of modern Japanese Buddhism, which I have certain misgivings about. Since I consider my own writings as part of this newer academic tradition, however, it may be even more urgently recommended to clarify in which sense my theoretical approach to the problem-complex of 'nation', 'nationalism' and 'national identity' differs from what is currently available in the field.

Limitations of space, of course, will not allow us to engage in an extended discussion of existing and, at times, mutually opposed approaches within the social sciences at large, and even less so in a discussion of the sociogenesis of the very terms 'nation' and 'nationalism'. Within the small group of those who have dealt with the complex of Japanese Buddhist nationalism, however, we may distinguish one approach that leaves the term 'nation' essentially undefined and treats 'nationalism' as a certain kind of irrational ideology and intolerant political fanaticism from which, for reasons that are all too obvious, critical scientists can only strive to dissociate themselves. It is thus characterized by a morally judgmental, highly negative attitude towards its object of investigation and finally comes close to an attempt at dragging some of pre-war Buddhism's major protagonists and apologists to a scientifically appareled war crime tribunal. Just or unjust, this approach – which has been adopted by more or less all eminent Japanese scholars of the older generation such as Ichikawa Hakugen 市川白弦 (1975), Tokoro Shigemoto 戸頃重基 (1966), and Fukushima Kanryū (or Hirotaka) 福嶋寛隆 (1986), and, in the West, in Peter Fischer's seminal anthology on 'Buddhism and Nationalism in Modern Japan' [Fischer (1979)], Brian Victoria's recent *Zen at War* (1997), and my own early attempt on Tanaka Chigaku's 田中智学 (1861–1939) so-called '*Nichirenism*' (*Nichiren-shugi* 日蓮主義) [Kleinen (1994)] – is mainly interested in the question of modern Buddhism's war responsibility. It utilizes the term 'nationalism' in a derogatory fashion, or as an insult, and, as such, is of rather limited use to our understanding of the complex socio-psychological and socio-political forces at work in the process of the adoption of a 'national identity'.

Yet, there is another major current in the aforementioned academic tradition. It, too, leaves the term 'nation' essentially undefined. On the other hand, it takes note of the historical phenomenon of Buddhist nationalism as such with slightly more calmness and treats well-known Buddhist apologists such as Shaku Sōen 釈宗演 (1859–1919), Nukariya Kaiten 忽滑谷快天 (1867–1934), and Suzuki Daisetsu 鈴木大拙 (1870–1966) as early protagonists of a *nihonjinron* 日本人論 -like cultural nationalism as it has been defined, among others, by the Japanese sociologist Yoshino Kōsaku 吉野耕作. In particular, authors like Robert Sharf (1993), Galen Amstutz (1997), James Ketelaar (1990) and others have sharpened our awareness that the considerably spiritualized and distorted image of Japanese Buddhism in general Western perception is an ahistorical construct *"predicated upon"*, as Robert Sharf has it, *"and inexorably enmeshed in, the nativist and imperialist ideology of late nineteenth- and early twentieth-century Japan."* [Sharf (1993), pp. 5f.]. To this, I would add – if this short anticipation may be permitted: just as in Buddhism's desire and struggle for status maintenance and social dignity, which entirely depended upon the possibility of national participation and integration. Now, Amstutz defining 'cultural nationalism' as the *"reactionary sense that Japanese culture is tied to some 'essential' ethnic characteristics of the Japanese"* [(1997), p. 65] and Sharf stating that *"[t]he* nihonjinron *polemic in Suzuki's work – the grotesque caricatures of 'East' versus 'West' – is no doubt the most egregiously inane manifestation of his nationalist leanings"* [(1995), p. 47], it is entirely clear that these authors, too, are not exactly sympathetic towards their respective objects of investigation. Political ethics, albeit somewhat unacknowledged, do figure prominently in their discourse.

At this point, I should better hasten to add that I do not have quarrels with the ethical standards or any of the empirical findings of my colleagues. In principle, my own writings on the history of modern Japanese Buddhism do not tell a different story. Rather, my point is that in the course of time I have come to treat 'nationalism' in a quite different fashion [see Kleinen (2000)], in particular that I have come to consider it misleading, at best, to exclusively treat it as chauvinism on the one hand, or, on the other hand, as culturalism – in the sense of cultural reductionism and determinism – or cultural chauvinism. Existing nationalisms, those exhibited by Japanese Buddhists being no exception, may and actually did develop in either direction, but, I feel inclined to add, they do and did not necessarily have to. Thus, I propose to not consider these developments as such an essential or constitutive element in our addressing them as 'nationalism'. So-called 'cultural nationalism' as Yoshino Kōsaku has it, is a kind of social practice that "*aims to regenerate the* national community *by creating, preserving or strengthening a* people's *cultural identity when it is felt to be lacking, inadequate or threatened. The cultural nationalist regards the* nation *as the product of its unique history and culture and as a collective solidarity endowed with unique attributes. In short, cultural nationalism is concerned with the distinctiveness of the* cultural community *as the essence of a* nation."* [Yoshino (1992), p. 1; my emphasis]. Well, what Yoshino actually does describe here, is nativism proper. Indeed, he concedes that "*[w]hether or not the writers of Japanese uniqueness are themselves cultural nationalists depends on the way in which the term nationalism, which has diverse connotations, is used*" [ibid., p. 36], and elsewhere adds that "*[t]he mode of explanation in the* nihonjinron *is best characterised as that of culturalism*" [ibid., p. 10]. Why then, I wonder, does he talk about nationalism at all?

As I see it, the problem here and much elsewhere in scientific discourse on 'nationalism' is, in short, an insufficient differentiation between the two concepts 'people' and 'nation'. It is well known that Max Weber, for his part, did not develop anything approaching what we might call a theory of the nation. For that reason, he is usually not considered to be the first address to turn to in search for clarification of the issues under discussion. Still, there is plenty to learn from his occasional comments in the chapter on ethnic community relationships of his major work on *Wirtschaft und Gesellschaft* ('Economy and Society'). As for one thing, Weber is unambiguous about the insight that the ethnogenesis of what we may call a 'people' always follows the development of rulership – a process which in his own words he refers to as an "*artificial way of the emergence of a belief in ethnic community [...which...] entirely corresponds to the pattern of reinterpretation of rational associative relationships [Vergesellschaftungen] into affectual communal relationships [Vergemeinschaftungen]*" [1] [Weber

---

[1] My translation. The key-terms "associative relationship" and "communal relationship" are adopted from Talcott Parsons [(1964), p. 136]. For a list including translations of all key-terms of Weber's *Outline of Basic Sociological Terms* [*Soziologische Grundbegriffe*] see also <http://www.ne.jp/asahi/moriyuki/abukuma/outline/outline_basic_concept.html>.

(1972), p. 237]. At the same token, he explicates that *"time and again, we find that the concept 'nation' directs us to political power. Hence, the concept seems to refer [...] to a specific kind of pathos, which is linked to the idea of a powerful political community of people who share a common language, or religion, or common customs, or political memories; such a state may already exist or it may be desired. The more power is emphasized, the closer appears to be the link between nation and state"* [2] [Weber (1972), p. 244].

Now, keeping in mind that purely affectual ties between social actors depend on the possibility of direct face-to-face contact, as it is given within the family and traditional small-scale village communities, we may draw several conclusions from Weber's observations. Firstly, both, 'people' and 'nation', are 'abstract' [James (1996)] or 'imagined communities', to use Benedict Anderson's (1983) famous – and often misunderstood – rendering. They are communities of strangers and, in this sense, do not differ from each other at all. Secondly, they entirely depend on constantly growing networks of agency-extended social communications, which, for their part, allow for the possibility of a reinterpretation of rational associative relationships into affectual communal relationships, but do not themselves exist outside the framework of rational associative relationships, the political embodiment of which is the modern state or a pre-modern state-like construct of rulership. In short, there is no 'people' and there is no 'nation' beyond the sphere of intersubjective perception within, or springing from, a state-like order. Again, there is no difference between 'people' and 'nation' at all. Thirdly, however, the concept 'nation' has an attribute which 'people' does not share: it is an abstract or imagined *political* community. For this reason, and in order to make provisions against conceptual confusion in the very definition of the term 'nation', I shall suggest to not equate 'people' with 'national community', 'nation' with 'cultural community', or 'national identity' with 'cultural identity' as such. [3] Cultural or ethnic

---

[2] This translation has been adopted from an article by David Little, United States Institute of Peace, on *Belief, Ethnicity, and Nationalism*, one of the very rare studies on Weber and his thoughts on national identity, nationalism and the nation; see Little (2001).

[3] Shmuel N. Eisenstadt and Wolfgang Schluchter have recently argued that *"the issues of nationhood and nationalism appear rather limited in scholarly terms if not seen against the backdrop of national identity being just one construction of collective identity, and in historical terms a rather late and by no means all-pervasive one. It is hardly an exaggeration to state that most theories of national identity and nationalism represent a*

characteristics are likely to enter the identity of any 'people', that is, they inform a consciously or unconsciously made selection of ascriptions which is taken from a potentially infinite number of empirical data and which is intersubjectively accepted by the most influential participants in public discourse within a given social order. "*Identity*", as Liah Greenfeld has it in the wake of Weber's methodological individualism, "*is perception. [...] It therefore either exists or does not; it cannot be asleep and then be awakened, as some sort of disease. It cannot be presumed on the basis of any objective characteristics, however closely associated with it in other cases*" [Greenfeld (1992), p. 13]. If a particular identity does not mean anything to an individual or a social collective in question, this individual or social collective does not have this particular identity.

What then does it mean to be a 'nation' and to have a 'national identity'? First of all, it is crucial to understand that the modern idea of the 'nation' is not identical with, but indeed based upon, the concept of the, or a, 'people'. 'Nation', as has been indicated, adds a specifically political notion to what only otherwise is a 'people' – which is why historian John Breuilly can be so unequivocal about the fundamental insight that "*nationalism is, above and beyond all else, about politics and that politics is about power.*" [(1993), p. 1]. It is generally acknowledged that until the French Revolution the dominant meaning of 'nation' was that of a 'community of aristocrats' which, for its part, was distinguished precisely by its "*status politicus*" [Schulze (1999), p. 117] or the political privilege of representation at one of Europe's various legislative assemblies. When the concept was transformed into the idea of a community not of the aristocracy, but of the people – who, according to Weber's idea, in any particular case consisted of a people culturally shaped within the framework of a state-like order – this meant that the people, formerly rabble at best, were conceptually, albeit only conceptually, elevated into the politically egalitarian, elitist, and thus homogeneous community, the older denotation of 'nation' had referred to. Now, in the course of the 19th century, in the case of power elites with a state apparatus at their disposal, to refer to their nation and thus to engage in nation-building in accordance with their particular national vision meant to

---

*restricted scholarly agenda, which should be replaced by one that is able to locate these forms of identity within a range of possible types of collective identity*" [(1998), pp. 13f.].

display a nationalist attitude as a legitimizing strategy for the sake of their claim to power. In the case of those being ruled over, on the other hand, to be aware of their being addressed as a nation or to address themselves as nation meant to develop a certain degree of consciousness for political agency and to lay claims to a moderate right to active participation in the political community and the social negotiation of its design – if not in a politically institutionalized form, then, at least, in the realm of public discourse. The struggle for social dignity or even cultural hegemony in public discourse is a form of participation in the realm of politics, too, albeit a somewhat more amorphous and subtle one. Being conscious of one's political capacity for participation in an abstract community addressed as nation is what in both cases, and in contrast to a merely cultural identity, a specifically national identity is about, regardless of the fact that cultural or ethnic questions are always likely to become subjects for socio-political negotiation over the dominant image of a nation. At the same token, it is save to claim that 'national identity' conceived of in this way does not essentially differ from 'nationalism' proper. It is, in short, a particular indi-vidual mode of perception that, due to its normative claim to validity for the whole community and apart from the fact that perception as such needs to be voiced in words anyway, leads to the necessity of negotiation in public discourse, and thus turns into a form of social practice. This social practice, for its part, may either take shape as official nation building or as a form of nation-alism in opposition to official interpretations.

Add to all this Nishikawa Nagao's 西川長夫 (1995) hint at the modular character of the nation-state as a 19th century embodiment of then all-powerful Western civilization and Liah Greenfeld's observations that "*the development of national identities [...] was essentially an international process*" and that "*societies belonging or seeking entry to the supra-societal system of which the West was the center had in fact no choice but to become nations[, as...] the sphere of influence of the core Western societies (which defined themselves as nations) expanded*" dramatically in the course of the 19th century [Greenfeld (1992), p. 14]. This should then make it perfectly clear why one would indeed have to go a long way to argue for the existence in Japan of something identifi-able as 'national identity' or 'nationalism' prior to the Bakumatsu and early Meiji periods. Only then did the concept of the 'nation' become available, only then could it be adjusted to already existing or, for the very sake of adjustment, newly invented traditions, only then did political elites in the center of power or at the periphery begin to consider it necessary to address the country as a nation-state and, consequently, its people as a nation, and only then could the people, or certain groups of people such as Buddhist clerics belonging to a particular denomination, begin to voice their interpretation of the political community against any officially prescribed image-clusters of the nation.

Japan is a typical example of a 19th century society on which in the course of some revolutionary events a state – which due to international pressure had no choice but to seek entry to the exclusive world of Western civilization, and thus make claims to represent a nation – was simply imposed from above by a formerly peripheral power elite, while almost all of its people had not yet developed anything like a national consciousness at all. Some individuals of the people, however, peripheral intellectual elites, for their part, as is almost always the case in the earliest formative stages of the nationalization of a people, were somewhat closer to acting socio-politically analogous to what has been referred to as 'nationalism' in the context of this paper than most of their contemporaries. This is not to say that these people would have consciously conceived of themselves as nationalists, or of their words and deeds as nationalism. As a matter of fact, for an indefinite number of years they did not even address the Japanese people as a 'nation'. Strictly speaking, we will hardly be able to find a Japanese term that may be translated as 'nationalism' – albeit with a strong undertone of nativism – prior to 1888, when the term *kokusui hozon shigi* 国粋保存旨義 first appeared in the magazine *Nihonjin* 日本人 published by the Society for Political Education (*Seikyōsha* 政教社).[4] This is, by the way, surprising for happening quite early rather than late, given that the term 'nationalism' itself had not been in use in the West throughout most of the 19th century [Koselleck (1992), p. 399]. On the other hand, 'nation' was not translated into the venerable old Sino-Japanese term *kokumin* 国民 – which only thereafter denoted somewhat more than simply *kuni no tami* 国の民 – much earlier than in Fukusawa Yukichi's 福沢諭吉 (1834–1901) famous writings of the 1870s, such as *Bunmeiron no gairyaku* 文明論之概略 and *Gakumon no susume* 学問のすゝ

---

[4] The very term *kokumin shugi* 国民主義, too, is a neologism dating from 1888. It was created and first used by the journalist Kuga Katsunan 陸羯南 (1857–1907) in his magazine *Tōkyō denpō* 東京電報; cf. Nishikawa (1998), p. 122.

め, where he states indeed that *"Nihon ni wa tada seifu arite mada kokumin arazu* 日本にはただ政府ありて未だ国民あらず ('There is only a government in Japan, but still no nation')" [cf. Nishikawa (1993), pp. 22f. and Maruyama (1992), pp. 109ff.].

Now, in order to finally turn to the case of Nishi Hongan-ji, let me give expression to my conviction that those Buddhist clerics of Bakumatsu and early Meiji belonging to, or rather informing, what I have labeled the Hongan-ji denomination's Chōshū-faction are such a peripheral intellectual elite whose words and deeds may be identified as an early example of Buddhist nationalism – in a somewhat ideal-typical fashion at least. In the remaining paragraphs of this paper I shall try to substantiate this. As for one thing, and to give an answer to the question posed at the outset of this paper, it is crucial to understand that there is simply no other Buddhist denomination which entered the Meiji period with such impeccable royalist credentials and intimate relations to some leading figures in the newly established government as the Nishi Hongan-ji. And one may indeed doubt that in the case of a Shimaji Mokurai 島地黙雷 these should not have been on a par, at least, with those exhibited by the few adherents to the National Learning (*kokugaku* 国学) and Restoration Shintō (*fukko shintō* 復古神道) traditions who, due to their capacity as *"ideologues of the anti-shogunate forces"* [Yasumaru (1979), p. 4], had been promoted to the very forecourt of state power. Whereas in Japan, however, this has been acknowledged by several generations of scholars belonging to both, the pre- and post-war periods,[5] English-language historiography is only *very* recently beginning to show an awareness of the fact itself, just as of possible inclinations for the interpretation of modern Japan's history of religion. The probably latest example being the volume on *Shinto in History* edited by John Breen and Mark Teeuwen in early 2000. Fukushima Kanryū 福嶋寛隆, to mention but one Japanese scholar, too, has more often than once pointed out that in early Meiji *"the Shin-sect has un-folded those activities on which, among the manifold movements within the Buddhist world, we should concentrate our main attention, in particular Nishi Hongan-ji which ever since the Bakumatsu period had made great contributions to royalism [kinnō* 勤王*] and maintained close relations with the new govern-*

---

[5] For the pre-war and war periods see e.g. Tokushige (1935), Kamine (1936) and Nunome (1942).

*ment"* [Fukushima (1986), p. 159]. This we should keep in mind, to understand why Nishi Hongan-ji clerics such as those of its Chōshū-faction may have exposed somewhat more of a specifically 'national' identity than most of their contemporary co-religionists. This was not the case, of course, because they would have been more nativist, more culturally or ethnically self-aware, more anti-Christian, hostile to foreigners or even chauvinistic than other Japanese Buddhists. They were definitely not. Likewise, it is safe to state that there were quite a few individual royalist priests who did not belong to Nishi Hongan-ji, the most famous probably being the Hossō 法相-monk Gesshō 月照 (1813–1857) of Kiyomizu-dera 清水寺, who was closely acquainted with Saigō Takamori 西郷 隆盛 (1827–1877). On the whole, however, some of the low-ranking priests of Nishi Hongan-ji branch temples in Suō 周防 and Nagato 長門 provinces exhibited apparently more of a political consciousness and apparently engaged more actively in drawing people of even the most humble social strata into active membership in, and positive identification with, the abstract community's public affairs than any other Buddhist group, thereby consciously infringing some of the most basic feudal rules of the contemporaneous society of orders. Mainly for such reasons, I consider it appropriate to identify these men as early protagonists of a Buddhist nationalism.

Due to historically entirely contingent circumstances, those Buddhist Chōshū activists who survived the political turmoil of the 1860s, after the revolution found themselves to have been comrades in arms and ideological allies on the winning party's side. This should not be forgotten when trying to find answers to the otherwise somewhat bewildering question complex, why, as for one thing, amidst the anti-Buddhist iconoclasm or so-called persecution of Buddhism in early Meiji, Shimaji Mokurai, one of the seemingly detested Buddhist clerics, of all protagonists on Japan's religious market place, should have been allowed, and urged indeed, to meet members of the Iwakura Embassy in London and frankly discuss politico-religious matters with Kido Takayoshi 木戸孝允 (1833–1877), Itō Hirobumi 伊藤博文 (1841–1909), and even Iwakura Tomomi 岩倉具視 (1825–1883). Or why, to give another example, as a formerly low-ranking *matsuji* 末寺-priest he was able, indeed, to establish himself as the single most influential advocate for the larger cause of early Meiji Buddhism with considerable influence on politico-religious developments at large, while actually not doing more than representing the this-worldly interests of his own denomination. As we know, Shimaji was not only instrumental in, first, the establishment and, later, the dismantling of the Great Teaching Institute (*Taikyōin* 大教院), but figured quite prominently in the government's very adoption of the infamous policy to regard Shinto as a non-religious cult [cf. Nitta (1997), pp. 47–92 and Fujii Takeshi's contribution to this volume]. Even before the so-called restoration of royal government (*ōsei fukko* 王政復古), Nishi Hongan-ji had let its young and daring pro-royal Chōshū activists assume command to a certain extend, and when in the course of 1868 it became quite clear that the Shogunate could not hold out against the revolutionary forces from Chōshū and Satsuma, the Buddhist establishment, with not a single exception I would know of, simply reacted by adopting the Nishi Hongan-ji's stance and ever since pledged itself to work for the 'unity of royal law and the Buddha-dharma' (*ōbō buppō furi* 王法仏法不離) – that is the vision of a political community informed by both, reverence for the monarchy and reliance on Buddhism as the major spiritual force for the protection of the country (*gokoku* 護国). In this broad sense, Nishi Hongan-ji's *ōbō ihon* 王法為本 and *shinzoku nitai* 真俗二諦 ideology, in short, its traditional acceptance of the dominance of royal law in the this-worldly realm which in 1871 was introduced as an official "dharma-*principle defining the proper relationship of members of the Hongan-ji to the state*" [Rogers/ Rogers (1990), p. 6], eventually became representative of modern Japanese Buddhism altogether.

One of the leading early architects of the linkage between Hongan-ji Buddhists and Chōshū VIPs such as Kido Takayoshi, Itō Hirobumi, or Yamagata Aritomo 山県有朋 (1838–1922) – and, at the same token, the probably most important Bakumatsu pioneer of a specifically Buddhist nationalism – is the so-called 'coastal defense priest' (*kaibōsō* 海防僧) Gesshō of Myōen-ji 妙円寺, a small Hongan-ji branch temple close to Yanai 柳井 city in Suō province. Gesshō, the ideological founder of the Chōshū-faction, was a personal acquaintance of reformer Murata Seifū 村田清風 (1783–1855) and radicals such as Yoshida Shōin 吉田松陰 (1830–1859) and Umeda Unpin 梅田雲浜 (1815–1859), to mention but a few, and also teacher of a number of young samurai retainers, peasants, and Buddhist novices alike, who were later to fight in Takasugi Shinsaku's 高杉晋作 (1839–1867) *Kiheitai* 奇兵隊 [cf. Umihara

(1972), pp. 135f.] or less well known units, among others Kusaka Genzui 久坂 玄瑞 (1840–1864) and the clerics Ōzu Tetsunen 大洲鉄然 (1834–1902) and Akamatsu Renjō 赤松連城 (1841–1919). Again, what leads me to address this low-ranking Hongan-ji cleric as an pioneering Buddhist nationalist is not so much the fact that he was indeed a xenophobic and chauvinistic anti-Christian with strong royalist and anti-Tokugawa leanings, but his very awareness of the necessity, and his actual endeavor, to bring the revolutionary political thought of *sonnō jōi* 尊王攘夷 ('revere the monarchy and expel the barbarians') and *tōbaku* 倒幕 ('overthrow the *bakufu*') ideology to the social level of the ordinary man – thus providing small fractions of Suō's populace with a humble sense of being a political subject of Japan's history and helping to create a starting point for the awakening of a national identity [cf. Umihara (1979), p. 127].

In conclusion, I would like to shortly refer to Gesshō's writing *Naikai kiyū* 内 海杞憂 ('Worry about the Inner Sea'), a memorandum to lord Mōri Takachika 毛利敬親 (1819–1871) of Chōshū domain, probably dating from early 1854 [cf. Murakami (1979), p. 240] and being used by Gesshō for reading practice and political education in his private academy Jishūkan 時習館. In a later and somewhat better known writing that in 1858 was published posthumously under the title *Buppō gokoku-ron* 仏法護国論 ('A Treatise on the Defense of the Country through the Buddha-*dharma*'), Gesshō elaborated his thoughts on the relationship of mutual dependence between Buddhism and the state and concluded in a *shinzoku nitai*-like fashion with a fervent appeal to his clerical co-religionists that "*living, as loyal and devoted subjects of the heavenly ruler, your names will be resplendent for a thousand years; dying, you will be reborn in the Pure Land as Buddhas, endowed with life for immeasurable eternity*" [English translation based on Earl (1964), p. 129; for a German translation see also Kleinen (1995), pp. 413f.]. In *Naikai kiyū*, on the other hand, he had already dealt at length with his suggestion to spiritually guide the populace towards an understanding of the necessity of their active participation in the defense not only of the domain, but also of the whole of Japan. And at the same token, he had demanded in no uncertain terms to permanently put the populace under arms, thus demonstrating his preparedness to provide social strata that were formerly excluded from public affairs with considerable means of interference at their own discretion: "*While urban retainers can hardly be brought in for farming, the common people may easily be kept under arms. In former times, peasants did indeed only march in so-called temporary troops* (gūhei 寓兵). *This, however, should not lead us to the conclusion that such measures would only be of use for the defense against the barbarians for a short period. They are, on the contrary, for all times the best way to protect our country*" [cf. Nakano (1971), p. 147]. Now, while Gesshō was probably not the first to appeal to the people's sense of responsibility for the welfare of the country and thus a community by far extending beyond a single peasant's horizon, and while he was probably not the first either to demand the military mobilization and the integration of all Japanese people, men and women alike, into a strong spiritual community, he nonetheless represents a rare and rather early example of this kind of political thought in Bakumatsu Japan. Years before the *Kiheitai* could actually demonstrate the effectiveness of a then still volunteer crack militia unit comprising men of all social strata, and years before men such as Ōmura Masujirō 大村益次郎 (1824–1869) and Yamagata Aritomo could realize the establishment of a modern, but already repressive system of universal conscription, it was a low ranking Hongan-ji cleric from Chōshū who had developed and propagated a vision of a Japanese military system (*tenka no heisei* 天下ノ兵制) which – as an ideological state apparatus[6] – from the outset had indeed a considerable impact on turning peasants and Buddhist clerics into Japanese.

### *Reverences*

Althusser (1994)
> Althusser, Louis: "Ideology and Ideological State Apparatuses (Notes Towards an Investigation)", in: Zizek, Slavoj (ed.): *Mapping Ideology*. London: Verso, 1994 [1970], pp. 100-140.

Amstutz (1997)
> Amstutz, Galen: "Modern Cultural Nationalism and English Writing on Buddhism: The Case of D.T. Suzuki", in: *Japanese Religions*, vol. 22/2 (1997), pp. 65-86.

---

[6] Cf. Althusser (1994), Nishikawa (1995) and Kleinen (2000).

Anderson (1983)
Anderson, Benedict: *Imagined Communities: Reflections on the Origin and Spread of Nationalism.* London: Verso, 1983.

Breuilly (1993)
Breuilly, John: *Nationalism and the State.* Manchester: Manchester University Press, 1993 [2nd edition].

Doak (1995)
Doak, Kevin M.: "Nationalism as Dialectics: Ethnicity, Moralism, and the State in Early Twentieth Century Japan", in: Heisig, James W./ Maraldo, John C. (eds.): *Rude Awakenings: Zen, the Kyoto School, and the Question of Nationalism.* Honolulu: University of Hawai'i Press, 1995, pp. 174-196.

Earl (1964)
Earl, David Magarey: *Emperor and Nation in Japan: Political Thinkers of the Tokugawa Period.* Seattle: University of Washington Press, 1964.

Eisenstadt/ Schluchter (1998)
Eisenstadt, Shmuel N./ Schluchter, Wolfgang: "Introduction: Paths to Early Modernities – A Comparative View", in: *Daedalus. Journal of the American Academy of Arts and Sciences.* [Issue on:] *Early Modernities.* [= Proceedings of the American Academy of Arts and Sciences; vol. 127, no. 3 (Summer 1998)], pp. 1-18.

Fischer (1979)
Fischer, Peter (ed.): *Buddhismus und Nationalismus im modernen Japan.* Bochum: Brockmeyer, 1979 [= Berliner Beiträge zur sozial- und wirt- schaftswissenschaftlichen Japanforschung; vol. 4].

Fukushima (1986)
Fukushima, Kanryū 福嶋寛隆: "Kokutai shingaku to kyōdan bukkyō no mosaku 国体神学と教団仏教の模索", in: Yasumaru, Yoshio 安丸良夫 (ed.): *Kindaika to dentō 近代化と伝統.* [= *Taikei bukkyō to nihonjin 体系 仏教と日本人*; 11] Tōkyō: Shunjūsha, 1986, pp. 142-178.

Gluck (1985)
Gluck, Carol: *Japan's Modern Myths: Ideology in the Late Meiji Period.* Princeton, New Jersey: Princeton University Press, 1985.

Greenfeld (1992)
Greenfeld, Liah: *Nationalism: Five Roads to Modernity.* Cambridge, Massachusetts: Harvard University Press, 1992.

Ichikawa (1975)
Ichikawa, Hakugen 市川白弦: *Nihon fashizumu-ka no shūkyō* 日本ファシ
ズム下の宗教. Tōkyō: Enuesu-shuppankai, 1975.

James (1996)
James, Paul: *Nation Formation: Towards a Theory of Abstract Community*. London, Thousand Oaks, New Delhi: SAGE Publications, 1996.

Kamine (1936)
Kamine, Tessei 神根恕生: *Meiji ishin no kinnō-sō* 明治維新の勤王僧. Kyōto: Kōkyō-shoin, 1936.

Ketelaar (1990)
Ketelaar, Edward James: *Of Heretics and Martyrs in Meiji Japan: Buddhism and its Persecution*. Princeton: Princeton University Press, 1990.

Kleinen (1994)
Kleinen, Peter: *Nichiren-Shugi: Zum Verhältnis von Nichiren-Buddhismus und japanischem Nationalismus am Beispiel von Tanaka Chigaku (1861–1939)*. [= *Miscellanea*, no. 7] Bonn, Tōkyō: Deutsches Institut für Japanstudien, 1994.

— (1995)
Kleinen, Peter: "Buddhismus und Nationalismus. Anmerkungen zur historiographischen Relevanz der Auseinandersetzung mit dem nationalistischen Diskurs des Bakumatsu-Buddhismus", in: Deutsches Institut für Japanstudien (ed.): *Japanstudien. Jahrbuch des Deutschen Instituts für Japanstudien, vol. 6*, München: Iudicium Verlag, 1995, pp. 387-427.

— (2000)
Kleinen, Peter: "Politics, Religion, and National Integration in Wilhelmine Germany and Meiji Japan. A Comparative View on the Kulturkampf and the 'Persecution of Buddhism'", in: Umesao, Tadao/ Fujitani, Takashi/ Kurimoto, Eisei (eds.): *Japanese Civilization in the Modern World XVI: Nation-State and Empire*. [= Senri Ethnological Studies; vol. 51] Senri, Ōsaka: National Museum of Ethnology, 2000, pp. 61-94.

Little (2001)
Little, David: *Belief, Ethnicity, and Nationalism*. <http://www.usip.org/research/rehr/belethnat.html#max>, (16.01.2001).

Kosellek (1992)

Kosellek, Reinhart: "Volk, Nation, Nationalismus, Masse XIII–XV", in: Brunner, Otto/ Conze, Werner/ Kosselleck, Reinhart (eds.): *Geschichtliche Grundbegriffe: Historisches Lexikon zur politisch-sozialen Sprache in Deutschland. Band 7. Verw.–Z.* Stuttgart: Klett-Cotta, 1992, pp. 380-431.

Maruyama (1992)

Maruyama, Masao 丸山真男: *'Bunmei-ron no gairyaku' o yomu (ge)* 「文明論之概略」を読む(下). [= Iwanami shinsho 岩波新書; no. 327] Tōkyō: Iwanami-shoten, 1992 [1986].

Murakami (1979)

Murakami, Iwatarō 村上磐太郎: "Gesshō to Akira Atsunosuke 月性と秋良敦之助", in: Misaka, Keiji 三坂圭治 (ed.): *Ishin no senkaku Gesshō no kinkyū* 維新の先覚月性の研究. Tokuyama: Matsuno-shoten, 1979, pp. 171-294.

Nakano (1971)

Nakano, Satoru 中野証: "Kindai Shinshū-shi ni okeru 'shinkyō jiyū undō' no mondai 近代真宗史における「信教自由運動」の問題", in: *Dendōin Kiyō* 伝道院紀要, vol. 11 (1971), pp. 136-151.

Nishikawa (1993)

Nishikawa, Nagao 西川長夫: "Kokka ideorogī toshite no 'bunmei' to 'bunka' 国家イデオロギーとしての「文明」と「文化」", in: *Shisō* 思想, vol. 827 (1993; no. 5), pp. 4-33.

— (1995)

Nishikawa, Nagao 西川長夫: "Nihon-gata kokumin kokka no keisei: Hikaku shiteki kanten kara 日本型国民国家の形成：比較史的観点から", in: Nishikawa, Nagao 西川長夫/ Matsumiya, Hideharu 松宮秀治 (eds.): *Bakumatsu- Meiji-ki no kokumin kokka keisei to bunka hen'yō* 幕末明治期の国民国家形成と文化変容. Tōkyō: Shinyōsha, 1995, pp. 3-42.

— (1998)

Nishikawa, Nagao 西川長夫: "Kokumin kokka to i-bunka kōryū: Bunka kōryū o samatageru mono to sokushin suru mono to no kankei ni tsuite no rironteki kōsatsu 国民国家と異文化交流：文化交流を妨げるものと促進するものとの関係についての理論的考察", in: Nishikawa, Nagao 西川長夫: *Kokumin kokka-ron no shatei: Arui wa 'kokumin' to iu kaibutsu ni tsuite* 国民国家論の射程：あるいは「国民」という怪物について. Tōkyō: Kashiwa-shobō, 1998, pp. 99-125.

Nitta (1997)

Nitta, Hitoshi 新田均: *Kindai seikyō kankei no kisoteki kenkyū* 近代政教関係の基礎的研究. Tōkyō: Taimeidō, 1997.

Nunome (1942)

Nunome, Yuishin 布目唯信: *Yoshida Shōin to Gesshō to Mokurin* 吉田松蔭と月性と黙霖. Kyōto: Kōkyō-shoin, 1942.

Parsons (1964)

Parsons, Talcott (ed.): *Max Weber: The Theory of Social and Economic Organization*. [translated by A. M. Henderson and Talcott Parsons] New York: The Free Press, 1964 [1947].

Rogers/ Rogers (1990)

Rogers, Minor L./ Rogers, Ann T.: "The Honganji: Guardian of the State (1868–1945)", in: *Japanese Journal of Religious Studies*, vol. 17/1 (1990), pp. 3-28.

Schulze (1999)

Schulze, Hagen: *Staat und Nation in der europäischen Geschichte*. [= Beck'sche Reihe; no. 4024] C.H. Beck: München, 1999.

Sharf (1993)

Sharf, Robert H.: "The Zen of Japanese Nationalism", in: *History of Religions*, vol. 33/1 (1993), pp. 1-43.

— (1995)

Sharf, Robert H.: "Whose Zen? Zen Nationalism Revisited", in: Heisig, James W./ Maraldo, John C. (eds.): *Rude Awakenings: Zen, the Kyoto School, and the Question of Nationalism*. Honolulu: University of Hawai'i Press, 1995, pp. 40-51.

Tokoro (1966)

Tokoro, Shigemoto 戸頃重基: *Kindai nihon no shūkyō to nashonarizumu* 近代日本の宗教とナショナリズム. Tōkyō: Fuzanbō, 1966.

Tokushige (1935)

Tokushige, Asakichi 徳重浅吉: *Ishin seiji shūkyō-shi kenkyū* 維新政治宗教史研究. Tōkyō: Meguro-shoten, 1935.

Umihara (1972)

Umihara, Tōru 海原徹: *Meiji ishin to kyōiku: Chōshū-han tōbaku-ha no keisei katei* 明治維新と教育：長州藩倒幕派の形成過程. Kyōto: Mineruba-shoten, 1972.

—     (1979)

Umihara, Tōru 海原徹: "Kyōikusha toshite no Gesshō 教育者としての月性", in: Misaka, Keiji 三坂圭治 (ed.): *Ishin no senkaku Gesshō no kenkyū 維新の先覚月性の研究*. Tokuyama: Matsuno-shoten, 1979, pp. 101-169.

Victoria (1997)

Victoria, Brian A.: *Zen at War*. New York, Tōkyō: Weatherhill, 1997.

Yasumaru (1979)

Yasumaru, Yoshio 安丸良夫: *Kamigami no Meiji-ishin: Shinbutsu bunri to haibutsu kishaku 神々の明治維新 : 神仏分離と廃仏毀釈*. Tōkyō: Iwanami-shoten, 1979.

Yoshino (1992)

Yoshino, Kōsaku: *Cultural Nationalism in Contemporary Japan: A Sociological Enquiry*. London: Routledge, 1992.

Weber (1972)

Weber, Max: *Wirtschaft und Gesellschaft: Grundriß der verstehenden Soziologie*. Tübingen: J.C.B. Mohr, 1972 [5th edition].

# Nationalism and Japanese Buddhism
# in the late Tokugawa period and early Meiji

FUJII Takeshi

In my paper, I will discuss the changes of religious policies in the period between 1868 (the beginning of Meiji) and 1889 (the year that the Meiji Constitution was issued), and the role of Shimaji Mokurai 島地黙雷 (1838-1911) in relation to this matter. He was a Buddhist priest of the *Nishi-Hongan-ji* 西本願寺 sect, which is the largest among the sects of *Jōdo Shin-shū* 浄土真宗, and made a clear logic on the relationship between religion and politics. With his logic, I think, the *Shin-shū* sects could influence the religious policy of the Meiji government and also influence the formation of the so-called State Shintō system. Thus I would like to emphasize Buddhists' influence and role on the religious policy in early Meiji. But before arguing the Buddhists' role in Meiji, I will discuss Buddhist thoughts in the latter half of the Tokugawa period because they had close relation to this theme. However, I will limit my arguments to discussing the role of the *Shin-shū* sects (especially the *Nishi-Hongan-ji* sect) to which Shimaji belonged. This is because in these days the *Shin-shū* sects were very active against the governments of Tokugawa and Meiji, and they alone tried to reject Shintō elements, which the Meiji government compelled them to receive.

## *Japanese Buddhism in the late Tokugawa period*

In general, modern Japanese nationalism was strongly influenced by National Learning (*kokugaku* 国学) and Shintō thoughts. In these thoughts, the emperor (*tennō* 天皇) was thought to be a descendant of gods which had been described in Japanese Classics such as *Kojiki* 古事記 and *Nihongi* 日本紀. As a descendant of gods, the emperor was sacred, and as the descendant of gods ruled Japan, Japan was a sacred country (*shinkoku* 神国, the 'country of gods'). These nationalistic thoughts were already established at the beginning of Tokugawa period[1], but in the 19th century they had come to influence political thoughts greatly.

One of the most influential figures among those nationalists was Hirata Atsutane 平田篤胤 (1776-1843), who was a famous scholar of National Learning and had many followers. He is usually thought to be the founder of the so-called school of 'Restoration Shintō' (*fukko shintō* 復古神道). After Hirata's time, Restoration Shintō became a religious-political movement rather than a school of National Learning, and influenced Meiji Restoration. Hirata and his followers insisted that foreign influences should be eliminated and the original culture and polity of Japan should be recovered. They also insisted that Shintō should be restored as the only and true Japanese religion. Naturally, they criticized Buddhism as a foreign religion. In other words, they denied the syncretism of Buddhism and Shintō. Kimura Ryūgyō 木村龍暁, one of the Buddhist priests of the *Nishi-Hongan-ji* sect, reported in his *Yudōben* 諭童弁 of 1866 that Hirata's followers often said Buddhism was only an illusion and Buddhist priests deceived honest people into spending money for that illusion. Buddhism was also blamed for destroying the country's old tradition.[2] According to this Buddhist priest, members of the Restoration Shintō were quite aggressive and had no hesitation in stating that Buddhism should be extinguished in Japan. These criticisms of the Restoration Shintō against Buddhism became stronger in the last years of the Tokugawa period.

Of course, many Buddhist priests, especially *Shin-shū* priests, tried to oppose the insistence of Restoration Shintō. To oppose it, Buddhist priests used some certain logic.[3] One of them was that in Japan the very syncretism was traditional and the so-called old tradition on which the Restoration Shintō insisted was not traditional (which is true in the history of Japanese religion).

Another logic was that Buddhism was useful for the stability of the social order, because Buddhist priests usually told their temples' members to obey this world's law and order. Furthermore it was said that Buddhism was useful against Christianity. During the last years of the Tokugawa period, there was a widespread fear of Western invasion, and in general, Christianity was thought to be used as the instrument for that invasion. Gesshō 月性 (1817-1858), a

---

[1] Cf. Yasumaru (1992), pp. 48-52.
[2] Kimura's text can be found in: Tokiwa (1935).
[3] On this logic, see Fujii (1987).

Buddhist priest of the *Nishi-Hongan-ji* sect, said in his *Buppō-gokokuron* 仏法護
国論 of 1856 that if only Japanese people believed in Buddha, Christianity could
not enter Japan.[4] Because of this reason, he wrote, Buddhism was useful for protecting Japan.

These Buddhist books, which were written against Restoration Shintō,
however contained one notable feature common to that movement. The
Buddhists who wrote these books also accepted the conception of sacredness of
the emperor and Japan. Gesshō wrote in his book that Japan had been established by the gods of heaven, and the emperors, who were the descendants of the
gods, inherited the rule. So Japan was the country of the gods and every
Japanese should pledge his loyalty to the emperor as long as he lived. Kimura
Ryūgyō wrote almost the same. Among the *Shin-shū* priests these ideas became
common in the 19th century. This was partly because of their compromise with
Shintō thought that spread increasingly as a nationalistic thought in those days.

But, we cannot attribute the cause of their acceptance of these ideas only to
their compromise, because on the other hand, the *Shin-shū* sect had been famous
for refusing to worship Shintō gods (*jingi-fuhai* 神祇不拝). Shinran 親鸞, the
founder of the *Shin-shū* sect, refused to depend on Shintō gods and emphasized
the ultimate salvation through the Buddha Amida 阿弥陀. As there had been the
tradition of syncretism in Japan, Shinran's thought was influenced by this
tradition. Therefore, after Shinran's death, there had been some complicated
attitudes toward this problem. In the Tokugawa period, especially in its latter
half, we can find that many *Shin-shū* priests told their temple's members not to
worship Shintō gods and rejected Shintō rituals.[5]

We should nevertheless notice that there were many *Shin-shū* priests in the
Tokugawa period and modern Japan, who refused to worship Shintō gods and
rejected Shintō rituals, but accepted the conception of the sacredness of the
emperor and even had reverence for the emperor, at the same time. For example
Seigai 誓鎧 (1753-1829), also a priest of the *Nishi-Hongan-ji* sect, wrote a book
of criticism against popular Shintō in 1817, titled *Shintō-zokudan-ben* 神道俗談
弁[6]. He was a scholar of *Shin-shū* teaching, and adhered to Shinran's thought of
refusing Shintō gods. But at the same time, he wrote that it was very important to

---

[4] Gesshō's text can be found in: Yasumaru/ Miyachi (1988).
[5] Cf. Fukuma (1964) and Kashiwabara (1976).
[6] Seigai's text can be found in: Fukushima (1977).

know that Japan was the country of gods (the Shintō gods). He said in his book that since Japan was the country of gods, *Shin-shū* could exist in this country guarded by them. We can see the influence of the Japanese tradition of syncretism here, but more importantly, an attitude to reject Shintō gods coexisted with an attitude to approve of the same Shintō gods. This ambivalence or contradiction about the Shintō gods can be found in many other books written by *Shin-shū* priests, including Shimaji Mokurai.

I think there was a special logic that made it possible for the *Shin-shū* priests to think of the coexistence to be natural. It was the logic about the existence of two kinds of truth, the 'ultimate truth' and the 'secular truth' (*shin-zoku nitai-ron* 真俗二諦論)[7]. This logic or idea was well known in the world of Buddhism and not limited to *Shin-shū* teaching. Its characteristic was to think that there were two kinds of truth of the world, or two aspects of truth. The 'ultimate truth' (*shintai* 真諦, the truth manifested through Buddha) was absolute and real. The 'secular truth' (*zokutai* 俗諦) on the other hand was relative and illusory. But in the latter half of the Tokugawa period, this logic had changed its character in the *Shin-shū* teaching. The ultimate truth had come to mean the *Shin-shū* teaching of the faith in salvation by Amida-Buddha and seeking rebirth in the Pure Land after one's death. On the other hand, the secular truth had come to mean the secular order, laws and morality. So generally the members of the *Shin-shū* sects were taught by the priests to accept both kinds of truth. The best way to live was to obey the social and political order of this world with *Shin-shū* faith in one's mind. In other words, while living, one should obey the secular order, that is to obey the orders of the rulers, had to work hard, had to keep the Confucian ethics, and so on. And after death one should live in the Pure Land forever. The point of this change is that the secular truth had come to be thought of as important. This change took place with relation to the Restoration Shintō's criticism against Buddhism. With this changed logic, *Shin-shū* priests insisted on the utility of Buddhism. When they emphasized that Buddhism was useful for keeping the social order, as I said previously, their arguments were commonly based on this logic.

According to this logic, Buddhists must live under two principles, the principle of Buddhism (that is *Shin-shū* teaching) and the principle of the secular

---

[7] On the *shin-zoku nitai-ron*, see Yamazaki (1996).

world. From the principle of *Shin-shū* teaching, the gods of Shintō should be rejected. But from the principle of the secular world, as long as the Shintō gods had relation with secular authority such as an emperor, they should not be rejected. I think the contradictory attitudes of *Shin-shū* priests toward the Shintō gods were also based on this logic.

Here, we must additionally consider the concept of Shintō. I think that Shintō was not a systematic religion until the end of the Tokugawa period. In other words, Shintō was not clearly defined as one religion. On the one hand, there were many Shintō priests who practiced Shintō rituals for people asking for their own benefits and welfare. In general, these Shintō priests accepted the syncretism of Shintō and Buddhism. On the other hand, Hirata and his followers rejected this syncretism and emphasized nationalistic aspects of Shintō. Furthermore, Hirata himself criticized Shintō rituals practiced for private purposes and Shintō priests who practiced those rituals.[8] For him, the true Shintō should have political and nationalistic aspects in relation to the sacredness of the emperor. Thus thoughts, rituals and priests of Shintō were not unified in the Tokugawa period. This was one of the reasons why the *Shin-shū* priests could take those different attitudes toward Shintō at the same time.

### Religious policy and Shimaji Mokurai in early Meiji

After the Meiji Restoration, the newly established Meiji government adopted the thoughts of Restoration Shintō as basic ideology of the state. This was because the Meiji government itself was established by nationalistic movements, which had close relationships with Restoration Shintō. In addition, the new government needed an authority for its rule, and the conception of sacredness of the emperor was very convenient for that purpose. It was prescribed that the emperor was sacred and inviolable, and the government acted for him. The government proclaimed that Japan had been founded by the Shintō gods and should be ruled by the emperor who was the descendant of the gods. Also they proclaimed that Japan should be unified around the sacred emperor. The sacredness of the emperor was emphasized, and the unity of religion and the state (*sai-sei-itchi* 祭政一致) was thought to be very important. Though the core

---

[8] Cf. Tsuda (1949), p. 297.

of this policy was not changed until 1945, the policy's details changed several times.

In 1868, the Department of Divinity (*Jingi-kan* 神祇官) was established. It conducted rites for the imperial ancestors and some other Shintō rituals. This Department was also expected to teach people the sacredness of the emperor and the Japanese nation. Also in 1868, an order, which required the complete separation of Buddhism from Shintō, was issued (*Shin-butsu bunri-rei* 神仏分離令). This order, which intended to deny the tradition of syncretism, was based on the thoughts of Restoration Shintō. As the order required to remove statues of Buddha and other Buddhist things from shrines – until the end of the Tokugawa period it was not so unusual to install Buddhist statues in a shrine –, Shintō priests caused movements of destroying Buddhist objects (*haibutsu-kishaku* 廃仏毀釈) in some regions. The Department of Divinity changed its status in 1871 and was renamed in Ministry of Divinity (*Jingi-shō* 神祇省), but the Shintō centered policy was not changed. We can say that from 1868 to 1872, Meiji government proclaimed that Shintō was the sole basis of the government. Through the rites and the teaching, the government wanted to unify the nation and national identity.

In these days, most of the Buddhists could not make effective criticism against the pro-Shintō government – the concept of religious freedom was not known yet. Some Buddhist priests such as Fukuda Gyōkai 福田行誡 (1809-1888), a priest of the *Jōdo* 浄土 sect, recognized spiritual decadence and financial corruption of Buddhism and tried to rebuild the morality of Buddhist priests.

As for the *Shin-shū* sects, the priests insisted on the utility of Buddhism as before. They continued to emphasize that Buddhism was useful for keeping the social order on the basis of the *shin-zoku nitai-ron*'s logic to which I referred previously. One notable point is that most of the Buddhist priests (including Shimaji at this time) did not, or, could not criticize Shintō. I think one of the reasons that prevented them from criticizing Shintō was that most of the Buddhist priests also accepted the sacredness of the emperor and the country.

At these points, the thoughts of Buddhist priests did not change. But obviously a new problem arose. According to the *shin-zoku nitai-ron*, as to the secular truth, one should obey the orders of rulers, but as to the religious truth, which had relation with one's inner mind and the world of after death, one could freely have Buddhist faith. But this logic did not expect the situation that rulers ordered the extinction of Buddhism. In the Tokugawa period, the authority of Restoration Shintō had been limited, so *Shin-shū* priests could reject it with their logic. But at the beginning of Meiji, the government adopted and authorized the thought of Restoration Shintō and became suppressive against Buddhism. Therefore logically, *Shin-shū* priests had come to be unable to reject it due to the 'secular truth' of their logic. In this sense, they faced a crisis. The Buddhists had to make a logic to reject the religious aspects of Shintō in order to protect the religious freedom of the Buddhists, and, at the same time, to accept the sacredness of the emperor that stood in relation to the political aspects of Shintō. But they could not find a new effective logic at this time, so they repeatedly only emphasized the utility of Buddhism.[9]

In 1872, the Meiji government had changed its religious policy. The Ministry of Divinity was abolished and the Ministry of Religion (*Kyobu-shō* 教部省) was established. From 1868 to 1872, the government had planned to spread the concept of the emperor's sacredness through the preaching of Shintō priests, but it had turned out to be difficult for Shintō priests to make effective preaching, because in the Tokugawa period, most of the Shintō priests used not to preach Shintō teaching but only to practice Shintō rituals. On the contrary, Buddhist priests, especially *Shin-shū* priests, often preached Buddhist teaching including the *shin-zoku nitai-ron* and developed their preaching skill in that period.[10] Therefore the government changed its policy and adopted Buddhist priests. Buddhist and Shintō priests together belonged to the Ministry of Religion and engaged in missionary work of the government. Although the government adopted Buddhists, it neither became favorable to Buddhists nor allowed them to preach freely. The Ministry of Religion issued the Three Great Teachings (*Sanjō no kyōsoku* 三条教則) as the basic standard of preaching in 1872. The Teachings were ① respect for the Shintō gods and love of country (*keishin aikoku* 敬神愛国); ② making clear the principles of Heaven and the Way of man (*tenri jindō* 天理人道); ③ reverence for the emperor (*kōjō-hōtai* 皇上奉戴). According to these Teachings, the government forced Buddhist priests to preach the faith in Shintō gods.

---

[9] On this point, see Fujii (1987).
[10] Cf. Sekiyama (1978).

Shimaji Mokurai 島地黙雷 wrote a notable criticism, titled *Sanjō no kyōsoku hihan kenpakusho* 三条教則批判建白書, against the Teachings and the government in about 1873 (the year of issue is not very clear).[11] He was a priest of the *Nishi-Hongan-ji* sect, born in the Chōshū domain (*Chōshū-han* 長州藩). Chōshū leaders played a major part at the Meiji restoration, together with the leaders of Satsuma domain (*Satsuma-han* 薩摩藩). Shimaji had close relations with these leaders who became the leaders of Japan after the Restoration. He participated in a movement to reform the system of *Nishi-Hongan-ji* before the Restoration, and insisted that Buddhist priests should work for the emperor and Japan, with the logic of *shin-zoku nitai-ron*. It is supposed that in this movement Shimaji met the leaders of Chōshū. This was one of the reasons why he could influence the religious policy of the Meiji government. After the Restoration he became one of the leaders of *Nishi-Hongan-ji* and played an important role in the organization's modernization. From 1872 to 1873, he went abroad to see the religious situation in Europe. At Paris, he heard of the Japanese government's new religious policy – the policy of the Ministry of Religion –and that Buddhist priests were forced to preach the faith in Shintō gods. It was then that he wrote the criticism and sent it to Japan.

In that criticism, he defined 'religion' and made it clear that religion and politics were different. His definition was rather simple, but I think this is the first definition of religion in the history of Japan. He said that the origin of religion was the intention of gods (*shin-i* 神意), and it was a matter of the inner life of man. Therefore, religion was essentially universal and no one could create religion. On the other hand, the origin of politics was the work of human hands (*jin-i* 人為), and the matters of politics were different in each country, not universal. Therefore, he wrote, these two were totally different. He criticized the policy from this point of view and said the government confused religion with politics. With his thought, the government could control the political matter, but could not interfere one's inner thought. According to his criticism against the Three Great Teachings, the respect for gods was a matter of religion and the love of country was a matter of politics. To make clear the principles of Heaven and the Way of man was a matter of education – which also is a matter of politics – and religion. The notable point is that Shimaji regarded the reverence for the emperor as the matter of politics.

---

[11] On that criticism, see Fujii (2000).

With this distinction between religion and politics, Shimaji could divide Shintō into two parts. One was the religious aspect of Shintō and another was the political aspect of Shintō, which was concerned with the sacredness of the emperor. According to him, religious Shintō was just a religion like Buddhism, and everyone had the freedom to have faith in it or not. In his criticism he regarded religious Shintō as an undeveloped religion, because it consisted of polytheism. But the reverence for the emperor, even if it was based on the sacredness derived from Shintō gods, was a matter of politics. If not, Shimaji said, the government could not demand the reverence from the Japanese people, because religious freedom should be recognized.

We can say that his new logic was not so different from the old logic of the *shin-zoku nitai-ron*. However, I think the important point is that Shimaji found the concept of religion in Europe and used that concept in his criticism. At that time, the most difficult problem for Buddhist priests was how to deal with Shintō, because from the late Tokugawa period, they had an ambivalent or con-tradictory attitude toward Shintō gods. As long as the character of Shintō was unclear for them, they could not criticize the pro-Shintō religious policy of Meiji government. Shimaji now divided Shintō into two parts, one was religious Shintō and another was political or nationalistic Shintō, in which the teachings of the sacredness of the emperor were very important. I think he could make this distinction according to the way he used the concept of religion. On the base of this distinction, he insisted on the religious freedom of Buddhists, and on the other hand, he insisted that the government should teach the sacredness of the emperor through education. In his logic, the teachings of the sacredness of the emperor were political, not religious. Thus, I think, Shimaji enhanced the *shin-zoku nitai-ron*, using the concept of religion to cope with the new situation.

Further, we can say that his logic that Shintō should be divided into two parts was almost the same logic that the government adopted in 1882. The logic of Shimaji was so effective that the government had to change its religious policy again. The Ministry of Religion was abolished in 1877, and the government began to seek a new policy. In 1882, it divided Shintō into Shrine Shintō and Sect Shintō. The Sect Shintō was characterized as religious, and the Shrine Shintō on the other hand was characterized as nonreligious. In 1889, the Meiji constitution was issued and religious freedom was guaranteed in it. But as the Shrine Shintō was technically nonreligious, every Japanese people was required to go and worship in Shintō shrines the Shintō gods that had relation with the imperial line. This new policy has been called the State Shintō (*kokka shintō* 国家神道) system.[12] In a sense, as I said above, I think Shimaji influenced the formation of the logic of the State Shintō system. And this logic in turn was also influenced by the *shin-zoku nitai-ron* of *Shin-shū* teaching.

### *Bibliography*

Fujii (1987)
    Fujii, Takeshi 藤井健志: "Shin-zoku nitai-ron ni okeru shintō-kan no henka 真俗二諦論における神道観の変化", in: Inoue, Nobutaka 井上順孝 / Sakamoto, Koremaru 坂本是丸 (ed.): *Nihongata seikyōkankei no tanjō 日本型政教関係の誕生*. Tōkyō: Daiichi shobō, 1987, pp. 199-244.

—    (2000)
    Fujii, Takeshi 藤井健志: "Shimaji Mokurai no Sanjō no kyōsoku hihan 島地黙雷の三条教則批判", in: Kobayashi, Takasuke 小林孝輔 et al. (ed.): *Kokka to shūkyō: jiyū na shinkō o motomete 国家と仏教：自由な信仰を求めて*. [*Gendai nihon to bukkyō 現代日本と仏教, vol. 2*] Tōkyō: Heibonsha, 2000, pp. 101-110.

Fukuma (1964)
    Fukuma, Kōchō 福間光超: "Kinseimakki no shinbutsu kankei 近世末期の神仏関係", in: *Ryūkoku-shidan 龍谷史壇*, vol. 52 (1964), pp. 27-44.

Fukushima (1977)
    Fukushima, Hirotaka 福嶋寛隆 (ed.): *Jinjamondai to shinshū 神社問題と真宗*. Kyōto: Nagata bunshōdō, 1977.

Kashiwabara (1976)
    Kashiwabara, Yūsen 柏原祐泉: "Shinshū ni okeru jingi-kan no hensen 真宗における神祇観の変遷", in: *Ōtani-gakuhō 大谷学報*, vol. 56/1 (1976), pp. 1-14.

Murakami (1970)
    Murakami, Shigeyoshi 村上重良: *Kokka-shintō 国家神道*. Tōkyō: Iwanami shoten, 1970.

---

[12] On the State Shintō, see Murakami (1970); Yasumaru (1979) and Sakamoto (1994).

Sakamoto (1994)
Sakamoto, Koremaru 坂本是丸: *Kokka-shintō keiseikatei no kenkyū* 国家神道形成過程の研究. Tōkyō: Iwanami shoten, 1994.

Sekiyama (1978)
Sekiyama, Kazuo 関山和夫: *Sekkyō no rekishi: bukkyō to wagei* 説教の歴史：仏教と話芸. Tōkyō: Iwanami shoten, 1978.

Tokiwa (1935)
Tokiwa, Daijō 常磐大定 (ed.): *Meiji bukkyō zenshū* 明治仏教全集 vol. 8: *Gohō-hen* 護法篇. Tōkyō: Shunyōdō, 1935.

Tsuda (1949)
Tsuda, Sōkichi 津田左右吉: *Nihon no shintō* 日本の神道. Tōkyō: Iwanami shoten, 1949.

Yamazaki (1996)
Yamazaki, Ryūmyō 山崎龍明 (ed.): *Shin-shū to shakai: 'Shin-zoku-nitai mondai' o tou* 真宗と社会：「真俗二諦」問題を問う. Kyōto: Daizō shuppan, 1996.

Yasumaru (1979)
Yasumaru, Yoshio 安丸良夫: *Kamigami no Meiji-ishin: Shinbutsu bunri to haibutsu kishaku* 神々の明治維新：神仏分離と廃仏毀釈. Tōkyō: Iwanami shoten, 1979.

— (1992)
Yasumaru, Yoshio 安丸良夫: *Kindai tennō-zō no keisei* 近代天皇像の形成. Tōkyō: Iwanami shoten, 1992.

Yasumaru/ Miyachi (1988)
Yasumaru, Yoshio 安丸良夫/ Miyachi, Masato 宮地正人 (ed.): *Shūkyō to kokka* 宗教と国家. Tōkyō: Iwanami shoten, 1988.

# The *chinkon kishin*: Divine help in times of national crisis

Birgit STAEMMLER

## *I.*

The Ōmoto 大本 is one of Japan's oldest and most influential new religions. It dates back to 1892 when Deguchi Nao 出口ナオ (1837-1918) experienced her first instance of spirit possession and started prophesying the immediate end of the world. In 1899 the later Deguchi Onisaburō 出口王仁三郎 (1871-1948) joined Nao and together they founded and lead the organisation later to be called Ōmoto. Cooperation between Nao and Onisaburō was not easy: Nao did not approve of Onisaburō's method of *chinkon kishin* 鎮魂帰神, a ritual of mediated spirit possession, which enabled anyone to experience spirit possession under his guidance. Onisaburō on the other hand did not agree with the impending rigorous renewal of the world, which Nao prophesied during her spirit possession.

Yet, in the years between 1917 and 1921 Nao's millenarian idea and Onisaburō's spiritual practice developed into an intimate and rather explosive mixture: the theory of the Taishō Restoration (*Taishō ishin setsu* 大正維新説) or the belief in the Second Opening of the Heavenly Rock Cave (*nidome no iwato biraki* 二度目の岩戸開き). Thus, I will now first introduce you to the *chinkon kishin* and a few of the Ōmoto's millenarian ideas. I will then describe the association established between these two through reference to old myths. And finally, I will make a first attempt at analysing the whole compound's significance with respect to national identity.

The Ōmoto's *chinkon kishin* is a ritual of what I termed mediated spirit possession, a ritual in which two people – mediator and medium – cooperate. The mediator needs to be well informed about matters of the spiritual and divine worlds, the medium may be any ritually pure layperson. First the mediator induces spirit possession into the medium by means of music or incantations. When the medium has become possessed the mediator identifies the possessing being, which may be difficult because lower spiritual beings tend to lie about their identity. He talks to it, asking a benevolent deity for advice or for information about some future event, for instance, or reproaching a malevolent spirit for its mean behaviour. Finally, the mediator has the possessing being go back to where it came from and the medium returns to his or her normal state of mind.

In Japan, the Shugendō's 修験道 *yorigitō* 憑祈禱 and the Ontakekyō's 御嶽教 *oza* お座 are examples for rituals of mediated spirit possession. And Honda Chikaatsu 本田親徳 (1822-1883), a nineteenth century Shintōist was well aware of these rituals when he invented the *chinkon kishin* after many years of travelling Japan's holy mountains in search of the perfect way to communicate with deities. Honda constructed his *chinkon kishin* as a method for inner contemplation and for communion with the divine. He based it partly on Ama no Uzume's 天宇受賣 dance, which is often believed to be the prototype of spirit possession in Japan, and which is also regarded as mythical predecessor to the court ritual *chinkonsai* 鎮魂祭 or *mitamashizume no matsuri*. This *chinkonsai* stood sponsor to the first half of the name Honda gave his new ritual. The second part of the *chinkon kishin*'s name, as well as most of its procedure, functioning and terminology, Honda derived from the account of Empress Jingū's 神功 ritual of spirit possession. Honda, thus, equipped his newly invented ritual with an alleged ancient parentage, but he did not embed it in any millenarian context, although he taught that he had revived it after it had fallen into oblivion many centuries ago.

Honda died in 1883 and did not teach Deguchi Onisaburō in person. But Onisaburō claimed that Honda's spirit had guided him on his journey through the spiritual worlds that had initiated his religious career in 1898. During this journey Honda's spirit had acquainted Onisaburō with the *chinkon kishin*, which Onisaburō then went to study with one of Honda's direct disciples. Onisaburō launched the *chinkon kishin* in the Ōmoto where it was practiced with vigour especially between 1916 and 1921, and even more so since it had been linked to a vibrant millenarian belief.[1]

---

[1] On the *chinkon kishin* in general see for instance my article Staemmler (2001) or the monographs by Tsushiro Hirofumi (1990) or Watanabe Katsuyoshi (1993).

The exact nature of the crisis Japan was believed to be facing according to the Ōmoto's millenarian teaching differed with different proponents:

Nao predicted the end and renewal of the world (*yo no tatekae tatenaoshi* 世の立替え立直し) to begin with the world's complete destruction. War with America and fire falling from the skies would destroy the whole country sparing only the Ōmoto's quarters in Ayabe 綾部. After about three years the world would then be reconstructed on an agrarian basis. People would live simply but happily on what they grew. They would all be equal – including the emperor – and only the world's creator, the deity Ushitora no Konjin 艮の金神 who had taken possession of Nao, would rule the world [Ooms (1993), pp. 75-107; Yasumaru (1977), pp. 192-225].

Onisaburō's idea of the ideal future world was more a political utopia than a religious vision: He foresaw an ideal agrarian state without taxes and with all property belonging to the emperor, its highest ruler. As one step towards the world's transformation Onisaburō predicted what he referred to as "Taishō restoration" – *taishō ishin* 大正維新 –, which would install the Sun-goddess's descendant, the Japanese emperor, in his natural position as true ruler over Japan. This the leaders of the Meiji restoration had been too egoistic and too concerned about their own power and wealth to accomplish, he said. Because of the emperor's prominent position in the world to come Onisaburō had changed the Ōmoto's official name to Kōdō Ōmoto 皇道大本, Imperial Way Ōmoto, in April 1916. He also identified Ushitora no Konjin with Kunitokotachi-no-mikoto 国常立尊 and made him ruler of the present world under orders of the Sun-goddess, the ancestress of the imperial house [Deguchi (1917); Lins (1976), pp. 62-74; Ōmoto (1964), pp. 364-371].

Asano Wasaburō 浅野和三郎 (1874-1937), one of the Ōmoto's most prominent members had joined to Ōmoto in 1916 because of his fascination with the *chinkon kishin*. He was influential among those who literally believed in Nao's teaching of the world's utter destruction prior to its renewal. To these people preparations for the impending catastrophe were urgently necessary. Some followers practiced living on grass and pine needles, expecting food to be unavailable after the rains of fire [Deguchi (1998), p. 70]. Asano on the other hand urged non-members to become members and members to prepare themselves spiritually through the *chinkon kishin*. He believed that only spiritual perfection could save anyone from destruction and that only those of a pure and sincere mind could achieve this perfection. In January 1919 Asano specified 1921 as the date for the world renewal — ironically the very year of the Ōmoto's first suppression [Asano (1919); Deguchi (1998), pp. 61-75; Lins (1976), pp. 76-80; Ōmoto (1964), pp. 396-406].

## II.

In April 1917, the second half of an article by Asano Wasaburō was published in the Ōmoto's monthly magazine *Shinreikai* 神霊界, entitled "About the *chinkon kishin*".[2] In its final section devoted to the *chinkon kishin*'s history, Asano wrote as follows [Asano (1917c), p. 33]:

> "*I want to close this part by finally describing very briefly the process of the* chinkon kishin *'s revival and perfection. In the beginning this method was an ancient imperial divinely transmitted mystic method (*ōko kintei no shinden hihō 往古禁廷の神伝秘法*). Examples of its being used in instances vital to running the country may be found repeatedly in the* Kojiki, Nihon shoki *and other old histories. Notable examples are Ame no Uzume's spirit possession during the episode of the heavenly rock cave; or when on the occasion of the conquest of the three Korean states Empress Jingū acted as medium (*kannushi 神主*) and Takeuchi no Sukune was in the sand garden (*saniwa ni ite 沙庭に 居て*)[3] requesting a divine message (*shinchoku 神勅*); or when Wake no Kiyomaro received an oracle from Hachiman in Usa. Since the middle ages contact between the divine and the human worlds was necessarily interrupted and the majestic mystery of our imperial house was eventually concealed. For well over one thousand years the method of communion (*kangō 感合*) between deities and humans remained extinct, but between Bakumatsu and the first years of Meiji the method came to revive. This happened thanks to the late Mr. Honda Chikaatsu, father of its revival. After more than 25 years of research and exertions his achievements are of sufficient value to record them in the histories to all eternity. On the other hand, in*

---

[2] The article's first half had been published a month earlier [Asano (1917a)].

[3] Asano himself gave the reading of 沙庭 as '*saniha*' which in Modern Japanese would be read '*saniwa*'.

*accordance with the cycles of the divine will (*ten'un 天運*) this man was used by the divine world as messenger to render the service of reviving [this method]. [...]*

*Under the direct guidance of Mr. Honda Chikaatsu's spirit Kotodama-hiko-no-mikoto Deguchi Onisaburō mastered the method of* chinkon kishin *through his one-week retreat on Mt. Takakuma. Since then about twenty years have gone by during which in thousand and ten thousand experiments and practical trainings he over and over again perfected this method and finally he faced the opportunity to conduct it widely in this world. [...] Today, that this method is perfected and may be executed at will, is the time when in this very world the heavenly rock cave will truly begin to open during the Taishō restoration and thus above everything the practice of this very method is necessary. People who see the realities of this world should certainly reflect upon themselves most thoroughly."*

This is one of several similar passages published in the *Shinreikai* between 1917 and 1920.[4] It linked the *chinkon kishin* to three mythical and historical events:

The first episode the *chinkon kishin* is connected with is Ame no Uzume's dance in front of the heavenly rock cave, one of the most famous of all Japanese myths: The Sun-goddess Amaterasu Ōkami 天照大神 had withdrawn into a heavenly rock cave following a series of misdeeds done by her brother Susanoo 素戔嗚. The other deities all consulted on how to induce her to leave the cave, because her absence had cast the world into complete darkness. Finally, Ame no Uzume danced an obscene dance of spirit possession in front of the cave and the merry laughter of all the onlooking deities successfully lured Amaterasu into the open again.[5]

The second episode is that of Empress Jingū's ritual of spirit possession prior to her planned expedition to the Kumaso in Kyūshū. The first time it was performed, Emperor Chūai 仲哀天皇, Empress Jingū's husband, played the *koto* 琴

---

[4] For other examples see Deguchi (1918a), p. 9 or Deguchi (1918b), p. 27. The latter article is signed by Onisaburō, but may well have been written by Asano Wasaburō. See also Tomokiyo (1918) or Asano (1917b).
[5] On this myth see NKBT, vol. I, pp. 80ff. and vol. LXVII, pp. 112f.; Watanabe (1993), pp. 30-39.

, the courtier Takeuchi no Sukune 武内宿禰 stood in the sand garden and requested divine orders and Empress Jingū herself was possessed by deities who gave their orders through the Empress's mouth: They were not to attack the Kumaso, but to go to a faraway land in the West instead, where they would find extraordinary treasures. As Emperor Chūai did not believe the divine utterances he died and the ritual had to be repeated without him after a series of purifying ceremonies. The deities' orders remained unchanged, however, and obeying them Empress Jingū went on a successful expedition to Korea.[6]

The third precedent is a historical incident:[7] Dōkyō 道鏡 (died 772), a Buddhist monk well versed in Esoteric Buddhism had become a favourite of Empress Shōtoku 称徳天皇 (718-770)[8] and promoted to highest posts at court. In the early summer of 769 (Jingo-keiun 神護景雲 3) Dōkyō claimed to have received an oracle from the Hachiman shrine at Usa (Usa Hachimangū 宇佐八幡宮) in today's Ōita prefecture. The oracle predicted that with Dōkyō as emperor, Japan would enjoy an era of peace and prosperity. Empress Shōtoku, however, dispatched Wake no Kiyomaro 和気清麻呂 (733-799) to Usa to confirm Dōykō's oracle. The oracle given to Wake no Kiyomaro differed entirely from the first one and utterly thwarted Dōykō's aspirations to the imperial throne as it emphasised that any Japanese emperor must necessarily stem from the Sun-goddess's line of descent.[9] Dōkyō was not amused by this new oracle and had Wake no Kiyomaro banned. After Empress Shōtoku's death, however, politics changed: Dōkyō was exiled and Wake no Kiyomaro pardoned.

---

[6] On this episode see NKBT, vol. I, pp. 228-231 and vol. LXVII, pp. 326-332; Blacker (1986), pp. 108-112; Naumann (1988), pp. 32-37.

[7] On Dōkyō, Wake no Kiyomaro and Empress Shōtoku see for instance Brown (1993), especially pp. 516f.; KSDJ, vol. XIV, pp. 884f. and vol. X, pp. 46f.; and NSDJ, vol. I, p. 719, vol. V, pp. 31f. and vol. VI, p. 1311.

[8] Empress Shōtoku reigned between 764 and 770 after she had already reigned as Empress Kōken 考謙天皇 between 749 and 758.

[9] Cf. the *Shoku-nihongi* 続日本紀 for the year 769 [*Kokushi Taikei* 国史大系, vol. II, p. 369]. An English translation of the oracle is provided by Delmer Brown [(1993), p. 516], a German translation by Nelly Naumann [(1988), p. 201].

*III.*

Of course none of theses examples is without its difficulties: The Ōmoto revered the *Kojiki* more than the *Nihon shoki*, although according to the *Kojiki* Ame no Uzume's spirit possession was only pretended. '*Saniwa*' 沙庭, the key term of Empress Jingū's ritual, is rather obscure and *Kojiki* and *Nihon shoki* differ considerably in their descriptions of the ritual. Hachiman was a deity very closely associated with Buddhism, and the *Nihon shoki* does not clarify the exact nature of his oracle.

Be this as it may, equating the *chinkon kishin* with these rituals and claiming that it had been lost for centuries and revived only several years ago through divine intervention, drew attention to the *chinkon kishin*'s claim to great antiquity. This claim had already been established by Honda Chikaatsu. And claims like these are typical characteristics of invented traditions. Similar to the *chinkon kishin* many apparently age-old traditions were invented during the Meiji period in Japan as well as in Western countries during comparable periods. Professing uncontaminated antiquity and divine origin were the two most important pillars of the *chinkon kishin*'s legitimacy.

But there was more to the above connections than mere claims to an unsullied heritage: At each of the cited mythical and historical occasions a situation critical for Japan had been resolved through divine intervention in the form of voluntary spirit possession. Linking the *chinkon kishin* to these events, which in Asano's words had been "vital to running the country" (*kokusei no daiji* 国政の大事), thus asserted its importance for the present period of national crisis: the Taishō restoration.

The episode surrounding Ame no Uzume's dance is invested with many layers of meaning: the deities involved were used to legitimate genealogies and political positions of several noble families; Ame no Uzume's dance is often presumed the prototype of all Japanese spirit possession; and last but not least the opening of the cave's door is frequently cited as a synonym for a resolved crisis or a major turning point. In the Ōmoto, too, an alternative name for the Taishō restoration was "second opening of the heavenly rock cave".

Empress Jingū's ritual was essentially an imperial ritual conducted by the empress herself for the sake of the whole country – although historically Empress Jingū's mere existence is at least uncertain. The accounts of *Kojiki* and *Nihon shoki* differ attributing important roles to members of various important families for example. Only the *Kojiki* mentions the Sun-goddess as one of the deities taking possession of the empress and thereby becoming directly involved in the fate of Japan. The ritual conducted by Empress Jingū is described as a ritual of mediated spirit possession, although the term used for the mediator, *saniwa*, is highly obscure. I have thus translated it literally as 'standing in the sand garden' in the article quoted above.

Hachiman was or is a deity closely linked to the imperial house.[10] He is identified with Empress Jingū and her son Emperor Ōjin.[11] Besides, the oracle he is believed to have given to Wake no Kiyomaro defeated Dōykō's attempt at succeeding to the throne. Its written record in the *Shoku-nihongi* 続日本紀 might also have impeded later overt endeavours of a similar nature. In linking the *chinkon kishin* to the incident of the oracle at the Hachiman Shrine in Usa Asano, thus, emphasised the *chinkon kishin*'s importance for the imperial family: In 769 it had saved Japan from the – for Asano in retrospect unbearable – crisis of a rupture threatening the imperial line and giving the throne away to a usurper. Adding insult to injury, the usurper would also have been a Buddhist priest!

Both, Onisaburō and Asano, taught that true communication with the divine and with it the power to save Japan in this time of national crisis was now unique to the Ōmoto. They did not restrict this communication to the *chinkon kishin*. Communication or communion with the divine was referred to abstractly as *shinjin gōitsu* 神人合一 or *shinjin kangō* 神人感合 and more concretely as *kamigakari* 神懸り. And – contrary to many anthropologists and other researchers – the Ōmoto did not distinguish analytically between the different forms this *kamigakari* could take. Anthropologists generally distinguish between ecstasy, that is a human being's soul leaving its body to travel to

---

[10] Cf. Martin Repp's contribution to this volume.
[11] On the Hachiman Shrine in Usa see Inoue (1999), pp. 326a-327c and pp. 611c-612a; Naumann (1988), pp. 198-206; KSDJ, vol. II, p. 65; NSDJ, vol. I, pp. 717f.; SDJT, vol. III, pp. 125f.

another world, and spirit possession, that is a spiritual being entering a human being's body. Generally only the latter is referred to as *kamigakari* in Japanese.

However, in the Ōmoto '*kamigakari*' was used to describe any kind of true communion or communication with a deity: It referred to Deguchi Nao's unsolicited prophetic spirit possession as well as to Deguchi Onisaburō's journey to the realms of the spiritual worlds. '*Kamigakari*' was also frequently used as alternative reading of the *chinkon kishin*'s '*kishin*' indicating that communion with the divine reached by means of the *chinkon kishin* was of comparable value to any other kind of *kamigakari*. The resulting communion mattered more than the way it had been accomplished by.[12]

There was, however, an essential difference between Nao and Onisaburō on the one hand and the Ōmoto's members on the other: Neither Nao nor Onisaburō had at all solicited or wanted their *kamigakari*. Their communication with the divine was not imbedded in a ritual. They had been chosen by the deities because of their inherent ritual purity that had qualified them for the task of preparing the world for its impending renewal. Both had lived a life of poverty. Nao had suffered through hard work and untoward circumstances, Onisaburō had worked as a peasant, which to him was the essence of a true Japanese.

No one else was believed to be similarly qualified by nature and thus anyone wishing to reach communion with the divine and prepare for the destruction of the world had to go through rituals of purification and study the Ōmoto's scriptures. Most importantly they had to practice the *chinkon kishin* under the guidance of a competent mediator, the *saniwa*. It was essential that the *saniwa* controlled the *chinkon kishin* and conducted the dialogue with the possessing being, because most mediums were hardly experienced lay people. Only the Ōmoto's most qualified members – notably Onisaburō and Asano – were permitted to act as mediator. It was the mediator, the *saniwa*, that made the *chinkon kishin* differ from other rituals of spirit possession.

---

[12] *Kamigakari* usually written as 神憑り is also used to refer to possession by evil or lowly spirits, which is regarded as highly dangerous and is thus not to be confused with communion with the highest divine ranks.

Anyone wishing to perform the *chinkon kishin* successfully even in the role of a medium necessarily had to be reverent to the deities, devoted to the emperor and loyal to Japan, said Onisaburō [Deguchi (1918a), p. 8]. Corresponding to his utopian view of the future world Onisaburō strove to prepare for it by turning the Ōmoto's headquarters in Ayabe into his utopia's miniature model: members there lived a communal live as one family sharing their resources, studying the Ōmoto's teachings and performing its rituals. It was Asano rather than Onisaburō who elevated the *chinkon kishin* above a ritual for spiritual self-perfection and healing to the single most important preparation for the world to come. To Asano essential prerequisites for successful *chinkon kishin* were profound knowledge about spiritual matters and a divine calling [Asano (1917c), p. 32]. By means of the *chinkon kishin* members would be able to attain communion with the highest deities. With the *saniwa*'s help they would realize that the First World War and other recent calamities were but divine warnings of the impending turmoils. They could then through further practice of the *chinkon kishin* polish and perfect their connections to the divine and thus prepare themselves spiritually for the world's renewal.

In view of the expected end of the world Onisaburō, Asano and others concluded that the Ōmoto with its various forms of divine communication had not developed by mere accident now of all times. They neither believed that it was due to any human achievement that the long lost ancient method of communication with the divine had been rediscovered. The initiative to reopen the channels of communication had lain with the spiritual worlds, because humans had until then been ignorant of its very necessity. Given the increasing deterioration of the human world, the predominance of materialism and the influence of a Western lack of morals to Japan, the deities had no longer been able to bear what they perceived. Especially Ushitora no Konjin had reappeared from 2000 years of seclusion to save the world. He had taken possession of Deguchi Nao in order to proclaim the world's renewal and urge humans to begin preparations.

Not only was the *chinkon kishin* regarded as a divine ritual, it was also connected directly to the imperial house: it had been performed on behalf of the imperial line's ancestress, the Sun-goddess; by Jingū, an early albeit mythical empress; and to save the imperial line from discontinuance. Although Deguchi Nao did not overly value the emperor because she held him partly responsible for the recent social misery, Onisaburō and Asano did. Very much in line with the Meiji and Taishō ideologists they emphasised the emperor's role for creating a unified Japanese national identity. To them the emperor was a divine figure due to his descent from the Sun-goddess and the only acceptable ruler for Japan. The laws and guidelines behind the emperor's rule were the essence of the *kōdō* 皇道, the Imperial Way. And this Imperial Way was now being revealed and taught through divine communication, preparing for its full implementation following the world's renewal.

Against the background of the Ōmoto's vibrant millenarianism connections with the three mythical and historical episodes substantiated the *chinkon kishin*'s professed position as a ritual through which Japan and its imperial house would once again be saved in a time of national crisis. Unfortunately for the Ōmoto, Japan's officials objected to having Japan and its imperial house saved from a presumed crisis. They regarded the Ōmoto as a socio-political threat because it mobilised thousands and thousands of people from all social strata. Thus, in February 1921 the police raided the headquarters in Ayabe. Most of the buildings were destroyed and Deguchi Onisaburō, Asano Wasaburō and several other senior members were imprisoned on equally invented charges of lèse-majesté and violation of the Press Law.

### References:

Asano (1917a)
  Asano, Wasaburō 浅野和三郎: "Chinkon kishin ni tsukite 鎮魂帰神に就きて", in: *Shinreikai* 神霊界, vol. 45, pp. 1-4.

—  (1917b)
  Asano, Wasaburō 浅野和三郎: "Rei no hatsudō to sono mokuteki 霊の発動と其目的", in: *Shinreikai* 神霊界, vol. 45 (1917), pp. 5-11.

—  (1917c)
  Asano, Wasaburō 浅野和三郎: "Chinkon kishin ni tsukite 鎮魂帰神に就きて", in: *Shinreikai* 神霊界, vol. 46 (1917), pp. 32f.

— (1919)
Asano, Wasaburō 浅野和三郎: "Taishō hachinen wo mukahu 大正八年を
迎ふ", in: *Shinreikai 神霊界*, vol. 77 (1919), pp. 18ff.

Blacker (1986)
Blacker, Carmen: *The Catalpa Bow: A Study of Shamanistic Practices in
Japan*. London: Unwin Paperbacks, 1986.

Brown (1993)
Brown, Delmer M.: "The early evolution of historical consciousness", in:
Brown, Delmer M. (ed.): *The Cambridge History of Japan. I: Ancient
Japan*. Cambridge: Cambridge University Press, 1993, pp. 504-548.

Deguchi (1998)
Deguchi, Kyotaro: *The Great Onisaburo Deguchi*. Translated by Charles
Rowe. Tōkyō: Aiki News, 1998.

Deguchi (1917)
Deguchi, Onisaburō 出口王仁三郎: "Taishō ishin tsukite 大正維新に就き
て", in: *Shinreikai 神霊界*, vol. 45, pp. 11-24.

— (1918a)
Deguchi, Onisaburō 出口王仁三郎: "Kishin ni tsukite 帰神に就きて", in:
*Shinreikai 神霊界*, vol. 61, pp. 7ff.

— (1918b)
Deguchi, Onisaburō 出口王仁三郎: "Reigaku kinkyū ni tsukite 霊学研究
に就きて", in: *Shinreikai 神霊界*, vol. 63 (1918), pp. 27-30.

Inoue (1999)
Inoue Nobutaka 井上順孝 et al. (eds.): *Shintō jiten 神道事典*.
Reduced-size edition. Tōkyō: Kōbundō, 1999.

KSDJ
*Kokushi daijiten 国史大事典*. 15 vol., Tōkyō: Yoshikawa Kōbunkan,
1979-1997.

Lins (1976)
Lins, Ulrich: *Die Ōmoto-Bewegung und der radikale Nationalismus in
Japan*. München: R. Oldenbourg Verlag, 1976.

Naumann (1988)
Naumann, Nelly: *Die einheimische Religion Japans. Teil 1: Bis zum Ende
der Heian-Zeit*. [Handbuch der Orientalistik, part V, vol. 4, sect. 1, no. 1]
Leiden: E. J. Brill, 1988.

NSDJ

*Nihonshi daijiten* 日本史大事典. 7 vol., Tōkyō: Heibonsha, 1992-1994.

NKBT

*Nihon koten bungaku taikei* 日本古典文学体系. 102 vol., Tōkyō: Iwanami shoten, 1957-1986.

Ōmoto (1964)

Ōmoto Nanajūnen Shi Hensan 大本七十年史編纂 (ed.): *Ōmoto nanajūnen shi* 大本七十年史. vol. 1, Kyōto: Tenseisha, 1964.

Ooms (1993)

Ooms, Emily Groszos: *Women and Millenarian Protest in Meiji Japan: Deguchi Nao and Ōmotokyō*. Ithaca: Cornell University East Asia Series, 1993.

SDJT

*Shintō daijiten* 神道大辞典. 3 vol., Tōkyō: Heibonsha, 1937-1940.

Staemmler (2001)

Staemmler, Birgit: "Das *chinkon kishin* der Ōmoto in der Taishō-Zeit", in: Gössmann, Hilaria/ Mrugalla, Andreas (eds.): *11. Deutschsprachiger Japanologentag in Trier 1999, vol. 1*. [Ostasien-Pazifik: Trierer Studien zur Politik, Wirtschaft, Gesellschaft, Kultur; vol. 13] Hamburg, London: Lit-Verlag, 2001, pp. 243-249.

Tomokiyo (1918)

Tomokiyo, Yoshisane 友清歓真: *Hito to kami to no sekai kaizō undō* 人と神との世界改造運動. Ayabe: Dainihon Shūsaikai, 1918.

Tsushiro (1990)

Tsushiro, Hirofumi 津城寛文: *Chinkon gyōhōron* 鎮魂行法論. Tōkyō: Shunjūsha, 1990.

Watanabe (1993)

Watanabe, Katsuyoshi 渡辺勝義: *Koshintō no higi: Chinkon to kishin no mekanizumu* 古神道の秘儀：鎮魂と帰神のメカニズム. Fukuoka: Kaichōsha, 1993.

Yasumaru (1977)

Yasumaru, Yoshio 安丸良夫: *Deguchi Nao* 出口ナオ. Tōkyō: Asahi Shinbunsha, 1977.

# Constructing the 'Other Modernity': Religion and 'Indigenous Identity' in Contemporary Japanese Cultural Discourse

Lisette GEBHARDT

## 1. Introductory Remarks: Japanese Cultural Discourse and the Issue of Religiousness

Since about the 1980s, the subject of 'religion' has played a central and determining role in Japanese cultural discourse. Intellectuals and artists have turned to religion in order to affirm a sense of Japanese identity that is said to have been lost in a modernization process that has been commonly understood as equivalent to Westernization. Politicians too fall back on an 'indigenous Japanese tradition', the revival of which, it is claimed, will provide the nation with fresh perspectives. Early in the year 2000, Prime Minister Yoshirō Mori 森喜朗, for example, proclaimed that Japan is 'kami no kuni' 神の国, 'land of the gods'.[1]

A short retrospective on Japanese intellectual history reveals that similar circumstances at the turn of the 20th century produced a similar reaction. In seeking a foundation for national unity, the Japanese leadership in the Meiji Period had looked to the role of Christianity in the nation-states of the West as a model; thus, for them, religion served a political-ideological function. For Japan's intellectuals and artists, on the other hand, religion served primarily to provide a possible means for securing a sense of personal identity and inner serenity in the otherwise inhospitable climate of a modernity, which they frequently regarded as a Western imposition, and which, shortly after its arrival, they were already trying to overcome. While the ruling circles sought to establish so-called

---

[1] It should be pointed out that the content of the controversial speech, delivered by the Prime Minister on May 15, 2000 to the delegation of Shintō parliamentarians (Shintō Seiji Renmei Kokkaigiin Kondankai 神道政治連盟国会議員懇談会), is far less provocative than one might immediately be led to conclude from his reference to kami-no-kuni, a phrase that evokes Imperial Japan during the war years. A more detailed and careful reading of his address makes clear that Mori, mindful of Japan's educational crisis and problems among the nation's youth, was (of course clumsy enough) making a case for a turn to religion – above all, the active practice of religion – as a means for reawakening awareness of moral values. On Mori's speech, see also Johann Nawrocki's contribution to this volume.

Shintōism as the national religion, intellectuals unable to warm to statist, col-
lectivist dogma, were looking for their own religion, one that would be
characterized by an inward-looking individualism. Among many Japanese
thinkers, skirmishes over philosophical outlook were intense. The search typically ended in either a plaintive heroicism, an aestheticized form of religion,
utopian schemes for a fantasy paradise, or vitalistic self-worship.[2] Statist religious politics and the religious aspirations of the intellectuals had at first glance
little in common; yet each influenced the other in their oscillating desires: the
one for power, the other for inner life of the spirit.

In August, 1945, Prime Minister Higashikuni Naruhiko 東久迩稔彦 called on
the Japanese population to engage in collective repentance (*ichioku sō-zange* 一
億総懺悔) [cf. Barshay (1998), p. 274]. This demonstration of penitence was
symptomatic, for after 1945 the questions of guilt, reconciliation, and forgive-
ness stood in the foreground; within intellectual circles, Christianity was again
expected to provide the model answers.[3]

Little is as yet known concerning the discussion, as carried out by Japanese
intellectuals on the subject of the religious after the war, that forms the background for the contemporary scene. In the following, I should like first to offer
some considerations for the 1950s and 1960s and ask in what context the case
was made for a nostalgic look back to 'indigenous religions' and how these were
then (re)constructed or perhaps simply 'invented.'

Already in the 1950s,[4] Japanese intellectuals were introducing into the discussion of Japanese identity the idea of an ethnic complex and, along with it, a new

---

[2] For a further analysis of this context in the writings of such *literati* as Kitamura Tōkoku 北
村透谷, Hagiwara Sakutarō 萩原朔太郎, Akutagawa Ryūnosuke 芥川龍之介 and Natsume
Sōseki 夏目漱石, see Gebhardt (1999).

[3] Some literary figures, e.g., Shimao Toshio 島尾敏雄 and Shiina Rinzō 椎名鱗三, became
postwar converts to Christianity, whose appeal at the time for many an intellectual may
have been the strong emphasis of that faith on remorse and penitence. Moreover, it
implicitly offered a model of sorts for what was for them two related issues: the abrupt
turning away (*tenkō* 転向) from a previous ideology, as seen in the coerced recantation of
arrested Japanese Communists under the militarist regime, and unswerving loyalty and
witness to one's convictions, as seen in the true-until-death courage of the Christian
martyrs.

[4] The intellectual turn to a Japanese tradition that would build the basis for a brighter future
was critically commented by Maruyama Masao 丸山真男 [see the introduction to
Maruyama (1988), pp. 14f.].

variant of so-called Japanese folk religion. Here the word *minzoku* 民族 – corresponding to *ethnikos*, people, or *Volk* – came in the postwar years to assume a connotation distinct from what it had previously had as a keyword in *tennō*-centristic propaganda. In 1952, the historian Ishimoda Shō 石母田正 (1912-86), for example, published *Rekishi to minzoku no hakken: Rekishigaku no kadai to hōhō* 歴史と民族の発見 : 歴史学の課題と方法 ('History and the Discovery of the People: Issues and Methodology in the Study of History'), in which he took up the cause of a revised historiology and a new history of oppressed peoples and groups. The oppressed were to collect and document materials of their own past – songs, legends and tales – in order to create a '*minzoku*-centered' history. This was to signal a liberation from narratives concerned with 'bourgeois modernization' [cf. Barshay (1998), pp. 312f. On the post-war concepts of the ethnic nation and the discourses of ethnic national culture (e.g. Maruyama Masao, Ishimoda), see the recent analysis of Gayle (2001)].

The ideological metamorphosis of an imperial master race into a simple 'indigenous people' made it possible to formulate the idea of a Japanese collective ethnicity that was, as it were, 'primeval', reconstituted after the war in all its pristine purity and having nothing in common with the collectivity that had carried out and lost the war. To be sure, many intellectuals and academics – including Ishimoda – intended to articulate criticism of the emperor system (*tennō-sei* 天皇制) and of those who had supported it without a murmur of protest. Yet by coming up with the notion of an 'indigenous Japan' that had been distorted and misused by the *tennō-sei*, they succeeded in creating a surface on which to project new visions of ethnic unity and a cultural discourse purged of imperialistic ideology. The regional and the rural now constituted a zone of freedom. The 'indigenous' (keyword: *dochaku* 土着) 'customs' and 'folk religion' offered a sense of identity.[5] Japanese intellectuals now had the opportunity to find a Japanese culture beyond that of the imperium-dominated metropolis, one

---

[5] Ideas of the 'indigenously Japanese' were and continue to be influenced by Japanese scholarly research into Japan's ethnic origins and the numerous theories that have been proposed in that regard: rice-cultivation culture, horse-rider culture, and the great Jōmon 縄文 debate, e.g., the beech culture theory and the *Kuroshio* 黒潮 (Black current) theory. These research efforts have in turn been influenced by historical trends. For an overview, see, for example, the work of Mark J. Hudson (1999).

that could provide sustenance, security, and, in their view, a good foundation for the country's further development.

## 2. The Rediscovery of Archaic Landscapes, Legends and Myths in the 1950s and 1960s

Among the first literary figures to turn their attention to the exploration of the Japanese periphery was Shimao Toshio 島尾敏雄 (1917-1986), a renowned postwar author, who in the 1950s investigated Ryūkyūan culture. This can be seen as a kind of 'guilt refurbishing' that typified the times.

During the war, Shimao was a young naval officer stationed on the island of Kakeromajima 加計呂麻島, where he met a woman named Miho ミホ, who would later become his wife. In much of his writing he deals with their marital problems, both as a private dilemma and as an allegory of the relationship between the Japanese mainland and the outlying island or as the collision of con-centric with regional thinking. In this regard, Shimao's major work, the novel *Shi no toge* 死の棘 (tr. 'The Sting of Death'), which, as Japanese critics note, is an anti-urban novel (*han-toshi shōsetsu* 反都市小説) that understands the me-tropolis of Tōkyō as the center of cultural imperialism. *Shi no toge* can be seen as an allegorical description of Imperial Japan, represented by the former naval officer Toshio, who as a private person perpetuates vis-à-vis his less privileged subjects the domineering posturing of the state.

Shimao Toshio describes Miho as a woman whose essence is intimately bound up with her southerly homeland and who can only recover from the neuroses from which she suffers if he takes her back to her native isle, thereby acknowledging both her sovereignty and his own betrayal of her (specifically, on the personal level, his adultery). The protagonist Toshio in *Shi no toge* is aware that Miho is endowed with 'uncanny powers' that put him in his place. He sees Miho's condition on the one hand as a trial to which the Christian God has subjected him and, on the other, as her 'enlightenment' and, according to some interpreters of the novel, her realization that she is a *yuta* ユタ or Ryūkyūan shaman [see Gabriel (1999), pp. 157ff.].

In his 1954 essay '*Okinawa' no imi suru mono* '沖縄'の意味するもの ('The Meaning of Okinawa') [Shimao (1980-83), vol. 16, pp. 11-16], Shimao regards the Ryūkyūs 琉球 as 'another Japan', from whose unique culture and heritage he hopes to gain salvation for the guilt-ridden mainland. Later in *Yaponesia no nekko* ヤポネシアの根っこ ('The Roots of Yaponesia', 1961) [Shimao (1980-83), vol. 16, pp. 190-93], he develops a Yaponesia-concept, with which he further advocates a culturally diverse Japan.[6]

The theme of island life, its 'primeval' folkways and religious worldview, is also taken up by Mishima Yukio 三島由紀夫 (1925-1970) in his novel *Shiosai* 潮騒 (tr. 'The Sound of the Waves', 1954), which likewise appeared at the beginning of the 1950s. Mishima's interpretation proceeds, however, in a different direction, and the setting of the novel, Utajima 歌島, is characteristically no distant southern isle: it lies in the Gulf of Ise. The religion of the island, the author implies, is a quasi-naturally born faith in Watatsumi no Mikoto 海神之尊, the god of the sea. The hero of the story, a young fisherman, embodies the mental and spiritual state of the local inhabitants: unspoiled, strong, and upright.

The portrayal of youthful male-bonding on the island and of the simple communal religious rites that infuse it with dignity, as well as the praises sung of hard physical labor offer an ideal picture of the collective, whose spiritual essence consists of a morality of righteousness and chastity and whose heroicized prototype the young fisherman represents. For Mishima, 'indigenous Japan' is one of natural and wholesome vitality. Here what is meant by religion is that which lies behind the picturesque façade of toriied shrines: a strict behavioral code that serves to regulate the communal life of the people. Mishima's clear intention is to describe the sublime condition of individuals who have submitted themselves to collective law. His account of the pure 'insular spirit' is

---

[6] Cf. Gabriel (1999), pp. 160-213. In an English-language outline of the Yaponesianism Shimao affirms: "*I was led to view Japan as Japanesia, that is, to assign greater significance to influence from the cultures of the South Pacific, by impressions I received from the Ryukyu Islands, the group which forms the southern end of the Japanese island bow. I first visited the Ryukyus more than 20 years ago, at the height of the war in the Pacific, when I was assigned to one of the islands, as a naval officer; and I sensed immediately, if vaguely, that this island society and culture were free of the tenseness and rigidity one always feels in Japanese culture. Then, 10 years ago, I made my home on one of the islands in this group, and I have become increasingly convinced that my original impressions were correct. Life on Ryukyu Islands is animated by a kind of internal vitality, and the islanders behave towards one another with a naturalness which has been forgotten on the Japanese mainland. Island society is unpoisoned by modern civilization; the islanders live a life so honest and unornamented that it recalls mediaeveal or even archaic Japanese society*" [Shimao (1973), p. 287]. Shimao, it may be briefly noted, also made reference to foreign researchers involved with the Ryūkyūs; in particular, he praises the work of the young Josef Kreiner; cf. Shimao (1980-83), vol. 17, pp. 62ff.

to be understood as an admonition to Mainland Japan that it should look to this society as an example to emulate.

The model of both positions is found again and again in the interpretations of the regional as they appear over the succeeding decades. Shimao refers to a 'feminine matriarchal island' as an alternative to the 'patriarchal insula'. Clearly following in the footsteps of Yanagita Kunio 柳田国男, he invokes the spirits of the island: the protagonist in *Shi no toge* associates with Miho, for example, *Kenmun* ケンムン, a mythological figure in the Ryūkyūan tales, and the island legends in which she is said to be revealed. With his grandiloquent island fantasy of the poor but manly fisherman who wins a beautiful and wealthy bride, Mishima fashions a vitalistic scenario: a man filled with *joie de vivre* is blessed by the deities and natural forces that rule the island; in his triumph he is even the equal of the gods and of *Natura omnipotens*.

The regional becomes an object of nostalgia,[7] a vital beacon of hope, for those who have conservative values as well as for those with a liberal outlook. The appeal to *densetsu* 伝説 (legend, though in the literal sense of oral tradition), *dochaku* 土着 (the indigenous) and the primeval faith (*genshūkyō* 原宗教) as a worldview of no lesser validity than that of urban Japan, together with the affirmation of a pure, energetic Japanese collectivity, a cohesive family- and village community,[8] represent – in regard to the concept of native religion – central lines of argumentation, which during the 1960s grew into a thick and massive network, whose strength and influence are felt even today.

In 1956 appeared another well-known atavistic vision of the village collective. *Narayama bushikō* 楢山節考 by Fukazawa Shichirō 深沢七郎 (1914-1987) is a ballad celebrating village life: as it is often said, it was received with astonishment by the contemporary literary scene because of its strikingly anachro-

---

[7] For a discussion of the Japanese 'invention' of the village, the rural and the regional, see the contributions of Jennifer Robertson (1998) and Marilyn Ivy (1995).

[8] The political scientist and Japanologist Wolfgang Seifert notes in regard to the renaissance in the postwar era of ethnic nativist nationalism (so-called *minzoku dochaku-ha* 民族土着派) that its representatives, e.g., Hayashi Fusao 林房雄, called for a return to Japan by opposing class divisions and insisting that family and village community should again be made the basis of society. There only, it was argued, could be nurtured those moral virtues on which obedience to the state and the emperor are predicated. Seifert points out that the stern and exhortative appeals to Japanese traditions and virtues became increasingly ineffective and that a counterattack on the conservatives was launched at the end of the 1960s, as social conflicts came to a head and the destruction of the environment had worsened. Cf. Seifert (1977), pp. 266ff.; for Mishima, see p. 48.

nistic theme. Still, the trend towards the archaic and the nostalgic had long since begun in earnest; together with such renowned representatives as Furui Yoshikichi 古井由吉 (b. 1937) and Nakagami Kenji 中上健次 (1946-92), it would prove to be one of the main currents of Japanese contemporary literature, art, and film.[9]

In 1952, the sculptor and writer Okamoto Tarō 岡本太郎 (1911-96) discovered the beauty of Jōmon 縄文 ceramics. Already in 1956 he had written _Nihon no dentō 日本の伝統_ ('Japanese Tradition'), and in 1958, a work with the characteristic title _Nihon saihakken 日本再発見_ ('The Rediscovery of Japan'). In 1959, he undertook a trip to Okinawa, and in 1961 published a collection of his impressions in a volume entitled _Wasurerareta Nihon 忘られた日本_ ('Forgotten Japan'). In 1964, _Shinpi Nihon 神秘日本_ ('Mystical Japan') was published. Okamoto, a cosmopolitan, had graduated from the University of Paris in folklore studies. His fresh perspective on Japanese culture sought to bring to light its original strata, to offer a 'return to our folkways' (_dozokuteki na mono e no kaiki_ 土俗的なものへの回帰), as Kurabayashi Yasushi 倉林靖 formulates it [Kurabayashi (1996), p. 18]; his attempts to grasp 'the vitality of the indigenous' are part of the tradition of avant-garde modernity and its yeah-and-nay ambivalence towards that same modernity: _kindai_ 近代 vs. _han-kindai_ 反近代.

Okamoto's travel notes in _Shinpi Nihon_, in which, for example, a single glimpse of the artwork inspired by esoteric Buddhism (_mikkyō_ 密教) is enough to make him aware of a 'primeval élan vital' (_genshiteki seimei no enerugī_ 原始的生命のエネルギー) [Okamoto (2000), p. 153], can be seen as among the first examples of a 'spiritual tourism' that would prove to be so emblematic of the 1970s and 1980s. Okamoto asks whether certain Japanese religious traditions other than Buddhism might still be living and whether these might offer potential and viable defenses against utilitarianism and modernity.

Since the mid-1960s, notes Aoki Tamotsu 青木保 in his depiction of _nihonron_ 日本論, 'Japaneseness' has again be seen as a distinctly positive quality [Aoki (1996), p. 77]. Aoki sees Mishima Yukio's _Bunka bōei ron 文化防衛論_ (1968), a restorative work, in which the author presents the emperor system (_tennō-sei_) as a cultural concept and affirms his allegiance to the Japanese soul, as characteristic of the era. Already in 1966, Hayashi Fusao 林房雄 (1903-1975), a pivotal

---

[9] As cinematic representatives of the search for an authentic Japan, Imamura Shōhei 今村昌平

representative of the new nationalism, had issued a similar call for a new cultural wholeness. In one of the last sections of his book *Midori no Nihon rettō* 緑の日本列島 ('The Green Archipelago of Japan'), published in 1966, he speaks of the 'rebirth of the gods' (*kamigami no fukkatsu* 神々の復活). He emphasizes that 'Shintō is Japan's indigenous folk-cult' (*Shintō wa Nihon no dochaku no kozoku de aru* 神道は日本の土着の古俗である) [Hayashi (1966), pp. 312f.] and that all attempts by the Western overlords to eradicate it have been in vain, just as Christianity has failed to banish the old gods in other non-Western countries.

In the same year that Mishima Yukio's *Bunka bōei-ron* appeared, Yoshimoto Takaaki 吉本隆明 published *Kyōdō gensō-ron* 共同幻想論, which offers a complicated analysis of Japanese social structure. It is intended to present an ideological critique, making reference to the *Kojiki* 古事記 and Yanagita Kunio's writings [10] and relying on anthropological and political theories. Although this was frequently invoked as a key to understanding the late Sixties, it can hardly be said to have undergone a detailed analysis. Yoshimoto's position is difficult to grasp.[11] His argumentation, which oscillates between a critique of 'primeval' Asiatic social forms and a critique of modernity, is typical of the ambivalence that is generally inherent in the discourse.

Whereas 'religion' is often criticized as an instrument of the powers-that-be, it can also serve – above all when it is that of a marginalized group – the cause of anarchy. The anarchist line within contemporary Japanese discourse on religion is represented by Takahashi Kazumi 高橋和巳. It was also in 1968 that the well-known literary figure and critic published his novel *Jashūmon* 邪宗門 ('Heretics' Gate'), a complex work that develops motifs relevant to the Japanese intellectual history of modernity and represents a critical view of Japan's modernizing phase.

---

and Shindō Kaneto 新藤兼人 may be mentioned.

[10] The theories of the folklorist Yanagita Kunio (1875-1962) on the origin of the Japanese and of Japanese culture had a decisive influence on Japanese cultural discourse. In the wake of his death, the 1960s saw a Yanagita boom. In the 1980s as well, there were frequent references to his work, though these must be understood in the spirit of the decades in which they were formulated, characterized as they are by an ethno-romantic impulse and the longing for national unity.

[11] In my view, Yoshimoto's role as an intellectual who in the course of the decades followed varied trends has hitherto not been sufficiently scrutinized; likewise, *Kyōdō gensō-ron* has not been adequately dissected and placed in its proper historical perspective.

### 3. Religion and the Avant-garde Counter Culture of the 1970s

With the collapse of the student movement and the 1973 oil crisis, which dominated the socio-economic scene in the early years of that decade, the ideology of progress and growth came to be critically questioned in Japan, too. As is generally noted, Japanese intellectuals increasingly withdrew into the private and personal realm. Many completed their retreat from involvement in public causes by seeking refuge in ethno-romanticism. Japanese identity finds itself located entirely within the sphere of the 'Asiatically spiritual'. With the shift into inwardness, the theme of religion gained increasing significance in the 1970s. This development, which also opened a new market for identity and religion, overlaps in its essentials with its counterpart in Occidental countries, in which hippy culture was commercialized and New Age enjoyed its heyday.

Japanese critics and artists next discovered, like their Occidental colleagues, an exotic, religious Asia – mostly India – or the culture of South America, into which they projected their longings for the 'primeval', the 'spiritual', and 'holistic' life. Characteristic of the decade are the works of the sociologist Mita Munesuke 見田宗介, who published as an essayist under the name of Maki Yūsuke 真木悠介, as well as the books of the graphic artist and bohemian of the 'spiritual world' (_seishin sekai_ 精神世界), Yokoo Tadanori 横尾忠則. In _Kiryū no naru oto: Kōkyō suru komyūn_ 気流の鳴る音 : 交響するコミューン ('The Sound of Airwaves: The Symphony of Communes', 1977), Maki Yūsuke writes Carlos Castañeda's Don Juan cycle, a key text of Occidental spiritual scene (and a neo-shamanistic fiction); he is equally enthralled by the way of life he finds in Ajisai Village 紫陽花邑, an alternative commune, whose leading figure is a Shintō priest. Ajisai Village supposedly gives us a vision of a community that, in its simple reverence for nature and man, has preserved the 'primeval faith' (_genshinkō_ 原信仰) [Maki (1986), p. 23].[12]

It did not take long before the mood of nostalgia was directed not only to distant lands and particular religious groups; Japan as a whole was rediscovered as a realm of indigenous creedal concepts. In addition to the archaeology boom,

---

[12] Mita/Maki describes the Japanese priest as a person who teaches how to walk the right path, a way of unity with all beings: "_The priest walks on his way, stands still time by time to listen to the voices. Stones, trees or the wind are calling on him. It seems to me that if we are with him, we too, will be able again to hear those words, which long existed before any language_" [Maki (1986), p. 24].

to which the mystery writer Matsumoto Seichō 松本清張 contributed, there was
a surging interest in 'indigenous religion', which in the academic sphere was
represented by the journal *Dentō to Gendai* 伝統と現代 ('Tradition and the Contemporary World'). The trend expanded all the more in the 1980s.

### 4. Bubble-Narcissism and Post-Aum-Paralysis

It is remarkable to what extent Japanese in the 1980s view their own culture
with the eyes of exoticists. They describe their homeland as the dwelling place
of ghosts and goblins, as an 'Occult Japan' such as Yamaori Tetsuo 山折哲雄
and Kamata Tōji 鎌田東二 suggest in a book with the same title, published in
1987 by Heibonsha. In this context, special attention should be drawn to the
newly coined term *ikai* 異界, a word widely used, but not listed in any representative dictionary.[13]

The concept *ikai* bespeaks the need in contemporary Japan for a
'counter-world' and a growing ethno-esoteric tendency in intellectual and artis-
tic circles. It was the post-modern camp that, in the 1980s, made a show of affirming indigenous Japanese religious sensibility as the basis for what was said
to be an imminent paradigm shift. The economic surge of the so-called bubble
favored a national introspectiveness. Post-modern and nationalist-conservative
thinkers, in particular such 'spiritual old boys' as Umehara Takeshi 梅原猛 and
Yamaori Tetsuo, shared an interest in the question of Japanese identity, which
became primarily one of religion. It was 'bubble narcissism' that first put the
spiritual nostalgia machine properly in gear. A new 'identity industry' brought
to the fore a multitude of texts on this theme as well as other neo-Japonesque
goods in the course of a retro-trend, stage-managed by huge department store
chains such as Seibu und Parco.

---

[13] The term literally translates as 'other, strange, alien world', but it would also be possible to
render it as underworld, occult world, ghost world, magic world, counter-world, liminal/
marginal world or twilight zone. In part, the term corresponds to other Japanese concepts of
the world of beyond such as *takai* 他界, *meido* 冥途 or *tokoyo no kuni* 常世の国. However,
*ikai* stands for more than 'traditional' Japanese beliefs. It has to be placed within the
framework of the criticism of modern Japan and its values; moreover, it implies an
extensive discussion of Japanese culture and society. For the concept of *ikai* and its
meaning within the Japanese cultural discourse, see Gebhardt (1996, 2000 and 2001).

In 1995 Japan was shaken by the Aum -shock, which brought with it a kind of paralysis. The 'spiritual intellectuals' were accused of obscurantism and lost some of their popularity. One of them, Nakazawa Shin'ichi 中沢新一, sees 1995 as a turning point. Marking as it did the 50-year mark since the end of the war, 1995 had been trumpeted as a symbol of Japan's break with the past. It came to be seen, however, not as the launching of a new era but rather as a traumatic uprooting. Now, Nakazawa would see Japan as a 'spiritual wasteland' (_seishin-teki arano_ 精神的荒野), devoid of any innovative developments. For Nakazawa, the Aum incident also signifies a debacle for religion and its leaders. Nakazawa goes so far as to say: "_With that, the curtain on whatever you might call 'Japanese religion' came down (Are de owatchatta, Nihon no shūkyō nante_ あれで終わちゃった、日本の宗教なんて)" [Nakazawa/ Setouchi (1997), p. 39]. As he puts it, he had been inspired by the optimism that pervaded the early 1980s. He cherished the hope that Japan would achieve a 'breakthrough' and find her spiritual potential recognized in the international community to the same degree that she had won acclaim for her economic accomplishments. Occidental interest in Japan peaked sometime after 1986, he claims, and then began to recede in 1988. With the fall of the Berlin Wall and the collapse of the Soviet Union had set in what he calls the European Revival (_Yōroppa no fukkō_ ヨーロッパの復興). The West was again self-absorbed. Japan, according to Nakazawa, had thereby lost an extraordinary opportunity.

Nakazawa's lament concerns the opportunity that Japan supposedly lost to hold its own at last against the West with a spirituality of its very own. It may be noted here that the ethno-romanticism and narcissism of many (would-be) representatives of Japanese culture – or rather those who claimed to be transmitting 'the' Japanese culture – hindered a genuine dialogue between Japanese and Western intellectuals and ultimately a constant and enduring interest on the part of the West in Japan. The image of a 'spiritually' superior Japan has, to be sure, a long tradition in the Western perception of Asia, but such cannot offer an adequate basis for a satisfactory intercultural exchange.

By constantly engaging for so many decades in a spiritual and indigenous religious self-verification that sought to claim for Japan an 'alternative modernity', the nation's cultural discourse has veered into a _cul-de-sac_. This, as Nakazawa now senses, has led to an isolation of the country and to stagnation within it.

## 5. Closing Comment: Selling Identity in Intercultural Salons

For lack of another 'grand narrative', there is still talk of a 'spiritual Japan'. The playing field of culturalistic argumentation has, however, shifted. Nowadays the players are less likely to be the 'colorful' intellectuals such as Nakazawa Shin'ichi, Kamata Tōji, Umehara Takeshi or Yamaori Tetsuo, who with their pithy theses had to face some criticism in magazines;[14] instead we see once again the *éminences grises* agitating on the international stage.

At gatherings in forums that I should like to call intercultural salon, representatives of current Japanese cultural discourse prefer to devote themselves to philosophical themes. For one thing, the complexity of philosophical matters makes it possible to come to conclusions relevant to the Japanese perspective that in the terminology of a scholar of religion, for example, would hardly be tenable. Under the pretence of wanting to carry on a new conversation, free of familiar boundaries, participants in these 'intercultural salons' reunite with some frequency, their real purpose being, it would appear, to strengthen old stereotypes about Far Eastern and Western worldviews and thereby to prepare the way for a new conservatism.[15] A fashionable shift to ethnology and cultural anthropology as guiding academic disciplines, together with 'intercultural philosophy',[16] lends credence to the assumption that the flow of words in the gallery will continue unimpeded.

Regardless of this development, it is important to elucidate the various forms of Japanese self-orientalism, which, as demonstrated since the 1950s, has been formulated primarily from the aspect of 'indigenous religion'. In this way it could be possible to expose the mechanisms of the 'nostalgic nationalism'[17] – as

---

[14] There is, for example, the severe criticism that the journalist Kimura Tatsuo 木村龍夫 lets loose in an article published in the well-known gossip magazine *Uwasa no shinsō* 噂の真相 ('The Truth Behind the Rumors'), entitled "Okaruto bunkajin オカルト文化人" ('Opinion Leaders with Occult Inclinations'); for a comprehensive discussion of the 'occult' and 'spiritual' interests of contemporary Japanese thinkers and writers, see Prohl (2000) and Gebhardt (2001).

[15] The Germanic scholar Mishima Ken'ichi 三島憲一 goes so far as to speak of a conservative revolution and in the process points to a parallel between the Japanese and German intellectual scenes; cf. Mishima (1996), p. 116.

[16] Representative of its problematic basis within 'intercultural philosophy' are the Japan-oriented views of Ōhashi Ryōsuke 大橋良介, as illustrated in a new collection of texts that have been translated into German; see, for further information, Gebhardt (2000a).

[17] On the subject of modern Japanese nationalism, the writings of the historian and novelist Nishikawa Nagao 西川長夫 are often taken up. As far as I know, he does not pursue to the

much molded by ideological ambitions as it is the product of the 'identity industry' – that crucially determines cultural discourse in today's Japan. Such would serve the cause of deepening understanding of Japan and, with the uniting of 'different modernities' in a globally understood future in the 21st century, help to protect the archipelago from intellectual and 'spiritual' isolation.

## References

Aoki (1996)

Aoki, Tamotsu: *Der Japandiskurs im historischen Wandel. Zur Kultur und Identität einer Nation.* [Monographien aus dem Deutschen Institut für Japanstudien, vol. 14] München: Iudicium Verlag, 1996.

Barshay (1998)

Barshay, Andrew E.: "Postwar Social and Political Thought, 1945-90", in: Wakabayashi, Bob Tadashi (ed.): *Modern Japanese Thought.* Cambridge: Cambridge University Press, 1998, pp. 273-355.

Gabriel (1999)

Gabriel, Philip: *Mad Wives and Island Dreams: Shimao Toshio and the Margins of Japanese Literature.* Honolulu: University of Hawai'i Press, 1999.

Gayle (2001)

Gayle, Curtis Anderson: "Progressive Representations of the Nation: Early Post-war Japan and Beyond", in: *Social Science Journal Japan*, no. 4/1 (2001), pp. 1-19.

Gebhardt (1996)

Gebhardt, Lisette: "Ikai: Der Diskurs zur 'Anderen Welt' als Manifestation der japanischen Selbstfindungs-Debatte". In: Hijiya-Kirschnereit, Irmela (ed.): *Überwindung der Moderne? – Japan am Ende des 20. Jahrhunderts.* Frankfurt/M.: Suhrkamp Verlag, 1996, pp. 146-171.

same degree aspects of cultural nationalism as a phenomenon of consumerism, lifestyle and mass media.

— (1999)

Gebhardt, Lisette: *Christentum, Religion, Identität: Ein Thema der modernen japanischen Literatur.* [Europäische Hochschulschriften: series 27, Asiatische und Afrikanische Studien; vol. 73] Frankfurt/M.: Peter Lang, 1999.

— (2000)

Gebhardt, Lisette: "'Die Herren der Geister': Volkskundliche Studien und Ethnofiktion oder warum man in Japan gegenwärtig soviel Geisterforschung betreibt", in: Manthey, Barbara/ Kleinen, Peter/ Distelrath, Günther/ Horres, Robert/ Lützeler, Ralph/ Ölschleger, Hans Dieter (ed.): *JapanWelten: Aspekte der deutschsprachigen Japanforschung. Festschrift für Josef Kreiner zu seinem sechzigsten Geburtstag von seinen Schülern und Mitarbeitern.* [Japan Archiv, vol. 3] Bonn: Bier'sche Verlagsanstalt, 2000, pp. 437-453.

— (2000a)

Gebhardt, Lisette: "Die 'Ekstase der Oktopusse': Anmerkungen zum japanischen Kulturdiskurs anhand der Reihe 'Japan und sein Jahrhundert'", in: *Japanforschung. Mitteilungen der Gesellschaft für Japanforschung e.V.*, year 2000, vol. 2, pp. 10-16.

— (2001)

Gebhardt, Lisette: *Japans Neue Spiritualität.* Wiesbaden: Harrassowitz, 2001.

Hayashi (1966)

Hayashi, Fusao 林房雄: *Midori no Nihon rettō: Gekiryū suru Meiji hyakunen* 緑の日本列島：激流する明治百年. Tōkyō: Bungei shunjū, 1966.

Hudson (1999)

Hudson, Mark J.: *Ruins of Identity: Ethnogenesis in the Japanese Islands.* Honolulu: University of Hawai'i Press, 1999.

Ivy (1995)

Ivy, Marilyn: *Discourses of the Vanishing: Modernity, Phantasm, Japan.* Chicago: The University of Chicago Press, 1995.

Kimura (1998)

Kimura, Tatsuo 木村龍夫: "Marukusu-shugi taichō no yoha de hasei shita okaruto bunkajin no ureubeki chōryō bakko マルクス主義退潮の余波で派生したオカルト文化人の憂うべき跳梁跋扈", in: *Uwasa no shinsō* 噂の真相, vol. 7 (1998), pp. 60–69.

Kurabayashi (1996)
Kurabayashi, Yasushi 倉林靖: *Okamoto Tarō to Yokoo Tadanori: Modan to han-modan no gyakusetsu* 岡本太郎と横尾忠則：モダンと反モダンの逆説. Tōkyō: Hakusuisha, 1996.

Maki (1986)
Maki, Yūsuke 真木悠介: *Kiryū no naru oto: Kōkyō suru komyūn* 気流の鳴る音：交響するコミューン. Tōkyō: Chikuma bunko, 1986.

Maruyama (1988)
Maruyama Masao: *Denken in Japan.* Herausgegeben und übersetzt von Wolfgang Schamoni und Wolfgang Seifert. [edition suhrkamp; no. 1398] Frankfurt/M.: Suhrkamp, 1988.

Mishima (1996)
Mishima, Ken'ichi: "Die Schmerzen der Modernisierung als Auslöser kultureller Selbstbehauptung – Zur geistigen Auseinandersetzung Japans mit dem 'Westen'", in: Hijiya-Kirschnereit, Irmela (ed.): *Überwindung der Moderne? – Japan am Ende des zwanzigsten Jahrhunderts.* Frankfurt/M.: Suhrkamp Verlag, 1996, pp. 86-122.

Nakazawa/ Setouchi (1997)
Nakazawa, Shin'ichi 中沢新一/ Setouchi, Jakuchō 瀬戸内寂聴: "Shūkyō no seiki e: Ōmu kara ninen 宗教の世紀へ：オウムから二年", in: *Chūō kōron* 中央公論, no. 4 (1997), pp. 28-45.

Okamoto (2000)
Okamoto, Tarō 岡本太郎: *Shinpi Nihon 神秘日本: Okamoto Tarō no hon* 岡本太郎の本 3. Tōkyō: Misuzu shobō, 2000.

Prohl (2000)
Prohl, Inken: *Die "spirituellen Intellektuellen" und das New Age in Japan.* [Mitteilungen der Gesellschaft für Natur- und Völkerkunde Ostasiens; vol. 133] Hamburg: Gesellschaft für Natur- und Völkerkunde Ostasiens, 2000.

Robertson (1998)
Robertson, Jennifer: "It Takes a Village: Internationalization and Nostalgia in Postwar Japan", in: Vlastos, Stephen (ed.): *Mirror of Modernity: Invented Traditions of Modern Japan.* Berkeley and Los Angeles: California University Press, 1998, pp. 110-129.

**Seifert (1977)**

Seifert, Wolfgang: *Nationalismus im Nachkriegs-Japan: Ein Beitrag zur Ideologie der völkischen Nationalisten*. [Mitteilungen des Instituts für Asienkunde Hamburg, No. 91] Hamburg: Institut für Asienkunde, 1977.

**Shimao (1973)**

Shimao, Toshio 島尾敏雄: "Kojin tokushū 個人特集", in: *UR. Existenz* [ed.: Yi, Seung Yun], vol. 3 (1973), Tōkyō: Tōhō shobō, pp. 287-409.

—   **(1980-83)**

Shimao, Toshio 島尾敏雄: *Shimao Toshio zenshū 島尾敏雄全集*. 17. vol., Tōkyō: Shōbunsha, 1980-83.

# Prophets of salvation coming out of the forests of Japan –
# Introducing some of the so called "spiritual intellectuals"[1]

Inken PROHL

Looking at the titles of some of the books on Japanese religion of the last dec-ade, it seems that the Japanese forest possesses a special meaning not only for the future of the Japanese, but also for the future of mankind. For an understand-ing of Japanese religion, it seems to be a must to retreat into the seclusion of Japanese woods and to experience the unique atmosphere: Kamata Tōji 鎌田東 二, for instance, tells us of his experiences of "holy nature" in the shrines hidden in the Japanese forest, together with Tsumura Takashi 津村喬 in their book *Tenkawa mandara: Chōshūkyō e no channeru* 天河曼陀羅 : 超宗教への水路 ('Tenkawa Mandala: The Channel to Super-Religion'; 1994). Other similar books have been published in recent years, such as Umehara Takeshi's 梅原猛 work *Mori no shisō ga jinrui wo sukuu* 森の思想が人類を救う ('The Philosophy of the Forest will Save the Human Race'; 1991) or *Mori no barokku* 森のバロッ ク ('The Barock of the Forest'; 1992) by Nakazawa Shin'ichi 中沢新一.

In my paper, I will outline some of the notions of Japanese religion as they are expounded by Umehara Takeshi, Nakazawa Shin'ichi and Kamata Tōji. These authors belong to a group called the "spiritual intellectuals" (*reiseiteki chishikijin* 霊性的知識人), a term coined by the scholar of religious studies Shimazono Susumu 島薗進 [cf. Shimazono (1993a, 1996)]. Part 1 of my paper will introduce some of the contents of the works of the 'spiritual intellectuals'. I will examine the 'spiritual intellectuals' use of such key terms as 'animism', 'shamanism' and 'spirituality' along with their views on the so-called 'indige-nous religion' of Japan, Shintō. The critical analysis of keywords as they figure in the visions of Japanese religious history elaborated by the 'spiritual intellectu-als' suggests that these texts can also be productively taken up as a type of *nihonjinron* 日本人論 ('discourses on Japaneseness'), more specifically as *nihonkyōron* 日本教論, i.e., 'discourses on Japanese religion'. Their treatment of the history of religion in Japan is characterized by the features typical of the

---

[1] The arguments of this paper have been developed at a greater length in Prohl (2000).

discourses on Japaneseness, for example ethnocentrism, the postulation of homogeneity, and their normative tendency [cf. Befu (1993)]. The way in which these authors freshen up their ideas with the help of popular terms from the so-called New Age will also be described. In part 2, the role and the function of their discourse will be discussed. It will be argued, that their texts function as a sort of civil religion for Japan. Some parallels between their notions and the teachings of the New Religions will be shown, as well as the influence of their notions on the teachings of certain New Religions. In the conclusion of this paper, I would like to draw attention to a new form of 'experiential–science' (*Erlebniswissenschaft*) in which the writing on religion is particularly popular and which may serve as an expression of cultural superiority.

## 1. The views of Umehara Takeshi, Nakazawa Shin'ichi and Kamata Tōji on Japanese religion

In his book "The Philosophy of the Forest will Save the Human Race" the religious philosopher Umehara Takeshi (former director of the International Research Center for Japanese Studies, Nichibunken) argues that the deep layer of Japanese religion, which he claims to be Shintō, goes back to the Jōmon 縄文 age (12.000 - 250 B.C.). This original set of beliefs was eclipsed by further development, but it is still to be found on Okinawa and among the Ainu today. The characteristics of this early Shintō (*kodai shintō* 古代神道; Umehara also uses the term *koshintō* 古神道 [cf. for instance Umehara/ Yamaori (1995), p. 200]), as still expressed in the religion of the Ainu and the Okinawans, are a belief in the spirit of trees, the idea of reincarnation (*saisei* 再生), the equality of all beings (*byōdō* 平等) and an emphasis on vitality (*seimei* 生命). Umehara depicts Japanese religion as polytheistic (*tashinkyō* 多神教) with the worship of the gods of nature playing an important role. He argues further that these characteristics have to be rediscovered. Shintō is portrayed as a religion of the forest, particularly of trees, a factor that, together with the coexistence of all beings with nature, constitutes its most significant element. The worship of nature and the idea of the coexistence of all beings have allegedly been preserved in Japanese Shintō up unto the present. Because of this, Japan is able to make an important contribution to the solution of the problems afflicting modern society [cf. also Umehara/ Yamaori (1995), p. 209]. This argument informs the title of his book "The Philosophy of the Forest Will Save the Human Race".

Umehara further stresses his opinion that Asia, and particularly Japan, will save the world because of its Buddhist traditions. He contrasts the harmonious Buddhist tradition with the putatively Christian tradition of the West, in which he claims to have discovered the "germ of destructive thinking". According to Umehara, Japanese Buddhism was influenced by those indigenous ideas characteristic of Shintō; as a result, Buddhism was transformed into 'animism' (_animizumu_ アニミズム), an animism that Umehara describes as pancosmic (_han'uchūteki_ 汎宇宙的). The notion of the equality of all things and beings in nature became essential to Japanese Buddhism, an expression of which we have in the phrase "mountains, rivers, plants, and trees are all enlightened" (_sōmoku kokudo shikkai jobutsu_ 草木国土悉皆成仏).

Another supporter of the idea of Shintō as a primeval religion (_genshintō_ 源神道) of the forest is the religious scholar Nakazawa Shin'ichi (Chūō University) [cf. Nakazawa (1992), p. 296]. The notion of gods, as Nakazawa elaborates in his _Mori no barokku_, is not to be found in early Japanese Shintō because ancient people were wiser than their modern-day counterparts and knew that the gods would be lost to men if they expressed their beliefs about them. For Nakazawa too, early Shintō is a religion of the forest. Entering a Japanese forest brings purification and 'mystic' (_shinpi_ 神秘) experience. According to him, the Japanese people learnt to understand from the network of relationships (_en no nettowāku_ 緑のネットーク) existing in the forest the so-called logos according to which human beings should live. For him, this logos forms the foundation of social life. In modern times the Japanese have lost the touch with this logos. Nakazawa also claims that the Japanese have also lost their feeling for spirituality which used to be expressed in terms such as _busshō_ 仏性 ('buddha-nature'), _yama no sekai_ 山の世界 ('the world of mountains') or _musubi_ 結び ('connection'). Like Umehara, Nakazawa criticizes "aggressive" Christian thought and identifies himself as Asian. In his thought, the gap between East and West is a very deep one. The differences between Christianity and Buddhism testify to the profundity of this gap: whereas the former is simple and bewitching, the latter is deep and complicated and nearer to truth [cf. Nakazawa (1993), pp. 67-70].

The religious philosopher Kamata Tōji (Musashioka Junior College) became famous in Japan for his support of the Tenkawa shrine 天河神社 in Nara. In his *Tenkawa mandara: Chōshūkyō e no channeru* Kamata argues that this shrine facilitates religious experiences, by which he means the experience of the holy silence (*sei naru seijaku* 聖なる静寂) of nature. This nature is inhabited by the gods in their 'pure' form, which is why the Tenkawa shrine makes it possible to experience 'Super-Religion' (*chōshūkyō* 超宗教). According to Kamata, 'Super-Religion' can be described as experiencing nature. He further claims that Tenkawa is the center of the Asian water-world, a world in which water symbolizes the connection between all beings and the bridge between this world and the other world. Kamata sees 'animism' (*animizumu*) along with 'shamanism' (*shāmanizumu* シャーマニズム) and 'polytheisms' (*tashinkyō*) preserved at Tenkawa. Like Umehara and Nakazawa, he argues, that Japanese Shintō is the primeval religion of Japan. For a better future he thinks it necessary to trace the 'spiritual' (*reiseiteki* 霊性的) roots of Japanese Shintō [cf. Kamata (1995)].

As we have seen, Umehara Takeshi, Nakazawa Shin'ichi and Kamata Tōji are particularly fond of using such 'scientific' terms as 'animism', 'shamanism' or 'mystic' – terms which belong to the long tradition of religious studies in the West. In the past, however, scholars of religion have also taken up the task of exposing the romantic and normative tendencies implicit in these terms by analyzing them and investigating their applicability to the historical and social realities of religion.

'Animism' is one example of the terms that are being subjected to intense scientific scrutiny. The term 'animism' was made popular by the British scholar of religion Edward B. Tylor (1832 - 1917) in his 1871 book *Primitive Culture*. As critics have pointed out, the term 'animism' speaks volumes about Tylor's fantasies about the thought and feelings of 'primitives' – heavily influenced as he was by Darwinism and evolutionary theory [cf. Bolle (1987), pp. 296-302] – and subsequent anthropological research could not substantiate Tylor's notion of 'animism' [cf. Schlatter (1988), pp. 473-476]. The use of the term 'shamanism' is also highly problematic. Ever since Mircea Eliade projected his famous theory in _Shamanism: Archaic Techniques of Ecstasy_ (1951), scholars of religion and anthropology have identified 'shamanistic' practices all over the world [cf. Bochinger (1994), p. 161]. While this term can be productively employed in discussions of the worldview prevalent among certain Siberian people, the indiscriminate use of it has robbed it of any accuracy it may have had [cf. Kohl (1998), p. 60].

Keeping in mind the origin of the term 'animism' and the way the Japanese scholars of religion use it, one fact should be clear: with its long historical development in Japan and its frequent changes and regional variations, it is highly improbable that the ancient Japanese possessed a belief system that can be accurately and usefully described as 'animistic'. Given the indiscriminate use of the term 'shamanism', it is unlikely to contribute much to a scholarly understanding of Japanese religion.

The authors introduced here use the term 'spiritual' to describe their alternative perceptions about the nature of Japanese religion. This is one reason why Shimazono has dubbed them the 'spiritual intellectuals'. However, none of the authors offer a definition for the term 'spirituality'. Objections can be raised against the use of the term 'spiritual', a term that is not defined either. The definition of the word 'spiritual' is far from clear once we have passed the borders of Christian theology (and even within these borders, there remains ample room for uncertainty). In Germany, the term came into frequent use in the 1960s as a codeword opposing a mechanistic, materialistic worldview [cf. Bochinger (1994), p. 377]. Lacking scientific accuracy, the use of the term 'spiritual' remains problematic as well. It seems that the use of these abstract terms leads to a focus on the categorization of religion, or, as the Buddhologist Hakamaya Noriyaki puts it:

> "_First of all, religious typologies such as polytheism, monotheism, and pantheism are neither more or less than a way to sort out and catalogue the phenomena we call "religions", much the same as a window–dresser arranges a display for a department store._"
> [Hakamaya (1997), pp. 114-115]

Different problems arise from the way, the 'spiritual intellectuals' envision the role of Shintō in Japanese history. Although research on the role and the significance of Shintō in the history of Japanese religion remains diverse and highly contradictory, the 'spiritual intellectuals' cling to the interpretation that Shintō is the primeval religion of Japan. To name only a few examples among many for an entirely different approach, let me point to the research of Kuroda Toshio (1993), Nelly Naumann (1988, 1994) and Klaus Antoni (1998). Kuroda Toshio 黒田俊雄, for instance, denies the existence of an independent Shintō before the Meiji period and suggests that the idea of Shintō in ancient Japan may be a "*ghost image*" [Kuroda (1993), p. 27].[2]

From these short considerations it should became clear that the writings of the 'spiritual intellectuals' effectively reread the entire Japanese religious tradition. Since they proclaim homogeneity on the basis of a vision of a unified and a super-historical Shintō that has shaped the Japanese mind, they support the view of 'orthodox Shintō' and arrive at normative effects. Thus their writings can be productively treated as a kind of religious *nihonjinron*. In declaring the superiority of Japan with regards to the salvation of the world, these authors contribute to a xenophobic cultural nationalism. This is a primary characteristic of all discourses on Japaneseness, a fact that for instance was already remarked upon by Yoshino Kōsaku 吉野耕作 [cf. Yoshino (1997)].

Shimazono Susumu has pointed out that since the 1990s, a special type of discourse on Japanese culture has became stronger, the *nihonkyōron*, that is to say writings in which the superiority of Japanese culture is explained by Japanese religion [cf. Shimazono (1995)]. The roots of this discourse may be traced back to the history of the debate on Japaneseness, which was initiated by Motoori Norinaga 本居宣長 and other early *kokugaku* 国学 scholars. The term *nihonkyōron* was coined by Yamamoto Shichihei 山本七平 who saw in the characteristics of the Japanese a religion itself [cf. Shimazono (1995), p. 9]. The term as I use it, may be translated as "discourse about Japanese religion". The main features of this discourse are the special Japanese 'animism' and 'shamanism' and their potential for the worship of nature, a vision of *koshintō* (ancient Shintō), and a critique of Western logic contrasting with Eastern

---

[2] In a recent article, Peter Fischer analyses the reasons for the influence of the image of 'orthodox shintō' outside Japan; cf. Fischer (2000/2001).

'spirituality'. Shimazono Susumu summarizes this discourse under the term *jiko shuchōteki nihonkyōron* 自己主張的日本教論, "self–assertive discourse on Japanese religion" [Shimazono (1993b), p. 152].

Not only Umehara Takeshi, Kamata Tōji and Nakazawa Shin'ichi but also scholars like Iwata Keiji 岩田慶治 or Yamaori Tetsuo 山折哲雄 (International Research Center for Japanese Studies, Nichibunken) engage in this kind of discourse, by attributing the superiority of Japan to Japanese religion. The book *Animizumu jidai* アニミズム時代 ('The Age of Animism'), written by the cultural anthropologist Iwata Keiji, is frequently quoted by other representatives of the 'spiritual intellectuals'. Iwata opens his book with a description of morning walks in his garden, where he greets his trees and senses their answers [cf. Iwata (1993), p. 7]. In doing so, he lives his concept of 'animism' – to feel the spirit living in all beings [cf. also Iwata (1996), pp. 14ff.]. According to Iwata, men are meant to encounter the power inherent in all things, a power which is at the same time linked with cosmic energy. 'Animism' is said to be the origin of all religion, but today it can still be experienced "especially in remote villages" in East Asia. For Iwata as well, 'animism' is going to be the religion of the future [cf. Iwata (1993), p. 10]. Yamaori Tetsuo, another religious scholar, has also contributed to the discussion of 'animism' in Japan. For him, 'animism' means harmony with nature as well as an open border between men and gods – a distinctive feature of religions in Japan, where the gods are easily accessible to human beings. Like Umehara and Nakazawa, Yamaori claims that because of these distinctive features, Japan will play an important role in solving the problems of modern society [cf. Umehara/ Yamaori (1995), p. 42]. Not only academics engage in the 'spiritual discourse', but also artists, as for instance, the painter Yokoo Tadanori 横尾忠則 [cf. Gebhardt (2001)] or the author Ōe Kanzaburō 大江健三郎, which Gebhadt labels a "new ager" [cf. Gebhardt (forthcoming)].

While engaging in this discourse, many of the authors also freshen up their writings with popular notions and ideas from the New Age[3]. The popularity of

---

[3] For the British scholar of religion Paul Heelas, the "lingua franca" of the global New Age Movement has to do with the *"human (and planetary) condition and how it can be transformed"*; Heelas (1996), p. 2. The American sociologist of religion Michals York has a similar understanding of the New Age [cf. York (1995), p. 2] and further characterizes it by a strong interest in older faith traditions and pagan beliefs and practices; on the term New

religious, esoteric and occult subjects shows that the New Age as a global development has also hit Japan.[4] The Japanese New Age (*seishin sekai* 精神世界, 'the spiritual world') is booming: new companies, both large and small, offer seminars and workshops about the 'spiritual' self and the proper way to attain it. A growing number of New Age shops sell *o-majinai* お呪い-goods, which is to say, goods with an 'occult touch', such as crystals, stones or pyramids. Almost any bookstore in Japan harbors a section of books labeled *seishinsekai* where one finds books, magazines and videos on a wide range of topics, including the occult, alternative healing, the 'secret' wisdom of archaic and world religion and psychotherapy. According to Shimazono, the main aims of the Japanese New Age Movement are the reformation of the self and the realization of 'spirituality', the quest for a new state of consciousness that exceeds modern science and western culture and for a unification of science and 'spirituality' [cf. Shimazono (1996), p. 51].

The 'spiritual intellectuals' borrow terms from the New Age as for instance 'deep ecology' – or, not to forget, 'spirituality' –, terms, which seem to resonate with meaning. As is typical of New Age thought, they discuss the future and the proper means to shape it. The 'spiritual intellectuals' stress the significance of Eastern religion in efforts to conceive a new paradigm of science, a notion that became popular in Japan through the translations of books by the New Age-authors like Fritjof Capra.[5] They expound on the general importance of experience, often even 'mystic experience', for the understanding of Japanese religion, a notion that is fundamental to New Age thinking. While New Age thought investigates so-called ancient wisdom for solutions of modern society, as, for example, the destruction of nature, the 'spiritual intellectuals' present a

---

Age see also Zinser (1997) and Bochinger (1994). While the process of defining the New Age is an ongoing one, in this article the term will be used to refer to the popularity of religious, esoteric, and occult ideas and practices across broad sectors of society striving for the transformation of the self and the planet.

[4] Cf. Shimazono (1996), Prohl (1997) and the special issue of the *Japanese Journal of Religious Studies*, with the title *The New Age in Japan* [JJRS (1995)].

[5] Fritjof Capra's 1975 book *The Tao of physics* (Ger.: *Das Tao der Physik. Die Konvergenz von westlicher Wissenschaft und östlicher Philosophie.* 1984) has been translated by Yoshifuku Shin'ichi 吉福伸逸 et al. into Japanese as *Tao shizengaku* タオ自然学 (1979); his 1982 book *The Turning Point: Science, Society, and the Rising Culture* was translated into Japanese as *Tāningu pointo* ターニング・ポイント (1984); both volumes have been published by Kōsakusha.

vision of Japanese religion where the worship of nature, and coexistence with it, plays an important role. All this is, of course, preserved in Shintō. However, there is little evidence that Japanese religion, or at least Japanese religious history, may hold solutions for the problems of modern society on offer, or, as the Buddhologist Matsumoto Shirō 松本史朗 elaborates on the subject of the worship of nature in Japanese religion:

> "Let us not forget, either, that the ecological movements of today were not generated by Eastern naturalism. They were initiated by Westerners, and founded on the traditions of rationalism and respect for human rights. It is simply not logically possible to derive the environmental movement and environmental ethics from an Eastern naturalism expressed in such phrases as "mountains, rivers, plants, and trees are all enlightened". Such 'naturalism' leads nowhere but to the 'natural state of doing nothing'. It does not direct us to think or actively to seek remedies to our problems." [Matsumoto (1997b), p. 403]

The categorization of religion together with a very special view of Japanese Shintō are freshened up with borrowings from New Age thought in order to make claims about the superiority of Japanese religion. In this sense, the texts of the three authors introduced here as well as other 'spiritual intellectuals' belong to the current discourse on Japanese religion that has strongly affirmative as well as nationalistic tendencies.

## 2. The functions of the discourse on Japanese religion

The question which functions these writings fulfill in Japanese society, remains. The authors introduced in this paper are not located on the fringes of Japanese society. Rather, they occupy prominent positions in the cultural mainstream. They are highly visible in the Japanese media and their books are published by powerful publishers such as PHP. As the _nihonjinron_ themselves, their writings or performances have become part of mass culture. Peter Dale describes the _nihonjinron_ as a "commercialized expression of modern Japanese nationalism" [Dale (1986), p. 14], a point which is also true for the writings of the 'spiritual intellectual', especially when they publish their views in glossy magazines like *Geijutsu shinchō* 芸術新潮 [cf., for instance, Umehara (1996)] or *Taiyō* 太陽 [cf., for instance, Yamaori (1988)]. As Shimazono points out, the discourse on Japanese religion popular during the 1990s, bestows upon its readers a feeling of safety and belonging to a group. According to Winston Davis, the *nihonjinron* act as a civil religion for Japan. He notes:

*"Many of the functions of the civil religion of pre-1945 Japan – the generation of national purpose, symbolic self-defense, value-consensus etc. – are now being assumed by the symbols, values, and imagery produced by the literature of Japan theory."* [Davis (1992), p. 269]

In an article of 1998, Davis specifies his view:

*"In countries like Japan, [...] national identity seems to have relatively little to do with conventional, institutional religion. The religion that remains important for the identity of the Japanese today is one that manifests itself in para-institutional, diffuse forms. While Japanese identity does not necessarily depend on religion, religion continues to be used to bear witness to the alleged uniqueness of the 'Japanese spirit'."* [Davis (1998), p. 169]

In this sense, one may call the International Research Center for Japanese Studies (国際日本文化研究センター, Nichibunken) in Kyōto – an institution with which many of the authors who participate in the 'spiritual discourse' are affiliated – the temple of the truly living Japanese religion of the 21st century. One could argue that some of the 'spiritual intellectuals' act like priests in a cult at the Nichibunken, an institution that provides *"a façade for the promotion of ideas of cultural supremacy"*, as Matsumoto Shirō puts it [Matsumoto (1997a), p. 359]. The cult they are engaged in is the cult of the superiority of the Japanese nation. Like a religious cult, the ideas formulated in this cult affect the resolution of social conflicts. Religion helps to balance these conflicts by transposing their solutions into the transcendental sphere. The texts of the 'spiritual intellectuals' perform a similar feat. The quest for harmony with nature can be construed as criticism of such negative aspects of modernization as alienation and rationalization.

The nationalistic tendencies in their visions have parallels in the teachings of some very popular New Religions in Japan, for example the *Kōfuku no Kagaku* 幸福の科学 ('Institute for Research in Human Happiness') or *World Mate* ワールドメイト.[6] The leader of World Mate, Fukami Tōshū 深見東州 claims, that Japan has a very special relationship with the world of gods. He postulates that under the roof of Shintō, universalistic values developed and will bring salvation to mankind.[7] It seems safe to argue that the 'spiritual intellectuals' provide the ideological foundations for the nationalistic notions of some of the new religions. On the other hand, the New Religions support the activities of authors and academics belonging to the 'spiritual intellectuals'. The best example is the International Shinto Foundation (*Shintō kokusai gakkai* 神道国際学会), an academic association that intends to enlighten the world about both, Shintō as Japan's indigenous religion and Shintō as a salvational religion for the world.[8] The above-mentioned Fukami Tōshū notes in the newsletter of the foundation:

> *"Shinto has been the essence of Japanese culture, and yet for the half century that has elapsed since the last war, Shintoists have been reticent in presenting their faith to the world, and seem to have been content to allow the word "Shinto" itself to go misunderstood or at best partially understood, in other Asian countries as well as in the West. A system of belief comparable to the great religions, Shinto has for two thousands [sic!] years been practiced and respected by the Japanese people, influencing their daily life and providing the source of their culture, but its true face has been allowed to go unrecognized. I perceived that there was a ground swell of feeling among serious practitioners and genuine scholars of Shinto that a way through this situation must be found to arouse international interest in Shinto. It was in February of 1994 that I resolved to take action, and began to consult with like minded people."* [Fukami (1996), p. 3]

Fukami Tōshū seems to have been very successful with his intention, because he was able to win many respected scholars as members of this association, as,

---

[6] On nationalistic tendencies in these two New Religions, see Shimazono (1993b).

[7] Cf., for instance, Fukami (1991). On World Mate, see Prohl (1999).

[8] See the homepage of the ISF <http://www.shinto.or.jp>, the *International Shinto Foundation Newsletter* and the publication of papers given at conferences of the IFS (announced on the IFS homepage). For further information see also Antoni (forthcoming).

for instance, Sonoda Minoru 蘭田稔 (Kyōto University), Ueda Kenji 上田賢治 (former president of Kokugakuin University), John Breen (University of London) as well as Kamata Tōji and Yamaori Tetsuo. The fact that this association is financially sponsored by *World Mate* is at least dubious. The fact that these scholars are willing to accept Fukami, leader of a new religion, as vice-president, might demonstrate the profundity of the need of cultural self-ascertainment among scholars of religion in Japan.[9]

### Conclusion

Why is it that religion, or to put it more accurately, the debate on religion, plays such an important role in the actual discourse on Japanese culture?

Firstly, the scholarly study of religion, *Religionswissenschaft*, has conjured up many terms that remain vague and act on an emotional level. As do magic formulas, they rely on assumptions that are not subject to critical analysis but are rather based on fascination and belief. Terms like 'animism' and 'shamanism' help to suspend the confrontation with social realities and to create awe of presumed other forms of reality. In employing these magic formulas, authors are able to assume transcendental positions – as for instance the uniqueness of the Japanese religion – that are not unlike the positions formulated by religious teachings themselves. Particularly the term 'spiritual' has proved to be a highly useful notion because of its vagueness and its reference to a particular state of mind. It indicates a special sort of experience, and in doing so allows a retreat to the last bastion of resistance against scientific analysis, the personal self. Therefore, this label helps to support the proclaimed newness and uniqueness of the findings of the 'spiritual intellectuals'.

---

[9] It is also interesting to note that the activities of Fukami Tōshū which he offered under the names *Cosmocoa*, *Cosmomeito* and *Cosmoworld* were not specifically hold religious by the group. It seems as if the possibility of tax exemption was one of the main motivations to unite the activities under the label 'religion' [cf. Mizoguchi (1995), Prohl (2001)]. Taking this development under consideration, it becomes even more clear that the underlying subject of Fukami Tōshū's teaching as well as the ISF is not necessarily religion but the construction of a positive, self-assertive image of Japan.

Secondly, religion seems to be something venerable und holy that should be treated with respect and not be subjected to criticism. Therefore, the subject of religion is particularly suitable to lend weight to claims of superiority.

Thirdly, speaking about religion possesses a certain level of entertainment value. The history of religion offers a wide variety of works of art that express aesthetic assertions about the world beyond. These aesthetic expressions can be used to increase the entertainment value of religion. With pictures or references to Buddha-statues, mandalas or Shintō-shrines, emotions and special frames of mind can be created – feelings that should however not be confused with religion itself. The subject of religion also offers performative qualities, which are particularly suitable for the discourse on Japanese religion acting as a kind of experiential science (_Erlebniswissenschaft_).

Speaking about religion not only bestows upon its audience the feeling that they learn something new, but also makes for good entertainment. The Japanese audience is assured that whatever problems the 21$^{st}$ century and globalization may hold, Japan will deal with them because of its unique religion, which has a salvational potential not only for the Japanese but for the human race. At least parts of the foreign audience are over–awed by this New Age celebration of Eastern-thought. They do not recognize the discourse on Japanese religion formulated by the 'spiritual intellectuals' as something familiar. It is in fact an orientalist discourse with reversed roles where the self-proclaimed Orientals are doing the orientalizing – or to put it in other words: the 'spiritual discourse' contains some sort of orientalizing of the self (_Selbstorientalismus_). The writings of the 'spiritual intellectuals' promise salvation on the basis of Japanese 'spirituality', which they declare to be superior. However nicely it is phrased, this promise implies the inferiority of other religious worldviews and one is therefore apt to see it as a kind of religious nationalism.

## References

Antoni (1998)
Antoni, Klaus: *Shintō und die Konzeption des japanischen Nationalwe-
sens (*kokutai*): Der religiöse Traditionalismus in Neuzeit und Moderne.*
[Handbuch der Orientalistik, part 5, vol. 8] Leiden: E. J. Brill, 1998.

—  (forthcoming)
Antoni, Klaus: "Shintō und der 'fremde Blick' auf Japan", in: Prohl/
Zinser (forthcoming).

Befu (1993)
Befu, Harumi: "Nationalism and Nihonjinron", in: Befu, Harumi (ed.):
*Cultural Nationalism in East Asia: Representation and Identity.*
University of California at Berkeley: Institute of East Asian Studies, 1993,
pp. 107-135.

Bochinger (1994)
Bochinger, Christoph: *'New Age' und moderne Religion: Religions-
wissenschaftliche Analysen.* Gütersloh: Gütersloher Verlagshaus, 1994.

Bolle (1987)
Bolle, Klees W.: "Animism and Animatism", in: Eliade, Mircea (ed.):
*Encyclopaedia of Religion.* New York: Macmillan, 1987, pp. 296-302.

Dale (1986)
Dale, Peter D.: *The Myth of Japanese Uniqueness.* New York: St.
Martin's Press, 1986.

Davis (1992)
Davis, Winston: *Japanese Religion and Society: Paradigms of Structure
and Change.* New York: State University of New York Press, 1992.

—  (1998)
Davis, Winston: "Religion and National Identity in Modern and
Postmodern Japan", in: Heelas, Paul (ed.): *Religion, Modernity and
Postmodernity.* Oxford: Blackwell, 1998, pp. 169-185.

Eliade (1975)
Eliade, Mircea: *Schamanismus und archaische Ekstasetechnik.* [Eng. orig.
1951] Frankfurt/Main: Suhrkamp, 1975. [Jap. transl.: Hori Ichirō 堀一郎:
*Shāmanizumu* シャーマニズム. Tōkyō: Tōjusha, 1974]

Fischer (2000/2001)
 Fischer, Peter: "Zu einigen Problemen der "Shintō"-Wörterbücher in
 westlichen Sprachen im Kontext der "Shintō"-Forschung allgemein", in:
 _Nachrichten der Gesellschaft für Natur- und Völkerkunde Ostasiens/
 Hamburg_, vol. 167-170 (2000/2001), pp. 347-381.

Fukami (1991)
 Fukami, Seizan [Tōshū 東州] 深見青山: _Kiseki no kaiun 奇跡の開運._
 Tōkyō: Gakken, 1991.

— (1996)
 Fukami, Tōshū: "Progress of the International Shinto Foundation", in:
 _International Shinto Foundation Newsletter_, No. 2 (1996), p. 3.

Gebhardt (2001)
 Gebhardt, Lisette: "'Okkultismus' als identitätsbildender Faktor oder
 warum es in Japan derzeit _en vogue_ ist, von den Geistern zu sprechen", in:
 Gössmann, Hilaria/ Mrugalla, Andreas (ed.): _11. Deutschsprachiger
 Japanologentag in Trier 1999, vol. 1._ [Ostasien-Pazifik: Trierer Studien
 zu Politik, Wirtschaft, Gesellschaft, Kultur; vol. 13] Hamburg: Lit Verlag,
 2001, pp. 703-714.

— (forthcoming)
 Gebhardt, Lisette: "Ein Nobelpreisträger als New Ager. Der Fall Ōe
 Kenzaburō", in: Prohl/ Zinser (forthcoming).

Hakamaya (1997)
 Hakamaya, Noriaki: "Scholarship as Criticism", in: Hubbard/ Swanson
 (1997), pp. 113-144.

Heelas (1996)
 Heelas, Paul: _The New Age Movement._ Oxford: Blackwell, 1996.

Hubbard/ Swanson (1997)
 Hubbard, Jamie/ Swanson, Paul L. (ed.): _Pruning the Bodhi Tree: The
 Storm over Critical Buddhism._ Honolulu: University of Hawai'i Press,
 1997.

Iwata (1993)
 Iwata, Keiji 岩田慶治: _Animizumu no jidai アニミズムの時代._ Tōkyō:
 Hōzōkan, 1993.

— (1996)
 Iwata, Keiji 岩田慶治: "Kuroi mizu no naka no kuroi sakana 黒い水のな
 かの黒い魚" In: _Bukkyō 仏教_, vol. 36/ 7 (1996), pp. 14-21.

JJRS (1995)
> *Japanese Journal of Religious Studies: The New Age in Japan.* Special
> issue, vol. 22/3-4 (1995).

Kamata/ Tsumura (1994)
> Kamata, Tōji 鎌田東二/ Tsumura, Takashi 津村喬 (ed.): *Tenkawa
> mandara: Chōshūkyō e no channeru 天川曼陀羅：超宗教への水路.*
> Tōkyō: Shunjūsha, 1994.

Kamata (1995)
> Kamata, Tōji 鎌田東二: *Shūkyō to reisei 宗教と霊性.* Tōkyō: Kadokawa,
> 1995.

Kohl (1998)
> Kohl, Karl-Heinz: "Der postmoderne Wilde", in: *Psychologie heute*,
> February 1998, pp. 58-63.

Kuroda (1993)
> Kuroda, Toshio: "Shinto in the History of Japanese Religion", in: Mullins,
> Mark R./ Shimazono, Susumu/ Swanson, Paul L. (ed.): *Religion &
> Society in Modern Japan.* Berkeley: Asian Humanities Press, 1993, pp.
> 7-30.

Matsumoto (1997a)
> Matsumoto, Shirō: "Buddhism and the Kami: Against Japanism", in:
> Hubbard/ Swanson (1997), pp. 357-373.

—    (1997b)
> Matsumoto, Shirō: "The *Lotus Sutra* and Japanese Culture", in: Hubbard/
> Swanson (1997), pp. 388-403.

Mizoguchi (1995)
> Mizoguchi, Osamu 溝口敦: "Wārudomeito: Seishinsangyō toshite no
> shūkyō ワールドメイト：精神産業としての宗教", in: Shimizu, Masato 清
> 水雅人 (ed.): *Shinshūkyō jidai 新宗教時代 3.* Tōkyō: Daizō, 1995, pp.
> 163-194.

Nakazawa (1992)
> Nakazawa, Shin'ichi 中沢新一: *Mori no barokku 森のバロック.* Tōkyō:
> Serika, 1992.

—    (1993)
> Nakazawa, Shin'ichi 中沢新一: *Shūkyō nyūmon 宗教入門.* Tōkyō:
> Madora, 1993.

Naumann (1988)
> Naumann, Nelly: _Die einheimische Religion Japans. Teil 1. Bis zum Ende der Heian-Zeit._ [Handbuch der Orientalistik, part 5, vol. 4, sect. 1, no. 1] Leiden: E. J. Brill, 1988.

— (1994)
> Naumann, Nelly: _Die einheimische Religion Japans, Teil 2. Synkretistische Lehren und religiöse Entwicklungen von der Kamakura- bis zum Beginn der Edo-Zeit._ [Handbuch der Orientalistik, part 5, vol. 4, sect. 1, no. 2] Leiden: E. J. Brill, 1994.

Prohl (1997)
> Prohl, Inken: "Zwischen 'Spiritualität' und Kommerz: Einige Anmerkungen zum New Age in Japan", in: _Spirita. Zeitschrift für Religionswissenschaft_, vol. 11/2 (1997), pp. 12-15.

— (1999)
> Prohl, Inken: "Inszeniertes Wissen: Zum Seminar- und Workshopangebot der japanischen New-Age-Szene", in: Schubert, Volker (ed.): _Lernkultur – Das Beispiel Japan._ Weinheim: Beltz - Deutscher Studien Verlag, 1999, pp. 265-276.

— (2000)
> Prohl, Inken: _Die "spirituellen Intellektuellen" und das New Age in Japan._ [Mitteilungen der Gesellschaft für Natur- und Völkerkunde Ostasiens; vol. 133] Hamburg: MOAG, 2000.

Prohl/ Zinser (forthcoming)
> Prohl, Inken/ Zinser, Hartmut (ed.): _Zen, Reiki und Karate: Japanische Religiosität in Europa._ [Bunka – Tübinger interkulturelle und linguistische Japanstudien/ Tuebingen intercultural and linguistic studies on Japan; vol. 2] Hamburg, London: Lit Verlag, 2001. [forthcoming]

Schlatter (1988)
> Schlatter, Gerhard: "Animismus", in: Cancik, Hubert et al. (ed.): _Handbuch religionswissenschaftlicher Grundbegriffe, vol. 1._ [4 vols.] Stuttgart: Kohlhammer, 1988, pp. 473-476.

Shimazono (1993a)
> Shimazono, Susumu: "New Age and New Spiritual Movements: The Role of Spiritual Intellectuals", in: _Syzygy: Journal of Alternative Religion and Culture_, vol. 1/1-2 (1993), pp. 9–22.

— (1993b)

Shimazono, Susumu 島薗進: "Kosumomeito to Kōfuku no kagaku: Jiko shuchōteki 'shintō' nashonarizumu to shinshinshūkyō コスモメイトと幸福の科学：自己主張的「神道」ナショナリズムと新新宗教'', in: *Shintō o shiru hon 神道を知る本.* [Bessatsu Takarajima 別冊宝島] Tōkyō: Takarajimasha, 1993, pp. 151-154.

— (1995)

Shimazono, Susumu 島薗進: "Nihonjinron to shūkyō 日本人論と宗教", in: *Tōkyō daigaku shūkyōgaku nenpō 東京大学宗教学年報,* vol. 13 (1995), pp. 1-16.

— (1996)

Shimazono, Susumu 島薗進: *Seishin sekai no yukue: Gendai shakai to shinreisei undō 精神世界のゆくえ：現代社会と新霊性運動. New Spirituality Movements in the Global Society.* Tōkyō: Tōkyōdō, 1996.

Tylor (1873)

Tylor, Edward B.: *Die Anfänge der Cultur: Untersuchungen über die Entwicklung der Mythologie, Philosophie, Religion, Kunst und Sitte.* 2 vols. (a + b). Leipzig: C.F. Winter'sche Verlagshandlung, 1873 [1871].

Umehara (1991)

Umehara, Takeshi 梅原猛: *Mori no shisō ga jinrui o sukuu 森の思想が人類を救う.* Tōkyō: Shogakukan, 1991.

— (1996)

Umehara, Takeshi 梅原猛: "Kamigami ga kataru nihonshi 神々が語る日本史", in: *Geijutsu shinchō 芸術新潮. Tokushū: Nihon no kamigami 特集：日本の神々,* vol. 47/3 (1996), pp. 200-234.

Umehara/ Yamaori (1995)

Umehara, Takeshi 梅原猛/ Yamaori, Tetsuo 山折哲雄: *Shūkyō no jisatsu: Nihonjin no atarashii shinkō o motomete 宗教の自殺：日本人の新しい信仰を求めて.* Tōkyō: PHP, 1995.

Yamaori (1988)

Yamaori, Tetsuo 山折哲雄: "Jigoku-kan no genryū 地獄観の源流", in: *Bessatsu Taiyō 別冊太陽,* no. 62 (1988), pp. 97-106.

York (1995)

York, Michael: *The Emerging Network: A Sociology of the New Age and Neo-Pagan Movements.* Boston: Rowmann & Littlefield, 1995.

Yoshino (1992)

    Yoshino, Kōsaku: *Cultural Nationalism in Contemporary Japan: A Sociological Enquiry.* London and New York: Routledge, 1992.

Zinser (1997)

    Zinser, Hartmut: *Der Markt der Religionen.* München: Wilhelm Fink, 1997.

# Hachiman – Protecting *kami* of the Japanese Nation

Martin REPP

*Introduction*[1]

The early Jesuit reports on Japan already portray Hachiman as the Japanese "deity of war". Vilela writes that the Japanese regard Hachiman "*as their guardian spirit [Patron] in their wars as we [Europeans] regard Santiago or St. George*" [Schurhammer (1923), p. 76]. Another report compares Hachiman with Mars.[2] This portrayal of Hachiman as war deity (*bushin* 武神) has endured into religious studies of the 20th century.[3] Recent research by Ross Bender and others, however, has drawn a different image of this *kami* 神 – Hachiman as the protecting deity of the Japanese nation. While Bender [(1979), p. 145] treated mainly what he calls the "*political meaning of Hachiman*" during the Nara period, in the following presentation I expand the investigation of Hachiman's political significance from the Nara to the Kamakura period in order to present a broader picture.

## 1. Origins of Hachiman belief

The origins of Hachiman belief are obscure. Nakano Hatayoshi [(1985), p. 28 and pp. 33-71; cf. (1986), pp. 3-34], the authority of Hachiman studies, suggests that the Hachiman cult developed as an amalgamation of Japanese animistic and Korean shamanistic elements and that it eventually came to be located in Usa

---

[1] The author wishes to express his gratitude to Robert Duquenne and Alexander Kabanoff for helpful suggestions and to Mark Meli for correcting the English.

[2] P. Francisco Pasio remarks about Hideyoshi's (1536-98) last will: "*Er wollte daher fortan unter den Camis sein, so heißen nämlich die großen Herren, die sich einst durch Kriegsruhm ausgezeichnet haben und die man nach deren Tod unter die Götter versetzt wähnt. Genannt werden aber wollte er Scinfaciman (Shin Hachiman), das heißt, der 'Neue Hachiman', denn wie einst bei den Römern Mars der Kriegsgott war, so gilt Hachiman bei den Japanern als Gott des Krieges.*" [Schurhammer (1923), p. 90].

[3] See for example Casal (1962) and Weinstein (1983). For a treatment of Hachiman as *bushin* see Nakano (1985), pp. 171-182.

(Kyūshū) during the 6th century. Especially the Usa 宇佐, Karashima 辛島 and Ōga 大神 clans and their belief in clan deities (*ujigami* 氏神) seemed to have played important roles in the formation of the cult. The fact that the Karashima clan originates from Korea, and the geographical proximity of Usa to the continent give an international flavor to the cult, in other words, Hachiman appears as a deity at the periphery who is able to mediate between the two countries. The Hachiman cult in Usa seems to be related first of all to metallurgy, but it also comprises diverse functions of mountain *kami*, sea *kami*, and also the *kami* of land and fertility, as phallic symbols at Usa suggest [cf. Casal (1962), p. 3, pp. 19f; Grapard (1986), p. 35].

Etymological explanations of Hachiman's name do not contribute much to the understanding of his origin and character. The original reading of the name was *yahata*, the pronunciation *hachiman* resulted from later Buddhist Sino-Japanese readings of the Chinese characters [Nakano (1985), p. 10]. Early documents refer to him as *ya-hata* or *yawata* 八畠, meaning the "eight fields" or, according to different kanji 八幡, "eight flags" or "banners".[4] For the latter case it is assumed that the name derives from the eight banners of traditional Chinese military formations. The number "eight" signifies the eight horizontal directions, according to which the formation of the army was structured and which were marked by eight banners.

Although the historical origins of Hachiman's worship and name remain obscure, one outstanding character of his cult seems to be clear from early historical records onwards, namely its oracular function. Hachiman pronounced oracles (*takusen* 託宣, *otsuge* お告) through possession of shrine maidens (*miko* or *fujo* 巫女), induced by music and dance, and deciphered by male interpreters (*saniwa* さ庭).[5]

Finally it may be noted that in present Japan at least one third of Shintō shrines are dedicated to Hachiman, these being surpassed in number only by

---

[4] Another rendering of *yahata* is 矢幡 ("arrow flag", or "arrow and flag"); cf. Nakano (1985), p. 64. For a discussion of various theories concerning the origins of the name see also Saigō (1986), pp. 8-12.

[5] According to Bender (1979), p. 136, this function is called *kanzukasa* 神祇官, which is to be distinguished from the *jingi-kan* (office for religious affairs at court), the Sino-Japanese reading of the same characters. For a brief outline of medieval oracular practice see Grapard (1999), pp. 558f. The oracles were later (since the Kamakura Period) collected in books like the *Hachiman Usa-gū gotakusen-shū* 八幡宇佐宮御託宣集 (14th century). Cf. ibid.; Nakano (1985), p. 39.

Inari shrines.[6] Hachiman shrines' main symbolic representations are the dove, a symbol for fertility, and the *mitsu tomoe* 三ツ巴, the threefold comma in a circle,[7] representing a whirl or whirlwind.

### 2. The Nara Period (710-784)

Hachiman's name does not appear in the *Kojiki* 古事記 and *Nihongi* 日本紀 [Casal (1962), p. 2]. His first historical record is found in the *Shoku-nihongi* 続 日本紀. It reports that in the year 737 offerings were sent to the Usa and some other shrines because of frictions with Silla [Bender (1979), p. 130]. Next, the *Shoku-nihongi* records that in 740 the deputy governor of Kyūshū, Fujiwara no Hirotsugu 藤原廣嗣, staged a revolt, and that the Yamato court ordered the general Ōno Azumabito 大野東人 to pray to Hachiman and then to subdue Hirotsugu. The deputy governor attempted to flee to Silla, but a storm prevented him from escape. Subsequently he was captured and decapitated. For the divine help, the Court rewarded the Usa shrine with donations such as land, horses, and servants, and a pagoda was built in its precincts [Bender (1979), p. 132]. The latter indicates an early affiliation of Hachiman worship with Buddhism, which is another indicator of its foreign connections. According to the *Jōwa engi* 承和 縁起, in 720 "*the priests of the Hachiman Shrine led a 'divine army' that successfully subjugated the rebellious Hayato in Osumi and Hyūga provinces*" [Guth (1985), p. 39]. The people from the southern part of Kyūshū apparently tried to resist the attempt by the Yamato court to unify and centralize the country.[8] In this case, the Hachiman shrine was instrumental in the central government's endeavor to get all parts of Kyūshū under its control. These early reports indicate certain patterns of Hachiman interventions, that – as a formidable spiritual power – he would be able to cope with external threats and internal revolts. It may be recalled that as a deity for metallurgy Hachiman was connected with casting of swords, and through this function he was naturally

---

[6] According to Nakano (1985), p. 10, among the 120,000 shrines in Japan today are 40,000 Hachiman shrines. Their number ranks second to that of Inari shrines. Cf. Casal (1962), p. 23. For differing accounts see Herbert (1967), p. 437.

[7] As such it represents a further development of the *yin-yang* 陰陽 sign (Jap. *in'yō*).

[8] While the *Shoku-nihongi* reports the uprising of the Hayato 隼人, it does not mention Hachiman's role in their defeat. Cf. Bender (1979), p. 131.

affiliated with warfare. This early pattern of Hachiman's dealing with external and internal threats will be also a characteristic of his future role.[9]

During the Nara period occurred two events of national significance in which Hachiman played a crucial role: the construction of Tōdai-ji 東大寺 and the so-called Dōkyō 道鏡-incident, a monk's attempt to usurp the throne.

First, the construction of the Tōdai-ji. According to the *Shoku-nihongi*, Hachiman was instrumental in the most ambitious building project of the Nara period, the construction of Tōdai-ji and its Daibutsu 大仏.[10] In 741 Shōmu 聖武 -tennō had issued an edict for constructing the *kokubun-ji* 国分寺, Buddhist state temples in each province. The temples for monks were called *konkōmyō shitennō gokoku no tera* 金光明四天王護国之寺, temples for the protection of the country by the four heavenly [guardian] kings of the Golden Light[-sūtra[11]]. These temples served the efforts of the *tennō* to unite the country. On the top of this provincial temple system Shōmu designed a central state temple in the capital, the Tōdai-ji in Nara, as symbol of national unity and imperial rule. It is not precisely clear how Hachiman contributed to this enormous construction project, but he surely was believed to have played an important role in it, probably through oracles in 747 and 749 promising the discovery of copper and gold for the casting of the huge Buddha statue [Nakano (1985), pp. 111f.]. Thereupon Hachiman announced by oracle in 749 that he wished to reside in the capital next to the Daibutsu. Subsequently, his divine body (*shintai* 神体) was brought in a procession from Usa to Nara and enshrined appropriately in the Hachiman-gū[12] on Tamuke-yama 手向山 next to Tōdai-ji.[13] When in 752 the

---

[9] Another example for Hachiman's role in spiritual warfare during the Nara period is his support in a fight against the Ainu, for which in 764 the Yahata-jinja in Yamagata-shi was erected. Cf. Herbert (1967), pp. 435f.

[10] The huge Buddha statue is a representation of (in Skt.) Mahā-vairocana, in Jap. Birushana, Roshana or Dainichi 大日.

[11] Together with the Lotus Sutra and the Ninnō-gyō one of the three sutras which are believed to protect the country.

[12] The transfer of a divine body (*shintai*) from one shrine to another is conceived of as a "*partition of the [divine] spirit*" (*bunrei* 分霊); cf. Herbert (1967), pp. 122f. Through such processes, a system of a main shrine and branch shrines could later be established.

[13] The fact that Hachiman was transferred from Kyūshū to Nara distinguishes him from a local deity, who was already dwelling at a certain place where a (foreign) Buddhist temple would be established and who then was enshrined and venerated as protecting deity (*jinushi no kami* 地主の神, *chinju no kami* 鎮守の神) of the respective temple. Hachiman's role at

dedication ceremony (*kaigan kuyō* 開眼供養) for the Daibutsu was held in Nara, Hachiman also received due recognition. According to the *Shoku-nihongi* the emperor issued an edict stating:

> "*In a recent year, we worshipped the Roshana Buddha at Chishikiji in the Agata district of Kōchi. Because we desired to construct such an image and yet were unable to do so, we appealed to the Great God Hachiman of the broad Ways who dwells in the Usa district of Buzen province.*"[14]

For his invaluable help, then, Hachiman was much honored: the emperor bestowed on the *kami* the first court rank. This event marks the rise of Hachiman from a local deity on the periphery to a national deity at the center of the state, endowed with the highest court rank. Accordingly, the priestess of Usa shrine received the second court rank, thereby exceeding the rank of the highest official at Amaterasu's shrine in Ise. It is also remarkable that in this event a native deity served as authorization for Buddhism, a religion foreign to Japan, which again served as religious legitimation for the state's unity and the emperor's authority. Thus, Hachiman became the *protector of state-protecting Buddhism*.

Second, after his involvement in the construction of the Daibutsu, Hachiman's political role reached another climax during the Nara period in the so-called Dōkyō-incident. Dōkyō 道鏡 was an influential Nara monk who healed the ex-empress Kōken 孝謙 in 761.[15] Subsequently, due to a power vacuum at court – the Fujiwara had temporarily lost influence at this time – Dōkyō was able to climb up in the court hierarchy and eventually in 765 became Chancellor (*daijō daijin* 大政大臣), that is, he held the highest office in the bureaucracy. In 766, Dōkyō received the title *hō-ō* 法王 (Dharma king) while the emperor or empress were traditionally called *hō-ō* 法皇; through his new title the monk was promoted to the same level as the empress.[16]

---

the Tōdai-ji seems to differ somehow because he serves on a political and national level as legitimation of state Buddhism (which is incorporated in Tōdai-ji) and as authorization of imperial rule.

[14] Bender (1979), p. 135. For a translation of the whole passage of the *Shoku-nihongi* (Tenpyō-shōhō 天平勝宝 1/12/27) see Bender (1979), pp. 135f. For a later (Kamakura period) report of this event see Brown/ Ishida (1979), p. 33.

[15] The daughter of Shōmu-tennō 聖武天皇 reigned under the name Kōken from 749-758, and again from 764-770 under the name Shōtoku 称徳.

[16] The *Shoku-nihongi* calls the relationship of the empress to the monk "affection" or "favor" (*chōkō* 寵), only later Heian traditions constructed a scandalous relationship.

During his time at court, Dōkyō fostered also a close relationship with the Usa shrine by repeatedly donating land [Bender (1979), pp. 140f.]. In 769, the *Shoku-nihongi* reports, a shrine priest *"fabricated a pronouncement of Hachiman,*[17] *which said: 'Let Dōkyō be made emperor and there shall be great peace in the realm'."*. The empress, however, after having a dream, sent Wake no Kiyomaro 和気清麿 to Usa to inquire about Hachiman's true intention. Kiyomaro, appealing to the kami that this is *"a matter of grave importance for the state"* [Bender (1979), p. 143; *Nihon-kōki* 日本後記, Enryaku 延暦 18/2/21], received the following oracle:

> *"Since the establishment of our state the distinction between lord and subject has been fixed. Never has been there an occasion when a subject was made lord. The throne of heavenly sun succession shall be given to one of the imperial lineage; wicked persons should immediately be swept away."* [Bender (1979), p. 142; *Shoku-nihongi*, Jingo-keiun 神護景雲 3/9/25]

When Kiyomaro returned and delivered this message, Dōkyō sent him immediately into exile. However, some time later, Dōkyō himself was exiled, and Kiyomaro rehabilitated.[18]

During the Dōkyō incident, Hachiman eventually provided the ultimate legitimation for the imperial family succession.[19] Hachiman prevented the Japanese imperial dynasty from being replaced by Buddhocracy.[20] It is also noteworthy

---

[17] A previous case for the abuse of Hachiman's oracle is reported for 755. According to the *Shoku-nihongi*, in this year the Usa priest Tamaro "conspired" with a priest of Yakushi-ji in Nara and "practiced sorcery" whereupon Tamaro and the priestess Morime lost their court rank and were exiled. This incident apparently had to do with improper acquisition of land for the shrine, because the *Shoku-nihongi* records an oracle by Hachiman for the following year stating: *"We do not desire that false pronouncements be made of Our will. There is no use for the excess lands and households that have been received, and they are as though abandoned on a mountain. They should be returned to the court, and only the permanent shrine lands should be retained ..."* [Bender (1979), p. 137; *Shoku-nihongi*, Tempyō-shōhō 天平勝宝 7/3/28].

[18] Some time after Wake no Kiyomaro's death a shrine was build for him in gratitude for his service to the throne, which later during the Meiji period (1886) was moved to the west side of the Gosho 御所 (Imperial Palace) in Kyōto with the new name Goō-jinja 護王神社, shrine protecting the *tennō*.

[19] Bender (1979), p. 146 calls Hachiman (during the Nara period) the *"ultimate arbiter of legitimacy"*.

[20] Bender (1979), p. 152 sees in the Dōkyō incident competing concepts of imperial legitimacy at work. He writes: *"Dōkyō's ascent exacerbated the Buddhist challenge to the native political tradition, and in the incident of 769 the underlying crisis of legitimacy came*

that it was not Amaterasu at Ise, the ancestral deity of the imperial family, who intervened, but a local deity from the periphery. We shall encounter the problem of the relationship between Hachiman and Amaterasu later again.

## 3. Heian Period (794-1185)

The Heian period witnessed several innovations in Hachiman belief. Before we turn to these, a few cases should be mentioned which show the continuity of Hachiman's role during the Nara and Heian periods in legitimizing imperial rule, in guaranteeing imperial succession and in subduing unrest in the realm.

In 939, for example, Taira no Masakado 平将門 staged a revolt in the Kantō area, declared himself as the New Tennō (*shinnō* 新皇) and justified his claim with his descent from emperor Kanmu 桓武 and an oracle from Hachiman. However, Masakado's attempt at the throne was subdued [Takeuchi (1999), p. 654]. Another case concerns Emperor Heizei 平城 (r. 806-809) who had to abdicate because of ill health in 809. Shortly afterwards, however, he claimed the throne again. His brother Saga 嵯峨 (r. 809-823) who had become his successor in the meantime, asked Kūkai 空海 to direct prayers to Hachiman. Eventually Saga was able to suppress the attempted coup [Guth (1985), p. 54]. Like the Dōkyō incident and Masakado's revolt, this case represents another example of Hachiman's role in solving problems of imperial succession.

As in the Nara period, also during the Heian period we encounter Hachiman as the *kami* who is invoked in times of internal unrest. In 1081, for example, during fights between the warrior monks (*akusō* 悪僧) of Enryaku-ji and Mii-dera, Emperor Shirakawa 白河 visited Iwashimizu Hachiman-gū and Kamō Shrine for prayers while being guarded by the brothers Minamoto no Yoshiie 源義家 and Yoshitsuna 義綱 against attacks by Mii-dera monks. It is well known that the hordes of violent monks, particularly later during the *insei* 院政 period, frequently threatened the court and endangered national stability. This unrest may have been the reason for Shirakawa's pilgrimage.[21]

---

to the surface. [...] The final oracle, however, reaffirmed definitely the native theory of imperial legitimacy.".

[21] Cf. Hurst (1999), p. 596. It may be noted that Hachiman's help was invoked also for other purposes. Emperors visited the Iwashimizu in order to pray for health, such as Go-Sanjō 御三条 in 1073, cf. Hurst (1999), p. 593. Another case is Saichō 最澄 who prayed for a safe

We now turn to the innovations which the Heian period contributed to the Hachiman belief: First, the Buddhist identification of Hachiman-*daijin* 大神 (great *kami*), as he was called until then, as a *bodhisattva*, resulting in his new name Hachiman-*dai-bosatsu* 大菩薩. Second, the establishment of a third important Hachiman shrine in Japan, the Iwashimizu Hachiman-gū southwest of Heian-kyō. Third, Hachiman's identification with the emperor Ōjin 応神, that is, Hachiman came to be perceived as the incarnation of an emperor. And fourth, the Minamoto clan's adoption of Hachiman as their *ujigami*.

First, the Buddhist interpretation of Hachiman *daijin* as *dai-bosatsu*. Amalgamations of the native cult in Usa with Buddhist elements are reported already in the Nara period. Here a pagoda and the Miroku-ji were built during the 8th century, marking one of the first known native-Buddhist amalgamations, which are called *jingū-ji* 神宮寺 (shrine-temple multiplex). Also, in 720, after the defeat of the Hayato by the "divine army", a *hōjō-e* 放生会, Buddhist festival for the release of animals, was held for the pacification of the souls of those who had died in battle. This represents the first occasion that this ceremony was held in Japan. After the establishment of the Iwashimizu shrine near Kyōto and the Tsurugaoka Hachiman-gū in Kamakura, the *hōjō-e* became a major festival in these places as well.

According to the *Nihon-kōki* [Bender (1978), p. 166], the Bodhisattva title was conferred to Hachiman in 809.[22] However, according to the *Jōwa-engi*, already in 783 Hachiman pronounced himself to be a Bodhisattva [Guth (1985), p. 42]. Moreover, according to this source, Hachiman revealed himself in an oracle to be the *gokoku reigen iriki jinzū daijizai-ō bosatsu* 護国霊験威力神通大自在王菩薩 (great sovereign Bodhisattva king who protects the country with miraculous, extraordinary and divine powers) [Nakano (1985), p. 31]. This long title also reveals other Buddhist influences. The term *gokoku* (protecting the country), for example, originates from the Buddhist scriptures. In other words, when Buddhists identified the *kami* Hachiman as a Bodhisattva, at the same time

---

trip to China at the Usa Hachiman-gū in 814 and who lectured on the Lotus Sūtra there upon his return, cf. Dykstra (1983), p. 32. Other monks prayed for the attainment of awakening, cf. Dykstra (1983), p. 50; Morrell (1985), p. 76.

[22] This makes him "*Japan's most ancient combinatory system incorporating a local, indigenous deity and imported buddhas and bodhisattvas.*", Grapard (1986), p. 24f.

they specified him as state-protecting Bodhisattva.[23] Thus his title *gokoku reigen iriki jinzū daijizai-ō bosatsu* clearly recognizes the role he had begun to play in fact already since the Nara period, the protection of the country.[24] This title also appears frequently in later sources, which suggests that it became the standard Buddhist title for Hachiman.[25] It may also be noted that with the Buddhist appropriation of Hachiman, the oracular practice also changed so that the receivers of oracles were no longer shrine maidens (*miko*) but Buddhist priests.[26] This implies, of course, an important transfer of religious and political power.

With the establishment of the new capital Heian-kyō, the state temples Tō-ji and Sai-ji were built in the southern part in imitation of Nara's Tōdai-ji and Saidai-ji. Hachiman was adopted as protective deity (*chinju-jin* 鎮守神) for the Tō-ji during the Enryaku period (782-805) [Guth (1985), p. 41]. The Tō-ji also has preserved the oldest Hachiman image, which is designed after a monk or Bodhisattva. This kind of depiction is called *sōgyō* 僧形 Hachiman (Hachiman in form of a monk).[27] That means, a national deity is converted to Buddhism.[28]

---

[23] According to Sonoda (1997), p. 412, this Buddhist interpretation implied the double process of transforming *kami* through its humanistic teachings resulting in anthropomorphic behavior and imagery of the Japanese deities, and transforming Buddhism by including *kami* as protective deities into its pantheon. It may be added that the Buddhist interpretation of Hachiman as Bodhisattva also meant a considerable extension of sphere of influence and power of an originally local deity.

[24] The Heian period put into words what in fact already had developed since the Nara period.

[25] For example, the *Teiō hennen-ki* 帝王編年記 (late Heian period) calls Hachiman *gokoku reigen ishin dai-jizai-ō bosatsu* 護国霊験威神大自在王菩薩 [cf. Nichiren-shū shūmu-in (1999), p. 315; Nakano (1985), p. 25], while the *Tōdaiji yōroku* 東大寺要録 (12th century) and the *Rokugō kaizan Ninmon daibosatsu hongi* 六郷開山仁聞大菩薩本紀 (compiled after the Mongol invasions) present him as *gokoku reigen iriki jinzū daijizai-ō bosatsu* 護国霊験威力神通大自在王菩薩 [cf. Nakano (1985), p. 31; Grapard (1986), p. 36].

[26] The *miko* or *fujo* were replaced by the *fusō* 巫僧 [cf. Nakano (1985), pp. 76f., pp. 95f.]. This occurred, according to Grapard (1999), p. 558, after the year 839; however, according to Nakano (1985), p. 76, this already happened at Usa between 552 and 587.

[27] In her study of Hachiman imagery, Christine Guth Kanda elaborates the significance of Hachiman statues in the following way: "Shinzō *[images] of Hachiman are among the earliest extant portrayals of kami and compromise one of the largest single groups of statues of any single deity.*", Guth (1985), p. 3. Between the 9th and the 19th century, Hachiman "*is one of the few deities to have been represented continuously during this time span. While other deities known in painting or sculpture have only a regional following, the Hachiman cult is nationwide, and its images are found throughout Japan.*", Guth (1985), pp. 3f. "*Images of Hachiman are among the earliest; they are also the largest single group ranging from Oita Prefecture in the south to Nagano Prefecture in the north. Their number and distribution reveal the pervasiveness of Hachiman worship.*", Guth (1985), p. 35.

The Tō-ji is also called Kyō-ō gokoku-ji 教王護国寺, temple that protects the country through the *Ninnō gokoku-kyō*.[29] This shows that Hachiman kept his official role as *protector of state-protecting Buddhism* also during the transition from the Nara to the Heian period.[30]

The second innovation of Hachiman belief during the Heian period can be seen in the founding of Iwashimizu Hachiman-gū, the third important Hachiman shrine after Usa and Nara.[31] In 858, the chancellor Fujiwara Yoshifusa 藤原良房 (808-858) had ordered the monk Gyōkyō 行教 to conduct prayers at Usa Hachiman-gū on his behalf that his grandson, a son of emperor Montoku 文徳, would succeed to the throne. The prayers were successful, and Yoshifusa's grandson became the next emperor, Seiwa 清和-tennō (850-881, r. 858-876). Seiwa was only 8 years old when ascending the throne, thus becoming the first of a number of child emperors in Japan. This peculiar form of imperial succession, as well as "marriage politics" enabled the Fujiwara to dominate the emperors through the office of regency. Soon after ascending the throne, Seiwa ordered the establishment of Iwashimizu Hachiman-gū on Otoko-yama 男山 southwest of Kyoto.[32] We can assume that behind the young emperor's order was the desire of the Fujiwara part of his family to express gratitude to the deity for the fulfillment of Yoshifusa's wish. Thus it may be concluded that while the

---

[28] Treatment and depictions of this 9th century Hachiman with attendants are found in Guth (1985), pp. 50-60. Hachiman statues and shrines normally appear in a triad together with his mother and his spouse.

[29] This information is taken from recent Japanese and English pamphlets of the temple.

[30] It may be noted that it is not a Buddhist, but a native deity who is trusted as ultimate protector.

[31] Also during the Heian Period, the imperial court maintained close formal relationship with the Usa Hachiman-gū, as the offerings at the occasion of enthronement (*sokui no hōhei* 即位の奉幣), the regular offerings (*kōrei no hōhei* 恒例の奉幣) and the offerings in times of emergency (*rinji no hōhei* 臨時の奉幣) show. Cf. Nakano (1985), pp. 152f.

[32] The choice of Otoko-yama as the place for Iwashimizu Hachiman-gū also had geomantic reasons: As the north-east direction (*kimon* 鬼門) is believed to exert dangerous influence, similarly the south-west is feared as *ura-kimon* 裏鬼門 (backside [of] devil's gate). Accordingly, the Sannō shrine on Mt. Hiei 比叡山 is believed to protect the capital from the *kimon*, while Iwashimizu is believed to do so against the *ura-kimon*. According to shrine tradition, Hachiman in Usa pronounced his wish to Gyōkyō to reside close to the new capital. 9th century shrine legends also tell that Hachiman asked Gyōkyō to pray for the protection of the country. According to the *Nihon sandai jitsuroku* 日本三代実録 (Jōgan 貞観 17/3/28), Gyokyō was sent to Usa to copy the Buddhist canon for Hachiman in order to bring "*peace to the realm.*", Bender (1979), p. 145.

Tamuke-yama shrine in Nara represented imperial rule, Iwashimizu rather symbolized Fujiwara rule at the Heian-court; accordingly, the Tsurugaoka Hachiman-gū later represented the new military rule in Kamakura. Thus, the Hachiman shrines in Tamuke-yama, Iwashimizu and Tsurugaoka became symbols of the shift of political power from imperial sovereign to Fujiwara regency, and eventually to the Kamakura *bakufu* 幕府.

The third innovation during the Heian period is Hachiman's identification with Emperor, or better, King Ōjin 応神. Ōjin (r. 270-310) was the son of Queen Jingū 神功 (r. 201-269?) who is said to have led a military invasion to Korea while being pregnant with the future king. Ōjin himself seems to have been a rather peaceful ruler. According to the *Jōwa engi*, Hachiman declared himself to be an incarnation of Ōjin in 584. However, this identification seems to have been generally acknowledged only after the establishment of Iwashimizu, probably by the end of the Heian period. According to the *Fusō ryakki* 扶桑略記 (12th century) Hachiman Dai-myōjin (!) declared himself to be Ōjin in the following way:

> *"In Buzen Province, Usa District, near Hishikata Pond of Mount Umaya, there lived an old metal worker. He was quite remarkable. Consequently, Oga Hige (went to Hishikata Pond), secluded himself in a hut and abstained from grain for three years. Then he made offerings and prayed: 'If you are truly a god, then appear before me.' Thereupon a three year old child appeared and said by oracle, 'I am the sixteenth emperor of Japan, Homuda Tennō Hirohata Hachiman-marō [i.e. Ōjin]. My name is Gokoku reigen [i]shin daijizaiō Bosatsu."*[33]

How is this identification of Hachiman and Ōjin to be understood? Bender [(1978), p. 167] calls it *"an attempt to integrate the god more closely with the imperial institution by making him an imperial ancestor"*. Accordingly, Iwashimizu was called *sōbyō* 宗廟, ancestral mausoleum, just like Ise![34]

---

[33] Guth (1985), p. 43. Guth mistakenly renders *ishin* (from 護国霊験威神大自在王菩薩) with *seishin*.

[34] It may be also noted that during the Heian period (11th century) a system of the 22 most important shrines was established in which Iwashimizu ranked second after Ise. Since the beginning of the 11th century commemorative rites for Ōjin, his mother Jingū and his wife were held here annually.

Finally, the Heian period witnessed another important development of Hachiman belief, when the Minamoto adopted Hachiman as their clan deity (*ujigami* 氏神).[35] Minamoto no Yorinobu 源頼信 (968-1048) is credited with being the first member of the clan to have worshipped Hachiman at Iwashimizu.[36] His son Yoriyoshi 頼義 (988-1075) attributed a decisive victory to Hachiman's help; in gratitude he then built a Hachiman shrine in 1063 in Yuigahama 由比ヶ浜 at the coast close to Kamakura. Yoriyoshi's son Yoshiie 義家 (1039-1106) was also called Hachiman Tarō because of his courage in combat. Subsequently he was believed to be an incarnation of Hachiman [Kitagawa/ Tsuchida (1990), p. 363]. Up to now we have already encountered two similar appropriations of Hachiman by certain groups during the Heian period, Hachiman as incarnation of Ōjin-tennō, whereby he was adopted into imperial lineage, and Hachiman as *bosatsu*, whereby he was adopted into the Buddhist pantheon. A descendant of Hachiman Tarō, Minamoto no Yoritomo 源 頼朝, brought forth the Kamakura period to which we turn now.

### 4. Kamakura Period (1185-1333)

The Kamakura period is characterized by the dual rule of court and *bakufu*, and by an increasing "militarization of life" in Japan.[37] It is in such a context that Hachiman came to be characterized as god of war. His military (and political) role is seen first in the Hachiman worship of the Kamakura *bakufu*, and second in the defeat of the Mongol army when Hachiman's spiritual warfare was believed to have caused the victory.[38]

---

[35] Minamoto 源 was originally a title given to imperial princes. Hence, the name of the respective emperor from which the Minamoto descended, was added to the name, such as Seiwa Genji 清和源氏 or Murakami Genji 村上源氏; cf. Takeuchi (1999), pp. 650f. During the Heian period the Seiwa Genji served as imperial guard. The afore mentioned Yoshiie and Yoshitsuna accompanying the emperor to Iwashimizu, belonged to the Seiwa Genji. Their grandfather was Minamoto no Yorinobu.

[36] His consciousness that his ancestor Seiwa-tennō had established this shrine may have brought him to worship Hachiman.

[37] This statement is derived from an observation Kamo no Chōmei 鴨長明 makes in his *Hōjō-ki* 方丈記, cf. Sadler (1975), p. 4.

[38] It should be kept in mind that even though Hachiman became a god of war during this period, his function ultimately was aimed at achieving peace and protection of the country.

First, the military and political character of Hachiman worship in the *bakufu*: The Kamakura period was brought forth by the Genpei 源平 war. This war between the Taira and Minamoto was triggered by Prince Mochihito's 以仁 call to fight the Taira in 1180. Upon hearing this call the influential courtier Kujō no Kanezane 九条兼実 noted in his diary:

> *"The safety of our country now rests with the will of the Great Gods of Ise, Hachiman and Kasuga."* [Sansom (1990), p. 280]

Kanezane believed that Mochihito's challenging the Taira endangered the country in such a way that only the joined forces of the three *kami*, Amaterasu, Hachiman, and the Kasuga Daimyōjin, could protect it. These deities represent the ancestral *kami* of three powerful families of the time, the imperial family, the Minamoto,[39] and the Fujiwara to which the Kujō belonged.[40]

Minamoto no Yoritomo learned of Prince Mochihito's call to fight the Taira in 1180 when he was in Kantō. According to the *Azuma kagami* 東鏡, he first prayed to Hachiman for help, then established his military headquarters in Kamakura, removed his ancestor's Hachiman shrine from Yuigahama to Kamakura, and made it the religious center of the new garrison town. Shortly after the relocation, Yoritomo held in the shrine a ceremony *"for the pacification and protection of the nation"* [41] (*chingo kokka* 鎮護国家). Then he started the Genpei War,[42] as it was called later, which eventually led to the downfall of the Taira and the establishment of the Kamakura Shogunate. Yoritomo attributed his victory over the Taira to Hachiman's help.[43]

Before the decisive fight at Dan-no-ura 壇之浦, the Taira had taken with them the young emperor as hostage and also the imperial regalia; however, during the

---

[39] The *Azuma kagami* 東鏡 called the Minamoto even the *"clan of the Great Bodhisattva Hachiman"*, cf. Collcutt (1996), p. 95.

[40] We shall encounter this triad later again.

[41] Collcutt (1996), p. 106. That means, that even after becoming *ujigami* of the Minamoto, Hachiman maintains his role as major protecting *kami* of the country.

[42] Not only in the shrine precincts at home, also in the battle field Yoritomo showed his belief in Hachiman. According to the *Heike monogatari* 平家物語, when the Taira fled, *"Yoritomo alighted from his horse, took off his helmet, washed his hands, and rinsed his mouth. Kneeling and facing the capital, he bowed his head down to the ground and said: 'I, Yoritomo, have not won by my own strength. It is the great bodhisattva Hachiman who has given me his victory'.",* Kitagawa/ Tsuchida (1975), p. 333; cf. p. 674.

[43] During the final battle at Dan-no-ura 壇之浦 auspicious signs of white banners were seen, whereupon Yoritomo's brother Yoshitsune exclaimed: *"This is truly a sign from the Great Bodhisattva Hachiman!"* [Guth (1985), p. 45].

battle the emperor drowned and one of the three regalia, the sword, was lost in the sea. Kanezane's brother Jien 慈圓 interprets the loss of the sword in his *Gukanshō* 愚管抄 as the emperor's entrusting his protection to the warriors, the Minamoto, and writes:

> *"to understand this event, I have come to the conclusion that since present conditions have taken such a form, and soldiers have emerged for the purpose of protecting the sovereign, the Imperial Sword turned its protective function over to soldiers and disappeared into the sea. ... But then the Sun Goddess and the Great Hachiman Bodhisattva reached this agreement: 'Clearly there is now a time [and] fate (jiun) which makes it impossible, since great military Shoguns have definitely gained control of the state, for the country's ruler to survive if he openly opposes the wishes of the great military Shoguns.' Consequently, the Imperial Sword no longer has a function to perform."*[44]

Amaterasu and Hachiman, (in this case) the two clan deities, had agreed on this change. According to this and other texts, the fundamental shift from court rule to military rule was ultimately brought forth by Hachiman, but at the same time these quotations maintain that the military rule still had to serve imperial rule.[45]

Yoritomo's self-consciousness and religious belief seem to share the same conviction, if we can trust a note in Kanezane's diary, which reports about his entering the capital and receiving high office in 1190:

> *"Tonight he was given the office of Grand Counsellor (Dainagon). During my interview with him the Minister Yoritomo said, 'An oracle from Hachiman told me to serve the sovereign wholeheartedly and guard the hundred princes. ... Therefore I must serve the present ruler with all my heart'."* [Sansom (1990), p. 330]

Here again, an oracle from Hachiman serves as legitimation for new political office and rule. Back in Kamakura, the Hachiman shrine prospered in pace with the political developments: Yoritomo's victory in 1185, his attaining the sover-

---

[44] Brown/ Ishida (1979), p. 144. The *Heike monogatari* offers a similar interpretation of this decisive event in Japan's history: *"The Heike had protected the imperial family and had maintained peace in the land. But now because they had disobeyed the emperor, they were to be deprived of command."* [Kitagawa/ Tsuchida (1975), p. 301]. And the Priest Nariyori (Mt. Kōya) commented: *"Ah, the prosperity of the Heike is finally nearing its end. ... I can understand why the great bodhisattva Hachiman should speak of giving the sword of command to Yoritomo."* [ibid.]

[45] Here we find an ambiguity of rule similar to that of the Fujiwara regency.

eign military power in Japan and his developing the military administration (*bakufu*). Being until then mainly a private family shrine (*ujiyashiro* 氏社) for the *ujigami* of the Minamoto, it now became the official shrine of the *bakufu* in which officials and documents from the court in Kyōto were formally received.[46]

When the shrine burnt down in 1191, at the same site a shrine known as Wakamiya was built, and above it, higher in the mountain, the new main shrine was constructed, the Tsurugaoka Hachiman-gū. At its opening ceremony, priests from Kyōto's Iwashimizu shrine brought a *shintai* and enshrined it there. This ceremony marks the fundamental change the Hachiman shrine in Kamakura underwent from a private family shrine to an official shrine.[47] The *hōjō-e* was performed here since 1187; it served like those in Usa and Iwashimizu as ritual to pacify the souls of those who have died in combat.

From the Tsurugaoka shrine in Kamakura the Hachiman cult also expanded among the *bushi* of the Kantō region who adopted him as *ujigami*. This common belief served to foster loyalty and unity among the Kamakura retainers [Collcutt (1996), p. 113]. Thus, the Kamakura developments connecting Hachiman belief and *bushi* contributed considerably to his image as "god of war" or "warrior deity".[48]

However, the war aspect is, as we have seen, only a part of the whole picture. Hachiman is believed to maintain peace in the realm, and both seemingly contradicting attributes, his peaceful and his warlike character, constitute him – at the latest from Heian times on – as the outstanding protective deity of the nation. Nichiren summarized this matter well when in 1262 he called Hachiman (together with Amaterasu) the "Protector of Japan" (*nihon shugo* 日本守護).[49]

---

[46] Collcutt (1996), p. 109, writes that the shrine *"increasingly took on quasi-official function. ... Clerical officials coming from Kyōto to serve in Kamakura were required to pledge their loyalty to the bakufu at the shrine. Official messengers from the court and documents issued by the emperor were formally received at the shrine.".*

[47] Important festivals which were performed here, include the *ninnō-e* 仁王会 (Benevolent Kings Ceremony) and the *hōjō-e*: The *ninnō-e*, conducted by 100 monks, consists of prayers for peace in Kantō and the whole country; cf. Collcutt (1996), p. 110.

[48] Cf. Bender (1978), p. 126, p. 167; Guth (1985), p. 44. In this connection the religious invocation *Namu Hachiman Daibosatsu* became the samurais' notorious war cry.

[49] Cf. Risshō Daigaku (1991), p. 246. It may be also mentioned that contrary to the contemporary (Kamakura) trend of the Pure Land movement to perceive Hachiman as incarnation (*keshin* 化身) of Amida Buddha, Nichiren maintained that he is an incarnation

At the same time, Hachiman also maintained his role of legitimizing imperial rule and high office as can be seen later in cases such as those of Yoritsune,[50] Oda Nobunaga and Hideyoshi.[51]

While Hachiman played a significant political and military role in internal strife for power during the Kamakura period, he also was believed to protect the nation from foreign threats. The Mongol attempts to invade Japan in 1274 and 1281 endangered the nation's sovereignty for the first time in its history. It is in such a national crisis that Hachiman came into the spotlight again, not paralleled by any other *kami*. After Mongol envoys charging Japan's submission in 1272 were sent home – which meant Japan's acceptance of war – the retired Emperor Go-Saga 御嵯峨 made a pilgrimage to Iwashimizu shrine in order to pray for protection [Sansom (1990), p. 442]. When the second invasion occurred, Emperor Kameyama *"proceeded in state to the Iwashimizu shrine and prayed for the safety of the country."*[52]. And when the second invasion was averted, the

---

of Shākyamuni. It seems that in the Heian Period Hachiman was first perceived to be an incarnation of Shākyamuni, cf. Nakano (1985), p. 203f.

[50] Jien wrote the *Gukanshō* in the beginning of the 13th century with the purpose to prove that the Kujō scion Yoritsune was the proper choice to unite in one person what had fallen apart by 1185, the court rule (Fujiwara regency) and military power (Shōgun). According to Jien, both Amaterasu and Hachiman, had decided that this would be the proper solution. He writes: *"The appointment of the young Lord Yoritsune of the regental house as the next Shogun has occurred because the Sun Goddess and Hachiman (sōbyō) felt that the state should now be governed for a while by returning to the ancient model of unity between the sovereign and his Regent or Chancellor."* [Brown/ Ishida (1979), p. 214]. *"The recent selection of the Minister of the Left Kujō Michie's son Yoritsune as the next great military Shogun was certainly made by the Great Hachiman Bodhisattva."* [Brown/ Ishida (1979), p. 217]. *"[W]e have come to a time when the state should be protected, and the sovereign guarded, by uniting the Regent/Chancellor house of Fujiwara with the military house of the Minamoto, thereby combining learning with military might. ... In understanding this way, the first thing to do is to probe deeply into the question of whether this appointment of the next Shogun from the Regent/ Chancellor house was in accord with the plan of the Great Hachiman Bodhisattva or was the doing of heavenly or earthly demons (tengu or chigu)."* [Brown/ Ishida (1979), p. 218]. *"The Sun Goddess enshrined at Ise Shrine and the Great Illuminating Kami enshrined at Kasuga certainly consulted together and decided (gijō) (how imperial rule was to be supported) in the distant past. And the Great Hachiman Bodhisattva and the Great Illuminating Kami of Kasuga consulted together and decided (how Imperial rule is to be supported) in the present. Thus the state was and is to be maintained. ... [The situation] requires that the sovereign have a guardian who has the power of both learning and military might."* [Brown/ Ishida (1979), p. 228].

[51] See for example Casal (1962), pp. 16f. and Schurhammer (1923), p. 90.

[52] Sansom (1990), p. 445. Of course, envoys were sent also to shrines of other *kami* to pray for protection of the nation. Hachiman did not have a monopoly in this role, but in this respect

*"retired Emperor Kameyama proceeded in state to the Iwashimizu shrine, where the victory was celebrated by a reading of passages from the ... Buddhist canon."* [Sansom (1990), p. 451]

In both cases, powerful typhoons had wrecked the Mongol fleet along Japan's shores. Both typhoons were called *kamikaze* 神風, divine storms, and were believed to have been sent by Hachiman, the great defender and protector of the nation. [53] Subsequently, shrines received reward for the spiritual warfare, especially the Usa Hachiman-gū[54] that, located on the periphery and close to the battlefield in North Kyūshū, had again demonstrated Hachiman's divine powers (*jinzū-riki* 神通力).

Finally, it should be mentioned that once the military aspect of the Hachiman belief became so dominant since the 13th century, tendencies to counterbalance this appeared. Especially Buddhists, after having appropriated Hachiman as Bodhisattva, found themselves in need to adjust his image to their own proper teaching. Now they had to deal with the apparent contradiction that a Bodhisattva was not supposed to be involved in killing living beings. For example, the *Rokugō kaizan Ninmon daibosatsu hongi* 六郷開山仁聞大菩薩本紀 ('Principal Record of the Great Bodhisattva Ninmon, founder of the Rokugō Cult Center'),

---

he is the most outstanding figure in Japan's pantheon. It may be noted that also in 1867 Emperor Kōmei 孝明 prayed several times at Iwashimizu Hachiman-gū for the expulsion of the barbarians. Cf. Casal (1962), pp. 22f.

[53] Later times claimed that it was not Hachiman but Amaterasu who sent the *kamikaze*, cf. Casal (1962), p. 22. Similarly, the *Sanja takusen ryakushō* 三社託宣略抄 ('Summary of the Oracles of the Three Shrines'; 17th century) claims, that an oracle of Amaterasu authorized Shōmu-tennō to build Tōdai-ji; cf. Bocking (2001), p. 47f. Such conflicting claims hint at apparent tensions developed between the two most powerful *kami* in Japan – or at least between their adherents. Amaterasu's relative absence (compared with Hachiman's presence) in times of grave national crises poses new questions concerning her proper role during Japan's history. Amaterasu is the sole ancestral deity only of the imperial clan who (at least during the period we treat here) did or could not exert her influence over the whole country and its people as Hachiman did.

[54] The *bakufu* sent a letter in 1284/2/28 to the Chief Priest of Usa Shrine acknowledging its role: "*Enclosed is the patent signifying the donation of Muratsuno Beppu in the province of Hyūga. We had offered a stewardship in the first year of Kenji (1275) for the purpose of repulsing the enemies, as a result of which all enemy ships were wrecked or sunk in the fourth year of Kōan (1281). Now, because it is rumored that enemies may come to attack us again, we would like to make a donation similar to the one given before. / We request that you say yours prayers with the utmost sincerity. On order of the Shogun, / Governor of Suruga Province (Hōjō Naritoki) / Governor of Sagami Province (Hōjō Tokimune)*", Hori (1991), p. 186.

a medieval *jisha-engi* 寺社縁起 compiled after the Mongol invasions, treats this problem explicitly. First it relates the legend which identifies Ōjin with Hachiman, and then, in a huge time leap, combines the revolt of the Hayato (719/720) and the Mongol invasion (1274/1281), which both were, according to this *engi*, subdued by Hachiman. In explanation of the meaning of the *hōjō-e*, Hachiman declares in the words of the *engi*:

> *"Because I set my mind on governing the world from generation to generation by means of forced conversion and all-embracing compassion, I have taken many lives. In order to bring these spirits to salvation, a ceremony to return living beings to freedom shall be performed."*

And:

> *"Killing shall henceforth be prohibited and the compassionate release of captive animals shall be practiced. However, when the nation faces great danger, this injunction shall be repealed for the sake of the country. There ought not to be any misgivings about this matter.*
> *I am a manifestation of the buddhas of the past and am endowed with the body of the Bodhisattva of Great Compassion."* [Grapard (1986), p. 47]

The author of this *engi* perceived the apparent conflict between Hachiman's warrior role and his (assumed) Buddhist identity as Bodhisattva. As a native *kami*, Hachiman was expected to fight spiritual wars for clan and country. But once being appropriated as a Bodhisattva who is supposed not to kill, a contradiction between native religion and Buddhism arises. While native beliefs clearly take sides with their nation in international disputes, this becomes difficult for Buddhism, which – although identifying itself to certain degrees with a nation – transcends national borders. For this reason it may be called a universal religion, which also includes the enemy in its own belief system. Therefore, in the very belief in Hachiman as state protecting *kami* and Bodhisattva, we encounter the conflict between national and international religious (and political) interests.[55]

---

[55] Another example of the softening of Hachiman's character as *kami* of war can be found in the Nō play *Yumi Yawata* 弓八幡, probably written by Zeami 世阿弥 (1363-1443) in the Muromachi period (1338-1573). The scenes of the play take place at Iwashimizu. A famous verse reads: *"Wrapping the bow in a sack, / Restoring the sword to its sheath, / These are the marks of an age of great peace."*, Bender (1978), p. 165, p. 173. The *Yuima Yawata* apparently rejects "the view of Hachiman as a god of war". Ross Bender (1978), p. 165,

## 5. Hachiman and the Japanese nation

After the invasion attempts of the Mongols, it seems that certain forms of nationalism[56] began to develop in Japan, to my knowledge, for the first time in its history. During the Heian period we can observe the development of (what I would call) a "national consciousness" over against the continent, especially China.[57] After the Mongol invasion attempts, however, nationalistic tendencies can be detected. This becomes manifest most clearly in Kitabatake Chikafusa's 北畠親房 (1293-1354) *Jinnō shōtō-ki* 神皇正統記 ('Chronicle of the direct descent of gods and sovereigns'), which argues that unlike other countries Japan is a "divine country" (*shinkoku* 神国) because it has an uninterrupted imperial lineage deriving directly from the kami.[58] Such a nationalistic tendency then also became a flavor of Hachiman belief. One such case can be found in the Nō play *Yumi Yawata* 弓八幡 which is attributed to Zeami 世阿弥. It relates an oracle by Hachiman claiming Japan's supremacy in the following way:

---

comments: "*Throughout the work Hachiman is depicted primarily as a deity who ensures a peaceful imperial reign.*" He further writes: "*the play 'advocates peace in a time of military rule; it lauds the imperial house at a time of shogunal despotism'.*", Bender (1978), p. 165. The play's "*view of Hachiman denies the contemporary association of the god with the ruling military house. It rather dramatizes an earlier conception of the deity, portraying a Hachiman who is intimately linked with the imperial institution.*", Bender (1978), p. 169.

[56] To apply the proper term "nationalism" to this period of Japanese history seems to be anachronistic, because the idea of a national state which forms its presupposition was formed in 19th century Europe and introduced to Japan during the Meiji period. Here I use the term in the broad meaning of the idea according to which the own country is elevated to an absolute value while other countries are placed in inferior positions. For a discussion of the term in the Japanese context see also Brown (1971), pp. 1-9 and Peter Kleinen's contribution in this volume.

[57] The inclusion of the name "Japan" into titles of works like *Nihon ōjō gokuraku-ki* 日本往生極楽記 by Yoshishige no Yasutane 慶滋保胤, and subsequent *ōjō-den* 往生伝 literature, or Genshin's 源信 sending his *Ōjō yō-shū* 往生要集 together with Yasutane's work to China, are indicators for an emerging national self-consciousness; cf. Brown (1971), p. 10, pp. 20f. After a long period of dependence on religious imports from Korea and China, these Buddhist authors maintain that also in Japan authentic religious experiences and insights can be gained and veritable Buddhist literature produced. However, this tone is quite different from the one to be heard after the invasion attempts by the Mongols. These events thus mark a change in Japanese history from national consciousness to nationalistic sentiments.

[58] For an introduction and English translation see Varley (1980). For the *shinkoku* discourse see also Kuroda (1996).

> *"Before foreign lands, our land;*
> *Before foreign peoples, our people."* [Bender (1978), p. 176]

The *Tōdai-ji Hachiman genki* 東大寺八幡験記, written in 1294, a few yeas after the invasion attempts of the Mongols, attributes this oracle to the Nara period, but neither such an oracle nor nationalistic tendencies can be detected in Nara documents [Bender (1978), p. 176]. In this oracle, Hachiman, hitherto the protector of the nation, for the first time appears to advocate nationalistic tendencies. It may be noted here that, similar to the reactions following the invasion attempts by the Mongols, also the subsequent two waves of foreign intrusions into Japan during the 16th/17th centuries and the 19th century caused considerable outbursts of antiforeign and nationalistic sentiments. Ideologically they were based partly on Kitabatake's work.

Finally it may be mentioned that the Meiji Government reversed the Buddhist appropriation of Hachiman, thereby eliminating his potentially critical or subversive role. Already in 1868 the government issued a law especially for Hachiman decreeing that he no longer was to be called *daibosatsu* 大菩薩, but *daijin* 大神, great *kami*.[59] To my knowledge, however, so far no oracle has been received from Hachiman authorizing this political decision.

### References

Bender (1978)
	Bender, Ross: "Metamorphosis of a Deity. The Image of Hachiman in Yumi Yawata", in: *Monumenta Nipponica*, vol. 33 (1978), pp. 165-178.

—	(1979)
	Bender, Ross: "The Hachiman Cult and the Dōkyō Incident", in: *Monumenta Nipponica*, vol. 34/2 (1979), pp. 125-153.

---

[59] The government ordered also the offerings of fish at Iwashimizu shrine, which is a proper sacrifice for a *kami*, but an offense to a Buddha or Bodhisattva. Cf. Lokowandt (1978), pp. 16f., pp. 252f.

Bocking (2001)
Bocking, Brian: *The Oracles of the Three Shrines*. Richmond, Surrey: Curzon Press, 2001.

Brown (1971)
Brown, Delmer M.: *Nationalism in Japan: An Introductory Historical Analysis*. New York: Russell & Russell, 1971 [1st ed., 1955].

Brown/ Ishida (1979)
Brown, Delmer M., and Ichirō Ishida (tr. & ed.): *The Future and the Past: A Translation and Study of the Gukanshō, an Interpretative History of Japan Written in 1219*. Berkeley: University of California Press, 1979.

Casal (1962)
Casal, U. A.: "Hachiman. Der Kriegsgott Japans", in: *Mitteilungen der Deutschen Gesellschaft für Natur- und Völkerkunde Ostasiens*, vol. XLI, part D (1962). Tōkyō: OAG.

Collcutt (1996)
Collcutt, Martin: "Religion in the life of Minamoto Yoritomo and the early Kamakura bakufu", in: Kornicki, P. F./ McMullen, I. J. (eds.): *Religion in Japan. Arrows to Heaven and Earth*. Cambridge: Cambridge University Press, 1996, pp.90-119.

Dykstra (1983)
Dykstra, K. Yoshiko (transl.): *Miraculous Tales of the Lotus Sutra from Ancient Japan*. Honolulu: University of Hawai'i Press, 1983.

Grapard (1986)
Grapard, Allan G.: "Lotus in the Mountain, Mountain in the Lotus: Rokugō Kaizan Ninmon Daibosatsu Hongi", in: *Monumenta Nipponica*, vol. 41/1 (1986), pp. 21-50.

—    (1999)
Grapard, Allan G.: "Religious practices", in: Shively, Donald H./ McCullough, William H. (eds.): *The Cambridge History of Japan Vol. II Heian Japan*. Cambridge: Cambridge University Press, 1999, pp. 517-575.

Guth (1985)
Guth Kanda, Christine: *Shinzō. Hachiman Imagery and its Development*. Cambridge (Mass.), London: Harvard University Press, 1985.

Herbert (1967)
Herbert, Jean: *Shintō. At the Fountainhead of Japan*. New York: Stein and Day Publishers (George Allen & Unwin Ltd), 1967.

Hori (1991)
Hori, Kyotsu: "The Economic and Political Effects of the Mongol Wars", in: Hall, John W./ Mass, Jeffrey P. (eds.): *Medieval Japan. Essays in Institutional History*. Stanford: Stanford University Press, 1991 [1st ed., 1974], pp. 184-198.

Hurst (1999)
Hurst, G. Cameron: "Insei", in: Shively, Donald H./ McCullough, William H. (eds.): *The Cambridge History of Japan Vol. II Heian Japan*. Cambridge: Cambridge University Press, 1999, pp. 576-643.

Kitagawa/ Tsuchida (1975)
Kitagawa, Hiroshi/ Tsuchida, Bruce T. (transl.): *The Tale of the Heike*. 2 vol., Tōkyō: University of Tōkyō Press, 1975.

Kuroda (1996)
Kuroda, Toshio: "The discourse of the 'Land of Kami' (shinkoku) in medieval Japan: National consciousness and international awareness", in: *Journal of Japanese Religious Studies*, vol. 23/3-4 (1996), pp. 353-385.

Lokowandt (1978
Lokowandt, Ernst: *Die rechtliche Entwicklung des Staats-Shintō in der ersten Hälfte der Meiji-Zeit (1868-1890)*. [Studies in Oriental Religions, vol. 3] Wiesbaden: Harrassowitz, 1978.

Morrell (1985)
Morrell, Robert E. (ed. & transl.): *Sand & Pebbles (Shasekishū): The Tales of Muchū Ichien, A Voice for Pluralism in Kamakura Buddhism*. New York: State University of New York Press, 1985.

Nakano (1985)
Nakano, Hatayoshi 中野幡能: *Hachiman shinkō 八幡信仰*. Tōkyō, Hanawa-shinsho, 1985.

—   (1986)
Nakano, Hatayoshi 中野幡能 (ed.): *Hachiman shinkō 八幡信仰*. [Minshu shūkyō-shi sōsho 民衆宗教史叢書, no. 2] Tokyo: Yūsankaku, 1986 [1st ed., 1984].

Nichiren-shū shūmu-in (1999)
Nichiren-shū shūmu-in 日蓮宗宗務院 (ed.): *Nichiren-shū jiten* 日蓮宗事典. Tōkyō: Nichiren-shū shinbun-sha, 1999.

Risshō Daigaku (1991)
Risshō Daigaku Nichiren Kyōgagku Kenkyūsho 立正大学日蓮教学研究所 (ed.): *Shōwa teihon Nichiren shōnin ibun* 昭和定本日蓮聖人遺文. 4 vol., Minobu: Kuon-ji, 1991 [1ˢᵗ ed., 1952-59].

Sadler (1975)
Sadler, A. L. (transl.): *The Ten Foot Square Hut and Tales of the Heike.* Tōkyō: Tuttle, 1975 [1ˢᵗ ed., 1972].

Saeki (1928-31)
Saeki, Ariyoshi 佐伯有義 (ed.): *Rikkoku-shi* 六国史. 11 vols. Ōsaka: Asahi Shinbun-sha. 1928-31.

Saigō (1986)
Saigō, Nobutsuna 西郷信綱: "Hachiman-shin no hassei 八幡神の発生", in: Nakano (1986), pp. 3-34.

Sansom (1990)
Sansom, George: *A History of Japan to 1334.* [Vol. 1] Rutland, Vermont, and Tōkyō: Charles E. Tuttle, 1990 [1st ed., 1974].

Schurhammer (1923)
Schurhammer S.J., Georg: *Shin-tō. Der Weg der Götter: Der Shintoismus nach den gedruckten und ungedruckten Berichten der japanischen Jesuitenmissionare des 16. und 17. Jahrhunderts.* Kurt Schroeder Verlag, Bonn und Leipzig, 1923.

Sonoda (1997)
Sonoda, Kōyū: "Early Buddha Worship", in: Brown, Delmer M. (ed.): *The Cambridge History of Japan, vol. I Ancient Japan.* Cambridge: Cambridge University Press, 1997 [1ˢᵗ ed., 1993], pp. 359-414.

Takeuchi (1999)
Takeuchi, Rizō: "The rise of the warriors", in: Shively, Donald H./ McCullough, William H. (eds.): *The Cambridge History of Japan, vol. II Heian Japan.* Cambridge: Cambridge University Press, 1999, pp. 644-709.

Varley (1980)
    Varley, H. Paul (transl.): *A Chronicle of Gods and Sovereigns. Jinnō Shōtōki of Kitabatake Chikafusa.* New York: Columbia University Press, 1980.

Weinstein (1983)
    Weinstein, Stanley: "Hachiman", in: *Kodansha Encyclopedia of Japan, vol. 3*, Tōkyō: Kodansha, 1983, p. 74.

# Land of the *Kami* and Way of the *Kami* in Yoshida Shintō

Bernhard SCHEID

In this essay I will investigate the relation of *shinkoku shisō* 神国思想 or Divine Land discourse and the conception of *shintō* 神道 in Yoshida Shintō 吉田神道.[1] In doing so I will first sketch the history of the two phrases based on the theories of Kuroda Toshio 黒田俊雄 and others. In the final analysis I will try to indicate some political implications in the genesis of Shintō that actually surfaced much later in Japanese religious history.

## *Different meanings of shintō*

In his famous essay "Shinto in the History of Japanese Religion" (1981) Kuroda Toshio discusses the evolution of the term *shintō*. Among the several possible meanings, isolated by Kuroda on the basis of Tsuda Sōkichi's 津田左右吉 studies (1949), I would like to focus on three which I consider the most important, namely: a) concepts and teachings concerning *kami* 神, b) 'the way of the *kami*' as a political or moral norm, and c) the power, activity, or deeds of a *kami*. The first definition, concepts and teachings, is probably closest to the modern understanding of *shintō*, in the West as well as in Japan. The second, *shintō* as political or moral norm, arouses associations of State Shintō, but can be traced at least back to the early Edo period [cf. Kuroda (1981), p. 19]. Finally the third definition, power or deeds of the *kami*, is mostly used as a synonym of the *kami* themselves without implying a specific way of venerating them or following their precepts. Not only Kuroda, but also for instance Nelly Naumann[2], argues that this was the common understanding of *shintō* in Japan up to the middle ages. Moreover, these scholars agree that the concept of *kami* religion as such – regardless of whether it went by the name *shintō* or not –

---

[1] 'Yoshida Shintō' refers to a Shintō sect headed by priests of the Yoshida family. Its doctrinal outlines were written down around 1485 in the *Yuiitsu shintō myōbō yōshū* 唯一神道名法要集 ('Essentials of Name and Law of the One and Only Way of the *Kami*'; hereafter *Myōbō yōshū*), by Yoshida Kanetomo 吉田兼倶 (1435–1511) [cf. Scheid (2001)].

[2] Cf., for instance, the preface of her two-volumed history of premodern indigenous religion [Naumann (1988), pp. IX-XIII].

hardly existed at that time. The shift from *shintō* in this ancient understanding to 'Shintō'[3] in the sense of an autonomous religion occurred, according to Kuroda, with the rise of Yoshida Shintō from the late 15th century onward [cf. Kuroda (1981), p. 18]. In the Edo period, new concepts of Shintō emerged under the influence of Neo-Confucianism. This implied a bias towards moral and political values that remained present in the discourse on Shintō also among the *kokugaku* 国学 ('National Learning') school, even though the *kokugaku* strove to clean Shintō from Buddhist as well as from Confucian influences and restore it as it was before the influence of foreign cultures in Japan. That effort finally solidified the notion of Shintō as the indigenous religion of Japan. However, according to Kuroda, it was not before the Meiji period, that this understanding of the term *shintō* gained common acceptance beyond limited circles of intellectuals and priests. Thus in Kuroda's historical sketch, the general meaning of the term *shintō* changed from a synonym of *kami* or 'power of the *kami*', to a mixture of 'concepts and teachings concerning *kami*', and 'way of the *kami* as political or moral norm'. This development of the term also reflects the evolution of Shintō as an independent autonomous religion. The aim of Kuroda's critical re-evaluation of the modern understanding of Shintō is to demonstrate its comparatively short history as an independent religion. Although *kami* worship is evident continually in Japanese religious history, the *kami* were revered mostly in the context of Buddhism, Kuroda argues.

### Shinkoku *in the medieval period*

In modern Japanese, the term *shinkoku* 神国 ('land of the *kami*' or 'divine land') has become a major catchphrase of ultra-nationalistic ideologies and is nowadays a clear indicator of reactionary political opinion.[4] In academic spheres, both apologetics and critics of Japanese nationalism have treated the concept of *shinkoku* widely and repeatedly have pointed to the long history of the term. Similar to the discussion of '*shintō*', they often implied that the meaning of *shinkoku* was always the same as in modern nationalist discourse. As can be expected, Kuroda Toshio (1975, 1996) also mentioned *shinkoku* but arrived at a quite different conclusion. Influenced by Kuroda's approach,

---

[3] By different writing, I try to differentiate Shintō in the conventional sense from *shintō* in other meanings.

[4] Cf. the contribution of Johann Nawrocki in this volume.

scholars like Satō Hiroo 佐藤弘夫 (1995, 1998), or Fabio Rambelli (1996), have recently published similar evaluations. Let me briefly take a look at these not yet very well known interpretations of _shinkoku_.

_Shinkoku_ first appears in the _Nihon shoki_ 日本書紀, in a report of a military campaign against the Korean kingdom of Silla, which is clearly shaped by patriotic or ethno-centric intentions.[5] From there on, the term surfaced here and there in ancient Japanese literature, but its occurrence is too infrequent to allow the reconstruction of a specific _shinkoku_ discourse. In the medieval period, however, the word _shinkoku_ suddenly appears in a wide range of texts.[6] This frequent use leads to the question, what connotations made the term attractive for the people of that time. Traditionally, the imminent Mongol invasion in the latter half of the 13th century has been seen as the reason for a significant growth of a national or nationalistic consciousness that in turn fostered the notion of Japan as 'land of the _kami_'. While not entirely rejecting this explanation, Kuroda indicates that _shinkoku_ was en vogue long before the Mongol threat. Moreover he characterizes _shinkoku shisō_ as 'essentially religious' [cf. Kuroda (1996), p. 376], pointing out, how well the concept of _shinkoku_ fitted into the common understanding of the relationship between Buddhist and native deities, the so-called _honji suijaku_ 本地垂迹 (original-trace) conception.

To illustrate this understanding by just one example, let me refer to a _setsuwa_ 説話-tale from _Shasekishū_ 沙石集, Mujū Ichien's 無住一圓 famous collection of entertaining anecdotes illustrating Buddhist doctrines. The tale in question holds quite a prominent place in _Shasekishū_ preceded only by two tales about the _kami_ of Ise.[7] The header of the story 'Praying to the Gods for Release from Birth-and-Death', contains already its didactic message, namely, how the _kami_

---

[5] I.e. the legendary conquer of Silla led by empress Jingū 神功皇后 (traditional dates of reign 201-269), a report designed to enlarge the prestige of Japan and its ruling dynasty [cf. NKBT 67, pp. 338f; Aston (1998) [vol. I], p. 230]. The anachronistic elaborations of the _Nihon shoki_ account are poignantly summarized by Naumann (1994), pp. 51f.

[6] Cf. Kuroda (1996), pp. 372ff. for the usage of _shinkoku_ in various doctrinal texts. See also Satō (1998), pp. 322ff. for examples from medieval _setsuwa_ 説話 collections like _Kokon chomonjū_ 古今著聞集, _Shasekishū_ 沙石集, or _Shintōshū_ 神道集, legends (_engi_ 縁起) like _Hachiman gudōkin_ 八幡愚童訓, historical reports like _Azuma kagami_ 吾妻鏡, doctrinal texts like _Yōtenki_ 耀天記, etc.

can lead people to Buddhist salvation. The story is about an illustrious abbot of the temple Miidera 三井寺, Kōken 公顯 (1110-1193), who performs every morning rituals dedicated to the *kami* donning the white robe of a Shintō priest. This practice is critically observed by a monk from Mt. Kōya 高野山 who sends a messenger to investigate the abbot's unorthodox behavior. To this messenger, the abbot explains his reasons in a long sermon. First he confesses his doubts regarding his abilities to attain Buddhist salvation by relying on his own 'self-power' (*jiriki* 自力). This weakness, however, is not only due to his individual fate (*karma*) or character, but also to the specific time and place he lives in. Japan is only an insignificant country, "*as remote from the centre [India, B.S.] as the small scattered millet seed*" [Morrell (1985), p. 78]. In this country, Buddhas and Bodhisattvas do not appear in their original form. Since the essence of Buddhism, the Dharma Body (jap. *hōshin* 法身, Skt. *dharma kaya*), is always different in terms of outer appearance according to the conditions of different societies, "*[i]n our country, as the land of the gods [*shinkoku, B.S.*], the provisional manifestations [*gongen 権現, B.S.*] of the Buddha leave their traces. Moreover, we are all their descendants; and it is no trivial fate to share with them a common spirit.*" [ibid.]. This argument, taken up repeatedly in the abbot's sermon, suffices to indicate his sincere Buddhist commitment when practicing *kami* rituals. The abbot is thus portrayed as an ideal model, how to 'pray to the *kami* for Buddhist salvation'.

This is only one among countless examples of *shinkoku* seen as a land, where the Buddhas found no other device than 'to leave their traces' as *kami*. According to Kuroda, the term had become an integral part of *honji suijaku* thought, and thus part of orthodox Buddhist reasoning in the medieval period. The conventional explanation holds that *shinkoku* was a vital, autochthon response to the pessimistic, Buddhist (= foreign) latter day thought (*mappō* 末法 = end of the Dharma).[8] Kuroda, by contrast, stresses the fact that *shinkoku* often referred to a land 'scattered like millet grain' (*zokusankoku* 粟散国) at the far periphery of the Buddhist cosmos [cf. Kuroda (1996), p. 374]. As Rambelli puts it: "*It is precisely because Japan was marginal and its people evil that the buddhas had to*

---

[7] I refer to the English translation of the story by Morrell (1985), pp. 76-79. For the original see NKBT 85, pp. 63f.

[8] Cf. for example, Naumann (1994), pp. 50f.

_manifest themselves in the forms of violent kami endowed with the power to convert and save particularly ignorant people in hard times._" [Rambelli (1996), p. 398]. Therefore, the 'land of the _kami_' could be regarded as a spatial counterpart to the notion of temporal decline in the 'latter days of the Dharma'.

Both notions, by the way, are not necessarily entirely pessimistic or optimistic. While the term _shinkoku_ itself undeniably does not contain any negative associations, historical analysis tells us, that _mappō_ too could become a source of new inspirations, as for instance in the various forms of Pure Land Buddhism. In times of decline, Pure Land adherents argue, it is futile to rely on inner strength or 'self-power' (_jiriki_) like people in the past. Only Amida's 'other-power' (_tariki_ 他力) is a trustworthy means of salvation. As we have seen from the above example, the reasoning of the abbot regarding his faith in the _kami_ was indeed quite similar.[9] Examples like this support Kuroda's view that _shinkoku_ discourse was essentially religious, and was primarily significant as a response to the rise of Pure Land Buddhism. It is not an anti-Buddhist reaction, however, but rather an attempt by the Buddhist establishment to cope with the challenge of heterodox Buddhist developments like radical Pure Land movements, which propagated various kinds of 'exclusive _nenbutsu_ practice' (_senju nenbutsu_ 専修念仏) often connected with a refusal to venerate the _kami_ (_jingi fuhai_ 神祇不拝). Medieval _shinkoku_ discourse was, in Kuroda's eyes, primarily a by-product of _honji suijaku_ syncretism, designed as an alternative to Pure Land Buddhism and has thus certain structural congruencies with the latter.[10] It was

---

[9] There is, by the way, an interesting historical connection with Pure Land Buddhism in this story: the monk from Mt. Kōya who initiated the investigation was abbot Myōhen 明遍 (1142-1224), widely respected for his knowledge and austerity in Shingon Buddhism, but also – according to Pure Land hagiography – a disciple of Hōnen 法然 (1133-1212), the founder of the Pure Land sect [cf. MKDJT, _sub voce_; Quenzer (2000), p. 170, pp. 272f].

[10] In this connection, Kuroda stresses the fact that the medieval notion of 'divine land' did not envision 'land' as 'state' or 'nation', but as sacred soil, much in the same way as Pure Land adherents envisioned Amida's paradise. _Shinkoku_ as for instance portrayed in the syncretistic collection _Shintōshū_ was a kind of 'Pure Land in this world' inhabited by the _kami_, which did not exclude, however, an even more important Pure Land in the other world, inhabited by Buddhas [cf. Kuroda (1975), pp. 296-299].

That the disregard of the _kami_ was seen as an offence against official Buddhist doctrine is already documented in the earliest critical treatise of Hōnen's teachings, the _Kōfuku-ji sōjō_ 興福寺奏状 by Jōkei 貞慶 (1155-1213), written in 1205. Among others, Jōkei charges 'the _nenbutsu_ followers' of being estranged from the _kami_ (described as _gonge suijaku_ 権化垂迹, 'provisional manifestations' of Buddhas and Bodhisattvas), and not paying their

therefore stimulated by inner-Buddhist antagonisms, not by an antagonism between universalistic Buddhist pessimists and patriotic Shintō optimists, Kuroda argues.

Whether one agrees with Kuroda's interpretation or not, one cannot deny its merit to draw attention to hitherto scarcely considered examples of *shinkoku* discourse such as the story from *Shasekishū*. Up to Kuroda most scholars focused on the *Jinnō shōtō ki* 神皇正統記 by Kitabatake Chikafusa 北畠親房[11] as the *locus classicus* of *shinkoku shisō*. Notably in the early Showa period (1925-1945) this treatise in defense of Go Daigo's 後醍醐 imperial restoration was presented as a model for modern nationalist ideology.[12] Although based on a different value scale, this view was taken over also by critics of nationalist ideology. Kuroda, on the other hand, hardly ever goes into the details of the *Jinnō shōtō ki* arguing that *shinkoku shisō* existed long before Chikafusa's treatise.[13] Regarding its loyalist intention, Kuroda points out that Buddhism and Tennōism (*tennō-sei* 天皇制) were by no means incongruous in the medieval period. Rather, the unstable balance between rival power centers of the ruling elites (the so-called *kenmon taisei* 権門体制, composed of religious and mundane institutions alike) was in need of symbolic center of the Tennō and thus persecuted all tendencies threatening the symbols of imperial sovereignty. The fact remains, however, that the *Jinnō shōtō ki* applied to ethno-centric, if not nationalistic sentiments in order to re-establish the Tennō's political authority. While it was probably not intentionally anti-Buddhist, its central concern was certainly not the defense of Buddhist 'orthodoxy'. And the object of its retrospective utopia was not the lifetime of Buddha Shakyamuni but the heydays of the early imperial rule up to the Nara period. It is this idealized past which serves as the

---

respects at the great shrines and imperial sanctuaries [cf. Morell (1987), p. 79; Kleine (1996), pp. 220ff].

[11] The *Jinnō shōtō ki* ('Report of the True Transmission of the Divine Ruler') was written by Kitabatake Chikafusa (1293-1354) in 1339, and is now generally known in its revised version from 1343. It was dedicated to the young emperor Go-Murakami 後村渋 of the Southern court, and was handed over to him in the year of his ascendance.

[12] For an example in a Western language see Hiraizumi (1938).

[13] Kuroda does not deny that Chikafusa's view was indeed the forerunner of modern Japanese nationalism. He stresses, however, that the shift from religious to merely political understanding represented a secondary development in medieval *shinkoku* discourse, which changed – to put it in a floppy expression – things from bad to worse [cf. Kuroda (1996), pp. 382f].

evidence that Japan is a 'land of the _kami_', as the _Jinnō shōtō ki_ stresses already in its first sentence. The precise fact that singles out Japan among all other nations is seen in the fact that its ruling dynasty was of divine origin and was never overthrown as the highest authority of the realm. Divine land is thus intimately connected with 'divine ruler' (_jinnō_), a term that is mentioned already in the title of the treatise.[14]

While I generally agree with Kuroda's emphasis on Buddhist impact on seemingly 'Shintōist' topics such as _kami_ worship and Tennō loyalism, it is obvious that he loses interest in pursuing the implications of _shinkoku shisō_, as soon as this discourse shifts entirely into the sphere of political ideology, that is, around the beginning of the Muromachi period. From that point onward Kuroda abandons his differentiated reconstruction and treats _shinkoku_ discourse in a generalizing way, regarding it as a more or less homogenous ideology up to its usage in modern nationalism. At the same time, he seems to play down chauvinist connotations of earlier _shinkoku_ discourse,[15] even if he summarizes it as a essentially 'reactionary' ideology [cf., for instance, Kuroda (1996), p. 377]. In the following, I would like to demonstrate that _shinkoku_ actually continued to change its functions and meanings, also after the _Jinnō shōtō ki_. Let me therefore take a closer look, how Yoshida Shintō integrated this illustrious term into its doctrinal system.

### Shinkoku _and 'tree theory'_

"_This country is a divine land_ [shinkoku]. _Its way is the kami way_ [shintō]. _The ruler of this country is the divine emperor_ [jinnō]." [_Myōbō yōshū_; cf.

---

[14] For a compact depiction of the _Jinnō shōtō ki_'s doctrinal quintessence cf. Naumann (1994), pp. 47-55.

[15] In this respect, we find actually quite contradictory statements by Kuroda. Regarding the territorial aspects of _shinkoku shisō_, for instance, Kuroda writes: "_[Shinkoku as a concept primarily concerned with territory] showed little if any explicit intent to draw comparison with other countries._" [Kuroda (1996), pp. 374f]. A little later we learn: "_Ultimately the_ shinkoku _concept was just a form of Buddhist doctrine and belief, but in it the desire to define Japan's peculiar status was clearly at work._" [ibid., p. 376]. And finally, a point to keep in mind is that: "_[shinkoku] functioned as a form of national consciousness within the framework of Japan's relations with other lands. Although essentially religious in nature, the_ shinkoku _concept, insofar as it constituted an awareness of Japan as_ kuni (_country_), _comprised a recognition by the Japanese of 'their land' as a part of the actual Asian world._" [ibid., p. 379].

Grapard (1992b), p. 158]. This emblematic formula, taken from Yoshida Kanetomo's *Yuiitsu shintō myōbō yōshū* conjures three catchphrases from *Jinnō shōtō ki*: *kami*-land, *kami*-way, and *kami*-ruler. All these expressions use the morpheme *shin/ kami* in the sense of a sacred or divine quality that seems – in this context – more or less identical with the essence of Japanese para-religious nationalism: *shintō*, the *kami*-way, is embodied by the Japanese emperor ruling his divine country.[16] This is indeed what traditional scholarship has pointed out as ideological kernel of the *Jinnō shōtō ki*. In the light of Kuroda's interpretation, it might be open to doubt whether the author, Kitabatake Chikafusa, indeed considered such a meaning consciously. Particularly the term *shintō* seems to be of much less value in the *Jinnō shōtō ki* than the other two terms, *jinnō* (divine ruler) and *shinkoku* (divine land).[17] Yet, put together into one slogan, as in the citation from the *Myōbō yōshū*, it is hard to deny that all three expressions combine into a more or less nationalistic and Tennō-centric message.

This combination of *shintō* and *shinkoku* is also found in a version of *Shintō taii* 神道大意, another text of Yoshida Shintō[18]:

> "*In this our country the gods appeared at the same time as heaven and earth. Therefore, this land is called Land of the Gods and its way is the Way of the Gods. This land is the origin of the thousand worlds. Therefore it is called 'origin of the sun' [Hi-no-moto written with the characters of Nihon]. India and China are shaped like stars. Therefore they are called moon-land and star-land.*" [*Shintō taii*, Kanenao-sen 兼直撰; ST 7/8, p. 3]

In this statement we find an explicit reference to the position of Japan in comparison to China and India. In spite of Kuroda's arguments my impression remains that this quest for a national identity vis-à-vis Japan's classical

---

[16] To avoid any misunderstanding, I should add that *shintō* actually had quite a diverse range of meanings in Yoshida Shintō. The present analysis is limited to its use in the context of the Yoshidas' peculiar depiction of Shintō ontology.

[17] Naumann [(1994), p. 49] points out that only one of the three mentions of *shintō* in the *Jinnō shōtō ki* allows for an interpretation beyond the ancient, narrow meaning of *shintō* as 'deeds of the *kami*' [see above, definition c)].

[18] *Shintō taii* is a peculiar genre of Yoshida texts, rather than an individual writing. It usually refers to a short essay on the nature of the *kami*. Yoshida Kanetomo wrote several such essays in the name of his predecessors to allude historical depths to his doctrine. His successors continued this tradition.

'master-nations' has always been a salient feature of *shinkoku* discourse, even if in many cases only implicitly present. In the course of *shinkoku* discourse, a peculiar Japanese quality was created as a standard response to this need for national identity: *kami*-ness – to coin a most general designation for what unites *kami*-land and *kami*-way. It is this quality that singles out Japan vis-à-vis India and China. In the writings of Yoshida Shintō, we encounter an even more explicit example to fill this need, the so-called 'tree-theory'. It relates to the three countries India, China and Japan and their respective teachings. The *Myōbō yōshū* recounts the tree theory in the following citation, which is alleged to Shōtoku Taishi 聖徳太子 (574–622):

> "*Japan produced the seed, China produced the branches and leaves, India produced the flowers and fruit. Buddhism is the fruit, Confucianism is the leaves, and Shintō is the trunk and the roots of all teachings. Buddhism and Confucianism are only secondary products of Shintō. Leaves and fruit merely indicate the presence of the trunk and the roots; Buddhism came east only to reveal clearly that our nation is the trunk and the roots of these three nations.*"[19]

As Nishida Nagao 西田長男 (1957) pointed out, neither this metaphor, nor its attribution to Shōtoku Taishi are Kanetomo's inventions. The metaphor itself can be traced back to China where it was applied to Buddhism, Confucianism and Taoism. In Japan, however, it was initially applied by Buddhist monks in an effort to combine Buddhist convictions, faith in the *kami*, and patriotism.[20] Thus, they replaced Taoism with the term *shintō* to indicate a Japanese way and they chose Shōtoku Taishi – who is otherwise known as one of the earliest mentors of Buddhism in Japan – as the originator of this saying. The purpose of the Buddhist tree-theory was therefore to show that Buddhism was actually not a foreign teaching but had its roots ultimately in Japan. *In nuce*, we encounter the same argument already in a well-known pun, allegedly coined by Saichō 最澄 (767-822): *Dai Nipponkoku* ('Great Land of Japan') = *Dainichi honkoku* ('origi-

---

[19] Translated by Grapard (1992b), p. 153. See also NST 19, p. 234; Scheid (2001), p. 350.

[20] One of the earliest examples of the tree theory in Japan can be found in the *Bikisho* 鼻帰書, a work from the so-called Ryōbu Shintō 両部神道 tradition written in 1324 only 15 years before the *Jinnō shōtō ki*. The *Bikisho* probably influenced the Shintō writings of Jihen 慈遍, in some respects a fore-runner of Yoshida Kanetomo [cf. Scheid (2001), pp. 87f, p. 219], who mentioned the tree theory in his *Kuji hongi gengi* 旧事本紀玄義 (written after 1329) [cf. Nishida (1957), pp. 387-390; SJ, p. 402].

nal land of Vairocana Buddha'): both expressions use the same characters 大日
本国. The endeavor to find the roots of Buddhism in Japan as illustrated by the
tree-theory exhibits a certain identity problem of Buddhist monks who were
caught by a kind of ethnocentric reflex when comparing their country with the
master nations India and China.[21]

Looking for specific sources of inspiration for the Yoshida's understanding of
'*kami*-ness', scholars univocally point at Ryōbu Shintō 両部神道 and Watarai 度
会 (or Ise 伊勢) Shintō. 'Ryōbu Shintō' is a general designation for syncretistic
efforts mostly of monks from esoteric branches of Shingon 真言 and Tendai 天
台 Buddhism who shared a common enthusiasm for the shrines of Ise.[22] On the
grounds of structural correspondence between the two shrines of Ise and the two
mandalas of Dainichi, they construed an identity of Dainichi and the Ise deities
(Amaterasu 天照 and Toyouke 豊宇気), and tried to reveal esoteric Buddhist
messages in mythological or pseudo-mythological accounts relating to the Ise
deities. These accounts and their interpretation were mostly attributed to
legendary historical personalities like Kūkai 空海, Saichō, or Shōtoku Taishi.
The proper authors of Ryōbu Shintō remained therefore in most cases anony-
mous, but it is generally assumed that Ryōbu monks had close relations to the
Watarai priests from the Outer Shrine of Ise, who worked out similar theories.
The Watarai, in turn, had an influence on Kitabatake Chikafusa, the author of the
*Jinnō shōtō ki*. All these politico-religious initiatives arose in a comparatively
narrow time frame between the late 13th and early 14th century. They mutually
influenced each other in their efforts to combine Indian and Chinese ideas with
patriotic sentiments and an endeavor to restore the imperial authority. While I
doubt Kuroda's general assessment that the ethnocentric or even nationalistic
impact of these medieval 'Shintō' currents can be explained simply by the
ideological needs of the ruling '*kenmon taisei*', it is important not to overlook
that, in general, the religious views of these initiatives were neither

---

[21] It would lead us to far to pursue this question any further. Suffice it to raise some doubts
regarding Kuroda's assumption that this kind of identity problem surfaced not earlier in
*shinkoku* discourse than at the beginning of the Muromachi period.

[22] For a general introduction into this still undeveloped chapter of Japanese religious history
see for instance Teeuwen and van der Veere (1998), pp. 4ff. In a more recent essay,
Teeuwen (2000) abandons the somewhat problematic term Ryōbu Shintō altogether,
speaking of 'esoteric Buddhist Shintō' instead. Cf. also Kadoya (1995) and Scheid
(forthcoming).

anti-Buddhist nor anti-Confucian, but aimed at a syncretistic worldview in which 'Shintō', however weakly defined, stood on the same footing as the other teachings.

My hypothesis is that prior to Shintō as an independent religion, there was the notion of 'Way of the *Kami*' as 'Way of Japan' or 'Way of our Country' which I would add to the initially mentioned possible meanings of the term *shintō*. '*Shintō*' as 'Way of Japan' differs from definition b), political or moral norms, in that sense that it does not necessarily define what this Japanese Way actually consists of. Rather, it is based on the assumption that there must be a 'Way' particular to Japan that is comparable to the Way of Buddha or the Way of Confucius. However, rather than an ethical or religious teaching, the salient feature of this 'Japanese Way' is seen in the fact that Japan was governed by one dynasty of divine origin since times immemorial – the quality of *kami*-ness mentioned above. While definitions a) (religious system) and b) (political or moral norms) are by no means incongruous with this notion of *shintō* as the 'Japanese Way', they are both somehow more specific.

The 'tree theory' provides the best example of this understanding of *shintō*. In the Edo period, when it circulated widely among Shintō intellectuals (probably due to its popularization by Yoshida Shintō), Buddhists also still applied it to defend the legitimacy of their convictions [cf. SJ, p. 402]. It is not difficult to surmise that in the Buddhist understanding, the notion of Shintō as 'roots and trunk' reflected a somehow primitive state of consciousness that was refined by the 'fruits' of Buddhism. Being based on a metaphor, the 'tree theory' provides not only one stringent xenophobic or xenophile interpretation, but also can be turned into both directions, which is probably one reason for its popularity.

For Yoshida Kanetomo, however, Buddhism was definitively a 'shallow and simplistic' provisional device that would be better replaced by the original, that is Shintō, which he considered 'deep and mysterious'.[23] And in contrast to his predecessors, he actually came up with a more or less systematic religious system. While I do not think that Kanetomo was actually the first to have a vision of Shintō as Japan's indigenous *kami* religion, he was certainly much more specific

---

[23] Cf. NST 19, pp. 236f; Grapard (1992b), p. 155; Scheid (2001), p. 354.

in defining what that *kami* way may actually consist of. He was thus the first who filled the attractive, but somehow ambiguous term *shintō* with a concrete content. This content was called Yuiitsu Shintō 唯一神道, the One-and-Only Shintō. It consisted basically of a system of esoteric – that is, secret – rituals, a pantheon based on the idea that *kami* where the original form of the Buddhas and not the other way around, and a cosmology based on Japanese mythology interpreted in terms of Yin and Yang and the Five-Phases conception.[24] From a modern perspective it is quite obvious that this Shintō was modeled largely on a Buddhist paradigm with the inclusion of certain Taoist conceptions and an iconography taken from Japanese myths. If we regard it from the perspective of the medieval *shinkoku shisō* or tree theory, however, Yuiitsu Shintō provided a plausible development of the axiomatic assumption that Chinese and Indian traditions both originated from Japan. In this perspective, Yoshida Shintō would have lost plausibility if it had no common features with Buddhism. The only requirement was to prove its antiquity and its genealogic legitimacy.

To prove the antiquity of his alleged family tradition, Yoshida Kanetomo reverted to pretensions that were probably only acceptable in the peculiar historical situation he lived in. I will mention these circumstances in a moment. Before, let me briefly analyze the general conception of Shintō as religion that can be gathered from the *Myōbō yōshū*. As I will try to show, this conception tells us more about the position of Kanetomo's Shintō in relation to *shinkoku shisō* and thus also has some political impact.

### *'Visible things' and 'hidden things'*

In defining his concept of religion, Kanetomo referred to the distinction of 'visible things' and 'hidden things', which he took from the so-called 'yielding of land' (*kuni-yuzuri* 国譲り) episode of the *Nihon shoki*. In this account, the god Ōanamuchi-no-mikoto 大穴牟遅命 surrenders to the Heavenly Grandson of Amaterasu who has just descended from Heaven to conquer the Earth. Ōanamuchi declares:

> *"From now on the visible things (*arawani-no-koto* 顕露事) which I was in charge of shall be directed by the Heavenly Grandson. I will*

---

[24] Cf. Scheid (2000 and 2001, chap. 6).

*retire and direct the hidden things.*" [NKBT 67, pp. 150ff.; Aston (1998) [vol. I], p. 80f.]

In a commentary on the *Nihon shoki* Kanetomo renders this declaration of Ōanamuchi in slightly different words: "*The visible kingly way (*ōdō 王道*) shall belong to the grandson of the sun deity. I shall direct the way of the kami (*shintō*)*". And he adds the commentary: "*The hidden things, that is* shintō. *They must be kept secret.*" [*Nihon shoki jindai shō* 日本書紀神代抄, Kubota (1959), p. 431]. In Kanetomo's interpretation the ominous term 'hidden things' is therefore a synonym for Shintō. This attribution reflects his understanding of Shintō as a basically esoteric teaching comparable to *mikkyō* 密教, Japanese eso- teric Buddhism. It is tempting to regard this interpretation as a feeble excuse for many structural congruities between Yoshida Shintō and *mikkyō*. However, as has been pointed out by Kubota Osamu 久保田収 already in the 1950's, the understanding of 'hidden things' as 'religious matters' in contrast to 'open things' as 'political matters' can be traced back to the writings of Kanetomo's spiritual mentor Ichijō Kanera 一条兼良 (1402-1481).[25] Thus, it was probably Kanera's idea to regard the 'visible things' and the 'hidden things' as expres- sions of a complementary system of political and spiritual authority that was initiated by the subjugation of Ōanamuchi. In contrast to Kanetomo, Kanera did not found a specific religious current but rather adhered to a pluralistic syncre- tism much in the same way as the afore mentioned Buddhist advocates of the tree theory. With them he shared the endeavor to put the *kami* at the basis of the syncretistic worldview and thus endow Japan with the afore mentioned quality of '*kami*-ness'.

At any rate, we have to underline two aspects in the understanding of Shintō, or rather Japanese religion, that Kanetomo drew from the *kuni-yuzuri* episode: First, not only Shintō, but all true religion belongs to the 'hidden things', that is to say it is secret and thus has much in common with esoteric Buddhism which was widely regarded as the ultimate form of Buddhism at that time. In a bold

---

[25] The renowned scholar and politician Ichijō Kanera compiled his views of Japan's mythological origin in the *Nihon shoki sansō* 日本書紀纂疏, an exegetical text on the *Nihon shoki* ( written in 1455 and revised in 1473) influenced by previous Urabe 卜部 priests and influencing subsequent Urabe (Yoshida) Shintō interpretations [cf. Kubota (1959), pp. 387-396; Scheid (2001), pp. 246f.].

reversal of intellectual influences, Kanetomo even pushed this idea to the pretension that Shingon Buddhism was actually the 'Shintō of India' [cf. Scheid (2001), p. 249]. Second, religion and politics are complementary 'Ways', both headed by separate authorities. This conception resembles the Buddhist understanding of *ōbō* 王法 and *buppō* 仏法, the kingly law and the Buddha law, which were seen as mutually sustaining each other but not as the same.

The adoption of this separation of spiritual and worldly authority is a significant turning point in the history of *kami* religion. At least in the tradition of court Shintō (to which Kanetomo belonged), it went without saying that the Tennō also represented the highest authority in the realm of stately *kami* ritual. Certainly, there were a number of priest families who specialized in the performance of rituals. But they did so much in the same way as other families specialized in the performance of dance or music. (Yoshida Kanetomo originated from the Urabe lineage, by the way, which was one of these traditional court ritual families.) On a symbolic level, however, the Tennō held the most important priestly function, as indicated, for instance, by his functions as the main ritualist of the *Daijōsai* 大嘗祭, the most prestigious courtly ritual performed only once during an individual Tennō's reign.[26] In Yoshida Shintō, by contrast, the *Daijōsai* – however 'esoteric' and sacred it may appear to us – is part of the 'visible things' and thus ultimately part of the profane and mundane. There is still an even more sacred and obscure counterpart of the *Daijōsai* in the esoteric, 'hidden realm' of Yoshida Shintō.[27]

---

[26] For general information about the *Daijōsai* cf. Naumann (1988), pp. 164-168. In spite of increasing Buddhist influences on court ritualism, and even on the imperial accession rites, to which the *Daijōsai* belonged, the Tennō's priestly functions remained untouched during the medieval period. "*It was inconceivable that a medieval emperor still on the throne would officially become part of a temple lineage by voluntarily passing through the rituals of affiliation with a temple social order. The emperor existed outside the Buddhist order; as a rule he could not function as a high-level ecclesial figure or as a performer of Buddhist rituals.*" [Kamikawa (1990), p. 245].

[27] Specifically, the temporary shrines erected during the *Daijōsai*, Yuki-den 悠紀殿 and Suki-den 主基殿, find their esoteric counterparts in two 'altars' of Yoshida Shintō called *bansō-dan* 万宗壇 ('altar of original spirits of the ten thousand phenomena') and *shogen-dan* 諸源壇 ('altar of sources of all living beings'). Cf. Grapard (1992b), p. 140; see also NST 19, pp. 214f; Scheid (2001), pp. 312f.

## The imperial regalia

In the same manner Yoshida Shintō interpreted also the so-called Imperial Regalia according to its twofold model of Shintō. The conventional set of three items, the sword, the mirror and the jewels which symbolize the Tennō's sacrosanct claim, had became the objects of various elaborate interpretations in the *Jinnō shōtō ki* as well as in all other 'Shintōistic' traditions of the medieval period. They were commonly referred to as *sanshu no jingi* 三種神器 ('three kinds of *kami* vessels') but also, for instance, as *sanshu no reihō* 三種霊宝 ('three kinds of spiritual treasures'), alluding to the three treasures of Buddhism (*sanbō* 三宝). This stress on the symbolic prestige of the Tennō can be regarded as expression of the 'union of government and ritual' (*saisei itchi* 祭政一致), which is already apparent in the *Jinnō shōtō ki* [28] and was regarded as a salient feature of the entire world of *kami* worship by 'nationalistic' scholars as for instance Hirata Atsutane 平田篤胤. Kanetomo, however, in spite of the nationalistic tones mentioned previously, clearly did not comply with this *saisei itchi* principle. This can not only be derived from his exegesis of the *kuni-yuzuri* narrative, but also from his interpretation of the Three Regalia as given in the *Myōbō yōshū*. Again he went back to Japan's mythological chronicles. The Three Regalia or Treasures are mentioned there in connection with the Heavenly Grandson's descent to Earth. In one of the chronicles, the *Sendai kuji hongi* 先代旧事本紀, however, we encounter not three treasures but ten treasures that should help the Grandson to establish an enduring rule on Earth.[29] Kanetomo accepts both versions as true and pretends that while the Tennō is in possession of the Three Treasures handed over to him from generation to generation from the Heavenly Grandson onward, the Ten Treasures are stored in the 'Inner Place'.[30] From the context it becomes clear that this ominous Inner Place refers to Kanetomo's own shrine, the Taigen-kyū 太元宮, which he had erected in honor of all *kami* of Japan. This implies that the one who is now in possession of the ten mythic treasures is the head priest of Yoshida Shintō. Moreover, the rela-

---

[28] Cf. Naumann (1994), p. 49.

[29] Up to the Edo period, the *Sendai kuji hongi*, known also as *Kuji hongi* or *Kujiki* 旧事紀, was regarded as the most ancient mythological chronology, issued by Shōtoku Taishi. Today it is regarded as an apocryphal text from the 9th century [cf. SJ, p. 569]. For the account of the ten treasures cf. ST 2/8, pp. 41f.

[30] Cf. NST 19, p. 219; Grapard (1992b), p. 143; Scheid (2001), p. 320.

tionship between Three Treasures and Ten Treasures is compared to the distinction between absolute and provisional forms of truth in Buddhism: They are two complementary aspects of the same thing.[31] Moreover, Kanetomo's main doctrinal text, the *Myōbō yōshū*, does nothing else than confront all commonly known aspects of court ritual with certain esoteric counterparts that had allegedly remained secret so far. It goes without saying that it was the Yoshida who were in charge of this secret tradition, which was said to contain the essence of Japan's original Shintō teachings.

It is this point where Yoshida Shintō diverts from the mainstream of *shinkoku shisō*. The Yoshidas' Shintō is no longer a matter of the Tennō, but rather a matter of his high priests. They are no longer only his loyal subjects. In religious matters they are his peers. Admittedly, this message cannot be found in an explicit statement of Yoshida Shintō. A thorough analysis of its implications on a symbolic level, however, cannot deny this impact. We have to ask now, why these implications did not disqualify Yoshida Shintō, at least among those contemporaries who were still loyal to the Tennō regime.

### *Historical setting*

Yoshida Shintō was born in the social environment of the *kuge* 公家, the ancient court nobility, who were also among its earliest followers. The restoration of the old social order from the Nara and Heian periods was certainly in line with the Yoshidas' natural political interests. However, while the return to a utopian past may have been a theoretical possibility in the eyes of Kitabatake Chikafusa, the author of the *Jinnō shōtō ki*, Yoshida Kanetomo witnessed what was probably the lowest point in the premodern history of the old nobility: the Ōnin War 応仁の乱 (1467-77). As we can see from his personal biography, Kanetomo accepted the regime of the *bushi* 武士 as a given fact.[32] It is therefore

---

[31] Admittedly, this is not too clear-cut a statement in favor of a division between religion and politics. Yet, to look for clear-cut statements in medieval Japanese religious discourse is a futile endeavor to begin with. For a more detailed analysis of the regalia in Yoshida Shinto cf. Scheid (2000), pp. 126-130 and (2001), pp. 236-242.

[32] Yoshida Kanetomo was, for instance, in close contact with Hino Katsumitsu 日野勝光 and his sister, the notorious Hino Tomiko 日野富子, wife of Shōgun Ashikaga Yoshimasa 足利義政 and sometimes rendered as 'female Shōgun' [cf. Hagiwara (1975), p. 638; Scheid (2001), pp. 123f].

quite understandable that he did not want to establish his religious tradition entirely within the framework of the ancient court, but rather that he wanted to incorporate the court using its symbolic prestige while presenting his own tradition as something that went beyond the traditional limitations of court ritualism. Therefore, Yoshida Shintō claimed to pertain to all *kami* of Japan not in the name of the Tenno, but in the name of Yuiitsu Shintō, the 'one-and-only way of the *kami*', that is, in the name of itself. Kanetomo was very explicit in this point: He maintained that his Shintō is actually the one and only religious tradition that originates from the Age of the Gods and was transmitted in only his family without any alteration up to the present day.[33] This radical 'invented tradition' would not have been possible, I believe, without the preceding destruction of virtually all Kyōto, which involved the annihilation of many historical records, documents and other scriptures pertaining to court ritualism. Yoshida Shintō is a typical product of post-war recovery ('*Wiederaufbau*'). One must add, though, that Kanetomo used the range of new possibilities at that time to develop indeed a comprehensive ritual system. This ritual system is the core of Yoshida Shintō, its secret part. The often pretentious claims for which Yoshida Shintō is famous actually are not its central issues but rather a kind of protective shield by which Kanetomo tried to legitimate his new ritual system.

## Conclusion

Let me conclude my considerations of the Yoshidas' novel usage of *shintō* and its relationship to *shinkoku*. As I have tried to show, the notion of Shintō as a 'Way' comparable to the 'Buddha Way' or the 'Way of Confucius' seems to have already existed before the propagation of Yoshida Shintō, and is best exemplified in the so-called tree theory, which can be traced back to the early 14th century. At that time, however, the term *shintō* was overshadowed by the term *shinkoku*, probably the most representative catch-phrase of "*Japan's quest for cultural identity and the search for an ultimate essence of things*" [Grapard (1992a), p. 46] in the late Kamakura and early Muromachi period. This so-called *shinkoku shisō* can be regarded as firmly established and widely known in educated circles in Yoshida Kanetomo's lifetime. The term *shintō* in its novel usage was probably something like a by-product of the Divine Land discourse; a kind

---

[33] Cf. NST 19, p. 239; Grapard (1992b), p. 157; Scheid (2001), p. 358.

of black box or container for a Japanese *kami*-ness yet lacking concrete contents. I believe that Yoshida Kanetomo based his own conception of Shintō precisely on this notion of *shintō* in the *shinkoku shisō*. As the religious dimension in Yoshida Shintō surmounted the political one, however, the word *shintō* surmounted *shinkoku*. At the beginning of my discussion of Yoshida Shintō, I cited two passages that may have given the impression that Yoshida Shintō doctrine was a direct successor of political texts such as the *Jinnō shōtō ki*. However, as I tried to point out later, Yoshida Shintō actually diverted from the Tennō-centric worldview of these predecessors. In fact, I could not find any other passages in Yoshida Kanetomo's texts containing the term *shinkoku* apart from the cited quotations. I am therefore quite sure that Yoshida Kanetomo made a conscious use of the ethnocentric connotations of *shin/ kami* in the Divine Land discourse, in order to promote the term *shintō*, but then used this term for different purposes. The most striking differences occur in two fields: The early *shinkoku* thinkers were proud of their country, proud of, or even loyal to, the Tennō but also acknowledged Buddhism. Kanetomo, on the other hand, rejected Buddhism and altered his own position vis-à-vis the Tennō since he strove for independence from both. Actually, the center of his concerns was his family tradition, which consisted partially of truly ancient traditions and partially of invented addenda. His aim was to establish this tradition as the most orthodox way of *kami* worship, while at the same time to gain freedom from the sacrosanct ritualism of the court, which always placed his family below the Tennō and one or two other priest families. Although the regime of the *bushi* is not mentioned with a single word in Yoshida doctrinal texts, Kanetomo certainly kept the political realities of his time well in mind and aimed to present himself as the spiritual leader of *kami* worship for the courtiers as well as for the warriors. In my view, this endeavor to restore and elevate his own family tradition was his strongest motivation for the propagation of the One-and-Only Shintō.

The Ōnin war and the so-called *ge koku jō* 下克上 ('low-beats-high') spirit of the time certainly favored the development of Yoshida Shintō. In the Edo period, Yoshida Shintō finally gained recognition as a kind of Shintō orthodoxy among *buke* 武家 authorities, while opposition among the courtiers constantly grew stronger. What is more, also intellectuals from various strata of society began to develop retrospective utopias with the Tennō in the center in the name of Shintō. While they took over the Yoshida's critical view of Buddhism and even drove it much further, they also developed the _saisei itchi_ paradigm of court Shintō. Yoshida Shintō, on the other hand, fell into doctrinal ossification and did not manage to develop its initiatives towards a religious system independent from political authorities any further. Thus, the _saisei itchi_ paradigm gained possession of the concept of Shintō. It was probably not before the 19th century that the conflict between the Yoshida paradigm of Shintō, which aims at building up a comprehensive religious system such as Buddhism, and the _saisei itchi_ paradigm which subordinates Shintō to politics, surfaced in open discussions. Implicitly, however, this conflict is already present in the development of Yoshida Shintō. In spite of its borrowings from other traditions, Yoshida Shintō actually provided a concept of _kami_ religion that was unified by a hierarchical structure and yet – in doctrinal theory, of course – independent from political authority.

### _References_

Aston (1998)
    Aston, William George: _Nihongi: Chronicles of Japan from the Earliest Times to A.D. 697._ Rutland, Vermont & Tōkyō: Tuttle, 1998. [[1]1972, first ed. in 2 vols. 1896].

Breen/ Teeuwen (2000)
    Breen, John/ Teeuwen, Mark (eds.): _Shinto in History: Ways of the Kami._ London: Curzon Press, 2000.

Grapard (1992a)
    Grapard, Allan G.: "The Shinto of Yoshida Kanetomo", in: _Monumenta Nipponica_ 47/1 (1992), pp. 27-58.

—    (1992b)
    Grapard, Allan G. [trans.]: "Yuiitsu Shintō Myōbō Yōshū (by Yoshida Kanetomo)", in: _Monumenta Nipponica_ 47/2 (1992), pp. 137-61.

Hagiwara (1975)
    Hagiwara, Tatsuo 萩原龍夫: _Chūsei saishi soshiki no kenkyū_ 中世祭祀組織の研究. Tōkyō: Yoshikawa kōbunkan, 1975 [[1]1962].

Hiraizumi (1938)
> Hiraizumi, H.: "Der Einfluß der Mappō-Lehre in der japanischen Geschichte", in: *Monumenta Nipponica* 1 (1938), pp. 58-69.

Kadoya (1995)
> Kadoya, Atsushi 門屋温: "Ryōbu shintō 両部神道", in: *Kokubungaku kaishaku to kanshō 国文学解釈と鑑賞* 60/12 (1995), pp. 61-66.

Kamikawa (1990)
> Kamikawa, Michio: "Accession Rituals and Buddhism in Medieval Japan", in: *Japanese Journal of Religious Studies* 17/2-3 (1990), pp. 243-280.

Kleine (1996)
> Kleine, Christoph: *Hōnens Buddhismus des Reinen Landes: Reform, Reformation oder Häresie?* Frankfurt am Main: Peter Lang, 1996.

Kubota (1959)
> Kubota, Osamu 久保田収: *Chūsei shintō no kenkyū 中世神道の研究.* Kyōto: Shintōshi gakkai, 1959.

Kuroda (1975)
> Kuroda, Toshio 黒田俊雄: *Nihon chūsei no kokka to shūkyō 日本中世の国家と宗教日本中世の国家と宗教.* Tōkyō: Iwanami shoten, 1975.

— (1981)
> Kuroda, Toshio: "Shinto in the History of Japanese Religion", in: *Japanese Journal of Religious Studies* 7/1 (1981), pp. 1-22.

— (1996)
> Kuroda, Toshio: "The Discourse on the 'Land of Kami' (*Shinkoku*) in Medieval Japan", in: *Japanese Journal of Religious Studies* 23/3-4 (1996), pp. 233-69 [Translation by Fabio Rambelli from "Chūsei no shinkoku shisō: kokka ishiki to kokusai kankaku 中世の神国意識：国家意識と国際感覚", a chapter from Kuroda 1975, ed. also in *Kuroda Toshio chosakushū 黒田俊雄著作集*, vol. II. Kyōto: Hōzōkan, 1994].

MKDJT
> Mikkyō jiten hensōkai 密教辞典編纂会 (ed.): *Mikkyō daijiten 密教大辞典.* Tōkyō: Hōzōkan, 1998 [¹1932].

Morrell (1985)
> Morrell, Robert E.: *Sand and Pebbles (Shasekishū): The Tales of Mujū Ichien, a Voice for Pluralism in Kamakura Buddhism.* Albany: State University of New York Press, 1985.

— (1987)
Morrell, Robert E.: *Early Kamakura Buddhism: A Minority Report.*
Berkeley: Asian Humanities Press, 1987.

Naumann (1988)
Naumann, Nelly: *Die einheimische Religion Japans. Teil 1: Bis zur Heian-Zeit.* [Handbuch der Orientalistik, part V, vol. 4, sect. 1, no. 1] Leiden: Brill, 1988.

— (1994)
Naumann, Nelly: *Die einheimische Religion Japans. Teil 2: Synkretistische Lehren und religiöse Entwicklungen von der Kamakura- bis zum Beginn der Edo-Zeit.* [Handbuch der Orientalistik, part V, vol. 4, sect. 1, no. 2] Leiden: Brill, 1994.

Nishida (1957)
Nishida, Nagao 西田長男: "Sankyō-shiyō-kajitsu setsu no seiritsu 三教枝葉華実説の成立", in his: *Shintōshi no kenkyū 神道史の研究,* vol. II. Tōkyō: Risōsha, 1957, pp. 370-394.

NKBT 67
Ienaga, Saburō 家永三郎 et al. (eds.): *Nihon shoki 日本書紀 jō 上.* [Nihon koten bungaku taikei 日本古典文学大系, vol. 67] Tōkyō: Iwanami shoten, 1967.

— 85
Watanabe, Tsunaya 渡辺綱也 (ed.): *Shasekishū 沙石集.* [Nihon koten bungaku taikei 日本古典文学大系, vol. 85] Tōkyō: Iwanami shoten, 1973.

NST 19
Ōsumi, Kazuo 大隅和雄 (ed.): *Chūsei shintō ron 中世神道論.* [Nihon shisō taikei 日本思想大系, vol. 19] Tōkyō: Iwanami shoten, 1977.

Quenzer (2000)
Quenzer, Jörg B.: *Buddhistische Traum-Praxis im japanischen Mittelalter (11.-15. Jahrhundert).* [Mitteilungen der Deutschen Gesellschaft für Natur- und Völkerkunde Ostasiens, vol. 132] Hamburg: OAG, 2000.

Rambelli (1996)
Rambelli, Fabio: "Religion, Ideology of Domination, and Nationalism: Kuroda Toshio on the Discourse of *Shinkoku*", in: *Japanese Journal of Religious Studies* 23/3-4 (1996), pp. 387-426.

Satō (1995)
Satō, Hiroo 佐藤弘夫: "Shinkoku shisō kō 神国思想考" [Some thoughts on Divine Land discourse], in: *Nihonshi kenkyū* 日本史研究 390 (1995), pp. 1-30.

— (1998)
Satō, Hiroo 佐藤弘夫: *Shin, butsu, ōken no chūsei* 神・仏・王権の中世. Kyōto: Hōzōkan, 1998.

Scheid (2000)
Scheid, Bernhard: "Reading the *Yuiitsu shintō myōbō yōshū*: A modern exegesis of an esoteric Shinto text", in: Breen/ Teeuwen (2000), pp. 117-143.

— (2001)
Scheid, Bernhard: *Der Eine und Einzige Weg der Götter: Yoshida Kanetomo und die Erfindung des Shinto*. Vienna: Verlag der Österreichischen Akademie der Wissenschaften, 2001.

— (forthcoming)
Scheid, Bernhard: "Both parts or only one? *Honji suijaku* syncretism challenged by 'orthodox Shinto' in the Edo Period", in: Teeuwen, Mark/ Rambelli, Fabio (eds.): *Honji suijaku*. London: Curzon (forthcoming).

SJ
Kokugakuin daigaku nihon bunka kenkyūjo 国学院大学日本文化研究所 (ed.): *Shintō jiten* 神道辞典. Tōkyō: Kōbundō, 1994.

ST 2/8
Kamada, Junichi 鎌田純一 (ed.): *Sendai kuji hongi* 先代旧事本紀. [*Shintō taikei* 神道大系 – *kotenhen* 古典編 8] Tōkyō: Shintō taikei hensankai, 1980.

— 7/8
Nishida Nagao 西田長男 (ed.): *Urabe shintō* 卜部神道, *jō* 上. [*Shintō taikei* 神道大系 – *ronsetsuhen* 論説編 8] Tōkyō: Shintō taikei hensankai, 1985.

Teeuwen (2000)
Teeuwen, Mark: "The Kami in esoteric Buddhist thought and practice", in: Breen/ Teeuwen (2000), pp. 95-116.

Teeuwen/ van der Veere (1998)
Teeuwen, Mark/ van der Veere, Hendrik: *Nakatomi Harae Kunge: Purification and Enlightenment in Late-Heian Japan.* Munich: iudicium, 1998.

Tsuda (1949)
Tsuda, Sōkichi 津田左右吉: *Nihon no shintō* 日本の神道. Tōkyō: Iwanami shoten, 1949.

# Matching *kami* with Modernity:
## an early Meiji intellectual's thought on electric light
Michael WACHUTKA

## 1. Introduction

The change of material culture in Japanese life under the impetus of Westernization in the early Meiji period brought with it the necessity to rationalize and integrate newly introduced items into the framework of one's own 'traditional' worldview. No matter how common these items are to all of us today, there was a time when they were new and astonishing to Japanese eyes. The need to cope with these articles from a different cultural sphere inevitably also challenged – and often triggered a change in – the common mental stance, resulting in an adaptation and redefinition of ones own cultural tradition. Certain mind-sets introduced from the Western countries in early Meiji, especially the ideas of enlightenment, freedom and equality no doubt were greeted with enthusiasm by a part of the young generation, but often the achievements and consequences of these thoughts were limited to a relatively small circle of intellectuals. In general, orthodox convictions prevailed. Items of a new material culture, however, quickly became 'visible' throughout all of society.

It was an often-heard opinion in those times that European or Western thinking might have advantages in technical and practical knowledge, but that Japan was clearly superior in the spiritual and moral sphere. The notion of 'Japanese spirit' versus 'Western knowledge', Japanese mental culture versus European material civilization was typically expressed in the popular term *seyō gijutsu tōyō dōtoku* 西洋技術東洋道徳 ('Western technology, Eastern morals'), coined by the Confucian scholar Sakuma Shōzan 佐久間象山 (1811-1864)[1]. A further popular term for those ideas was *wakon yōsai* 和魂洋才 ('Japanese spirit, Western knowledge'). It was modified in the Meiji period from the expression *wakon kansai* 和魂漢才 ('Japanese spirit, Chinese knowledge'), traditionally attributed to Sugawara no Michizane 菅原道真 (845-903). This term expressed

---

[1] Sakuma was a retainer of the Matsushiro 松代 domain in Shinshū 信州, i.e., the province Shinano 信濃, now Nagano-ken 長野県.

the "*ideal of using knowledge gained from China in accordance with Japan's native cultural traditions*"[2] that can be sensed in written sources since the earliest contacts between these two countries. In its 'modern' Meiji modification, the term was advocated as a guiding principle for the adoption of Western culture, because "*the adaptation of Western technology was an inevitable, necessary step towards the pursuit of envisioned national growth. The wish to maintain traditional moral values produced the position of compromise known as* wakon yōsai. *This term exemplifies the process by which traditional Japanese culture and Western technology were woven together in modern Japanese civilization.*"[3]

From the viewpoint of the recipient it is undeniable that – especially when introduced from a foreign nation – 'spiritual culture' is far more difficult to accept than 'material culture'. However, it is clear that distributing commodities not only means crossing regional boundaries, but simultaneously breaking through the closed barriers that separate groups and their innate habitual behavior, traditional values and views. Therefore, when importing and adopting foreign goods to simplistically speak of the culture of the West as 'material' and that of the East as 'spiritual' is of course susceptible to questionable inferences, as the dichotomy between spiritual and material is hardly ever valid – yet, it reveals a lot about the manner in which these concepts are perceived, as Shibusawa Keizō 渋沢敬三 wrote:

> "*There ware [sic] Japanese in the late Tokugawa and the early Meiji periods who proposed to adopt the material culture of the West but retain the traditional spiritual culture of Japan. As long as one accepts the idea that material culture and spiritual culture are separate utilities, this sounds reasonable enough, but subsequent events more than amply demonstrated the naireete [sic] of this type of thinking.*"[4]

It always was and is a common reaction to integrate strange items into familiar concepts and value-systems, in order not to be overwhelmed by their sheer incomprehensibility. One of the basic problems of human mind all over the world is to meaningfully anchor oneself in the eternal flow of time, which lets

---

[2] KEJ, vol. 8, p. 221a.
[3] KEJ, vol. 8, p. 221a-b.
[4] Shibusawa (1958), p. 3.

people in their rationalized comparisons easily fall back on common 'traditional answers' to new questions and problems. Describing this phenomenon, the social philosopher Hermann Lübbe writes: *"Die Leistungen des historischen Bewußtseins sind Leistungen zur Kompensation eines änderungstempobedingten kulturellen Vertrautheitsschwundes."*[5]

This kind of rapid 'loss of cultural familiarity' at the dawn of the Meiji period, to a great extent caused by the uncontrollable influx of unfamiliar Western thoughts and goods, generated a specific 'historical awareness' of what is Japanese. It triggered the need to hold on to one's own 'traditional spiritual culture' in opposition to Western culture – in this context mostly seen as merely material and therefore inferior. A need that was felt by many Japanese in early Meiji when confronted with, at times, awe-inspiring and at first sight inconceivable new foreign matters.

One example of this whole process with its underlying antagonistic view of 'tradition' versus 'modern' – illustrating a specific historical and to a large extent also 'national' awareness or identity – is Iida Takesato's 飯田武郷 (1828-1900) short essay on the newly introduced electrical lamp, *Denkitō* 電氣燈, written in the early half of the Meiji period.

## 2. Iida Takesato's life and background[6]

Iida Takesato was born on Bunsei 文政 10/12/6[7] [22 January 1828], in the Edo-residence of the lord of Suwa 諏訪 in Shinshū – the same province as the

---

[5] 'The achievements of a historical awareness are achievements to compensate a loss of cultural familiarity caused by the pace of change.' (cited in: A.V. Cheruskia zu Tübingen (ed.): *Mitteilungsblatt*. No. 100 (March 1999), p. 6).

[6] Only a concise overview is given to provide a better understanding of the possible origin of Iida's thoughts. For more thorough information on his background and ideas, see Wachutka (2001). An extensive biographic study of Iida Takesato, focusing also on the contemporary role of his accademic circle *Ō-yashima gakkai* 大八州學會, is under preparation.

[7] I.e., on the 6th day of the 12th month of the 10th year of the era named *bunsei* (held by emperor Ninkō 仁孝). Until shortly after the Meiji-restoration when the Western calendar was adopted, the months and days of the Japanese lunar-based calendar did not correspond with the ones in the Western solar-based calendar. Those Japanese dates are given here in an abbreviated form as shown above, followed by this date converted into its Western form.

above named Sakuma Shōzan, who coined the term *seyō gijutsu tōyō dōtoku* ('Western technology and Eastern morals').

At the age of 11 Iida entered the school of Hattori Gensai 服部元濟, to study Chinese literature (*kangaku* 漢学). However, after he came in contact with some of Motoori Norinaga's 本居宣長 works, Iida was very impressed by their ideas and stopped his learning with Hattori, entering Hirata Atsutane's 平田篤胤 school shortly after the latter's death in 1843. After many years of exposure to nativist thoughts, Iida on Kaei 嘉永 5 [1852], at the age of 25, began to write the *magnum opus* that was going to occupy the rest of his life – the manuscript of his *Nihonshoki-tsūshaku* 日本書紀通釋. With its 4000 pages in 70 volumes, it is the largest commentary work on *Nihongi* 日本紀 ever written and represents what Iida Takesato is known for today.

The next decade and a half, Japan was faced with extremely turbulent years. At least since the threat of Perry's arrival, the discourse on *sonnō jōi* 尊王攘夷 ('reverence for the emperor, expulsion of the barbarians') spread throughout the country. During this time, Iida was among the patriots loyal to the Emperor whom Iwakura Tomomi 岩倉具視 (1825-1883) secretly rounded up in Bunkyū 文久 2 [1862] for the purpose of building a conspiracy to restore the imperial power and overthrow the Shogunate (*tōbaku* 討幕). Others belonging to that group were inter alia such prominent figures as Saigō Takamori 西郷隆盛 (1827-1877), Ōkubo Toshimichi 大久保利通 (1830-1878), Kido Takayoshi 木戸孝允 (1833-1877) and Sagara Sōzō 相良總三 (1839-1868).[8] All in all, these chaotic years saw the death and succession of five Shoguns and three changes of imperial era names, until finally with the fourth change a new era in Japan's history emerged: Meiji 明治.

During the 8th month of Meiji 2 [ca. September 1869], Iida returned to his home domain Takashima-han in Shinshū, to become the head of the Institute for Imperial Studies (*kōgakusho* 皇學所), also called *kokugakkō* 國學校. When offered the position of Professor at that Institute, Iida was said to have replied that "*for a long time it has earnestly been my heart's desire to teach the younger people of this domain our nation's nobility and the spiritual founding of the state*

---

[8] Cf. "Iida Takesato den 飯田武郷傳" [Appendix of Iida (1922-26)], p. 1f.

[kokutai no sonki to chōkoku-seishin 國體の尊貴と肇國精神]."[9] In this school, every month a celebration was held for the souls of the four great figures of the nativist movement – Kada no Azumamaro 荷田春満 (1669-1736), Kamo no Mabuchi 賀茂真淵 (1697-1769), Motoori Norinaga (1730-1801) and Hirata Atsutane (1776-1843) – together with an exhortation sermon on different duties for the students. The textbooks used included most of the old Japanese classics so prominent in *kokugaku* 国学 ('national learning').[10] However, in October 1872, due to a general governmental land reform that eliminated the domains and installed the prefectures (*haihan-chiken* 廃藩置県), the Takashima domain was abolished, and with it, also the Institute for Imperial Studies.

About half a year later, in Meiji 6/3 [March 1873][11], Iida Takesato was appointed chief-priest of the Great Shintō-shrine (*kampei-taisha* 官幣大社)[12] Kehi-jingū 気比神宮. Despite Iida's actual inclination to diligently fulfill his function as shrine priest for a long time, a sudden telegraphic instruction from the Ministry of Education (*kyōbushō* 教部省) called him to the capital. Due to the lack of written evidence, there is no clear reason why Iida was called back to Tōkyō hardly a month after his appointment at Kehi-jingū. However, the Ministry of Education became substitute office of imperial rule when on 5 May 1873 a fire partially burned down the Emperor's palace. It is said that due to that fire many of the collected books, charts and maps on the genealogy of the reigning line and the historical geography of government were lost, and as a result on 8 May every province and prefecture was ordered to gather and copy materials concerning these topics to present to the throne.[13] It can be assumed that because people with expertise in the Japanese classics and ancient history to inspect and verify these materials were urgently required at that time, Iida Takesato was asked for his assistance.

---

[9] Sakamoto (1944), p. 136.
[10] Cf. ibid. (1944), p. 137f.
[11] From this time, due to a calendar-reform in the beginning of that year, the Japanese days and months correspond to the Western Gregorian-calendar.
[12] The highest class in the prewar ranking of shrines that received government offerings (*kanpei*).
[13] Cf. Sakamoto (1944), p. 148f.

This important assignment was followed by appointments as chief-priest at Suwa-jinja 諏訪神社 (a *kampei-taisha)* and Nukisaki-jinja 貫前神社 (a middle-ranked national shrine, *kokuhei-chūsha* 国幣中社) in 1874, and additionally at Asama-jinja 浅間神社 (a *kokuhei-chūsha)* in 1875. Iida engaged diligently in his duties at these shrines and *"served the promulgation of the Imperial way* [kōdō no senpu 皇道の宣布]"[14]. The following year in April however, Iida quit all his posts of chief-priest and permanently moved his home to Tōkyō. The reason for doing so was his appointment as teacher at the Great Teaching Institute 大教院 (*Daikyōin).*[15] This Institute was part of a governmental endeavor to create a unified state religion – not initially identified as Shintō – through the so-called 'Great Promulgation Campaign' (*daikyō senpu undō* 大教宣布運動).[16] This campaign (*undō)* to promulgate (*senpu)* to the people a 'great teaching' (*daikyō)* was announced by an imperial edict on 3 February 1870, and its dogmas were basically the same as the ones of Hirata-Shintō.[17] The campaign consisted of three major components: of a corps of evangelists or 'teachers of ethic' (*kyōdōshoku* 教導職) since a modification in March 1872; 'Three Great Teachings'[18] that were announced on 28 April 1872 for those evangelists to promulgate; and the 'Great Teaching Institute' (*Daikyōin),* established in 1873 for the training and education of these evangelists. In order to provide proper training within this Institution, someone well versed in the Japanese classics was in need and Iida was invited to be a teacher.[19]

Retiring from that duty after two years in Meiji 11 [1878], Iida at the age of 52 became government official at the Great Council of State's College of Historiography (*Daijōkan-Shūshikan Goyōgakari* 太政官修史館御用掛). At that time, already about 20 years had passed since Japan opened its ports to foreign contact, whose influence so profoundly changed the country. One of the major aims of this College was, *"feeling that the ideas and thoughts of the people of this country are also on the verge to be changed, to make the people understand*

---

[14] Ibid. (1944), p. 150.
[15] Cf. ibid. (1944), p. 158 and p. 193.
[16] On this campaign and some of the institutions and people involved, see: Antoni (1998), p. 203ff and Hardacre (1989), p. 42ff.
[17] Cf. Muraoka (1988), p. 205.
[18] Variously called *daikyō* 大教, *kyōsoku sanjō* 教則三條, *sanjō no kyōsoku* 三條の教則 or *sanjō no kyōken* 三條の教憲. On the content of these three teachings see Fujii Takeshi's contribution to this volume, p. 113.
[19] Cf. Sakamoto (1944), p. 158.

*the essence and true meaning* [shinsui 神髓] *of our national history*"[20]. Arriving on the urgent need to have an expert on the Japanese classics – also due to the occasion of carrying out the mending of imperial tombs, the preservation of spots 'honored by the imperial presence' of successive emperors (*rekichō no seiseki-hozon* 歷朝の聖蹟保存), the raising of the status of shrines, etc. – Iida was worked there for about two years until 1880.[21] That year he became a Professor at Tōkyō University with expertise on the Japanese classics, staying there for about six years until Meiji 19 [1886].[22] At the age of 62, in December 1888, Iida became lecturer at the Institute of Japanese Literature (*Kōten-kōkyūjo* 皇典講究所)[23] and additionally, in February 1891, Professor at the private Keiō University (*Keiō-gijuku-daigaku* 慶應義熟大學) founded by Fukuzawa Yukichi 福沢諭吉 (1835-1901).[24] Further, in 1893 Iida was also asked to become lecturer at Jingūkyō-kō 神宮教校. *Jingūkyō* was originally one of the sects of Shintō that emerged in the late Edo and early Meiji period, but was dissolved in 1900.[25] It had headquarters in Tōkyō and Ise, and this additional school in Tōkyō where education in the Imperial way (*kōdō kyōiku* 皇道教育) was conducted.[26] Then, at the age of 70 in 1896, Iida after ten years returned to the Imperial University (Teikoku daigaku 帝國大學) in Tōkyō to become lecturer at its Philological Department (*bunka* 文料). Falling ill however, he resigned about a year later, ending his academic career as Professor for Japanese Classics at various institutions.

---

[20] Ibid. (1944), p. 159.

[21] Cf. ibid. (1944), p. 159f.

[22] In 1886 Iida Takesato established a 'Great Japan Academic Association' (*Ō-yashima gakkai* 大八州學會). Among its members were many (later to be) outstanding persons – professors and politicians alike – such as inter alia Kimura Masakoto 木村正辭, Motoori Toyokai 本居豐穎, Kume Motobumi 久米幹文, Yano Harumichi 矢野玄道, Kurokawa Mayori 黒川真頼 or Mozume Takami 物集高見.

[23] This Institute, specializing in research in Japanese classics, was established in 1882 and renamed the 'Institute for National Learning' (*Kokugakuin* 國學院) in 1890. In 1906 it became the present Kokugakuin University.

[24] Cf. Sakamoto (1944), p. 165.

[25] Karl Florenz writes that: "*In 1882, six sects were recognized [by the government]. One of them, the Jingū-kyōkwai, which stood in close relation to the Grand Shrine of Ise, had to dissolve itself in 1900, when the 'shrines' were separated from the 'religions'. By further eight sects becoming recognized, the number now is thirteen.*" [Florenz (1925a), p. 345].

[26] However, after some talks, in April 1896 this school was fused with Kokugakuin [cf. Sakamoto (1944), p. 166f].

Iida nevertheless passionately continued his research, and in 1899 finished his *Nihonshoki-tsūshaku* 日本書紀通釋. It took him 48 years to write and can be compared – not only in size and in time-span for completion – to Motoori Norinaga's life work *Kojiki-den* 古事記傳. Soon after completion, Iida Takesato died on 26 August Meiji 33 [1900] at the age of 74.

### 3. Iida's essay as an example of significant Meiji thoughts

#### The electric lamp

*Everybody mentions that the sun is the embodiment of fire, the moon the embodiment of water etc., although it goes without saying that from the beginning [they have been] in the middle of this firmament[27]. Plants, trees and stones, furthermore living beings – there is nothing among the things in this world that does not comprise the essence [ki] of water and fire. The great lights putting those suffusing fire and water up high in the middle of heaven and illuminating this world, hinge on the august deeds of the deities of sun and moon. Therefore, for large and small alike, the principle of condensation indeed is augustly prescribed by the* kami. *The people of the West, being industrious in everything, developed a way to replace the oil-lamp [by] assembling light and manufacturing this into a marvelous apparatus that may also be called a 'small sun'. Truly, when having one of these lamps, radiating a light excelling many a thousand fires, in an appropriate way it makes one also realize that there are opportunities in the world. Nevertheless, as might be suspected, their folk as well has not the faintest idea that there exists the fire of the deity Kagutsuchi's blood, deigned to be cut and sprinkled over all the 10 000 things in our age of gods. [They will] perceive that 'how can it be embarked upon' as dispositional root, indeed is a mere useless, empty theory. While in the near future various marvelous apparatuses will be manufactured, we have reason to bravely say that yet there are numerous who recognize that there is nothing of which the source not already was revealed in our Age of Gods. Do they know that the electric lamp hinges on the fire deity's august deeds?[28]*

---

[27] The characters for *ōzora* 大空, rendered here as 'firmament' (literally 'great air'), with the reading *daikū* are also used in the sense of 'ether' or, in a more Buddhist connotation, as 'great emptiness' and 'all-embracing nothing'.

[28] *Denkitō*
*Hi wa. Hi no karada nari. Tsuki wa mizu no karada nari nado wa. Dere mo iu koto naredo.*

Most likely, Iida Takesato for the first time saw an electric light when the rather famous light at Ginza No. 2 – hung on a pole 50 feet high and run by a five horsepower steam-operated generator – was put into operation on October 28, 1882. Contemporary newspapers estimated the light given off to be equal to that of 2000-4000 wax candles.[29] Although by that time gaslights for instance were known from long before, when looking at the scene captured in different woodblock prints – for instance, Eisai Shigekiyo's 栄斎重清 three-part print of 1883: *Tōkyō Ginza-dōri denkitō kensetsu no zu* 東京銀座通電氣燈建設之圖 ('View of the inauguration of the street lighting at Tōkyō's Ginza avenue') – showing a marveled audience gazing with open mouths at that incomprehensible

---

Moto yori kono ōzora no naka wa sara-nari. Yo no naka ni aru mono. Kusaki ishimura.
Mata iki toshi ikeru mono. Izuremo suika no ki o fufumanu wa arazaru nari. Sono
michimichitaru himizu o. Ame no monaka ni takaku kakagete. Kono yo o taraseru ōinaru
tomoshibi wa. Hi-kami tsuki-kami no miwaza ni yoreri. Sareba ōkiku mo chiisaku mo.
Atsumureba atsumaru kotowari o zo kami no sadame tamaerishi. Sore o nishi no kuni-bito
ga. Yorozu ni hakarite ayashiki utsuwa ni tsukuri ide. Ko-nichirin to mo ii-tsubeki sama
shitaru hikari o atsumete. Abura-hi ni kōru waza o namu kōgae idetaru. Geni kono hitotsu
no tō areba. Hyaku-sen no hi ni masaru hikari idekite. Yo ni bin aru mo saru kata ni
sakashiki chi nari kashi. Shika wa aredo. Sasuga ni kare no kuni-bito mo. Waga kamiyo ni
Kagutsuchi-no-kami no kirare-tamaishi chi no. Man no mono ni sosogite kaku hi wa aru to
iu koto o ba yume ni mo shirazu. Ika ni shite kakaru zo to iu sono tachi no moto o ba. Tada
itazura naru kūri ni nomi zo omoi toreru. Chikaki koro wa kusagusa no ayashiki utsuwa
domo o tsukuri idete. Ware takeku iu mo kotowari ni wa aredo. Nao sono moto o waga
kamiyo no den ni akasamu ni wa. Koto ni mo arazu oboyuru ga ōshi. Denki no tomoshibi no.
Hi no kami no go-waza ni yoru koto o ba shiru ya shirazu ya.
電氣燈
日は。火の體なり。月は水の體なりなどは。誰もいふことなれど。もとよりこの大空の
中はさらなり。世の中にあるもの。草木石むら。また生きとしいけるもの。いづれも水
火の氣をふゝまぬはあらざるなり。その滿ち滿ちたる火水を。天のもなかに高くかゝげ
て。此世を照せる大なるともし火は。日神月神の御わざによれり。されば大きくも小さ
くも。集むれば集まることわりをぞ神のさだめたまへりし。それを西の國人が。よろづ
にはかりてあやしき うつはに造りいで。小日輪ともいひつべきさましたる光を集めて。
あぶら火にかふるわざをなむかうがへいでたる。げにこの一つの燈あれば。百千の火に
まさる光いできて。よに便あるもさるかたにさかしき智なりかし。しかはあれど。さす
がに彼の國人も。わが神代に迦具土神のきられたまひし血の。萬の物にそゝぎてかく火
はあるといふ事をばゆめにも知らず。いかにしてかゝるぞといふその質のもとをば。たゞ
徒なる空理にのみぞ思ひとれる。近きころは種々のあやしき器どもをつくりいでゝ。わ
れたけくいふもことわりにはあれど。なほそのもとをわが神代の傳にあかさむには。こ
とにもあらずおぼゆるが多し。電氣のともし火の。火の神の御業によることをば知るや
知らずや。[Iida (1903), p. 272f].

[29] Cf. Shibusawa (1958), p. 142f.

spectacle, one can imagine the impact that such event must have had on the common people.

Picture 1: *Eisai's depiction of the electrical light at Ginza*

A hardly known but interesting aspect about the introduction of electrical light in Japan deserves to be mentioned at this point. On the scenic grounds of Iwashimizu Hachiman-gū 岩清水八幡宮 south of Kyōto, a monument to the memory of Thomas Alva Edison (1847-1937) can be found. The commemorative plaque explains that after developing the electric light bulb in 1879, for more than a decade the bamboo growing on the ground of this shrine was used to produce the necessary filaments[30] for Edison's carbon-filament lamps. This Iwashimizu Hachiman-gū, together with Ise-jingū 伊勢神宮 and Nara's Kasuga-taisha 春日大社 (some documents instead have Kamo-jinja 賀茂神社 in Kyōto), are the so-called *sansha* 三社. These 'three (major) shrines' for many centuries stood in close relation to the imperial court and its legitimization rituals. It is therefore also likely that Iida had his first encounter with the electric lamp at this shrine, during one of his many visits to Kyōto's historico-culturally important vicinity due to his writing of *Nihonshoki-tsūshaku*.

---

[30] For the production of filaments cellulose was dissolved to form a syrupy liquid, which was then extruded through a nozzle into a coagulating bath. The resulting thread was then wound on formers, shaping it as a characteristically looped curved, and carbonized by baking.

Our concern however is not so much the physical object 'electric lamp' as such, but rather the modes of ambivalence and explanation that are set off by this innocuous item in an exemplary fashion. It has to be reminded that Iida's essay in this respect should be seen as only one possible reaction and rationalization among early Meiji intellectuals when confronted with unfamiliar Western items. Limitation of space does not provide to deeply dive into all of his thoughts, but some of the concepts expressed in this short essay deserve a closer look.

Interestingly, instead of merely rejecting the electrical lamp by judging, Iida tries to explain by exploring and comparing to 'widely known' and traditionally established concepts. The first thing he does at the opening of the text, is to confirm the familiar and widely used concept of the Taoist *gogyō* 五行 ('five elements') doctrine, which belongs to the complex of *in-yō-dō* 陰陽道 ('the way of yin and yang'). This teaching of the cosmic dual forces divides and categorizes all natural phenomena into opposing poles, for instance, day and night, male and female, sun and moon. These dual forces are the origin of everything, a universal principle imbuing the whole cosmos. The *gogyō* are the five elements water, fire, wood, metal and earth, to which all things in the cosmos can be reduced. These two concepts can be combined on a fixed scheme, resulting in Iida's characteristic association of the sun being the embodiment of fire and the moon the embodiment of water. Similarly, the concept of the fire and water's *ki* 気, the essence or venereal, all-transcending energy of which everything – be it plants, trees, stones or living beings – is comprised, belongs to this complex as well. This 'Chinese' influenced general introduction of the text is soon expanded by the particular notion that nevertheless everything in the world is dependent on the Japanese deities and their deeds. Iida now is associating sun and moon not with a basic element but with specific deities administering them.

The deity Kagutsuchi-no-kami 迦具土神, on whom Iida centers his explanation, is the source of fire in Japanese mythology. His notion that herbs, trees and stones are 'naturally' filled with fire, is directly taken from the mythological part about this deity in *Nihongi* 日本紀.[31] After Izanami was burned and died while

---

[31] It is interesting to note that Iida in this essay uses the characters for Kagutsuchi as found in *Kojiki* 古事記, although the explanation of why the element of fire is inherent in all things

giving birth to Kagutsuchi, Izanagi out of anger cuts him to pieces with a sword. Many deities emerge from his slain parts and his blood, which is also sprinkled about on plants and stones, filling them with his fire.[32] This specific part, variant 8 of the 4th myth-sequence in *Nihongi*, reads:

> "*Izanagi no Mikoto cut Kagutsuchi no Mikoto into five pieces [...]. At this time the blood from the wounds spurted out and stained the rocks, trees and herbage. This is the reason that herbs, trees and pebbles naturally contain the element of fire.*"[33]

Consistent with this story, Iida in his *Nihonshoki-tsūshaku* explains that the blood that was dripping down on things, is to be taken as fire.[34] Already Hirata Atsutane refers to the relation between fire and blood. For instance he explains that the red color of the people's blood stems from the color of the fire, because fire and blood are originally the same.[35]

In the texts of *Nihongi* and *Kojiki*, Izanami is burned while giving birth to Kagutsuchi. This gives rise to the assumption that Kagutsuchi not only is the deity administering the fire, but indeed the real, physical fire itself. It is a common assumption by Japanese nativist scholars that *kami* not only control or inhabit things, but also are those things as such.[36] In the case of Kagutsuchi, in the *Norito* 祝詞 on the 'Ritual for the pacification of fire' (*Hoshizume no matsuri* 鎮火祭) it is even explicitly written that Izanami gave birth to the physical fire, not its deity.[37] This lack of distinction suggests that in ancient times the visible fire as such was venerated.

There is however a further long-standing connection between fire, sun and also the 'core' of Meiji Japan's national consciousness, the Emperor. Iida writes: "*the word* hi 火 *[fire] is identical with the* hi 日 *[sun] of the word* ten-hi 天日 *[the*

---

after sprinkling his blood, to which Iida refers, is only found in *Nihongi*. There this deity's name is written as 軻遇突智.
[32] Cf. NKBT, vol. 67, p. 99, l. 8f.
[33] Aston (1993), p. 29.
[34] Cf. Iida (1922-26), vol. 1, p. 207.
[35] Cf. ibid., vol. 1, p. 265.
[36] Motoori Norinaga for instance writes that: "*Amaterasu [is] the Great Sun God of the Heavens, who rules the Plain of High Heaven and who for all eternity, as at this very moment, illuminates the world [...]. How can one doubt that Amaterasu Ōmikami is the great ancestress of the emperors, as well as the sun in the heavens that illuminates this world.*" [Teuween (1995), p. 13f].
[37] Cf. NKBT, vol. 1, p. 428, l. 15f.

sun or sunlight, i.e., 'heavenly fire']. Surely from the beginning they are the same. The only difference is that the fire restricts its effect on the 10 000 things on earth, while the sun in heaven [amatsu-hi 天ッ日] with its mighty light illuminates the universe"[38]. Therefore, according to Iida, the Japanese word *hi* denotes at the same time the fire and the sun – and this correspondence hints to an inner connection that existed between fire and sun in traditional Japanese belief.[39]

The imperial succession traditionally is called *amatsu-hi-tsugi* 天つ日嗣 ('heavenly sun succession'). Customarily the origin of this term is explained from the fact that the imperial dynasty derives its origin and legitimacy from the deity of the sun, Amaterasu-ōmikami ('heaven-illuminating great deity'), and continues to pass on this legitimacy according to this deity's order.[40] As mentioned above, the word *hi* however denotes either 'sun' or 'fire'. It is therefore possible to see a connection between this title – ultimately denominating the nation's self-assessment of the Japanese Emperor and Empire as being derived from the gods – with an ancient fire-cult in Japan. From the beginning, all over the world, fire was a venerable object, and it also played an important role in Japan's conception of self, culture and nation.[41] Aston in his study on Shintō also refers to this ancient fire-cult and its source for legitimization and continual succession, as it is conducted at the shrine in Izumo: "*At the present day, when the office is transmitted from one high priest to his successor, they proceed to the 'Shrine of the Great Precinct', where the ceremony of 'divine fire' and 'divine water' is held. [...] This ceremony is called* hi-tsugi *(fire-continuance). It is curious that the same term (*hitsugi*) is constantly used of the succession to the Mikado's throne, and that the delivery of the sun-mirror formed part of the ceremony used on his accession. Hi* means either sun or fire"[42]. Fire, sun and light traditionally is closely related to the imperial family, its succession and legitimization – and therefore, according to the official state-ideology as promoted by the Meiji government, also with the self-assessment of the whole nation and its people. The role that the important late Tokugawa and early Meiji

---

[38] Iida (1922-26), vol. 1, p. 173
[39] Cf. also Aston (1905), p. 159, where he writes: "*The domestic fire renders important services to mankind, and its relation to the sun is unmistakable. Indeed the Japanese call fire and sun by the same name*, hi".
[40] Cf. Motoori (1926), vol. 2, p. 687.
[41] Cf. Nakayama (1987), part 2, p. 237f.
[42] Aston (1905), p. 258.

period conception of *kōshitsu chūshin shugi* 皇室中心主義 ('the imperial line as central principle') held in Iida Takesato's thoughts – despite all his progressiveness in other aspects – might not be clearly sensed from his essay on the electric light, but maybe from his short work *Kokutai-ron* 國體論, published in July 1892, where he writes: *"Indeed, since the earliest foundation of the Empire [creation of this nation], the way of ruler and ruled was firmly determined. [...The] great deity [Amaterasu-ōmikami] is the great august ancestor of the present Emperor. [...] Because the ruler exists also the people exist, and this is the foundation of the nation."*[43]

Having all this in mind, Iida naturally must have been impressed and shaken alike by the skill of the Western people to collect the light of the powerful fire in the sky – the 'sun' Amaterasu, the ancestral deity of the imperial line illuminating the universe – and manufacture it into a small 'little sun' able to easily illuminate every corner of the most ordinary person's home in Japan and abroad. The 'common citizen' of Tōkyō probably did not have much ambivalent feelings towards the electric lamp besides initial fascination when Ginza for the first time was bathed unfamiliarly in bright light during the evening of October 28, 1882. Nevertheless, many people of the *wakon yōsai* faction among the Meiji elite were of a different opinion. But maybe only for someone like Iida Takesato, constantly researching and being absorbed in *Nihongi* and its mythological world-view for many decades, the underlying connection with its possible power to challenge the 'spiritual core' of Japanese nationhood might have been immediately obvious.

The inherent dichotomous tension and paradox between the Japanese nation's strive for a Western-style (technical) 'modernity' and the simultaneous danger of a loss of cultural familiarity, independent spiritual identity and 'traditional' stance as feared by many intellectuals in the Meiji period, can therefore be exemplarily sensed even by the seemingly innocuous introduction of the electric lamp.

---

[43] Iida (1903), p. 312f.

## 3. Conclusion

It is a common socio-historical assumption nowadays that political or cultural constructions are in need of a 'spiritual' idea, because they cannot base their stability on political-economic interests alone. Be it the holiness or divinity of the kings, the class-mission of the party, the national identity of the whole people or the spiritual foundation to fight for freedom and democracy – for the accomplishment of (not only political) innovations it has always required such goals and values that not only appeal to practical interests, but especially to the heart and soul of the people as well.

One such aspect is the ideal of adopting and applying Western learning and knowledge in conformity with native Japanese cultural and spiritual traditions, referred to since the introduction of European items in the late 16th century. It again gained currency in the Meiji period as Western knowledge and technology began to be adopted on a large scale in Japan. This intellectual undercurrent of Meiji times – expressed in the popular slogans *seyō gijutsu tōyō dōtoku* and *wakon yōsai* – tried to call attention to the importance of the native cultural heritage and the unique spirit said to be inherent in Japanese civilization. This 'mainstream' of cultural-nationalist thoughts was centered on the foundation myths of *Kojiki* and *Nihongi*, especially the institution of the Emperor as direct descendent of the (Japanese) gods and therefore 'spiritual father' of the whole country, people and nation.

Individual nations do display certain special cultural traits and tendencies, but most developments and concepts are of course not singular. In certain aspects comparable to the Japanese concept of *shinkoku* 神国 ('divine country') and the divine imperial line of *amatsuhi-tsugi*, European monarchies as well legitimized themselves and their 'divine right of kings' by the fusion of Christian symbols with nationalistic ideas of a divine nation. However, such national-religious concepts of a noble and chosen *Volksgemeinschaft* cannot be interpreted with one-dimensional patterns of explanation. A rather complex model of narration is required to be able to trace the various religious-historical paths of development of modern nation-states. To this end, different habitual aspects of cultural identity-constructions via religious emotions and syncretistic fusions of old symbols or traditional thoughts with new political slogans, need to be analyzed on the basis of preferably various sources.

A valuable further step on the path towards a wider picture and more comprehensive understanding of the underlying concepts from a global perspective is provided by taking into account the various reactions of common people or intellectuals alike when faced with ungraspable, interesting, shocking or awe-inspiring new material items introduced from abroad – one example being Iida Takesato's essay *Denkitō* and the way he tries to make this marvelous foreign object intelligible to himself and others according to his own cultural tradition. Despite a recent general focus on such questions and problems, the many processes of linking religion and national identity have only been considered marginally when it comes to everyday commodities and their capacity to trigger enormous consequences.

In this respect it is correct to say that in the case of Japan the government and economy that eventually emerged in the Meiji period *"were a far cry from what the Tokugawa and early Meiji leaders had in mind when they spoke of retaining the traditional spiritual culture of Japan. It all started with the appearance of a few material objects lifted out of Western culture and carried boldly to Japan, but one thing lead to another, and eventually there occurred something that can only be described as a spiritual revolution."*[44]

## References

Antoni (1998)
> Antoni, Klaus: *Shintō und die Konzeption des Japanischen Nationalwesens (Kokutai): Der religiöse Traditionalismus in Neuzeit und Moderne.* [Handbuch der Orientalistik, part V, vol. 8], Leiden, Boston: Brill, 1998.

Aston (1993)
> Aston, William George: *Nihongi – Chronicles of Japan from the earliest times to A.D. 697.* London: Tuttle, 1993 [reprint of 1896].

Florenz (1925)
> Florenz, Karl: "Die Japaner; Teil A: 'Shintō' ", in: Berthold, Alfred/ Lehmann, Eduard: *Lehrbuch der Religionsgeschichte*, Bd. I, 4th ed., Tübingen, 1925, pp. 262-348.

---

[44] Shibusawa (1958), p. 3f.

Hardacre (1989)
Hardacre, Helen: *Shinto and the state, 1868-1988*. Princeton, 1989.

Ichimura (1929)
Ichimura, Minato 市村咸人: *Ina sonnō shisō shi* 伊那尊王思想史. Tōkyō, 1929.

Iida (1903)
Iida, Takesato 飯田武郷: *Hōshitsu-shū* 蓬室集. [Iida Sueharu, ed.] Tōkyō, 1903.

Iida (1922-26)
Iida, Takesato 飯田武郷: *Nihonshoki-tsūshaku* 日本書紀通釋. [6 vols.] Tōkyō: Daishōkaku, 1922-26.

KEJ
*Kodansha Encyclopedia of Japan*. [9 vols.] Tōkyō: Kodansha, 1983.

Motoori (1926)
Motoori Norinaga 本居宣長: *Kojiki-den* 古事記傳. [4 vols.] Tōkyō: Kōbunkan, 1926.

Muraoka (1988)
Muraoka, Tsunetsugu: *Studies in Shinto Thought: Classics of Modern Japanese Thought and Culture (Nihon-shisōshi-kenkyū)*. New York: Greenwood, 1988.

Nakayama (1987)
Nakayama, Tarō 中山太郎: *Nihon minzokugaku jiten* 日本民俗學辭典. [2 parts] Tōkyō: Parutosu-sha, 1987.

NKBT
Takagi, Ichinosuke 髙木市之助 et al (ed.): *Nihon koten bungaku taikei* 日本古典文学体系. [102 vols.] Tōkyō: Iwanami shoten, 1957-86.

Sakamoto (1944)
Sakamoto, Tatsunosuke 坂本辰之助: *Iida Takesato okina-den: Ishin no resshi kokugaku no taito* 飯田武郷翁傳：維新の烈士國學の泰斗. Tōkyō: Meibunsha, 1944.

Shibusawa (1958)
Shibusawa, Keizō: *Japanese Life and Culture in the Meiji Era*. [transl. Charles S. Terry] Tōkyō: Ōbunsha, 1958.

**Teuween (1995)**

Teuween, Mark (transl.): *Motoori Norinaga's The two shrines of Ise: an essay of split bamboo (Ise nikū sakitake no ben)*. [Izumi: Quellen, Studien u. Materialien zur Kultur Japans; vol. 3] Wiesbaden: Harrassowitz, 1995.

**Yamasaki (1956)**

Yamasaki, Setsuko 山崎節子: "Iida Takesato 飯田武郷", in: Kobayashi, Toraji 小林寅次 (publ.): *Kindai-bungaku kenkyū sōsho 近代文学研究叢書*, vol. 4 (1956), Tōkyō: Showa Joshi Daigaku, pp. 283-324.

**Wachutka (2001)**

Wachutka, Michael: *Historical Reality or Metaphoric Expression? – Culturally formed contrasts in Karl Florenz' and Iida Takesato's interpretations of Japanese mythology*. [BUNKA – Tuebingen intercultural and linguistic studies on Japan, vol. 1] Hamburg: Lit-Verlag, New Brunswick: Transaction Publishers, 2001.

# The Emperor, Shintō Ultranationalism and Mass Mobilization

## Walter A. SKYA

In his essay *The Ideology and Dynamics of Japanese Fascism*, Maruyama Masao 丸山真男, the renowned Japanese political scientist, discussing the distinctive characteristics of the ideology of State Shintō, noted that *"The basic characteristic of the Japanese state structure is that it is always considered as an extension of the family"*[1] as other Meiji ideologues such as Hozumi Yatsuka 穂積八束 and Inoue Tetsujirō 井上哲次郎 had theorized. Maruyama goes on to say in this article written in the late 1940s that this notion *"is maintained [by fascists] not as an abstract idea but as an actual historical fact that the Japanese nation preserves unaltered its ancient social structure based on blood relationship."*[2]. He further noted that this emphasis on the idea of the family was so important that it defined the social context of Japanese fascism, and concluded his statement on this particular point saying: *"The insistence on the family system therefore may be termed a distinctive characteristic of the Japanese fascist ideology; and it is connected with the failure of Japanese fascism as a mass movement."*[3]

Ishida Takeshi 石田雄, another well-known early postwar scholar, took up the issue of the ideology of State Shintō in his work *Meiji seiji shisō-shi kenkyū 明治政治思想史研究* ('A Study of the History of Meiji Political Thought').[4] He sought to explain the intellectual structure of State Shintō through the linkage of German organic state theory and Confucian family ideology. Although Ishida's formulation of State Shintō differs from Maruyama's, a point in common to both Maruyama and Ishida is that they saw the family-state concept as fundamental to the ideology of State Shintō. More recently, Irokawa Daikichi 色川大吉, a scholar of Japanese History, challenged both Maruyama's and Ishida's analysis of the intellectual structure of State Shintō. While Irokawa too considered the family-state concept essential to State Shintō, his chief concern was the validity of the ideological mechanism connecting the family and the emperor in the intel-

---

[1] Maruyama (1969), p. 36.
[2] Ibid. p. 36.
[3] Ibid. p. 37.

lectual structure of State Shintō constructed both by Maruyama and Ishida. Although for Irokawa as well as Maruyama and Ishida the family-state concept was a core component of State Shintō ideology, Irokawa raised the following objection to both Maruyama's and Ishida's theory in his essay *The Emperor System as a Spiritual Structure*[5]:

> *"What [...] was the link that allowed two such disparate elements [the family and the emperor] to be joined? Ishida proposes imported organic theory as the bonding agent, whereas his teacher, Maruyama, invoked the whole indigenous tradition since the Jomon period to account for it. Neither approach, it seems to me, satisfactorily explains the connection established between the family and the state under the emperor system."*[6]

That is to say, for Irokawa, neither Maruyama's nor Ishida's explanation of the mechanism linking the family and the emperor satisfactorily accounts for the reason the Japanese people would be so willing to risk their lives for the emperor in the same way that they would for their own family. Irokawa insists that there must be something else that allows the powerful emotional attachment the individual naturally has for his family to be transferred to the emperor. In short, Irokawa proposed four 'ideological intermediaries' to join the family or the household to the state in the Meiji period: the imperial myth, the religious tradition of ancestor worship, the social structure of the family system, and the customary heritage of folk morality.

But, again, what Maruyama, Ishida and Irokawa all had in common was that they assumed the family-state concept to be an essential component of the intellectual structure of State Shintō throughout the prewar period. In other words, they maintained the view that there had been no significant change in the ideology of State Shintō between the late Meiji period and the end of the Second World War. American scholars too seem to have followed their Japanese counterparts and accepted, for the most part, their arguments at face value.

This paper challenges the accuracy of this interpretation of the nature of State Shintō's ideology in prewar Japan. Such an interpretation raises a number of important questions that have not been adequately addressed by scholars of prewar

---

[4] See Ishida (1954).
[5] See Irokawa (1985).
[6] Ibid, p. 282.

Japanese political thought. How could a premodern theory of absolute monarchy appeal to the newly politicized Japanese masses in the first two decades of the twentieth century? How could a premodern theory of absolute monarchy constructed by Hozumi Yatsuka (whom Maruyama cited as the chief architect of the family-state concept) in the late Meiji period in the 1890s, serve as an effective ideological force in mobilizing the Japanese masses for total war in Asia and the Pacific in the 1930s and 1940s? It was with such questions in mind that I began to examine the writings of State Shintō theorists of the 1920s and the 1930s to find out if they too had followed their Meiji predecessors in conceptualizing the Japanese state in terms of a traditional patriarchical family-state. It did not take me long after I had begun my research to find out that this was certainly not the case. There was much more to the story of the emperor-centered ideology of State Shintō than what scholars like Maruyama, Ishida and Irokawa had put forward. As evidence, this paper examines the state theory of Uesugi Shinkichi 上杉慎吉, a leading constitutional legal scholar and Shintō ultranationalist of the Taisho period.

### A New Theory of the Japanese State

"*The state is ultimate morality*" (*kokka wa saikō dōtoku nari* 国家は最高道徳 なり). These are the first words of Uesugi Shinkichi's book *Kokka shinron* 国家 新論 ('A New Theory of the State'). Written in 1921, this work set forth the theoretical framework of a theory of state that had a profound influence on ultranationalist thought in the prewar Showa period. The idea that the state is ultimate morality was at the heart and the center of his theory of state. What did he mean by asserting that the state was ultimate morality?

Uesugi's theory of state was built upon a moral philosophy that rested on a theory of metaphysics. A prerequisite for the knowledge of ultimate morality was the possibility of knowledge of the ultimate nature of Being. If we were to deconstruct his theory of Being into its constituent elements and discern its special characteristics, we would come up with something like the following. First, in Uesugi's ontology, that is, his theory of the nature and relations of Being, Being in its totality could not be defined in terms of the self as a complete entity in distinction or differentiation from other selves. It could not be conceived of in its entirety as an entity existing independently of the existence of other selves. The self thus was merely a part of a greater 'Being as a totality'.

Being was Being only in so far as it formed an organic part of an irreducible aggregate of Beings. To put it another way, the affirmation of the existence of the self, one's own Being, was possible only in the recognition of the inter-dependent existence of the self with other selves as an organic totality.

Second, in Uesugi's ontology, Being did not simply denote what might be referred to as static-given Being. One's individual Being – as a constituent element of 'Being as a totality' – had movement. This movement of Being relating in a cause-and-effect relationship to the movement of other Beings in a spatial environment was what Uesugi called man's *sōkan* 相関.[7] Being's movement, however, did not only involve this spatial relationship. It involved this inter-relationship with other Beings in a spatial totality in time, which he called man's *renzoku* 連続.[8] The movement of Being in this spatial-temporal relationship was not generated by the type of dialectic found in Hegel's ontological category of negativity. We do not find in Uesugi's ontology the idea of conflicting forces resolved in a dialectic synthesis. Instead, we find Being as becoming Being in terms of a continual and never-ending process of development. Each Being, as part of 'Being as a totality' mutually and interdependently developing and perfecting the self in relation to other selves in a definite spatial-temporal matrix was what Uesugi called *hito no sōkan to renzoku* 人の相関と連続.[9] This mutual development and perfection of Beings in this spatial-temporal matrix was what Uesugi defined as morality.

Third, this perfection, or the object of Being's becoming, was what he called man's *honsei* 本性 ('essential Being').[10] Man's essential Being constituted the real Being, which inherently contained in it a moral nature that was to be per-fected. It was the purpose of moral man to work towards a moral end. Thus, Uesugi's conception of Being rested also upon a teleological thinking as well as the union of Being and morality in an imagined metaphysical order. That is to say, the essence of man's Being also constituted at the same time the end or goal of Being itself. The supreme goal of morality was accordingly this: realize your own essential Being, which was of course, at the same time, your innate nature. This teleological conception of essential Being was therefore the basis of the essential unity of Being and ultimate morality.

---

[7] Cf. Uesugi (1921), pp. 5f.
[8] Cf. ibid, p. 7.
[9] Cf. ibid, p. 8.
[10] Cf. ibid, pp. 5-8.

The full realization of Being's essential nature was the goal of man's Being. The closer one progressed to one's essential Being, the closer one came to the fulfillness of Being, and the closer to ultimate morality. It was the motivation for action and the ultimate purpose of existence. The problem was to determine which actions correspond to man's essential Being. Uesugi's ontology presupposed that man's Being is essentially social, and that man's Being is perfected in society. This society of Beings interacting in an organic totality leading towards essential Being was what constituted the state. In other words, state and society were theoretically identical. Therefore, Being reached its fulfillment only in the state; the ideal of man could be perfected only in the state. Man was a part of state just as the state was a part of man. Uesugi – echoing Aristotle's dictum that 'man is a political animal' – stated that 'man is a statist animal'[11]. The state is what leads man to his ideal that originated in his essential Being. _"If there were no state, one could not develop and perfect one's essential Being."_[12]. The ideal state was of course the state of ultimate morality. The state of ultimate morality would encompass the totality of man's life and embrace it in its entirety.

Accordingly, Uesugi denounced the idea that the society could be disconnected from the state. Having traveled to China, he observed that the problem with China, which had disintegrated after the failure of the 1911 republican revolution, was that the concept of society was separate from the concept of state: _"Probably the most striking thing about present-day China is the separation of state and society. It is in a situation where there is almost all society and no state."_[13]. In Uesugi's understanding of Chinese political thought, Chinese society and culture would continue on in tact even without the state, because the family, not the state, was at the core of society. Uesugi noted that the Japanese, in contrast to the Chinese, had never conceptualized Japanese society and the Japanese state as separate entities. He claimed that whenever a Japanese spoke of Japan, he had in his mind the notion of one state, one society, and one ethnic group.

A key concept Uesugi used to clarify the nature of the Japanese state was _taisei ishi_ 体制意志 ('organizational will').[14] This organizational will was the source of state cohesion and national solidarity. It was the will that organized

---

[11] Cf. ibid, p. 93.
[12] Ibid, pp. 93f.
[13] Ibid, p. 60.
[14] Cf. ibid, pp. 62-65.

each individual into the state. It was a mode of thought, a consciousness of what one should do and not do. However, this organizational will was not the will of each individual, nor was it the sum of total of all wills. It was the will existing in an irreducible totality, the will of one power. But it was also inherent in the essential Being of the individual as well as in the founding of the state. Organizational will included man's *sokan* and *renzoku*, that spatial-temporal matrix of social solidarity, and man's essential Being, that inner force drawing man to his perfection. Organizational will was a moral force, since *sokan* and *renzoku* constituted moral bonds and essential Being a teleological moral vision. Organizational will was this moral force that drove man to cooperate with his fellow man, to continuously progress and develop, to strive to moral perfection. In this metaphysical conception of Being, where the individual Being was an organ of Being in its totality, the moral development of the self automatically translated into the moral development of all the other selves in the totality of the state. What constituted moral action corresponding to man's essential Being was that which contributed to the collective 'Being as a totality'. The result was the elimination of contradictions between the individual self and all other selves. Accordingly, sacrifice of the self for the good of 'Being as a totality' was not really sacrifice in the sense of giving up something in order to attain something else, but it was tantamount to the realization of one's own essential Being.

Ultimately, the emperor was the source of organizational will. He alone possessed the ideal and perfect qualifications for the embodiment of the organizational will. The emperor was the state, the emperor's will was the organizational will in man's spatial-temporal matrix. To obey the emperor's will was the highest realization of the self, the realization of one's 'essential Being'. To absorb the self into the emperor, to become a part of the emperor was to accomplish man's essential Being. That is to say, organizational will was the emperor, man's essential Being, ultimate morality. This was the special characteristic of the Japanese state, the essence of the *kokutai* 国体.

Opposed to Uesugi's emperor-centered organic organizational theory of state was a conception of the state built upon what he called 'mechanistic organization' (*kikai-teki soshiki* 機械的組織)[15]. The mechanistic organizational theory of the state rested on a metaphysics that perceived the individual as a self-sufficient

---

[15] Cf. ibid, pp. 73ff.

and complete entity in itself. He charged that from this mechanistic theory of state organization, individuals were isolated from each other and also from the whole, and that this was the source of aggressive selfishness and vanity, personal advantage seeking at the expense of the state at large. It was a theory of organization in which the whole of society was sacrificed to the personal profit of a part of the whole in some form or another. It was a theory created by those who assumed that conflict was at the basis of society. And it was a theory in which the very spiritual root of sociality was denied, and thus contradicted the whole meaning of human nature. It was a theory of organization that contradicted the belief that man had a natural inclination toward mutual help and cooperation.

Uesugi attacked the mechanistic theory of organization as a theory of social Darwinism, the 'struggle for existence' that Darwin had found in nature, applied to man's social life as well. According to social Darwinism, man too was engaged in a constant struggle against his fellow men from which only the fittest emerged victorious. It was a theory in which free economic competition, laissez faire at its most extreme, performed the same function in society as natural selection performed in nature. For Uesugi, social conflict was artificial and transitory, while social harmony was the natural condition of man. It is noteworthy that in connection with his criticism of the mechanistic theory of organization, Uesugi chastised Katō Hiroyuki 加藤弘之 and even his own teacher Hozumi Yatsuka for incorporating ideas of social Darwinism in their state theories. According to Uesugi, social Darwinism, a Western concept introduced into Japan in Meiji times, was not consistent with Japanese tradition in which social organization was based on mutual cooperation. Uesugi was heavily indebted to the thought of the Russian anarchist Peter Kropotkin for this idea that the true character of man was not the struggle for existence but mutual cooperation.

Uesugi went to great lengths to deny that the authoritarian structural relationship was at the core of the Japanese state. In connection with this, he devoted one chapter of _A New Theory of the State_ to clarifying the nature of politics. For him, politics was non-rule. He charged that no one should use the state to permit the rule of others. The fundamental source of national solidarity was essential Being. The purpose of politics was to develop and perfect man's moral nature, man's essential Being. Politics, unlike in the West, were not power relationships. Neither did the motivation of politics lie in the private benefit of individuals. Uesugi tried to channel the political energies of the masses into a non-Western political mode. It was not that he objected to the involvement of the masses in the affairs of the state. He certainly favored this. In fact, he claimed that it was the moral duty of the individual to serve the emperor, giving him advice on matters pertaining to the affairs of state. He charged that the *"responsibility of serving the emperor by giving him advice on matters pertaining to the affairs of state does not rest solely on the ministers of state."*[16]. It was the responsibility of all subjects to assist the emperor. This idea of service to the emperor was the ideal behind the Constitution of the Empire of Japan. In other words, the Constitution had broadened the way for the subject to assist imperial rule.

Finally, following his teacher Hozumi, Uesugi posited that the Japanese state must be an 'ethnic state' (*minzoku kokka* 民族国家)[17], a state composed of members from the same ethnic stock. In other words, he maintained that the state and the ethnic group should be identical. The ethnic state was also the only natural state. He defended this idea of the ethnic state on the grounds that people everywhere, both in the East and West, and from ancient times to the present, tried to form a state based on ethnicity, even though no purely ethnic states in fact existed. Accordingly, even though the term 'ethnic state' was of recent origin, it was not peculiar to the modern period. The nation-state should be an ethnic group composed of individuals related by ancestry and share common feelings and sentiments of their own identity. He also suggested that the members of the ethnic state must be consciously aware that they are of one ethnic group and have the desire to maintain that ethnic unity and promote ethnic purity. Uesugi noted that among the various states in the world the Japanese state was the most ethnically pure, and that the Japanese people maintain their solidarity through their consciousness that they are brothers and sisters united in the feeling of love and attachment. This was the reason why their ancestors established the state, it was the reason why it should be maintained, and the reason why it should be handed down to their descendants. Uesugi claimed that only in the ethnic state could one develop and perfect oneself and realize his essential Being. Consequently, ethnic purity was also inextricably linked to his theory of

---

[16] Ibid, p. 84.
[17] Cf. ibid, p. 40.

ultimate morality. The Japanese state, consisting of ethnic Japanese, constituted one body under the rule of the emperor. Other criteria of the state such as territorial mass, land features, customs, religion, and industrial production did not constitute a basis on which to establish the value of the state.

In this march toward moral perfection, the Japanese state was superior to all other states. It alone sought and had the inner capacity to attain the ultimate morality. It alone could achieve the total unity of the people. Uesugi believed that the total unity of the people could be achieved only by the Japanese state, because it alone was governed by the emperor, a 'living deity' (_arahitogami_ 現人神)[18]. According to the doctrine of the emperor as a 'living deity', the emperor was the perfect Being. In the emperor, there is no distinction between man's existential Being and his essential Being, man's existence and his essence. The emperor is the essential Being, the ultimate norm, the ultimate morality. In man's essential Being dwells the emperor, for all Beings were descendants of _Amaterasu Ōmikami_ 天照大神. As superior Being, the emperor was also the goal of all created Beings. The emperor was the final activity towards which all Japanese must work. In short, much like God is to man in Christian theology, the emperor was the glory of all creation. The state was called into existence by the will of _Amaterasu Ōmikami_ who was at the origin of the Japanese state, and who was also the final end to which all activities of the Japanese state were directed.

Derived from the doctrine of the emperor-as-god, only the emperor, as the embodiment of ultimate morality, could rule with absolute fairness and impartiality, totally disinterested from any personal profit or considerations. By contrast, the human Western king or emperor, or elected head of state, could not rule with this total impartiality and represent the will of the people entirely. He could only hope to express the will of the majority of the people. The Japanese state was able to do precisely what no Western state could claim: rule with a total impartiality that expressed the will of _all_ the people.

The promulgation of the Constitution of the Empire of Japan on February 11, 1889 was an important event in modern Japanese history. Uesugi regarded the Meiji constitution as a sacred text. He called it, along with the Imperial Rescript on Education, the "_two great canons_"[19] of the state. However, these state docu-

---

[18] Cf. ibid, chapter 12 titled _Tennō_ 天皇.
[19] Uesugi (1916), p. 2.

ments were sacred to Uesugi not because of their inherent content, but solely for the reason they were the words of the emperor. Conveniently forgetting that the Constitution was drawn up in secret by Itō Hirobumi 伊藤博文 and his colleagues and his German constitutional legal advisor Hermann Roessler in 1889, he regarded it as the action of the emperor, and for Uesugi, *"the will of the emperor is absolute, and the standard of behavior of Japanese subjects depends solely on his will."*[20]

In a 1915 essay titled *Kempō seitei no shushi* 憲法制定ノ趣旨 ('The Primary Intent in Establishing the Constitution')[21], Uesugi stated that the Constitution was established to mobilize all power in the nation to actively assist the sovereign emperor in pursuing the essence of the state. The essence of the state was the will of the emperor, which, of course, was identical to the pursuit of ultimate morality. Stressing the importance of Article 4 of the Constitution – that states: The Emperor is the head of the Empire, combining in Himself the rights of sovereignty, and exercises them, according to the provisions of the present Constitution –, Uesugi declared that *"the emperor is the sovereign of our Japanese empire."*[22]

*"What is sovereignty?"*[23] asked Uesugi. For him it was more than just the location of ultimate power or authority in the state. The rule of the sovereign existed to fulfill the ethical purpose of the state. In other words, the state and the emperor had a mission. It had a mission to expand and perfect the good and the moral to the 'total of human society' (*ningen-shakai zentai* 人間社会全体)[24] throughout 'the entire universe' (*uchū zentai* 宇宙全体)[25]. In other words, according to Uesugi's emperor ideology, the Japanese state had the right, indeed, the moral duty to spread emperor ideology on a global scale. This was the goal of *"our imperial ancestors."*[26]

Uesugi believed that the function of the parliament was *"to approve this great aim of the emperor"*[27]. Furthermore, Uesugi actively sought to use the politicized masses to support the emperor. Unlike Hozumi Yatsuka, who had an

---

[20] Ibid, p. 8.
[21] See ibid., pp. 257-291.
[22] Ibid, p. 257.
[23] Ibid, p. 257.
[24] Cf. ibid, p. 258.
[25] Cf. ibid, p. 258.
[26] Ibid, p. 276.
[27] Ibid, p. 280.

instinctive mistrust of the masses, he tried to incorporate them into his emperor ideology. From Uesugi's perspective, the Constitution of the Empire of Japan was designed to ensure that state power could be mobilized for the unlimited expansionism of the Japanese state on a global scale.

### Totalitarian Ideology

In the late Meiji period, constitutional legal scholar Hozumi Yatsuka had worked out an 'orthodox' ideology of State Shintō in support of absolute monarchy. It was a state ideology in which the subject was a kind of political child, personally subordinated to the paternal emperor. The family was the model for describing most political and social relationships, not only between the emperor and his subjects, but also between all superiors and subordinates throughout the whole society. In other words, personal dependent hierarchical relationships constituted the ligaments that held the state together and made it work. It was a state in which the masses were not supposed to be involved in politics.

However, despite Hozumi's efforts to keep the masses depoliticized, a decade or so later this task proved impossible. The masses were rapidly becoming politicized. The traditional bonds of society were loosening and the patriarchal construction of society was breaking down. By the end of the first decade of the twentieth century, the Japanese masses had already revealed their power in various demonstrations. This was evident even to observers closer to those times. For instance, Yoshino Sakuzō 吉野作造 wrote that the Hibiya Riot (_Hibiya yakiuchi jiken_ 日比谷焼打事件) of 1905 signaled the emergence of the Japanese masses on the political stage. And, as Andrew Gordon demonstrated in his work _Labor and Imperial Democracy in Prewar Japan_, 1905 was the beginning of a series of mass disturbances that would culminate in the Rice Riots of 1918.[28] Other historians also saw the importance of the Hibiya Riot in terms of the beginning of mass participation in politics.

---

[28] Cf. Gordon (1991), p. 1. Gordon states: "_In the first two decades of the twentieth century, crowds of city-dwellers took to the streets of Tokyo and launched the most vigorous urban protests yet seen in Japan. At least nine times from the Hibiya riot of 1905 to the rice riots of 1918, angry Tokyoites attacked policemen, police stations, and national government offices, smashed streetcar windows and beat the drivers, marched on the Diet, and stormed the offices of major newspapers. They destroyed public and private property, launching both symbolic and substantive attacks on the institutions of the established order of imperial Japan._".

Uesugi, keenly aware of this, had constructed his theory of state on the assumption that the masses were already becoming politicized, and that no force could hold back this process. He could see that the people, through their actions in the streets, were capable and willing to take matters into their own hands. Accordingly, he formulated a state theory based on very different sorts of human relationships from that of patriarchy. His theory of *sokan* and *renzoku*, man's relationship in a spatial-temporal matrix, linked people with one another in a horizontal social structure, not in a vertical patriarchal structure. People were linked by new bonds of mutual cooperation and affection, respect and consent. Uesugi was a revolutionary in this respect. In effect, he sought the reconstruction of the basic social relationships of society.

Nevertheless, Uesugi seemed to have had the same fundamental aim of Hozumi: the control of the masses. He sought to do this by displacing politics with morality, the political state with a moral state. He sought to insure that the masses were no longer political in the sense of representing different sorts of interests in society and different ideas of how the state ought to be managed. He sought to channel the politicized masses into one mold. Ultimately, the goal of Uesugi's *A New Theory of the State* was to displace power politics with absolute morality.

### Conclusion

Through this brief introduction to the state theory of Uesugi Shinkichi, I have tried to show that an important transformation in the internal structure of State Shintō ideology had occurred between the Meiji period and the Taishō period. Uesugi's idea of the Japanese state as an undifferentiated mass of people interacting in a spatial-temporal matrix in pursuit of ultimate morality represented a fundamental transformation of the ideology of State Shintō. Accordingly, it is a glaringly obvious mistake to claim, as Maruyama Masao and others had done, that the patriarchical family system is a central feature of Japanese 'fascism' that distinguishes it from German Nazism or Italian Fascism. The idea of the Japanese state as an extension of the primary family group had been official state ideology from the beginning of the Meiji period, and it was certainly integral to Hozumi Yatsuka's state theory, but this was not in a period of fascism. On the contrary, the development of the intellectual structure of extreme nationalist ideology from the Meiji period to Taishō and Shōwa periods leads to a rejection of the family principle as a fundamental component of State Shintō ideology. Uesugi's metaphysics totally displaced the family principle as a key component of State Shintō ideology. He clearly understood that the theoretical focus on the family system and family consciousness would actually work against the creation of 'mass man' with total devotion to the emperor. He knew that when the consciousness of the family, man's primary social group, is strengthened, identification of the self and one's own being with the emperor is necessarily weakened. Under Hozumi's patriarchal theory of the state, the emperor was not identical with the self. The emperor remained ultimately something external to the self, thus not achieving an absolute control over all spheres of the individual's life. Under Uesugi's state theory, the emperor had become totally internalized and the separation between the emperor and the individual had been closed theoretically. Thus, State Shintō ideology had become ultranationalist and totalitarian.

This ideology had a major impact on the ultranationalist movement in the 1920s and 1930s. For instance, it inspired the members of the Imperial Way Faction of the military and other civilian rightists who staged the violent revolt of February 26, 1936. It is not difficult to understand the reasons for this. One must remember that Uesugi's theory of state involved a dynamic process. He sought to organize the masses and set them in a perpetual state of motion in pursuit of the imperial way. Further, it was man's moral duty to strive relentlessly to close the gap between existential being and essential being. Seeking actualization of one's essential being became, in effect, the search for total identity with the emperor, which morally justified – indeed required – the destruction of all existing institutions of government separating the emperor from the masses. That is to say, his thought both theoretically and morally justified terrorism, for it made it the individual's duty to eliminate 'wicked advisors, corrupt politicians, capitalists and weak-kneed bureaucrats' separating the masses from the emperor. In short, Uesugi's thought was the intellectual foundation behind one of the most extreme forms of ultranationalism in prewar Japan.

*Bibliography*

Gordon (1991)
> Gordon, Andrew: *Labor and Imperial Democracy in Prewar Japan.*
> Berkeley: University of California Press, 1991.

Irokawa (1985)
> Irokawa, Daikichi: "The Emperor System as a Spiritual Structure", in:
> *The Culture of the Meiji Period.* [transl. ed. by Marius B. Jansen]
> Princeton: Princeton University Press, 1985, pp. 245-311.

Ishida (1954)
> Ishida, Takeshi 石田雄: *Meiji seiji shisō-shi kenkyū* 明治政治思想史研究.
> Tōkyō: Miraisha, 1954.

Maruyama (1969)
> Maruyama, Masao: *Thought and Behavior in Modern Japanese Politics.*
> [ed. by Ivan Morris] London: Oxford University Press, 1969.

Uesugi (1916)
> Uesugi Shinkichi 上杉慎吉: *Kokutai kempō oyobi kensei* 国体憲法及び憲
> 政. Tōkyō: Yuhikaku-shobō, 1916.

— (1921)
> Uesugi Shinkichi 上杉慎吉: *Kokka shinron* 国家新論. Tōkyō: Keibunkan,
> 1921.

# The Cosmology of Shintō
# and National Identity in Modern Japan

ENDŌ Jun

## Introduction

Concerning the relation between religions and national identity in Modern Japan, a considerable number of studies have been made on State Shintō (*kokka shintō* 国家神道) over the past few decades.

It is certain that the Meiji government set religious policies to develop a national consciousness in its early years. Shintō took a leading role of all in this respect. Because Buddhism was the most popular religion in those days and thought to bring the salvation after death, Shintō had to take its place and to develop a theology in connection with the next world.

As a matter of fact, these kinds of Shintō theologies can already be found in the later 18th or the first half of the 19th century, before the Meiji Restoration: the thought of Motoori Norinaga 本居宣長, the cosmology of Hattori Nakatsune 服部中庸 and the cosmology of Hirata Atsutane 平田篤胤. The purpose of this paper is to review both the background and the development of these theologies and to examine their influence on the theological discussions of Shintō in the Meiji era.

## Cosmology, Geography and National Identity in Tokugawa Japan

Generally a national identity is inseparable from the representation of other nations. The representations of the own nation and of others together form the total image of the world.

First of all, we will refer to the Buddhist cosmology among various others. Although the cosmology of Mt. Sumeru (*Shumisen-setsu* 須弥山説) – where mountains and seas surround a sacred mountain named Sumeru one after the other – is the most basic cosmology of Buddhism, the image of the world consisting of three countries (*sangoku sekaikan* 三国世界観) is more important for us in order to examine the national identity of Japan. These three countries are India, China, and Japan, which showed the steps of Buddhist mission. This image was connected with the historical idea of three stages of Buddhism in the 14th century and became a Buddhist value both on time and space. Judging from this idea, Japan was considered to be inferior in its location and in its historical stage.[1] Buddhists in Japan called their country *mappō no hendo* 末法の辺土 (the isolated district of the latter days of Buddhism).

The notion of *shinkoku* 神国 (the land of gods) also came from the three countries image of Buddhism (*sangoku shisō* 三国思想).

It was justified by Shintō-Buddhist syncretistic ideas: in Japan, Buddha and Bodhisattvas often appear as gods, so Japan is the land of gods as well as of Buddha.

Since the later 16th century, Buddhist temples started to enter into association with different *ie* イエ (households), widely formed among the common people. The Tokugawa Shogunate adapted the temple registration system from these relations for the purpose of family registration and control over religions. Buddhism became more familiar to the people through these relations and spread into local communities. As funerals and ancestor worship were central to the temple registration system, it enabled Buddhism to acquire the monopoly of the salvation after death.

The most popular representation of the next world in Buddhism is Pure Land (*gokuraku-jōdo* 極楽浄土). While it was supposed to be in the west, it did not necessarily have an exact position on the geographic representation of the three countries. The cosmology of Mt. Sumeru then became less important to people, except Buddhists, in the Tokugawa period.[2]

Let us now turn to Confucianism, which had a great influence on Tokugawa Japan. Though it was supposed in Confucian tradition that the sky was round and the land was square (*ten-en chi-hō setsu* 天円地方説), it was also general not to mention the shape of the cosmos. As for more specific images, the value of *ka-i* 華夷 (chin.: *hua yi*) was influential in geographical understandings.[3] The value of *ka-i* is the perspective to discriminate between China as the center of

---

[1] Cf. Ōji (1996), pp. 145-148.
[2] Cf. Sawai (2000), p. 212.

civilization and surroundings as the primitive periphery. Confucians early in the Tokugawa period did not distinguish between Confucianism and the discourses on gods of Japan,[4] and they regarded their country as the nation (or the land) of gods. But as they digested Confucianism, questions came up where to locate Japan under the *ka-i* perspective and how they could harmonize the image of the nation of gods with the Confucian one.[5]

## Cosmology and Theology in National Learning

National Learning and Shintō discourses oriented to nativism appeared against the *ka-i* perspective in Confucianism and attempted to be an alternative to the representation of the next world in Buddhism.

National Learning rose from studies on Japanese classics and developed a tendency to understand Japanese tradition without the influences of foreign cultures and thoughts. Kamo no Mabuchi 賀茂真淵, a scholar of National Learning, thought that the poems in the *Man'yōshu* 万葉集 showed the feelings and ideas of the ancient Japanese. He denied the importance of civilization stressed by Confucianism, and instead gave weight to the conception of nature. This also led to an objection against the *ka-i* perspective, and opened the way for the development of new cosmologies in National Learning.[6]

We are going to examine the thoughts of three scholars, Motoori Norinaga, Hattori Nakatsune and Hirata Atsutane, which offer the key to understand the relationship between national identity and the representations of the world.[7]

---

[3] The following explanation about the relationship between the value of *ka-i* and images of the world is based on the work of Sawai (2000).

[4] Cf. Kurozumi (1994), pp. 278f.

[5] Katsurajima [(1999), pp. 167-172] divides the answers to these questions among Confucians into three types: ① Japan belongs to the periphery judging from universal values embodied in China; ② Japan is superior to other surrounding countries in these universal values; ③ the universal values in the *ka-i* perspective was realized just in Japan. He also points out that behind these answers lay the common premise that the civilization China had realized, shows the supreme value.

[6] Cf. Katsurajima (1999), pp. 180-186.

[7] I already examined the relation of works of these three persons and their cosmologies in Endō (1995). Though we should not find a lineal relationship between master and pupil among the three, we may describe their thoughts as the development of a cosmology, considering that Hattori's theory was based on Norinaga's writings and that Hirata constructed his cosmology according to their theories.

Motoori Norinaga is well known for marking an epoch in the interpretation of the *Kojiki* 古事記. He fully accepted the story of the *Kojiki* as true on one hand, and he attempted to clarify the exact meaning of this text with a philological method on the other. As far as the cosmology is concerned, it is important that Motoori considered the structure of the world to be described in the *Kojiki*. He took notice of the places of the gods' activities and discovered that the world consists of three parts: *ten* 天, *chi* 地 and *yomi* 黄泉. He regarded all beings, including animals and plants, as lifeless, made to work like puppets by the gods. This view leads to a denial of the Confucian understanding of the world, where the world is filled with *ki* 気 and everything has vitality in itself.

This brings us to the question of which god makes the world work. Motoori introduced the gods of *musuhi* ムスヒ as the gods of Creation, who created the world and animated all beings, despite that discourses on Shintō often set Kunitokotachi クニトコタチ at the root of the world. In line with the story of the *Kojiki*, unmarried gods like Ame no minakanushi アメノミナカヌシ and Kunitokotachi came up in the beginning, disappeared soon and did not appear in the other parts – except the gods of *musuhi*. Instead the gods of *musuhi* often appeared and took some actions in following parts of the text as well. The discovery of the gods of *musuhi* as the cause of the Creation led to the complete rethinking of the characters of gods. Motoori denied both, the worldviews that stressed Kunitokotachi and the organic representation of Confucianism.

According to Motoori, the gods also rule the whole world once it was created. In the *Nihonshoki* 日本書紀, Takamimusuhi タカミムスヒ assigned the rule of the visible world (*arawanaru-koto* 顕) to Amaterasu アマテラス, and the invisible world (*kakuretaru-koto* 幽) to Ōkuninushi オオクニヌシ. Motoori regarded the visible world as of human and the invisible world as of gods, and he thought that Amaterasu and Ōkuninushi had shared the universe and ruled each world. He also thought that Amaterasu was both the sun and the highest god of the universe, and that Japan was superior to the other countries, because the Emperors, descendants of this god, succeeded the supremacy up to the present. This explanation started off on a premise completely different from the *ka-i* perspective. While Suika Shintō 垂加神道 had connected the gods and the Emperor with the world or the universe through Confucian concepts like *kei* 敬 (piousness), Motoori considered the world as a direct result of activities of gods and _discovered_ a mythical or religious relation between the real Emperor and the world. This contains the paradox that the gods are universal as the master of the universe, whereas they were born in a particular country, Japan.

Motoori identified the afterworld with _yomi no kuni_ 黄泉国 instead of the Pure Land or the Buddhist hell (_jigoku_ 地獄), but did not clearly criticize Buddhism. It is Hattori Nakatsune who attempted a more detailed explanation of the creation of the universe. Hattori tied the three parts of the world in the _Kojiki_ to the revolution of the heavenly bodies in western astronomy in his writing, the _Sandai-kō_ 三大考.

Motoori drew the activities and movements of gods in a chart named _Ten-chi zu_ 天地図, where he identified _ten_ 天, _chi_ 地 and _yomi_ 黄泉 with the sun, the earth and the moon, but he did not set them in the context of their revolution. Hattori illustrated his view, and later on he added other planets to his cosmology. After Motoori's death, his official heirs regarded Hattori as heresy, but Motoori in his life appreciated the works of Hattori.

Hattori drew the process of the creation in a row of ten charts (see Figure 1). Something, which appeared in an empty space, broke up into the upper, the middle and the lower, and they became the sun, the earth and the moon. The births and activities of gods overlap with the creation of heavenly bodies.

The question now arises why Hattori thought he could connect the myth of the _Kojiki_ with western astronomy without contradiction.

Western thought including astronomy and geography had gradually spread in Japan since the 18th century, and it made an impact on traditional perspectives on the world in Japan.

Nishikawa Joken 西川如見, who had his roots of thought in Confucianism, was supposed to draw the image of the world based on the _ka-i_ perspective, but once he got in contact with western astronomy, he tried to draw a new representation of the world. He accepted the rotation of the ball-shaped earth and insisted that Japan was superior to the other countries for the reason that Japan was in the east, the best direction to where the sun came first. Though it may have been against the Confucian thought, where the upper and lower means superiority and inferiority, he did not abandon Confucianism. One of the reasons for this _successful_ connection is that there was no logical relation between the fundamental understanding of the universe from the view about *ki* and the *ka-i* perspective.[8]

Motoori, the master of Hattori, thought that human perception was finite and the gods were beyond. Hattori shared this view and insisted as follows: western thought is superior to Confucianism in the knowledge of present recognizable things, but its knowledge is limited, so it has nothing about the past. It is the *Kojiki* that tells the past activities of gods, left only in Japan. This is the reason why he connected both systems. He was convinced that the truth had rightly been passed on only in Japan, which caused the sense of superiority of Japan.

In addition to this, we must not ignore the circumstances of translation in Tokugawa period. Among astronomical books based on the Copernican system, some explained the generation of heavenly bodies from the viewpoint of the Creation in Christianity. Japanese translators avoided such parts in their translation considering the prohibition against Christianity.[9] It caused an intended blank in the translated books. On the other hand, Motoori regarded the *musuhi* gods as the creators of the world, and Hattori thought to fill the blank with the *musuhi*.

This connection necessarily brought new modes of discourses on the universe and the world. The first is that a myth had to be not only a story as a sequence of events, but also a story covering time and space as a whole. Western knowledge such as astronomy or geography had a tendency to describe and illustrate every part of the universe or the world and, as a result, gave the knowledge covering the present world. By contrast, the *Kojiki* shows the chronology of the creation. The connection between astronomy and the *Kojiki* imposed the task of exhaustive descriptions of the world in any time and anywhere.

The second is that everything had to be illustrated. For example, there arose the necessity to represent ideas like the superiority of their own country in the representation of the world. While Nishikawa Joken proved the superiority by the sacred direction, the east, Hattori regarded Japan as the point of the separation of earth and sun, in order to show its superiority on his charts. Modern astronomy and geography are basically free of any value judgment, and the attempts of Nishikawa and Hattori were destined to be a failure.

---

[8] Cf. Sawai (2000), pp. 217-221.
[9] Cf. Nakayama (1974), pp. 89ff.

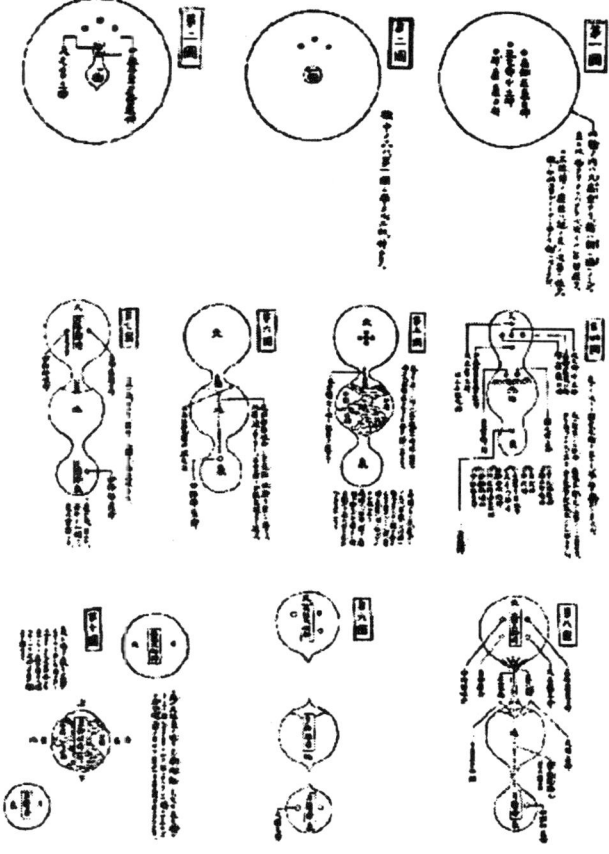

Figure 1: Hattori's ten charts from *Sandai-kō*

It is Hirata Atsutane, a scholar in the 19th century that advanced his new theory by correcting the theory of Hattori. Hirata explained in his early work *Tama no mihashira* 霊能真柱 the development of the universe with charts similar to those of Hattori. Hirata followed Motoori and Hattori on the point of considering that gods created the universe. But he stressed the importance of three gods of Creation (*zōka no sanshin* 造化三神), especially Ame no minakanushi as a center of the world. He did so more clearly however in his later works. The *Tama no mihashira* described Japan as the point of separation like the *Sandai-kō*, and explained that the Emperor was the tycoon of the world.

It is a characteristic of his representation that it was designed for identifying the location of the next world where spirits went after death. Though both Motoori and Hattori shared the belief that everything in the world was a result of the activities of gods, Hirata thought it applied even during the life of a person, that is to say, both this life and the next had to be consistently explained from the movements of gods. At this point, it is clear that the *enemy* he imagined is Buddhism, which had almost occupied the notion of salvation after death. The term *anjin* 安心 that Hirata adopted to mean the salvation, had been originally used in *Jōdo-kyō* 浄土教 (the religion of Pure Land) as a word that meant the confidence to reach the Pure Land after one's death. His dominant motive to describe the world was the desire to replace Buddhism as the provider of the salvation after death.

Motoori thought nobody could avoid the death and going to *yomi*, the impure land after one's death, but Hirata did not. Of course he accepted the premise that the universe consists of the sun, the earth and the moon, which Motoori and Hattori had shared. If the next world was not the moon as representation of *yomi*, it would be nowhere in the universe as a consequence. On the other hand, Hirata had an absolute confidence in the existence of spirits. In order to resolve this contradiction, he *discovered* the distinction between visible and invisible as a new segment of the world. This was based on the interpretation of *arawanaru-koto* and *kakuretaru-koto* in the *Nihonshoki*. While Motoori, as we have seen, regarded them as the world of humans and the one of gods, Hirata understood them as the world of the living and the one of the dead. He was *successful* in securing the position of the world of spirits in a cosmology consisting of heavenly bodies.

This caused Ōkuninushi to assume a fresh importance. Hirata identified the *kakuretaru-koto* as the next world, so he regarded Ōkuninushi, the god ruling the *kakuretaru-koto*, as the master of the next world and made a point of it. This was the attempt to exclude the discourses of Buddhists, which were dominant in the popular idea of the next life, and to explain everything in the world from the gods in Japan. This may be a kind of nationalism, which includes some paradox: the death is universal to all mankind, but the god who rules the death is peculiar to Japan.

Concerning Amaterasu, on the other hand, Hirata basically followed the view of Motoori, but it became subtly different from it. When Motoori thought that Amaterasu ruled human beings and Ōkuninushi the gods, these two gods were not supposed to compete with each other, because the gods and mankind were on different levels. Hirata however made these two gods share the two parts of a person, so it became uncertain which world was more important.

We can summarize the outlines of Hirata's theology as follows: ① three gods of Creation (_zōka no sanshin_), especially Ame no minakanushi, are the masters of the world; ② the Emperor, who is a descendant of Amaterasu, is at the absolute center of this world; ③ Ōkuninushi rules the life after death.

Hirata oriented these theses to the one cosmology. He thought that these gods were born in Japan and that the activities and statements of gods were rightly passed down only in Japan. Also for foreign countries he considered their founders to have been the Japanese gods. Monopoly of all the origins gave ground for a national identity, with a sense of superiority to other nations, where the general cosmology was connected to a particular nation.

As for the total order of gods, it is a kind of progress in which Hirata's theology developed their organization. It did not necessarily lead to a unified order of gods, and it contributed the divergence of theology.

Considering his theses, each god had a potential to gain predominating influence over the whole world. According to Hirata, Ame no minakanushi was the ruler of the universe and presided over everything in it. He could have been the ultimate principle. On the other hand, if departed souls profoundly influence the living in the Shintō theology, as in Buddhist thought, Ōkuninushi will rise in his status as mentioned above. Of course, Amaterasu, who was identified with the sun, was considered as the supreme god by Motoori, and Hirata generally agreed with him.

It made a difference in opinion among the followers of Hirata which side of the relation between gods and human or the universe was considered to be more important. Tsurumine Shigenobu 鶴峯戊申, Suzuki Shigetane 鈴木重胤 and Suzuki Masayuki 鈴木雅之 attached great importance to Ame no minakanushi, whereas Mutobe Yoshika 六人部是香 and Yano Harumichi 矢野玄道 made much of the state of Ōkuninushi.[10] Ironically, each god grew more universal, and the division of the Shintō theologies became deeper.


### The Varieties of Theology and National Identity in the Meiji Era

The Emperor gradually became more significant as a representation for the movement against the Shogunate. The consciousness of the reverence for the Emperor (sonnō 尊皇) enabled the protesting people to unite together, and mitogaku 水戸学, a school of political thought under the influence of Confucianism, deeply affected its development. Aizawa Yasushi 会沢要 (also called Seishisai 正志斎), a scholar of the Mito school, insisted on the formation of national consciousness among people, according to imperial rites centered on Amaterasu. His concern was rather realistic than religious.

Ibuki no ya 気吹舎 (the school of Hirata) had a considerable influence on the sonnō consciousness. They participated in that political movement with their religious faith in gods.

The new government, which had been established under the influence of this movement, was planning to invent the unity of the nation around the Emperor, and focused popular religious faith. Now the entry of Shintō into the salvation of the soul became not only the theological but also the political issue.

Different groups, including a staff of National Learning and a staff with Confucian background among others, made up the religious section of the government. In the staff of National Learning, the members from Tsuwano-han 津和野藩 held an advantage over the Hirata school.

In the early years of the Meiji era, Ono Nobuzane 小野述信, with Confucian background, gained control of the religious section, and gave a trial lecture for the Emperor and the staff of the government. In this lecture, he advocated his own theology, in which Amaterasu was the highest god as the Creator and ruled the world of the dead as well. Amaterasu therefore acquired the characters of zōka no sanshin and of Ōkuninushi.[11] The Hirata School opposed this view. We can easily find a revival of the problem of universality here. The Hirata School

---

[10] Cf. Katsurajima (1992), pp. 29-32 and Hara (1996), pp. 67-103.
[11] Cf. Haga (1994), pp. 167ff.

was in opposition to the Tsuwano group, and shortly after that, it was driven out of the government.

The *Kyōbu-shō* 教部省 (Ministry of Doctrine) was established to carry out the religious enlightenment to form a national consciousness, and for that purpose it proclaimed the 'Twenty-eight themes' (*nijūhachi-kendai* 二十八兼題). Though these themes show some influence of the Hirata School, the religious enlightenment did only have little success, because of the variety of the staff. The attempt to form a national consciousness according to Shintō theology ended in failure, but another way was to be opened later. Apart from the formation of a national identity, theological arguments became the main problem for the Shintōists and would lead to the controversy of which gods to deify (*saijin ronsō* 祭神論争) in the 1880's, where the status of Ōkuninushi was the main issue.

## Conclusion

Generally, the identity of a nation-state has various aspects: economical, political, ideological and cultural integration.[12] Myths are important as cultural resources, and very often they include explanations for the creation of the world. Some kind of universality is needed here, and as modern science became popular, the myths were required to be consistent with it.

The cosmologies in National Learning, which was established against Confucianism and Buddhism, searched their evidences among Japanese myths and connected them with the astronomy and geography of Europe.

If a national identity demands both the universality and the peculiarity of the nation – and it must express both of them at one time – its representation may appear as a cosmology or a worldview expressing both characters.

The cosmologies of National Learning are good illustrations for that.

---

[12] See, e.g., Nishikawa (1995).

## Selected Sources

**Endō (1995)**

Endō, Jun 遠藤潤: "Hirata Atsutane no takai-ron saikō: 'Tama no mihashira' o chūshin ni 平田篤胤の他界論再考：『霊能真柱』を中心に", in: *Shūkyō kenkyū* 宗教研究, vol. 69/2 (1995), pp. 93-117.

**Haga (1994)**

Haga, Shōji 羽賀祥二: *Meiji-ishin to shūkyō* 明治維新と宗教. Tōkyō: Chikuma-shobō, 1994.

**Hara (1996)**

Hara, Takeshi 原武史: *'Izumo' to iu shisō* 「出雲」という思想. Tōkyō: Kōjinsha, 1996.

**Katsurajima (1992)**

Katsurajima, Nobuhiro 桂島宣弘: *Bakumatsu minshū-shisō no kenkyū* 幕末民衆思想の研究. Kyōto: Bunrikaku, 1992.

**—　(1999)**

Katsurajima, Nobuhiro 桂島宣弘: *Shisōshi no 19-seiki: 'tasha' toshite no Tokugawa-nihon* 思想史の19世紀：〈他者〉としての徳川日本. Tōkyō: Perikan-sha, 1999.

**Kurozumi (1994)**

Kurozumi, Makoto 黒住真: "Jugaku to kinsei nihon shakai 儒学と近世日本社会", in: Asao, Naohiro 朝尾直弘 et al. (ed.): *Iwanami-kōza Nihon tsūshi* 岩波講座日本通史, *vol.13, Kinsei* 近世, *no. 3*. Tōkyō: Iwanami shoten, 1994, pp. 251-302.

**Maruyama (1952)**

Maruyama, Masao 丸山眞男: *Nihon seiji shisōshi kenkyu* 日本政治思想史研究. Tōkyō: Tōdai Shuppankai, 1952 [= Studies in the Intellectual History of Tokugawa Japan. University of Tokyo Press and Princeton University Press, 1974].

**Nakayama (1972)**

Nakayama, Shigeru 中山茂: *Nihon no tenmon-gaku* 日本の天文学. Tōkyō: Iwanami shoten, 1972.

Nishikawa (1995)
Nishikawa, Nagao 西川長夫: "Nihongata kokumin-kokka no keisei: hikaku shiteki kanten kara 日本型国民国家の形成：比較史的観点から", in: Nishikawa, Nagao 西川長夫/ Matsumiya, Hideharu 松宮秀治 (ed.): _Bakumatsu, Meiji-ki no kokumin-kokka keisei to bunka-hen'yō_ 幕末・明治期の国民国家形成と文化変容. Tōkyō: Shinyōsha, 1995.

Ōji (1996)
Ōji, Toshiaki 応地利明: _E-chizu no sekai-zō_ 絵地図の世界像. Tōkyō: Iwanami shoten, 1996.

Sawai (2000)
Sawai, Keiichi 澤井啓一: _'Kigō' toshite no jugaku_ 〈記号〉としての儒学. Tōkyō: Kōbōsha, 2000.

# Shintō and *kokutai*:
# Religious Ideology in the Japanese Context

Klaus ANTONI

## 1. Introduction[1]

The subject of 'Shintō' marks one of the essentials of Japanese cultural history. Inside and outside of Japan, Shintō is not only seen as the Japanese national religion, but it is often used as a metaphorical expression for the alleged immutability of the Japanese culture or even for the Japanese 'national polity' (*kokutai* 国体) itself. To give a popular example of this common view, let me cite Joseph M. Kitagawa, who wrote in the *Japan-Handbuch* (translation by Ludwig):

> *"Shintō ist im eigentlichen Sinne die dem japanischen Volk zugrunde liegende Wertorientierung, denn er ist das Zusammenwirken der divergierenden und doch einzigartigen japanischen Sensitivitäten, der religiösen Überzeugungen und der kulturellen Haltung, die seit der frühesten Zeit bis auf heute ganz und gar das Erleben des japanischen Volkes geprägt haben."*[2]

Definitions like this one show the great dilemma of an approach, which tries to preclude the historical aspect and unreflectingly postulates an ahistorically valid Shintō. Yet, this religious system has developed historically, and has united most heterogeneous elements throughout the course of its development up to the ideology of the religiously based Japanese nationalism of the modern age (*kokutai-shintō* 国体神道).

---

[1] For a more detailed and expanded German version of this article see Antoni (2001); for an elaborated argumentation on the whole topic cf. Antoni (1998).

[2] Hammitzsch (1981), p. 1633. Eng. transl.: *"Shintō is in fact the underlying value orientation of the Japanese people, because it is a combination of divergent and yet unique Japanese sensitivities, religious principles and cultural attitudes, which have shaped completely the experience of the Japanese people from the earliest time until today.".*

A generally valid Japanese 'national religion' as postulated by Kitagawa and others, can therefore only be verified as an ideal and a construction of modern times. One author remarks in that context restrictively, that the term 'Shintō' might only be used for the designation of religion in a narrower sense. He elaborates that *"Der Begriff 'Shintōismus' hingegen wird nur dann verwendet, wenn es sich um die durch Ideologisierung bzw. die Politisierung entstanden shintōistisch orientierte Sozial- oder Staatsgedanken handelt"*[3] [Miyasaka (1994), p. 236, n. 214]. Yet, such a differentiation, which sets a politically free Shintō – in the sense of a religiously indigenous folk religion – apart from its negative ideologically contaminated counterpart – the Shintō of modern times –, misjudges in my opinion the facts relating to its (ideological) history. The political aspect is constituent for the 'Shintō' system from the beginning on, and it cannot be separated from an idealized Japanese religion – both are the two sides of the same coin.

Precisely such seemingly value-free assertions, like the one brought forth by Miyasaka in his recent work of scientific standard, show how in the present time it is absolutely necessary to have a historical-critical study of this subject.

Dealing with 'the' Shintō, much more than with any other subject, means to question Japanese culture and its self-conception: Is it a national religion or a construct of the modern age? Is it archaic ancestor worship or an all-Japanese folklore? Is it an esoteric doctrinaire religion or syncretistic ritualism? Or, is it eventually an ethno-centrist nationalism or peaceful nature worship?

Any cliché with regard to Japanese culture will also be found in the debate over 'the' Shintō: Shintō in the ideological development of the modern age has to function as a nativist synonym for the 'unaltered', 'homogeneous', 'unique', and finally 'ultimate' Japanese culture, which is freed from all foreignness, allowing a view into allegedly 'true' Japan. In this respect, the postulation of a Japanese national religion implicitly freed from all foreign elements, is already a product of this modern Japanese auto-stereotype, which, as the allegedly authentic form of cultural self-expression, is able to shape Japan's image – also abroad – until this very day.

---

[3] Eng. transl.: *"The term 'Shintōism' on the other hand is only to be used if it concerns the shintōistic oriented social or national thought which developed out of ideologization and politicalization, respectively."*.

On the whole, it demonstrates that an evaluation of the claim made by Shintō to represent Japan's virtually natural 'national religion' is not possible without a thorough examination of the historical development.

## 2. Historical development: The "primeval religion of Japan"

Let us begin our short trip through the history of Shintō with yet another definition. Here it is no longer the question of a homogeneous religious ethno-centrism, but rather, as the Japanese scholar Ōbayashi Taryō 大林太良 defines the alleged national religion of Japan: "*Shintō [ist] im weiteren Sinne die Urreligion Japans, im engeren Sinne ein aus Urreligion und chinesischen Elementen zu politischen Zwecken ausgebautes System*"[4] [Ōbayashi (1982), p. 135].

If we take this definition as the basis of our considerations, two questions are brought up: ① What is to be understood by a Japanese 'primeval religion'?; and ② What does the scholar refer to by 'political purposes'?

Let us therefore go back in time as far as resources allow. This is where the oldest written records of Japan are of critical importance: the *Kojiki* 古事記 ('Records of ancient matters') from the year 712 AD and the *Nihongi* 日本紀 ('Chronicles of Japan') from the year 720 AD. These works – conceived as historical works – supply information on the official conception of history at that time by describing the country's history from the mythological primal beginnings until the time of recording. Simultaneously, they, especially the *Kojiki*, are to a certain degree regarded as the 'holy books' of Shintō by traditional Shintō circles of modern times. How is this circumstance to be explained?

There is no doubt to the fact that pre-Buddhist religious forms did exist in Japan, but it should not be ignored that the source material available is not sufficient in order to be able to draw an unambiguous – and above all, homogeneous – picture. On the contrary, all information has to be arduously concluded and interpreted from the handed down records. A fundamental study of these prob-

---

[4] Eng. transl.: "*Shintō [is] in the broader sense the primeval religion of Japan, in the narrow sense a system constructed for political purposes from primeval religion and Chinese elements.*".

lems has been presented in Nelly Naumann's research of the primeval religion of Japan.

Besides deductions from results of archaeological research – it is for instance possible to conclude specific afterlife ideas from the conducted type of funerals –, the myths in the old records such as *Kojiki* and *Nihongi*, provide the underlying approach to understanding. Precisely these myths, arranged by statesmen of the 7th and 8th century in a systematic order for the purpose of legitimizing the imperial rule, permit valuable findings on the earliest Japanese belief systems – hence 'primeval religion(s) of Japan' – by examining single elements.

The mythology of the *Kojiki* was only later made a sacral tradition by Shintō theologians and ideologists, such as is shown in the historical analysis. A homogenous 'indigenous religion' as postulated by the *kokugaku* 国学 (National School) of the Edo period, cannot be found in the old records. 'The' Shintō at the dawn of its well-known history presents itself in an ambiguous and manifold appearance – at this point, there was no hint of a uniform thread of a homogenous indigenous religion of Japan. Thus, by a thorough examination, the source materials show the diverse origins and homogenous character that were made into this allegedly single, uninterrupted 'tradition' of mythological tradition by the compilers of official documents in the 8th century.

In this context it is remarkable that the mythological matter is presented considerably much more differentiated in the second of the mentioned old records, the *Nihongi*, than in the *Kojiki*. The whole matter in the *Kojiki* is presented as a single, continuous purposive plot, whilst the *Nihongi* usually also presents differing variations of a specific episode. The different variations in the Nihongi proof that one was aware of different branches of traditions, which showed great variances. The modern Shintō doctrine of 'one homogenous tradition' primarily referring to the *Kojiki* – which was adopted by the *kokugaku* of the modern times and realized in the Meiji period – is an illusion from its beginning on: something that was made artificially for the purpose of political authentication.

The modern Japanese ideology of an incomparable 'unique' national polity (*kokutai*) was eventually entirely based on legitimatizing statements of handed down mythology from records of the 8th century. Apparent from several cases, an objective scientific research of these myths – especially in an ethnological-comparative sense – was predestined to collide with the sacrosanct understanding of the state from the Meiji period to the year 1945: Any proof of connections between the native mythology to traditions of the continental mainland or the southern archipelago shook the dogma of a self-sufficient 'land of gods'.

Thus, the liberal effect of free scientific research in mythology after the war, cannot be over-estimated. Without this critical, cultural-historical analysis [for instance, Matsumura et al. (1954-58), Naumann (1971, 1988), Ōbayashi (1973, 1988)], dogmatic doctrines of modern State Shintō might, left unexamined, apply even today. These researches provide the comprehension of an extremely complex and historically thoroughly graded genesis of the Japanese culture, whose origins have been liberated from the artificially constructed isolation of the modern age after the year 1868 and put in an overall context, not only of the east-Asian human history but also of human history in general. Therefore, the idea of Japan's homogeneity, ideologically justified and rooted in the tradi-tionalistic constructions of pre-modern times, cannot be upheld anymore. Japan is indeed geographically an island (_shimaguni_ 島国), but not so in respect of culture.

## 3. Legitimation of the imperial house

With regard to 'political purposes' as stated by Ōbayashi, the beginning chap-ters of both, the _Kojiki_ and the _Nihongi_, are of eminent importance, because they contain the already mentioned mythological traditions of the country and thereupon the religiously binding foundation of the 'official' Shintō. Here we can find the records of the creation of the world, of the gods and their deeds, of the origin of the imperial house and the strengthening of its power. This shows already one characteristic feature of Japanese mythology: it primarily serves the purpose of legitimizing the power of the imperial house, and as such it indeed serves 'political purposes'.

The center of China's Confucian state doctrine was always the ideal state, led by an equally ideal ruler, the _t'ien-tzu_ 天子 (jap. _tenshi_, 'Son of Heaven'). Yet, only a truly virtuous ruler could secure the prosperity of the state – and thus the basic principles of Confucianism –, because ruler and state were deeply inter-linked in mystical ways. If an emperor lost his individual virtue, he lost the right way, in which case the people did not only have the right but practically the moral obligation to dethrone this ruler who had suddenly become hazardous to public welfare. These thoughts were clearly represented by the Confucian philosopher Meng-tzu 孟子 (Menzius; jap. Mōshi) and also came to Japan in ancient times as a result of Japan's penetration with Chinese ideas.

Typically enough, it was precisely in this respect – the dethronement of an emperor – that Japan did not follow the Chinese role model. The Japanese rulers – meanwhile called *tennō* 天皇 ('Heavenly Ruler') – felt entirely equal in rank to the Chinese emperors.[5] Accordingly, the court invented its own kind of legitimation of imperial power, which was deliberately disassociated from Confucianism.

This legitimation was found in the handed down myths of the ruling family, which reported of the heavenly origin of the imperial house and designated the living emperor as a direct descendant of the Sun Goddess. Thence, the Sun Goddess gave her grandson and his descendant, the first human emperor, the heavenly order (*shinchoku* 神勅) to rule over the land of Japan. To be more precise: to rule for all times as one single dynasty.[6] Never ought there to be a change of dynasty, such as it was common in China, and they ought never to renounce their claim to power. The more the state became Sinicized, the clearer the court invented an image of a specific Japanese ruler in the sense of a divine descendant of sacred nature – and everything else descended and derived its meaning from him and his ancestors, respectively.

This deification of the emperor and eventually of the whole country (*shinkoku, kami-no-kuni* 神国, 'land of the gods') is the substance of what is called Shintō – the 'Way of the Gods' of Japan. Nelly Naumann stated already thirty years ago that *"Die Bedeutung des Wortes* shintō *kann [...] konkret erfaßt werden in der Idealvorstellung des japanischen Gott-Kaisertums, welche die Göttlichkeit der regierenden Kaiser und ihren von der Sonnengöttin verliehenen Herrschaftsauftrag umfaßt."* [Naumann (1970), p. 13][7].

---

[5] This is already shown by the famous letter Empress Suikō 推古 wrote to the Chinese Emperor, addressing him as the Emperor of the West who respectfully is greeted by the Emperor of the East, i.e., Suiko-tennō counts herself as equal in value to the Chinese Son of Heaven. Cf. *Nihongi*, Suiko-tennō 推古天皇, 16/9 [NKBT, vol. 67, p. 192].

[6] Cf. *Nihongi* [NKBT, vol. 67, p. 147]; *Kojiki* [NKBT, vol. 1, pp. 126f.]; *Kogoshūi* [GSRJ, vol. 25, p. 5]; Florenz (1919), p. 246 and Antoni (1998), p. 77, n. 48.

[7] Eng. transl.: *"The meaning of the term* shintō *can concretely be [...] comprehended in the ideal concept of the Japanese heavenly emperorship, which comprises the reigning emperors' divineness, and their ruling mandate bestowed upon them by the Sun Goddess"*.

An individual theology of Shintō did not develop until the Japanese middle ages. Although the emperor lost the direct ruling power to the military aristocracy and the *bakufu* 幕府, which ruled nominally in the name of the imperial house and continued to maintain this rule until the year 1868, a more and more prominent idea of Japan as a country under special protection of the gods (*shinkoku*) developed among circles of the Shintō-theology. Extreme supporters of this way of thinking eventually concluded from the handed-down myths that not only the imperial house is of divine descent, but the whole Japanese nation.[8] For them, Japan was a country whose nature was different from all other parts of this world, being endowed with a unique, indigenous Japanese spirit – *Yamato-damashii* 大和魂, the 'spirit of Yamato'.

On this basis, Shintō-theology again turned to politics since the 18th century at the latest. We will deal with these questions in the following.

## 4. Shintō in modern times and modern age

### 4.1 Confucian Shintō

At the beginning of this development stood Shintō-Confucian syncretism or Confucian Shintō (*juka-shintō* 儒家神道)[9], which on a level of theoretical-theological discussions to a large extent succeeded the Buddhist Shintō of the middle ages.[10] The conception of a unity of Shintō and Confucianism (*shinju-itchi* 神儒一致)[11] made (neo-) Confucianism the spiritual core and developed a definitely opposing attitude towards Buddhism (*haibutsu* 排仏).

Influential Confucian philosophers of that period like Fujiwara Seika 藤原惺窩 (1561-1619) and Hayashi Razan 林羅山 (1583-1657), were representatives of this newly Confucian oriented Shintō. The doctrines of Watarai- 度会 (Ise- 伊

---

[8] On the concept of human beings and mankind within the context of Japanese mythology, cf. Antoni (1991), pp. 60-75.

[9] Cf. Sugiyama/ Sakamoto (1994); Abe (1972); Boot (1992); Kishimoto (1993), pp. 47-69 and Kracht (1986). For the philological sources cf. Taira/ Abe (1972), pp. 9-262; KJRE, *Jingi-bu* 神祇部 II/44, Shintō vol. 2, pp. 1359-1455.

[10] Concerning the *jingūji* of the Edo-period cf. Seckel (1985), pp. 29f. and 74-77.

[11] Cf. Kishimoto (1993), pp. 49-58; Sugiyama/ Sakamoto (1994), p. 16.

勢)[12] and moreover Yoshida-Shintō 吉田神道 of the middle ages were reinterpreted as well, and hence further developed in the sense of the new power relations in Edo period. The house of Yoshida considerably shaped the development of Shintō in the early Edo period under the influence of new social and political structures. The Yoshida doctrine logically also went through far-reaching developments in that context, at the end of which stood a Neo-Confucian shaped Shintō of modern times that hardly showed any correspondence to the medieval doctrines of Yoshida Kanetomo 吉田兼俱 (1435-1511).

Moreover, the Yoshida house received its outstanding importance for Edo period's Shintō due to its particularly powerful position in the system of Shintō shrines, as well as due to its fast achieved closeness to the Tokugawa's center of power of.[13]

### 4.2 The 'National School' (kokugaku)

Confucian Shintō, on the one hand, which flourished together with Confucianism of modern times, developed into the mainstream of Edo period Shintō.[14] Yet on the other hand, a new interpretation of Shintō in the context of the 'National School' (kokugaku 国学) did slowly develop since the middle of the Edo period.

The kokugaku originated in a countermovement to the increasing advancement of Japan's Sinicization. This school – represented by its main supporters Kada no Azumamaro 荷田春満 (1668-1736)[15], Kamo Mabuchi 加茂真淵 (1697-1769)[16], Motoori Norinaga 本居宣長(1730-1801)[17] and finally Hirata Atsutane 平田篤胤 (1776-1843)[18] – developed in the course of the Edo period

---

[12] For an introduction to the medieval Watarai-Shintō cf. Teeuwen (1993, 1996), Naumann (1994), pp. 29-56; Picken (1994), pp. 306-310; Kishimoto (1993), pp. 31-37.

[13] Cf. Antoni (1998), chap. II. 2. 2. 1. 2. 2.

[14] Cf. Sugiyama/ Sakamoto (1994), p. 17.

[15] On Kada Azumamaro cf. Dumoulin (1940); Nakamura (1984).

[16] On Kamo Mabuchi cf. the works of Heinrich Dumoulin (1939b, 1941a, 1941b, 1943a, 1943b, 1953, 1955, 1956a 1956b).

[17] On Motoori Norinaga cf. Allessandro (1964); Brownlee (1988); Dumoulin (1939a); Hino (1983); Matsumoto (1970); Motoori (1919-27); Nishimura (1987, 1991); Satō-Diesner (1977); Stolte (1939).

[18] On Hirata Atsutane cf. Devine (1981); Hammitzsch (1936); Keene (1953, 1978); McNally (1998); Miki (1990); Odronic (1967); Schiffer (1939); Tahara (1990); Watanabe (1978).

from a purely philological-literary school to a deliberately political-agitatorial ideology.

The *kokugaku* mainly chose native classical literature of Japan as their research objective. The study of the literature of Japanese ancient times, especially the *Kojiki*, by Motoori Norinaga, a student of Kamo Mabuchi, led to the pushing aside of hitherto syncretistic interpretations of Shintō. Thus a nativist doctrine developed, i.e., a philosophical-political Shintō, which began to contest with the Confucian-Shintō syncretism over predominance.

On the basis of its philological and theological studies, the *kokugaku* towards the close of the 18th century eventually tried to convert its postulates into politics by greatly emphasizing a renaissance of the Japanese emperorship according to the shintōistic doctrines of the imperial house's genealogical origin.

The *kokugaku* regarded the principle of historical truth and reality of the old records, including the chapters concerning the 'era of the gods' in the oldest Japanese documents, as their theoretical axiom.

These traditions were understood, in its lexical meaning, as 'facts' (*jujitsu* 事実): the accounts on the origin of the world, the gods of heaven and earth, the establishment of an emperorship, the origin of the powerful noble lineages – for the philosophers of the 'National School' all these mystic occurrences became descriptions of realities in a historical sense. When in that context Hirata Atsutane, an extremely influential theorist and ideologist of the late *kokugaku*, called Japan the 'land of the gods', he thus followed a literal understanding of the handed-down written records in the sense of a 'shintōist fundamentalism' – if it was more scheming or yet naïve remains to be seen. In Atsutane's case, this viewpoint led to fanatical nationalism and to the conviction of Japan's special status above all other countries. He was convinced, that "w*e all are undoubtedly descendents of the deities*"[19]. Therefore, even the people were elevated to divine descendants, and they regarded themselves adopted into the lineage of the Emperor as an *arahitogami* 現人神 (or 荒人神), i.e., a 'deity that is presently visible as a human being'.

---

[19] Hirata (1927-29), p. 1; cf. Hammitzsch (1936), pp. 20ff. and Antoni (1991), p. 66.

### 4.3 The conception of 'national polity' (kokutai)

By the end of the Edo period, *kokugaku* ideology entered into an astonishing combination with Confucian ideology, and again we meet the handed-down structures of Japanese syncretism. The core of those national-religious speculations of the Bakumatsu period was formed by the idea of a 'national polity' (*kokutai* 国体).[20] This idea described all those 'national characteristics' that a country ought to have. Japan's 'national polity' was seen to be based on the allegedly unique fact of being a 'divine country' (*shinkoku, kami-no-kuni*), founded by the Sun Goddess Amaterasu 天照, and being ruled by her direct descendants – the human emperors. Thus, the divine *tennō* became the personification of Japanese identity.[21]

Historical analysis shows that the usage of the term *kokutai* as a synonym for Japan was already common at that time, at least in the circles of the imperial court of Kyōto.[22] It should also be recalled that already Hirata Atsutane saw the 'true Shintō' (*makoto no shintō* 真の神道) embodied in the *kokutai*.[23] Yet, the adoption of this concept as a national religious state ideology by the majority of the people did not take place until after the Meiji restoration.

Three phases of *kokutai*-ideology can be clearly identified: ① formative phase (approx. 1825-1890); ② classic phase (1890-1937); ③ phase of hybris (1937-1945). The beginning of the formative phase was the early 19th century, documented by Aizawa Seishisai's 会沢正志斎 work *Shinron* 新論 of 1825.[24] The end of that period came in 1890, the year of the proclamation of the *Kyōiku chokugo* 教育勅語 ('Imperial Rescript on Education'), which was decisive for the further development and which marked the beginning of the second, the classic phase.

By looking on these particular dates, it becomes clear that this first, formative phase falls into the era of the great transformations of Japanese history: the decline of the Tokugawa state, the opening of the country to the outside world, the

---

[20] Cf. Antoni (1987, 1991, 1998).

[21] Cf. Stanzel (1982), pp. 53ff.; concerning the Japanese identity debate, cf. also Naumann (1987).

[22] Cf. Meyer (1997), p. 135, p. 140 and p. 141, n. 23.

[23] On Hirata's opinion of the 'true kami way' (*makoto no shintō*) being embodied in the Japanese *kokutai*, cf. Hirata (1976), p. 87 and Schiffer (1939), p. 227.

[24] Concerning the *Shinron*, cf. Stanzel (1982) and Wakabayashi (1982).

establishment of a modern Japanese empire with the *tennō* being the sacrosanct head of state – even placed above the constitution – as an incarnation of the state itself.

As is generally known, the philosophers of the so-called Mito school (*mitogaku* 水戸学) had a substantially spiritual and political influence. Through their interpretation of the national school, they broadened the land-of-the-god-doctrine of Shintō by the canon of Confucianist maxims, which dominated at that time. Herein lies the intrinsic difference to the purist national school, which strictly opposed all things of Chinese origin.[25]

In combination with the shintōist land-of-the-gods-ideology of the national school, this ended in a familistic conception of *kokutai*: a definition of the Japanese nation as a society of real descent, as a family of commonly divine origin with the emperor being the natural head.[26]

### 4.4 Religion and ideology in the Meiji period

The spiritual core of modern Japan's? national idea was therefore least but not last given in the ideological-religious postulate of a homogeneous Japanese family state. This idea found its formulation since the Meiji period in the concept of 'familism' (*kazoku-shugi* 家族主義), i.e., through the comprehension of Japan as a nation state whose people are united by being one single family. At the head of this family, in the role of the father, stood the *tennō*.[27] It seems remarkable that the most radical version of familism did not understand this intimate relationship between *tennō* and people as family in a figurative sense, but more as a real ethnical-genetically defined extended family whose members are connected with each other through their same origin in the divine ancestors.

The picture of a Japanese culture that we can find with philosophers such as Inoue Tetsujirō 井上哲次郎[28], as being manifested in Shintō and excelling due to

---

[25] Cf. Antoni (1998), p. 170. For an introduction into Mito thought cf. Imai (1973), Koschmann (1987), Kracht (1975) and Webb (1958).

[26] Even the *Nihongi* (Yūryaku 雄略 23/8/7) knew a comparison between the relationships of ruler/vassal and father/child. The effective identification of both pairs of relationship was completed only in the 19th century. Cf. Lokowandt (1978), pp. 60ff.; Tsurumi (1970), pp. 103-109; Fridell (1970), pp. 828-833; Bellah (1985), p. 104 and van Straelen (1952), p. 83.

[27] For an introduction into the ideology and thought of the Meiji period cf. Gluck (1985) and Harootunian (1995).

[28] Cf. Antoni (1990, 1998) and Nawrocki (1998).

its history throughout which at its core stood the person and institution of the *tennō* who is inseparably connected with the – homogeneous – people by a quasi genetically transmitted national ethic (*kokumin dōtoku* 国民道徳), was spread especially by the commentaries on the Imperial Rescript on Education from 1890 until its nationalistic climax with the publication of the *Kokutai no hongi* 国体の本義[29] in the year 1937.

Insights into the historical reality, which stood apart of the ideology of *kokutai*-Shintō, remained to a large extent unheard in this context. In the Meiji period it has been successfully ideologically dismissed that throughout the whole course of its historical development Japan always was a country mainly marked by complexity and disintegration in cultural, social, territorial, and especially religious regards – to an extent that the new view of an ethnically and culturally homogenous country could rise to the absolute dogma of *kokutai*-Shintō.[30]

Precisely because the country was always divided in particular groups, the utopia of homogeneity appeared very promising from the viewpoint of a new, central state in the Meiji period. In that context Shintō occupied a key position, because this religious world that used to be heterogeneous and complex, comprehended now as the only authentic Japanese religion, was more and more identified as spiritual core and foundation of the Japanese culture. Logically, this ended in a concept of Shintō embodying Japanese culture itself, as it shaped the country from late Meiji period until the decline in the year 1945.

Despite the official renunciation of his divine status by Shōwa-tennō 昭和天皇 on January 1, 1946, the Japanese emperorship receives its whole spiritual and religious authority, now as before, from the religious-political ideology of Shintō. On a regular basis opinion polls proof the Japanese people's great approval of the institution of the *tennō*.[31] But almost none of the interviewed people seemed to consciously think of 'religion' in that context, because the *tennō* for most Japanese citizens is just what has been attributed to him by the constitution: a 'symbol' of Japan. According to this concept, Japan can be sure

---

[29] Cf. Monbushō (1937); Gauntlett/ Hall (1949). Partial translations in: Tsunoda (1964), vol. II, pp. 278-288; Wittig (1976), pp. 127-130, doc. no. 33. See also Antoni (1998), p. 219 and Miller (1982), p. 92.

[30] On the term *kokutai*-Shintō in Inoue Tetsujirō's writings, cf. Nawrocki (1998), pp. 152-158, pp. 162f. and pp. 220f.; Antoni (1998), p. 229, pp. 274-277, p. 309 and p. 330. Even Gerhard Rosenkranz [(1944), p. 100] uses this term; cf. Antoni (1998), p. 309.

of its inner unity as long as the emperor resides in his palace's mysterious seclusion, like on an island in the middle of Tōkyō, and performs his daily rites.

## 5. Résumé

In the present context, the historical development could not be considered in more detail. Let me instead point to my summarized description of neoteric and modern developments [Antoni (1998)].

Yet it remains to be hoped for that this short introduction to the problem field of Shintō conveyed at least an impression that an ahistorical-static approach cannot contribute to the understanding and explanation of this question. It shows that Shintō just like Buddhism, Confucianism and other complex systems, is neither clearly defined nor an invariable entity. However, it is still possible to determine characteristics, which document an undoubted continuity of the system 'Shintō'. In the center of this continuity lies the function to legitimize the ruling position of the imperial house since the days of *Kojiki* and *Nihongi*. This 'political purpose' – which outshines everything else – is the actual core of what we call Shintō. It can be seamlessly followed through the history of Shintō: from the constructions of a standardized mythology of ancient times, via the *shinkoku* ideology of the middle ages and the nativist ideological concepts of the *kokugaku*, up to the modern conception of *kokutai*. Of central importance in this context is the perception that the philosophical structures of modern age Japan have their own differentiated development, reaching far back into pre-modern times, and are only to be comprehended from there.

Thus, the philosophical structures of the Japanese modern age are founded on the development in Japanese pre-modern times – drawn up by theological and philosophical circles of Buddhism, Confucianism and Shintō – and were put into practice only since the Meiji period together with imported conceptions of the Western modern age. The world of Shintō was attributed with a decisive importance for the identity formation of modern Japan.

As cultural scientists, we are called upon to undertake the arduous work to reveal these lines of tradition. In order to understand the constructions of the modern age, we have to turn to the authentic sources of pre-modern times: the

---

[31] Cf. Antoni (1991), p. 24.

language and literary-documentary traditions of ancient and classic Japan. Thus, the hermeneutical analysis of pre-modern times supplies the most certain basis for the comprehension of the present. Even though such a philological-hermeneutical approach is much more complicated on the whole than a great ahistorical design in the sense of Kitagawa's definition of Shintō quoted in the beginning, science cannot withdraw from this challenge. Most of all, Japanology has been attributed with an extremely important function. As a science about Japan, it is supposed to pursue unbiased fundamental research about this subject. A Japanology however, which closes its eyes to the research of historical processes and their philological resources, cannot accomplish this task.

## *Bibliography*

Abe (1972)
> Abe, Akio 阿部秋生: "Juka-shintō to kokugaku 儒家神道と国学", in: Taira/ Abe (1972), pp. 497-506.

Allessandro (1964)
> Allessandro, Casero: *Das Naga no Hire des Ichikawa Kakumei Tazumaro: Eine kritische Auseinandersetzung mit der Wissenschafts-auffassung des Motoori Norinaga.* [M.A. Thesis] München: Universität München, 1964.

Antoni (1987)
> Antoni, Klaus: "Kokutai – Das 'Nationalwesen' als japanische Utopie", in: *Saeculum – Jahrbuch für Universalgeschichte*, vol. 38/2-3 (1987), pp. 266-311.

— (1990)
> Antoni, Klaus: "Inoue Tetsujirō und die Entwicklung der Staatsideologie in der zweiten Hälfte der Meiji-Zeit", in: *Oriens Extremus*, 33rd year, no. 1 (1990), pp. 99-116.

— (1991)
> Antoni, Klaus: *Der Himmlische Herrscher und sein Staat: Essays zur Stellung des Tennō im modernen Japan.* München: iudicium, 1991.

— (1992)
Antoni, Klaus: "Tradition und 'Traditionalismus' im modernen Japan: Ein kulturanthropologischer Versuch", in: Deutsches Institut für Japanstudien (ed.): *Japanstudien: Jahrbuch des Deutschen Instituts für Japanstudien der Philipp-Franz-von-Siebold-Stiftung*, vol. 3 (1992), pp. 105-128.

— (1997)
Antoni, Klaus (ed.): *Rituale und ihre Urheber: 'Invented Traditions' in der japanischen Religionsgeschichte.* [Ostasien – Pazifik. Trierer Studien zu Politik, Wirtschaft, Gesellschaft, Kultur; vol. 5] Hamburg: Lit-Verlag, 1997.

— (1998)
Antoni, Klaus: *Shintō und die Konzeption des japanischen Nationalwesens (kokutai): Der religiöse Traditionalismus in Neuzeit und Moderne Japans.* [Handbuch der Orientalistik, part V, vol. 8] Leiden: Brill, 1998.

— (2001)
Antoni, Klaus: "Shintō", in: Kracht, Klaus/ Rüttermann, Markus (eds.): *Grundriß der Japanologie.* [Izumi – Quellen, Studien und Materialien zur Kultur Japans; vol. 7] Wiesbaden: Harrassowitz, 2001, pp. 115-147.

Bargatzky (1997)
Bargatzky, Thomas: *Ethnologie: Eine Einführung in die Wissenschaft von den urproduktiven Gesellschaften.* Hamburg: Buske, 1997.

Bellah (1985)
Bellah, Robert Neelly: *Tokugawa Religion: The Cultural Roots of Modern Japan.* New York: Free Press, 1985 [1957].

Boot (1992)
Boot, Willem Jan: *The Adoption and Adaptation of Neo-Confucianism in Japan: The Role of Fujiwara Seika and Hayashi Razan.* [Ph. Diss.; 2nd ed.] Leiden: Rijksuniv., 1992.

Brownlee (1988)
Brownlee, John: "The Jeweled Comb-Box: Motoori Norinaga's 'Tamakushige'", in: *Monumenta Nipponica*, vol. 43/1 (1988), pp. 35- 61.

Devine (1981)
Devine, Richard: "Hirata Atsutane and Christian Sources", in: *Monumenta Nipponica*, vol. 36/1 (1981), pp. 37-54.

Dumoulin (1939a)
Dumoulin, Heinrich: "Motoori Norinaga", in: *Nippon*, vol. 5 (1939), pp. 193-197.

— (1939b)
Dumoulin, Heinrich: "Kamo Mabuchi: 'Kokuikō'. Gedanken über den 'Sinn des Landes'", in: *Monumenta Nipponica*, vol. 2/1 (1939), pp. 165-192.

— 1940
Dumoulin, Heinrich: "Sō-gakkō-kei: Kada Azumamaro's Gesuch um die Errichtung einer Kokugaku-Schule", in: *Monumenta Nipponica*, vol. 3/2 (1940), pp. 590-609.

— (1941a)
Dumoulin, Heinrich: "Zwei Texte zum Kadō des Kamo Mabuchi: 'Uta no kokoro no uchi' – 'Niimanabi' [part I]", in: *Monumenta Nipponica*, vol. 4/1 (1941), pp. 192-206.

— (1941b)
Dumoulin, Heinrich: "Zwei Texte zum Kadō des Kamo Mabuchi: 'Uta no kokoro no uchi' – 'Niimanabi' [part II]", in: *Monumenta Nipponica*, vol. 4/2 (1941), pp. 566-584.

— (1943a)
Dumoulin, Heinrich: "Die Erneuerung des Liederweges durch Kamo Mabuchi", in: *Monumenta Nipponica*, vol. 6 (1943), pp. 110-145.

— (1943b)
Dumoulin, Heinrich: *Kamo Mabuchi (1697-1769): Ein Beitrag zur japanischen Religions- und Geistesgeschichte.* [Monumenta Nipponica Monographs, no. 8] Tōkyō, Sophia University, 1943.

— (1953)
Dumoulin, Heinrich: "Kamo Mabuchi und das 'Manyōshū'", in: *Monumenta Nipponica*, vol. 9/1 (1953), pp. 34-61.

— (1955)
Dumoulin, Heinrich: "Zwei Texte Kamo Mabuchis zur Wortkunde", in: *Monumenta Nipponica*, vol. 11/3 (1955), pp. 268-283.

— (1956a)
Dumoulin, Heinrich: "Kamo Mabuchis Erklärung des Norito zum Toshi-goi-no-matsuri [part I]", in: *Monumenta Nipponica*, vol. 12/1-2 (1956), pp. 121-156.

— (1956b)
Dumoulin, Heinrich: "Kamo Mabuchis Erklärung des Norito zum Toshigoi-no-matsuri [part II]", in: *Monumenta Nipponica*, vol. 12/3-4 (1956), pp. 269-298.

Florenz (1919)
Florenz, Karl: *Die historischen Quellen der Shinto-Religion: Aus dem Altjapanischen und Chinesischen übersetzt und erklärt von Dr. Karl Florenz*. Göttingen: Vandenhoeck & Ruprecht, 1919.

Fridell (1970)
Fridell, W. M.: "Government Ethics Textbooks in Late Meiji Japan", in: *The Journal of Japanese Studies*, vol. 29/4 (1970), pp. 828-833.

Gauntlett/ Hall (1949)
Gauntlett, J. O./ Hall, R. K. (transl.): *Kokutai no hongi: Cardinal Principles of the National Entity of Japan*. Cambridge: Harvard University Press, 1949.

Gluck (1985)
Gluck, Carol: *Japan's Modern Myths. Ideology in the Late Meiji Period*. Princeton: Princeton University Press, 1985.

GSRJ
Hanawa Hokiichi 塙保己一 (ed.): *Gunsho ruijū 群書類従*. 30 vols., Tōkyō: Zoku gunsho ruijū kansen kai, 1959-60 [3rd ed.].

Haekel (1971)
Haekel, Josef: "Religion", in: Trimborn, Hermann (ed.): *Lehrbuch der Völkerkunde*. 4th ed., Stuttgart: Ferdinand Enke Verlag, 1971.

Hammitzsch (1936)
Hammitzsch, Horst: "Hirata Atsutane: Ein geistiger Kämpfer Japans", in: *Mitteilungen der Deutschen Gesellschaft für Natur- und Völkerkunde Ostasiens*, vol. 28, part E (1936), Tōkyō: OAG, pp. 1-27.

— (1981)
Hammitzsch, Horst et al. (ed.): *Japan-Handbuch*. Wiesbaden: Franz Steiner, 1981.

Harootunian (1988)
Harootunian, Harry D.: *Things Seen and Unseen: Discourse and Ideology in Tokugawa Nativism*. Chicago: University of Chicago Press, 1988.

— (1995)
Harootunian, Harry D.: "Late Tokugawa Culture and Thought", in:
Jansen, Marius B. (ed.): *The Emergence of Meiji Japan*. Cambridge:
Cambridge University Press, 1995, pp. 53-143.

Hino (1983)
Hino, Tatsuo 日野龍夫 (ed.): *Motoori Norinaga shū* 本居宣長集.
[Shinchō nihon koten shūsei 新潮日本古典集成; vol. 60] Tōkyō:
Shinchōsha, 1983.

Hirata (1927-29)
Hirata, Atsutane 平田篤胤: *Kodō taii* 古道大意. [Shinchū kōgaku sōsho
新註皇學叢書, vol. 10] Tōkyō: Kōbunko kankōkai, 1927-29.

— (1976)
Hirata, Atsutane 平田篤胤: *Taidō wakumon* 大道或問. [Hirata Atsutane
zenshū 平田篤胤全集, vol. 8] Tōkyō: Meicho shuppan, 1976, pp. 77-93.

Hobsbawm/ Ranger (1983)
Hobsbawm, Eric/ Ranger, Terence (ed.): *The Invention of Tradition*.
Cambridge: Cambridge University Press, 1983.

Imai (1973)
Imai, Usaburō 今井宇三郎 et al. (ed.): *Mitogaku* 水戸學. [Nihon shisō
taikei 日本思想大系; vol. 53] Tōkyō: Iwanami, 1973.

Inoue (1994)
Inoue, Nobutaka 井上順孝 (ed.): *Shintō jiten* 神道事典. [Kokugakuin
daigaku Nihon bunka kenkyūjo hen] Tōkyō: Kōbundō, 1994.

Inoue (1897)
Inoue, Tetsujirō 井上哲次郎: *Nihon yōmeigakuha no tetsugaku* 日本陽明
學派之哲學. Tōkyō: Fuzanbō, 1897.

— (1918)
Inoue, Tetsujirō 井上哲次郎: *Teisei zōho Nihon kogakuha no tetsugaku*
訂正増補日本古學派之哲學. Tōkyō: Fuzanbō, 1918.

— (1945)
Inoue, Tetsujirō 井上哲次郎: *Teisei zōho Nihon shushigakuha no
tetsugaku* 訂正増補日本朱子學派之哲學. Tōkyō: Fuzanbō, 1945.

Keene (1953)
Keene, Donald: "Hirata Atsutane and Western Learning", in: *T'oung Pao*,
vol. 42 (1953), pp. 353-380.

— (1978)
Keene, Donald: *Some Japanese Portraits.* Tōkyō: Kodansha, 1978.

Kemper (1967)
Kemper, Ulrich: *Arai Hakuseki und seine Geschichtsauffassung: Ein Beitrag zur Historiographie Japans in der Tokugawa-Zeit.* Wiesbaden: Harrassowitz, 1967.

Kishimoto (1993)
Kishimoto Yoshio 岸本芳雄: *Shintō nyūmon: Shintō to sono ayumi* 神道入門：神道とそのあゆみ. Tōkyō: Kenpakusha, 1993 [1972].

*Kogoshūi* 古語拾遺 [GSRJ; vol. 25].

*Kojiki* 古事記 [NKBT; vol. 1].

KJRE
*Jingūshichō zōhan Kojiruien* 神宮司庁蔵版古事類苑. 51 vols., reprint: Tōkyō: Yoshikawa kōbunkan, 1977.

Monbushō (1937)
*Kokutai no hongi* 国体の本義. Tōkyō: Mombushō, 1937.

Koschmann (1987)
Koschmann, J. Victor: *The Mito Ideology: Discourse, Reform and Insurrection in Late Tokugawa Japan, 1790-1864.* Berkeley: University of California Press, 1987.

Kracht (1975)
Kracht, Klaus: *Das Kōdōkanki-Jutsugi des Fujita Tōko: Ein Beitrag zum politischen Denken der Späten Mito-Schule.* Wiesbaden: Harrassowitz, 1975.

— (1986)
Kracht, Klaus: *Studien zur Geschichte des Denkens im Japan des 17. bis 19. Jahrhunderts: Chu-Hsi-konfuzianische Geist-Diskurse.* [Veröffentl. des Ostasien-Instituts der Ruhr-Universität Bochum, vol. 31] Wiesbaden: Harrassowitz, 1986.

Krusche (1990)
Krusche, D.: *Hermeneutik der Fremde.* München: iudicium, 1990.

Krusche/ Wierlacher (1985)
Krusche, D./ Wierlacher, Alois (ed.): *Literatur und Fremde: zur Hermeneutik kulturräumlicher Distanz.* München: iudicium, 1985.

**Kubota (1989)**
Kubota, Osamu 久保田収: *Chūsei shintō no kenkyū* 中世神道の研究.
Kyōto: Shintōshi gakkai, 1989.

**Lokowandt (1978)**
Lokowandt, Ernst: *Die rechtliche Entwicklung des Staats-Shintō in der ersten Hälfte der Meiji-Zeit, 1868-1890.* (Studies in Oriental Religions, vol. 3). Wiesbaden: Harrassowitz, 1978.

**Matsumoto (1970)**
Matsumoto, Shigeru: *Motoori Norinaga 1730-1801.* Cambridge: Harvard University Press, 1970.

**Matsumura (1954-58)**
Matsumura, Takeo 松村武雄: *Nihon shinwa no kenkyū* 日本神話の研究. 4 vol., Tōkyō, 1954-58.

**Matsunaga (1969)**
Matsunaga, Alicia: *The Buddhist Philosophy of Assimilation: The Historical Development of the Honji-Suijaku Theory.* Tōkyō: Sophia University Press, 1969.

**McNally (1998)**
McNally, Mark Thomas: *Phantom History: Hirata Atsutane and Tokugawa Nativism.* [Ph. Diss.] UMI: University of California, 1998.

**Meyer (1998)**
Meyer, Eva-Maria: *Japans Kaiserhof in der Edo-Zeit: Unter besonderer Berücksichtigung der Jahre 1846 bis 1867.* (Ostasien-Pazifik: Trierer Studien zu Politik, Wirtschaft, Gesellschaft, Kultur; vol. 12). Hamburg: Lit-Verlag, 1998.

**Miki (1990)**
Miki, Shōtarō 三木正太郎: *Hirata Atsutane no kenkyū* 平田篤胤の研究. [Shintō-shi sōsho 神道史叢書, vol. 5] Tōkyō: Rinsen shoten, 1990 [1969].

**Miller (1982)**
Miller, Roy Andrew: *Japan's Modern Myth: The Language and Beyond.* New York: Weatherhill, 1982.

**Minamoto (1992)**
Minamoto, Ryōen 源了圓: *Tokugawa shisō shoshi* 徳川思想小史. [Chūkō-shinsho 中公新書; vol. 312] Tōkyō: Chūō-kōronsha, 1992 (1973).

Miyasaka (1994)
Miyasaka, Masahide: *Shintō und Christentum: Wirtschaftsethik als Quelle der Industriestaatlichkeit.* Paderborn: Bonifatius, 1994.

Motoori (1919-27)
Motoori, Norinaga 本居宣長: *Kojiki-den* 古事記傳. [Motoori Norinaga zenshū 本居宣長全集, vol. 1] Tōkyō: Yoshikawa kōbunkan, 1919-27.

Murayama (1972)
Murayama, Shūichi 村山修一: *Honji suijaku* 本地垂迹. [Nihon rekishi sōsho 日本歴史叢書; vol. 33]Tōkyō: Yoshikawa kōbunkan, 1972.

Nakamura (1984)
Nakamura, Hirotoshi 中村啓信: "The Kojiki with Revisions Added by Kada no Azumamaro", in: *Nihon bunka kenkyūsho kiyō* 日本文化研究所紀要, vol. 54 (1984), pp. 128-242.

Naumann (1970)
Naumann, Nelly: "Einige Bemerkungen zum sogenannten Ur-Shintō", in: *Nachrichten der Gesellschaft für Natur- und Völkerkunde Ostasiens/ Hamburg*, vol. 107/108 (1970), pp. 5-13.

— (1971)
Naumann, Nelly: *Das Umwandeln des Himmelspfeilers: Ein japanischer Mythos und seine kulturhistorische Einordnung.* [Asian Folklore Studies Monograph, No. 5] Tōkyō, 1971.

— (1985)
Naumann, Nelly: "Shintō und Volksreligion: Japanische Religiosität im historischen Kontext", in: *Zeitschrift für Missions- und Religionswissenschaft*, vol. 69 (1985), pp. 223-242.

— (1987)
Naumann, Nelly: "Identitätsfindung – das geistige Problem des modernen Japan", in: Martin, Bernd (ed.): *Japans Weg in die Moderne: Ein Sonderweg nach deutschem Vorbild?.* Frankfurt, New York: Campus, 1987, pp. 173-192.

— (1988)
Nelly Naumann: *Die einheimische Religion Japans, Teil 1: Bis zum Ende der Heian-Zeit.* [Handbuch der Orientalistik, part V, vol. 4, sect. 1, no. 1] Leiden: Brill, 1988.

— (1994)
Nelly Naumann: *Die einheimische Religion Japans, Teil 2: Synkretisti-sche Lehren und religiöse Entwicklungen von der Kamakura- bis zum Beginn der Edo-Zeit.* [Handbuch der Orientalistik, part V, vol. 4, sect. 1, no. 2] Leiden: Brill, 1994.

— (1996)
Naumann, Nelly: *Die Mythen des alten Japan: Übersetzt und erläutert von Nelly Naumann.* München: Beck, 1996.

Nawrocki (1998)
Nawrocki, Johann: *Inoue Tetsujirō (1855-1944) und die Ideologie des Götterlandes: Eine vergleichende Studie zur politischen Theologie des modernen Japan.* [Ostasien-Pazifik: Trierer Studien zu Politik, Wirtschaft, Gesellschaft, Kultur; vol. 10]. Hamburg: Lit-Verlag, 1998.

Nell (1998)
Nell, Stephanie: *Die Rezeption des Buddhismus im Spiegel des Nihonshoki: Eine kritische Analyse ausgewählter Textpassagen von Kimmei-Tennō bis Suiko-Tennō.* [M.A.-Thesis] Universität Trier, 1998.

*Nihongi* 日本紀, vol. 1 [NKBT, vol. 67].

Nishimura (1987)
Nishimura, Sey: "First Steps into the Mountains: Motoori Norinaga's 'Uiyamabumi'", in: *Monumenta Nipponica,* 42/4 (1987), pp. 449-493.

— (1991)
Nishimura, Sey: "The Way of the Gods: Motoori Norinaga's 'Naobi no Mitama'", in: *Monumenta Nipponica,* vol. 46/1 (1991), pp. 21-41.

NKBT
Takagi, Ichinosuke 高木市之助 et al. (ed.): *Nihon koten bungaku taikei* 日本古典文学大系. 102 vol. Tōkyō: Iwanami shoten, 1957-86.

Nosco (1984)
Nosco, Peter: "Masuho Zankō (1655-1742): A Shinto Popularizer between Nativism and National Learning", in: Nosco, Peter (ed.) *Confucianism and Tokugawa Culture.* Princeton: Princeton University Press, 1984, pp. 166-187.

— (1990)
Nosco, Peter: *Remembering Paradise: Nativism and Nostalgia in Eighteenth-century Japan.* [Harvard-Yenching Institute Monograph Series; no. 31] Cambridge: Harvard University Press, 1990.

Ōbayashi (1973)
Ōbayashi, Taryō 大林太良: *Nihon shinwa no kigen* 日本神話の起源.
Tōkyō: Kadokawa, 1973.

— (1982)
Ōbayashi, Taryō: *Ise und Izumo: Die Schreine des Schintoismus*. [Die
Welt der Religionen; vol. 6] Freiburg, Basel, Wien: Herder, 1982.

— (1986)
Ōbayashi, Taryō 大林太良: *Shinwa no keifu: Nihon shinwa no genryū o
saguru* 神話の系譜 : 日本神話の源流をさがる. Tōkyō: Seidosha, 1986.

— (1997)
Ōbayashi, Taryō: "Der Ursprung der shintōistischen Hochzeit", in:
Antoni (1997a), pp. 39-48.

Odronic (1967)
Odronic, Walter J.: *Kodō Taii (An outline of the Ancient Way): An anno-
tated translation with an introduction to the Shinto Revival Movement
and a sketch of the live of Hirata Atsutane*. [Ph. Diss.] UMI: University of
Pennsylvania, 1967.

Ōkubo (1969)
Ōkubo, Toshiaki 大久保利謙 et al. (ed.): *Kindaishi shiryō* 近代史史料.
Tōkyō: Yoshikawa kōbunkan, 1969 (1965).

Ooms (1985)
Ooms, Herman: *Tokugawa Ideology: Early Constructs, 1570-1680*. New
Jersey: Princeton University Press, 1985.

Picken (1994)
Picken, Stuart D. B.: *Essentials of Shinto: Analytical Guide to Principal
Teachings*. [Resources in Asian Philosophy & Religion Series] Westport,
Conn.: Greenwood, 1994.

Rosenkranz (1944)
Rosenkranz, Gerhard: *Der Weg der Götter (Shintō): Gehalt und Gestalt
der japanischen Nationalreligion*. München: Arbeitsgemeinschaft für
Zeitgeschichte, 1944.

Rothermund (1989)
Rothermund, Dietmar: "Der Traditionalismus als Forschungsgegenstand
für Historiker und Orientalisten", in: *Saeculum – Jahrbuch für
Universalgeschichte*, vol. 40/2 (1989), pp. 142-148.

Satō-Diesner (1977)
Satō-Diesner, Sigmara: *Motoori Norinaga: Das Hihon tamakushige. Ein Beitrag zum politischen Denken der Kokugaku.* [Ph. Diss.] Universität Bonn, 1977.

Schiffer (1939)
Schiffer, Wilhelm: "Hirata Atsutane: Taidō Wakumon – Es fragte einer nach dem Grossen Weg...", in: *Monumenta Nipponica*, vol. 2 (1939), pp. 212-236.

Seckel (1985)
Seckel, Dietrich: *Buddhistische Tempelnamen in Japan.* [Münchener Ostasiatische Studien, vol. 37] Stuttgart: Steiner, 1985.

Smith (1973)
Smith, Warren: *Confucianism in Modern Japan: A Study of Conservatism in Japanese Intellectual History.* Tōkyō: Hokuseido Press, 1973.

Stanzel (1982)
Stanzel, Volker: *Japan – Haupt der Erde: Die 'Neuen Erörterungen' des Philosophen und Theoretikers der Politik Seishisai Aizawa aus dem Jahre 1825.* Würzburg: Königshausen & Neumann, 1982.

Stolte (1939)
Stolte, Hans: "Motoori Norinaga: 'Naobi no Mitama' – Geist der Erneuerung", in: *Monumenta Nipponica*, vol. 2/1 (1939), pp. 193 -211.

Sugiyama/ Sakamoto (1994)
Sugiyama, Rinkei 椙山林継/ Sakamoto, Koremaru 坂本是丸: "Kinsei no shintō 近世の神道", in: Inoue (1994), pp. 13-18.

Tahara (1990)
Tahara, Tsuguo 田原嗣郎: *Hirata Atsutane* 平田篤胤. [Jinbutsu sōsho 人物叢書, vol. 111] Tōkyō: Yoshikawa kōbunkan, 1990 [1963].

Taira/ Abe (1972)
Taira, Shigemichi 平重道/ Abe, Akio 阿部秋生 (ed.): *Kinsei shintō-ron zenki-kokugaku 近世神道論前期国学.* [Nihon shisō taikei 日本思想大系, vol. 39] Tōkyō: Iwanami, 1972.

Teeuwen (1993)
Teeuwen, Mark: "Attaining Union with the Gods: The Secret Books of Watarai Shintō", in: *Monumenta Nipponica*, vol. 48/2 (1993), pp. 225-245.

— (1996)
Teeuwen, Mark: *Watarai Shintō: An Intellectual History of the Outer Shrine of Ise.* [CNWS Publications, vol. 52]. Leiden: Research School CNWS; School of Asian, African, & Amerindian Studies, 1996.

Thiel (1984)
Thiel, Josef Franz: *Religionsethnologie: Grundbegriffe der Religionen schriftloser Völker.* [Collectanea Instituti Anthropos, vol. 33] Berlin: Dietrich Reimer, 1984.

Tsunoda (1964)
Tsunoda, Ryusaku et al. (ed.): *Sources of Japanese Tradition.* 2 vol., New York: Columbia University Press, 1964.

Tsurumi (1970)
Tsurumi, Kazuko: *Social Change and the Individual: Japan Before and after Defeat in World War II.* Princeton: Princeton Univ. Press, 1970.

van Straelen (1952)
van Straelen, Henry: *Yoshida Shōin: Forerunner of the Meiji-Restoration.* Leiden: Brill, 1952.

Watanabe (1978)
Watanabe, Kizō 渡邉金造: *Hirata Atsutane kenkyū* 平田篤胤研究. Tōkyō: Hō shuppan, 1978.

Webb (1958)
Webb, Herschel F.: *The Thought and Work of the Early Mito School.* [Ph. Diss.] UMI: Columbia University, 1958.

Wittig (1976)
Wittig, Horst E.: *Pädagogik und Bildungspolitik Japans: Quellentexte und Dokumente von der Tokugawa-Zeit bis zur Gegenwart.* München: Reinhardt, 1976.

# 'Nihon no kuni wa tennō o chūshin to suru kami no kuni'
## (日本の国は天皇を中心とする神の国)
## The Divine Country Debate 2000

### Johann NAWROCKI

The idea of the national- and state-divinity came into being in ancient Japan and it is principally seen as a classical thought of Shintō tradition which in the past stood always for the most vital element of the *kokutairon* 国体論, the theory on Japanese original national polity. Indeed the belief that identifies Japan with a sacred-divine country and with a unique in the world holy-land of the Gods originates in Shintō mythology and it appears in written sources for the first time already in *Nihongi* 日本紀.[1] Its modern, prevalent imperialistic interpretation witnessed its renaissance in the Late Edo era as an ideological reply to the Western colonialism and obviously as its challenge in the Far East. The concept was put into political practice as the official state ideology during the first half of the 20th century and it seemed to fall finally into oblivion with the war defeat in 1945 [cf. Antoni (1998); Nawrocki (1998)].

Nevertheless on May 15, 2000, the new designated prime minister Mori Yoshirō 森善朗 suggested in his speech to some 400 participants of the Council of the Shintō Political Federation of Diet Members (*Shintō seiji renmei kokkai giin kondankai* 神道政治連盟国会議員懇談会) celebrating its 30th anniversary, that Japan is a divine nation centered around the Emperor. Well, at least this was an official English translation of Mori's remark. This statement – reviving memories of wartime ideology and infringing the constitution – sparked outrage, both at home as well as abroad, and caused a fiery debate on its admissibility and validity in modern Japan facing the 21st century.

---

[1] *"I have heard that in the East there is a divine country named Nippon, and also that there is there a wise sovereign called the Tennō. This divine force must belong to that country. How could we resist them by force of arms?"* [Aston (1990), p. 230]; *"Imashi, samete ieraku, are kiku, himugashi ni kami no kuni ari, Yamato to iu. Mata hijiri no ōkimi ari, sumera mikoto to iu. Kanarazu sono kuni no miikusa naramu. Anitsu wa mono o agete fusegu bekemu yato.* 乃今、醒めて日らく、吾聞く、東に神国有り、日本と謂う. 亦聖王有り、天皇と謂う. 必ず其の国の神兵ならむ. あにつは兵を挙げて距ぐ可けむやと." [Shinten (1942), *Nihon shoki* 日本書紀, pp. 363f.].

However the usage of the term *kami no kuni* 神の国, which was above all confronted with harsh critics from abroad, overshadowed the more controversial part in premier's remark placing the Emperor Akihito within the meaning of the pre-war *kokutai*-Theory and State-Shintō (*kokka shintō* 国家神道) as a sacred spiritual and religious center of the Japanese nation. Doi Takako 土井たか子, chair of the Social Democratic Party, Hatoyama Yukio 鳩山由紀夫, chairman of the Democratic Party of Japan and many other opposition leaders criticized this remark favoring Shintō as a quasi-state religion for being clearly contradictory to the post-war constitution which prescribed the freedom of belief, the separation of church and state and the guarantee that the nation's sovereign power resides with the people and not with the Emperor.[2] Even though the prime minister was not finally induced to resign, the incident damaged the already poor image of the ruling coalition and certainly influenced the election to the Lower House on June 25th.

Mori apologized for causing confusion already in the Diet session on May 17th and once again at a press conference on May 26th, but in both cases he refused to retract his controversial comments. He stated on May 17th: "*It is a matter of course that I must protect the principles of people's sovereign rights and freedom of religion as prime minister. I feel sorry that my remarks have caused misunderstanding. [...] My remarks were not aimed at promoting certain religions. The position of the Emperor has changed from time to time. In that particular remark, I referred to the Emperor as the symbol of the unity of the people.*" [*Mainichi Daily News* (18.05.2000)]

On May 26th he said among others: "*Deeply reflecting on the misunderstanding my remarks caused, I apologize from the bottom of my heart. [...] As a prime minister I naturally respect the sovereign power of the people and freedom of religion as provided in the Constitution. [...] I have never thought of reviving state Shintoism with the Emperor as a sovereign and I never intended to connect the Emperor with God.*" [*Mainichi Daily News* (27.05.2000)]. In the interview Mori said furthermore that he only meant to say religious and moral

---

[2] Article 20: (1) Freedom of religion is guaranteed to all. No religious organization shall receive any privileges from the State, nor exercise any political authority. (2) No person shall be compelled to take part in any religious acts, celebration, rite or practice. (3) The State and its organs shall refrain from religious education or any other religious activity. Article 89: No public money or other property shall be expended or appropriated for the use,

education is important at a time when teen-agers are committing more and more crimes, but asked by a journalist if he is going to withdraw the comment he answered: "*I said nothing wrong.*" [ibid.].

Well, what actually did prime minister Mori say on May 15th last year and how can his remark be interpreted? Was it just a simple slip of the tongue as widely asserted, a profound religious conviction or maybe something else? He said exactly:

"*In our times the value of the gods is going to be forgotten, which meant always an inducement for our federation. Now that I am in government, matters that have been pushed behind the scenes should be brought out into the open. I want to make sure that we firmly teach the whole nation to recognize that Japan is a land of the Gods with the Emperor at its center. Thirty years passed since I have been working for that idea. Human life is given by parents, but frankly speaking, life is a gift from the Gods. Therefore we cannot terminate the human life by ourselves. The society, schools and parents that do not impart this fundamental principle to the children are wrong. There came some proposals from children at a meeting, which took place during the Okinawa summit. There were proposals concerning the importance of the natural environment but not stressing the human life. The death of Prime Minister Obuchi happened to be announced there. Let's think about where the human life comes from. Doubtlessly we get it from our parents. But there is nothing more mysterious than the human body. Yet, is not everyone believing that it can only be something received from the Gods? Religion presents a culture that dwells in our spirit, no matter whether it is about Shintō deities or Buddhas, so why is it not advocated at the educational level to put more value on religion? One should not be silent because of the freedom of religion. Is it not important because we have freedom of faith and speaking from the contemporary discourse on Japanese spirit, to tell at school as well as at home to value every religion? Local communities prosper centered around Shintō-shrines. I would like all of you to be encouraged to form orderly communities where children of today can feel in their body the Shintō deities and Buddhas. Moreover, I think that we the members of the Parliament also have to understand the*

---

benefit or maintenance of any religious institution or association, or for any charitable, educational or benevolent enterprises not under the control of public authority.

*origin of what is the most important and conduct our political activities accordingly.*"[3]

The authoritative article in the following debate written by Gregory Clark, the president of Tama University and a famous author of *Yunīku na Nihonjin* ユニークな日本人 ('The Unique Japanese') and of *Gokai sareru Nihonjin* 誤解される日本人 ('The Misunderstood Japanese'), commented the incident at first lax as a clear misunderstanding: "*According to the English-language media, Japan's*

---

[3] "*Kami sama o daiji ni shiyō to iu koto o yo no naka ga wasurete iru, to iu no ga kessei no dōki datta. Seifu gawa ga oyobi koshi ni naru yō na koto o zenmen ni dashite, Nihon no kuni wa tennō o chūshin to suru kami no kuni de aru to iu koto o shikkari to kokumin no mina sama ni shōchi shite itadaku, sono omoide katsudō shite sanjū nen ni naru. Hito no inochi wa chichihaha, tanteki ni ieba kami sama kara itadaita mono. Dakara jibun wa mochiron, hito no inochi mo yamete wa naranai. Sono kihon o kodomo tachi ni oshiete inai oya, gakkō, shakai ga ikenai. Okinawa samitto ni kanren shita kodomo kara no teigen o kiku kai ga ari, shizen kankyō o taisetsu ni shiyō to iu teigen wa atta keredomo, inochi o taisetsu ni shiyō to iu teigen wa nai. Soko e Obuchi shushō no fuhō ga todoita. Hito no inochi wa doko kara kita no ka o kangaeyō. Chichihaha kara itadaita no wa machigainai. Shikashi ningen no karada hodo shinpi teki na mono wa nai. Yahari kore wa kami sama kara itadaita mono da to iu koto shika nai, sō minna de shinjiyō ja nai ka. Kami sama de are butsu sama de are, shūkyō to iu no wa jibun no kokoro ni yadoru bunka na no dakara, daiji ni shiyō to iu koto o kyōiku no genba de naze ienai no ka. Shinkyō no jiyū dakara ienai no dewa naku, shinkyō no jiyū dakara, dono shūkyō mo daiji ni shiyō to iu koto o, gakkō de mo katei de mo iu koto ga, ima no Nihon no seishinron kara ieba daiji na no dewa nai ka. Jinja no chūshin ni chiiki shakai wa sakaete iku. Yūki o motte, ima no kodomo tachi ga kami sama to ka butsu sama to ka o karada de oboete iku chitsujo aru chiiki shakai o tsukuri dasu tame, mina sama ni katsuyaku shite moraitai. Mata wareware kokkai giin no kai mo, nani ga ichiban taisetsu na no ka no genten o haaku shite seiji katsudō o shite ikanakereba to kangaete iru.* 神様を大事にしようということを世の中が忘れている，というのが結成の動機だった．政府側が及び腰になるようなことを前面に出して，日本の国は天皇を中心とする神の国であるということをしっかりと国民の皆様に承知して戴く，その思いで活動して三十年になる．人の命は父母，端的に言えば神様から戴いたもの．だから自分はもちろん，人の命も殺めてはならない．その基本を子供達に教えていない親，学校，社会がいけない．沖縄サミットに関連した子供からの提言を聴く会があり，自然環境を大切にしようという提言はあったけれども，命を大切にしようという提言はない．そこへ小渕首相の訃報が届いた．人の命はどこからきたのかを考えよう．父母から戴いたのは間違いない．しかし人間の体ほど神秘的なものはない．やはりこれは神様から戴いたものだということしかない，そうみんなで信じようじゃないか．神様であれ仏様であれ，宗教というのは自分の心に宿る文化なのだから，大事にしようということを教育の現場でなぜ言えないのか．信教の自由だから言えないのではなく，信教の自由だから，どの宗教も大事にしようということを，学校でも家庭でも言うことが，今の日本の精神論から言えば大事なのではないか．神社を中心に地域社会は栄えていく．勇気をもって，今の子供達が神様とか仏様とかを体で覚えていく秩序ある地域社会を作り出すため，皆様に活躍してもらいたい．また我々国会議員の会も，何が一番大切なのかの原点を把握して政治活動をしていかなければと考えている．" [*Jinja Shinpō* (22.05.2000), p. 1].

prime minister Yoshirō Mori is in trouble for having said that Japan is a 'divine nation'. But Mori did not say Japan was divine. He said Japan was 'kami no kuni', which translates as 'country of the gods'. 'Divine nation' is a pre-1945 translation, when kami no kuni was supposed to imply that Japan has some god-given superiority over all others. Mori was using the term in a very different context, namely the need he and many other Japanese conservatives feel for today's largely agnostic Japan to have some kind of spiritual identity. [...] Within Japan, Mori's main error is seen as seeming to endorse Shintoism, with the Emperor system at its core, as Japan's official religion. This grates heavily on the ears of Buddhist and others who remember how state Shintoism was an instrument of oppression and nationalism in prewar years. But for Mori and his conservative friends, even this problem is secondary to that of trying to rescue Japan from what they see as a slide into decadence, apathy and hedonism. They worry much about the youth and Mori's call relates directly to the current debate on education reform initiated by former prime minister Keizō Obuchi. [...] One respects the sincerity of Mori and the other conservatives. They really do believe that all this, plus respect for national flag and anthem, pumped into the closed world of school and family will, as in the past, somehow turn the youth into obedient and diligent citizens." [*The Japan Times* (02.06.2000)].

Well, to judge it properly maybe we should trace the topic back and look at what was actually stressed at the mentioned meeting on May 15th that took such a, let say, somehow confusing course doubtlessly under the impression of the death of Obuchi Keizō 小渕恵三. Obuchi who was laying in a coma already for several weeks died just a day before, on Sunday afternoon May 14th. The chairman of the Council of the Shintō Political Federation and speaker of the Lower House Watanuki Tamisuke 綿貫民輔 opened the gathering with an offer of condolence on death of the former prime minister. Furthermore Watanuki said: "*Centered around the imperial family we really succeed to preserve our traditional culture. We want to carry on a government which has a right view on our national history.*"[4]

---

[4] "*Kōshitsu o chūshin to shita dentō bunka o mamoru koto ni jisseki o agete kita. Tadashii rekishi kan o motta kokusei o tsuranuite ikitai* 皇室を中心とした伝統文化を守ることに実績を挙げてきた. 正しい歴史観を持った国政を貫いていきたい." [*Jinja shinpō* (22.05.2000), p. 1].

After Watanuki spoke Murakami Masakuni 村上正邦, a member of the Upper House and a secretary-general of the concerned Shintō-Council. Murakami described the work of the Shintō-Federation in a historical perspective mentioning the achievements, among others: the enactment of the national flag and anthem law in 1999. Regarding future-plans, he talked about the legalized renaming of the *Midori no hi* 緑の日 into *Shōwa no hi* 昭和の日, the important role of the diet-committee working on the new independent constitution for Japan, the necessity to reform the education system backed by a national movement, and finally, he pointed out the overdue requirement to nationalize the Yasukuni shrine [cf. *Jinja shinpō* (22.05.2000), p. 1].

Murakami was followed by the well-known philosopher Umehara Takeshi 梅原猛, former director general of *Nichibunken* (*Kokusai Nihon Bunka Kenkyū Sentā* 国際日本文化研究センター) in Kyōto, now its honorary advisor, who stressed in his lecture the imperative aspect of the internationalization of Shintō in order to achieve the goal towards its universal leading role in the coming era of the world-globalization [cf. *Jinja shinpō* (22.05.2000), p. 1]. Prime minister Mori following these three lectures apparently tried to adjust his speech to his predecessors.

In this intellectual debate that kept Japan busy through the whole summer, politicians, scholars and journalists of the entire ideological and political spectrum participated. The subject was taken up positively just by organizations like *Jinja Honchō* 神社本庁 or *Shintō seiji renmei* itself, which apparently sympathized with Mori [cf. *Jinja shinpō* (29.05.2000), p. 3; (05.06.2000a; b), p. 1]. The opposition parties welcomed Mori's comment as an useful weapon in a political campaign shortly before the general election. Buddhist and Christian circles reacted with more or less stressed indignation depending on their distance to the governing coalition. The artificially overheated debate exposed generally one major shortcoming, namely the obvious lack of objective, impersonal argumentation. Both, supporters and opponents of Mori's comments, at home as well as abroad, did not presented a convincing, effective arguments [cf. *Jinja shinpō* (10.07.2000b), p. 6; (21.07.2000), p. 9].

Mori's remarks were sharply criticized in China and Korea without any serious diplomatic steps or lasting consequences. The Washington Post issued on June 4th an article under the title: 'Japan's Two Nationalisms' stating Mori's comment as follows: "*When Japan's prime minister describes his nation as a divine country with an emperor at its center, American policy makers need to sit up and pay attention. The remarks show the power of nationalist feeling in Japan; and despite the prime minister's strenuous efforts at damage control, they show that this nationalism includes nostalgia for the mystical chauvinism that drove Japan's expansionist drive into Asia and ultimately its war with America."* [*Washington Post* (04.06.2000); cf. *Jinja shinpō* (10.07.2000a), p. 5].

Just a few days later, Gregory Clark tended suddenly also to change his previous appeasing opinion of misunderstanding, moved by Mori's another slip of the tongue during a lecture in Nara on June 3rd: *"When prime minister Yoshirō Mori said that Japan is a 'kami no kuni' (country of the gods), it can be argued he was doing little more than expressing a personal religious belief before a group of like-minded, Shinto-supporting Diet members. U.S. media claims that he was trying revive Japanese nationalism hinge on mistranslation that have him saying Japan was a 'divine nation'. But his more recent claim that Japan is a 'kokutai' (a national polity) based on the Emperor in which the Communist Party has no place really is alarming. It is a direct throwback to Japan's prewar fascism and throws severe doubt on Japan's claims to be a Western-style democracy. [...] Mori made waves with the word 'kokutai'. But the much-used term 'kokumin' (national people) is just as alarming. Like the word Volk (people) as used in pre-1945 Germany, it implies a nation united by sentiment in which dissent is unwelcome."* [*The Japan Times* (11.06 2000)].

An American Shintō-scholars of highest renown, Daniel Holtom, expressed already in 1938 his opinion on the idea of divinity compiling his paper on 'The National Faith of Japan'. He finally stated in this book: *"No other word in the entire range of Japanese vocabulary has a richer or more varied content and no other has presented greater difficulties to the philologist than the word* kami.*"* [Reader (1993), p. 77].

Ueda Kenji 上田賢治, presently the leading Shintō-Professor at Kokugakuin Daigaku translated 1996 the interpretation of the divine idea found in the writings of Motoori Norinaga 本居宣長 as follows: *"I do not yet completely understand the meaning of the term* kami. *The word* kami *refers, in the most general sense, to divine beings of heaven and earth that appear in the classics. More particularly, the* kami *are spirits that abide in and are worshiped at the shrines. In principle human beings, birds, animals, trees, plants, mountains, oceans – all may be* kami. *According to ancient usage, whatever seemed strik-*

*ingly impressive, possessed the quality of excellence, or inspired a feeling of awe was called kami.*" [Ueda (1996), p. 35].

Holtom wrote under the impression of the Pacific War furthermore in 1943: "*The true members of the Japanese race regard themselves as the offspring of the gods. They believe that their state was brought into being by the* kami *and that the people are the descendants of these ancestral deities.*" [Holtom (1943), p. 157]. And: "*Japan is the Land of the Gods. This is the name that patriots throughout a long history have liked to give to their homeland. It does not mean merely that the gods are many, that unseen spirits haunt the mountains and valleys, the streams and woodlands. More than this, it means that the very islands themselves, the people, their racial characteristics, and the unique form of their national life are something more than the resultants of ordinary geographical and historical forces.*" [ibid., p. 13].

As a result of the debate, everyone – and especially former prime minister Mori – knows meanwhile for sure the ambivalent implications of the remark *tennō o chūshin to suru kami no kuni*. The term according to the majority of its advocates is as old as Japan itself and consequently must be interpreted as a cultural acquisition of the national tradition [cf. *Jinja shinpō* (05.06.2000), p. 1]. At the same time however, all of them had to admit that when hearing the term nowadays everyone associated it still with the pre-war imperialistic ideology and the expansionistic policy. Even if some argued that the Japanese meaning of the word *kami* does not correspond with the Western understanding of the transcendental, absolute God, there was no voice saying that both have absolutely nothing in common [cf. *Jinja shinpō* (19.06.2000a; b; c; d; e), p. 1-6].

The general critique appearing in Japanese sources has to be also taken into account. It is true that popular Western phrases like: 'God save the queen', 'God bless America', 'In God we trust' or, the German equivalent to that, 'Gott mit uns' (God with us) alike just present manifestations of the national culture and tradition and basically involve similar connotations as the Japanese term. But if so, why there was not a Chancellor in post-war Germany singing in public the first stanza of the old German anthem, and on the other hand the Japanese themselves tumble so easy in this irresolutely looking unsolvable debate, without which the incident would probably not be noticed abroad? Even though several leading politicians in Japan are widely known for making reactionary comments or using inappropriate terms in their lectures and interviews, no one is going to blame just them alone. Above all, the past debate revealed once again after more than half a century the symptomatic syndrome of an unsolved historical and ideological controversy still existing in the Japanese society itself.

## References

Antoni (1998)
> Antoni, Klaus: *Shintō und die Konzeption des japanischen National-wesens* (kokutai)*: Der religiöse Traditionalismus in Neuzeit und Moderne Japans*. [Handbuch der Orientalistik, part V, vol. 8] Leiden, Boston, Köln: Brill, 1998.

Aston (1990)
> Aston, William George: *Nihongi: Chronicles of Japan from the Earliest Times to A. D. 697*. Tōkyō: Charles E. Tuttle, 1990.

Holtom (1938)
> Holtom, Daniel C.: *The National Faith of Japan*. London, 1938.

— (1943)
> Holtom, Daniel C.: Modern Japan and Shinto Nationalism: A Study of Present-day Trends in Japanese Religions. Chicago, 1943.

*The Japan Times* (02.06.2000)
> "Mori's point misunderstood", online (last accessed 13.07.2001) at: <http://www.japantimes.co.jp/cgi-bin/getarticle.pl5?eo20000602gc.htm>.

— (11.06.2000)
> "Mori casts doubt on Japanese democracy", online (13.07.2001) at: <http://www.japantimes.co.jp/cgi-bin/getarticle.pl5?eo20000611gc.htm>.

*Jinja shinpō* 神社新報 (22.05.2000)
> "Shinsei-ren kokkaigiin-kon sanjū shūnen kinen shukuga-kai 神政連国会議員懇３０周年記念祝賀会 ('The 30th anniversary of the Council of the Shintō Political Federation of Diet Members')".

— (29.05.2000)
> "Shushō hatsugen: Seisō no tsubusa ni suru na! Rongi fūsatsu no ronchō ni igi 首相発言: 政争の具にするな! 論議封殺の論調に異議 ('Do not make Mori's remark to a political dispute! The objections to the tone of the force-out arguments')".

— (05.06.2000a)
"Myōnendo yosan nado kimaru: Jinja-honchō hyōgiin-kai. Shushō hatsugen de kinkyū ketsugi mo. 明年度予算等決まる: 神社本庁評議員会. 首相発言で緊急決議も ('The budget for the next year will be decided: Meeting of the Jinja Honchō board. The urgent resolution on prime minister's remark')".

— (05.06.2000b)
"Kami no kuni e no ketsugi saitaku: Ketsugi-bun o Watanuki kaichō ni 神の国への決議採択: 決議文を綿貫会長に ('The adoption of the resolution on the divine country: The resolution-letter to chairman Watanuki')".

— (12.06.2000)
"Mori shushō no kami no kuni hatsugen to Koiso shushō no tenjō-mukyū tōben 森首相の神の国発言と小磯首相の天壌無窮答弁 ('The divine country remark of prime minister Mori and the tenjō mukyū reply of prime minister Koiso')".

— (19.06.2000a)
"Shinsei-ren chūō-iinkai: Konnendo katsudō hōshin kimeru. Shushō hatsugen no zenmen-shiji hyōmei 神政連中央委員会: 今年度活動方針決める. 首相発言の全面支持表明 ('The central committee of the Shintō Political Federation: Deciding an active policy this year. The demonstration of general support to prime minister's remark')".

— (19.06.2000b)
"Mori shushō hatsugen kōsei ni tsuite: Shintō seiji-renmei 森首相発言攻勢について: 神道政治連盟 ('The offensive on prime minister Mori's remark. The Shintō Political Federation')".

— (19.06.2000c)
"Shinkoku-shisō koso hokoru beki: Nihon o koe, banbutsu ni kami o mini wareware no kongen-teki na shinkōshin no hyōmei 神国思想こそ誇るべき: 日本を越え, 万物に神をみに我々の根元的な信仰心の表明 ('Indeed we should be proud of the divine country-idea: Between all things the attitude to God presents a manifestation of our original faith and spirit')".

— (19.06.2000d)
"Baatari-teki hihan de naku mirai o misueta giron o 場当たり的批判でなく 未来を見据えた議論を ('The controversy as seen in the future without showy critiques')".

—  (19.06.2000e)
"Kami no kuni hatsugen ni omou: GHQ ga jōsei shita kauntaa-ideorogī 神
の国発言に思ふ: ＧＨＱが醸成したカウンター・イデオロギー ('Thinking
about the divine country-remark: The counter ideology created by
GHQ')".

—  (10.07.2000a)
"Maku o tojita kami no kuni sōdō: Kōtaigo-heika hōgyo no kanashiimi no
naka de 幕を閉じた神の国騒動: 皇太后陛下崩御の悲しいみの中で ('The
closed curtain on the divine country-dispute: In the midst of the mourning
after death of the Empress Dowager')".

—  (10.07.2000b)
"Ikei o wasureta Nihonjin: Gaikoku kara mita Nihon 畏敬を忘れた日本
人: 外国から見た日本 ('Japanese who have forgotten the reverence: Japan
as seen from abroad')".

—  (21.07.2000)
"Nihon wa kami no kuni dewa nai desu ka 日本は神の国ではまいですか
('Is not Japan a divine country?')".

*Mainichi Daily News* (18.05.2000)
"Mori defends 'divine' speech", online (last accessed 13.07.2001) at:
<http://www.mainichi.co.jp./english/news/archive/200005/18/news01.html>.

—  (27.05.2000)
"Mori sorry for 'divine' remark", online (last accessed 13.07.2001) at:
<http://www.mainichi.co.jp./english/news/archive/200005/27/news01.html>.

Nawrocki (1998)
Nawrocki, Johann: *Inoue Tetsujirō und die Ideologie des Götterlandes:
Eine vergleichende Studie zur politischen Theologie des modernen Japan.*
[Ostasien-Pazifik: Trierer Studien zu Politik, Wirtschaft, Gesellschaft,
Kultur; vol. 10] Hamburg: Lit-Verlag, 1998.

Reader(1993)
Reader, Ian et al. (ed.): *Japanese Religions: Past and Present.* Sandgate,
Folkestone, Kent: Japan Library, 1993.

Shinten (1942)
Ōkura seishinbunka kenkyūjo 大倉精神文化研究所 (ed.): *Shinten* 神典.
Tōkyō: Sanseido, 1942.

Ueda (1996)
Ueda, Kenji: "Shinto", in: Tamaru, Noriyoshi/ Reid, David (eds.): *Religion in Japanese Culture: Where Living Traditions Meet a Changing World*. Tōkyō, NY, London: Kodansha International, 1996.

*Washington Post* (04.06.2000)
"Japan's two nationalisms", online (last accessed 13.07.2001) at: <http://newslibrary.krmediastream.com/cgi-bin/search/wp>.

# The Contributors

**Klaus ANTONI** is Professor and chair of the Japanese Department at Tübingen University, specializing on cultural anthropology. Being trained in Japanology, Sinology and Ethnology, his research is focused on the history of thoughts and religion in Japan, while his main interest centers on the mutual relation of religion (Shintō) and ideology in (early-) modern times. In addition he is interested in cultural theories on Japan (e.g., researching cultural stereotypes) and the cultural-historic role of Japan in Asia.

**AWAZU Kenta** 粟津賢太 graduated from Soka University and received post-graduate training at Sōka University and the University of Essex. Currently he is lecturer and co-operate researcher at the National Museum of Japanese History and the Institute for the Study of Oriental Philosophy in Tōkyō.

**ENDŌ Jun** 遠藤潤 is Research Fellow in the International Institute for the Study of Religions in Tōkyō, Japan. He is the author of "Late Tokugawa Society and Religious Restorationist Movements" (Transactions of the IJCC, Kokugakuin Univ., 1999), and the co-author of *The History of Shinto* (2001). He is currently writing a study of Hirata Atsutane's thought and researching Japanese religious thoughts in the 19th century.

**FUJII Takeshi** 藤井健志 is Professor at Tōkyō Gakugei University and has long been interested in the modern history of Japanese religions, especially Buddhism and new religious movements. These days his research focuses on the Buddhists' thought in the early Meiji period and on the overseas missionary works of Japanese religions. Currently he collects data concerning the activities of the Japanese new religion Tenrikyō in Taiwan.

**Lisette GEBHARDT** currently is substitute Professor of Japanese Studies at Martin Luther University in Halle-Wittenberg, Germany. Researching Japanese (modern) literature, she is focusing on its relationship with religion and the history of thoughts. Her fields of interest and ongoing projects include identity discourses of Japanese intellectuals and the New Age in Japan.

**Peter KLEINEN** (1964) received an M.A. in Japanology, Philosophy, and Comparative Studies of Religion from Bonn University, where he is currently research associate (Wissenschaftlicher Mitarbeiter) at the Department of Japanese Studies. He focuses on the history of church-state-relations in early modern and modern Japan and is particularly interested in Buddhism's contributions to the discursive construction of Japanese national identities. His publications include "Nichiren-Shugi: Zum Verhältnis von Nichiren-Buddhismus und japanischem Nationalismus am Beispiel von Tanaka Chigaku (1861-1939)" (DIJ Tōkyō, 1994) and "Politics, Religion, and National Integration in Wilhelmine Germany and Meiji Japan: A Comparative View on the Kulturkampf and the Persecution of Buddhism" (National Museum of Ethnology, Ōsaka, 2000). He is also author of the forthcoming volume *Im Tode ein Buddha. Anmerkungen zu Gesshō (1817-1858) und der Genese buddhistisch- nationaler Identität in Japan* (Lit Verlag).

**KUBOTA Hiroshi** 久保田浩 studied Theoretical Physics at the Science University of Tōkyō, and Comparative Religions at International Christian University, Tōkyō; the University of Tōkyō and Tübingen University. Currently he is lecturer at the Department for Japanese Studies in Tübingen. His research focuses on comparative religions, the disciplinary history of religious studies, Christian-nationalistic religious movements and the modern history of religion in Germany and Japan.

**Johann NAWROCKI** studied law at the University of Warsaw, Poland, and received his Ph.D. from the University of Hamburg, Germany, where he studied Japanology, Sinology and political science. Between 1991 and 1992 he has been a lecturer of Japanese at Hochschule Bremen, Germany, from 1993 to 1995 a research fellow at the University of Tōkyō, and from 1998 to 2000 he was research associate at the German Institute for Japanese Studies in Tōkyō. Since August 2001 he is Director of the Tübingen University Center for Japanese Language at Dōshisha University in Kyōto.

**ŌTANI Eiichi** 大谷栄一 is a research fellow at the International Institute for the Study of Religions in, Tōkyō, Japan. He takes an interest in the relation between religion and nationalism in modern Japan, especially on developmental processes of the Nichiren Buddhist movements. His current research focuses on the views of Nichiren as expressed by his biographies and novels in modern Japan.

**Inken PROHL** received her Ph.D. (Religious Studies) from Free University of Berlin. Between 1995 and 1997 she did research on the Japanese New Age and New Religions at Tōkyō University and is currently research associate (Wissenschaftliche Mitarbeiterin) at the Institute for Religious Studies, Free University of Berlin, Germany. Her research interests include the study of New Age in Germany and Japan, the history of Japanese Buddhism in the 20th century as well as the theory of ritual. She is at present engaged in research on the so-called New New Religions in Japan.

**Ian READER** is Professor and Head of the Department of Religious Studies, Lancaster University. Previously he has held academic positions in Scotland, Denmark, Hawaii and Japan. Among his most recent books are *Religious Violence in Contemporary Japan: The Case of Aum Shinrikyo* (Curzon Press, UK and University of Hawaii Press, USA, 2000) and *Practically Religious: Worldly Benefits and the Common Religion of Japan* (co-authored with George J. Tanabe, University of Hawaii Press 1998). He is currently writing a book on pilgrimage in Japan.

**Martin REPP** is Associate Director of the NCC Center for the Study of Japanese Religions (Kyōto) and editor of its journal *Japanese Religions*. His research focuses on medieval Japanese Pure Land tradition, especially Honen, and on contemporary new religions in Japan, particularly Aum Shinrikyō.

**Bernhard SCHEID** graduated from Vienna University and is research fellow at the Institute for Asian Studies, Austrian Academy of Sciences. He recently published *Der Eine und Einzige Weg der Götter. Yoshida Kanetomo und die Erfindung des Shinto* (Wien, 2001).

**Walter SKYA** teaches in the History Department at Kenyon College in Columbus, Ohio. He received his undergraduate degree from the Far Eastern & Russian Institute (currently the Henry M. Jackson School of International Studies), University of Washington, and his doctorate in history from the University of Chicago. He also studied and worked in Japan from 1975 to 1984. His field of research is modern Japanese political thought.

**Birgit STAEMMLER** received her BA in Japanese in 1992 (SOAS) and her MA in Japanese and Anthropology in 1995 (Heidelberg University). Currently she is working on a Ph.D.-thesis about "*Chinkon Kishin*: Spirit Possession in Three Japanese New Religions". She is a member of the research project on Japanese religions and the Internet at Tübingen University.

**Michael WACHUTKA** obtained his BA in Japanology and Sinology from Tübingen University, Germany, and his MA in Comparative Cultures/ Asian Studies from Sophia University, Tōkyō. Being a Ph.D. candidate at the Japanese Department in Tübingen, he currently is a research fellow at the German Institute for Japanese Studies (DIJ) in Tōkyō, working on his thesis on the life, ideas and 'behind-the-scene' influence of the *kokugaku* scholar Iida Takesato. In addition, he is interested in the adaptation of western academic ideas and methods by Japanese scholars in early Meiji Japan and the shifting interpretation of Japanese mythology throughout the nativist movement. His most recent publication is: *Historical Reality or Metaphoric Expression? – Culturally formed contrasts in Karl Florenz' and Iida Takesato's interpretations of Japanese mythology.* [BUNKA vol. 1] Lit-Verlag, 2001.